Conditio Judaica 49
Studien und Quellen zur deutsch-jüdischen Literatur- und Kulturgeschichte

Herausgegeben von Hans Otto Horch
in Verbindung mit Alfred Bodenheimer, Mark H. Gelber und Jakob Hessing

D1720302

Mary Cosgrove

Grotesque Ambivalence

Melancholy and Mourning
in the Prose Work of Albert Drach

Max Niemeyer Verlag
Tübingen 2004

Bibliografische Information der Deutschen Bibliothek

Die Deutsche Bibliothek verzeichnet diese Publikation in der Deutschen Nationalbibliografie;
detaillierte bibliografische Daten sind im Internet über *http://dnb.ddb.de* abrufbar.

ISBN 3-484-65149-0   ISSN 0941-5866

Gedruckt auf alterungsbeständigem Papier.
Druck: Laupp & Göbel GmbH, Nehren
Einband: Nädele Verlags- und Industriebuchbinderei, Nehren

Content

Chapter 1

Introduction 1
  1.1 Albert Drach: Revolutionary Poet and Bearer of Death 1
  1.2 »O Ophelia«: The Encounter with the Cadaver 10
  1.3 *Status Nascendi* versus *Status Quo*: In defence of *Nature Morte* 12
  1.4 Positions 15
  1.5 The Child in Flight 22

Chapter 2

The Grotesque: Topography of Transgression, Morphology of Emptiness ... 25
  2.1 Body Language 25
  2.2 An Entire Thematics of Mortality and Vitality 34
  2.3 Subterranean Spaces 43

Chapter 3

Grotesque Discourses: Mourning and Melancholia 51
  3.1 Constellation of Cross-Contamination 51
  3.2 From System to Process: The Semiotic, the Symbolic
      and the Thetic 55
  3.3 Anaphora of Nothing 64

Chapter 4

Floating Documents 73
  4.1 The Protokoll: Epic of the In-Between 73
  4.2 Outside the Text: Creating the Catachrestic Space 80

Chapter 5

Ex-centrics, Evil Eyes and Missing Persons: The Optics of Mimicry in
  Das Goggelbuch 107
  5.1 Grotesque Surplus: Mimic Man 107
  5.2 Representing the In-Between: The Secret Art of Invisibility 114
  5.3 Fallible Frames 121
  5.4 Aphanisic Faders 131

Chapter 6

»Z. Z.« das ist die Zwischenzeit: Paralysis of the Powerless 151
  6.1 Diverging Paths: A Theoretical Re-evaluation 151
  6.2 Writing Apotheosis 160
  6.3 In the Shadow of the Egocrat: A Micro-Physics of Power 173
  6.4 The Ventriloquist's Dummies 183

Chapter 7

The Time of Evil Children 187
  7.1 The Spectre of Absolute Negation 187
  7.2 Divine Intoxication: Simulating Infantile Sovereignty 198
  7.3 Infernal Sobriety: Apotheosis of the Eternal Present 204
  7.4 Contours of the Culpable 208
  7.5 Suffer Little Children 216

Conclusion

Concentration Camps of the Mind and the Child in Flight 219

Bibliography 221
Index 229
Acknowledgements 231

Chapter 1
Introduction

> [...] »Art« takes on murder and moves through
> it. It assumes murder in so far as artistic prac-
> tice considers death the inner boundary of the
> signifying process. Crossing that boundary is
> precisely what constitutes »Art«. In other words,
> it is as if death becomes interiorized by the sub-
> ject of such a practice; in order to function he
> must make himself the bearer of death.
>
> (Julia Kristeva)

> In jedem Wort sitzt der Tod.
>
> (Albert Drach)

1.1 Albert Drach: Revolutionary Poet and Bearer of Death

Albert Drach has often been associated with the grotesque, his works an expression of uncompromising cynicism and relentless criticism of existing social orders.[1] The everyday banalities of culturally produced grotesquerie and
horror are recurring thematic topoi of his prose work. Characteristic for Drach's
use of the grotesque is also the distinct lack of pathos in the comically vivisect-
ing gaze of the narrating perspective, whether focalised through the innocent
but discerning eyes of a young child, or whether transmitted through the radically alienated perspective of the persecuted self.[2] In particular, Drach's use of

---

[1] »Drachs erzählerisches Mittel ist die Groteske: Alles, was komisch verzerrt, absurd, über-
steigert und wunderlich ist, nützt er in der Fülle seiner Episoden und Figuren und Na-
men.« Matthias Settele: Der Protokollstil des Albert Drach. Recht, Gerechtigkeit, Sprache, Literatur. Frankfurt a. M.: Lang 1992 (Europäische Hochschulschriften; 1/1343),
p. 158. »Drachs Wirklichkeitsmodellierungen deformieren alle vernunftgemäßen, das
einzelne Faktum in einen übergreifenden Sinnzusammenhang integrierenden Absich-
ten als einen Zynismus, als eine Fortsetzung der zynischen Geschichte mit den Mitteln
der Logik.« André Fischer: Inszenierte Naivität. Zur ästhetischen Simulation von Geschichte bei Günther Grass, Albert Drach und Walter Kempowski. München: Fink
1992 (Theorie und Geschichte der Literatur und der schönen Künste; 85), p. 216.

[2] Cf. Albert Drach: Lunz. Eine Erzählung. In: id., Ironie vom Glück. Kleine Protokolle und Erzählungen. München, Wien: Hanser 1994, p. 7–34. Cf. id., Unsentimentale
Reise. Ein Bericht. München: Hanser 1988.

unresolved contradiction as a tool of representation in his work broadly affiliates him to the grotesque tradition. Add to this the recurring motif of deceased bodies accompanied by an incommensurable admixture of comic investment and it would seem that we have a *quod erat demonstrandum* case of the grotesque in all its contradictions, incompatibilities and cynical exposure.[3]

In the case of Albert Drach, however, one must ask whether the scope of these features suffices to adequately capture the economy of the grotesque as it is manifested in his work. As shall become clear throughout this work, Drach's rendition of the grotesque in fact forces a revision and expansion of current theories. Beyond the dull crudity of the material moment, beyond the representation of the frail dismembered human body in all its powerless and pathetic incapacitation, beyond the image of a world grotesquely alienated from any awareness of the extent of its self-alienation,[4] Drach's *sui generis* use of the grotesque primarily as a vessel of language ambivalence testifies to a level of calculated subtlety not normally associated with the grotesque.[5]

In the following chapter, I aim to develop a theory of language grotesquerie as a form of language ambivalence. Using Julia Kristeva's theory of revolutionary poetic language as a basis for the expansion of the grotesque, I hope to highlight the proximity of the grotesque and the notion of unresolved contra-

---

[3]   André Fischer has correctly pointed out the role played by Drach's grotesque style in the problematic reception of his work in post World War II society. Cf. Fischer, Inszenierte Naivität (note 1), p. 214–217. Eva Schobel has moreover drawn an enlightening comparison between the troubled publishing history of the German-Jewish writer, Edgar Hilsenrath, and Drach's own situation. Again, here the problem is a scandalous use of the comic in a particularly philosemitic social context (Eva Schobel: Albert Drach. Ein lebenslanger Versuch zu überleben. In: Albert Drach. Hg. von Gerhard Fuchs und Günther A. Höfler. Wien, Graz: Droschl 1995, p. 329–375, here p. 363). Indeed, letters of rejection from publishing houses of the time testify to a mainly socio-historically based complete lack of understanding of this style: »Zwischen überzeichneter Karikatur und verwischten Umrissen schwankt das Buch und wird vom Übel.« Letter from H. J. Mundt, Kurt Desch Verlag, Munich, to Albert Drach, 30 December 1957, Nachlaß Albert Drach, Österreichisches Literaturarchiv der österreichischen Nationalbibliothek (ÖLA), Wien.

[4]   In this respect, Drach is an author of the (in Theodor W. Adorno's sense) anti-realist, post-war novel, in which the artistic approximation of grotesque reality in the twentieth century necessitates the relentless use of aesthetic distance. See Theodor W. Adorno: Standort des Erzählers im zeitgenössischen Roman. In: id., Noten zur Literatur I. Hg. von Rolf Tiedemann. Frankfurt a. M.: Suhrkamp 1981 (Suhrkamp-Taschenbuch Wissenschaft; 355), p. 4–48.

[5]   Matthias Settele underestimates the literary consequences of Drach's use of the grotesque when he separates narrative plot, time and characterisation from the grotesque: »Neben der eher konventionellen Handhabung von Ort und Zeit und der Figurenzeichnung steht die besondere Bedeutung der Groteske und Episodenfülle.« (Settele, Der Protokollstil des Albert Drach [note 1], p. 155) I would argue that Drach's use of the grotesque along with his language grotesquerie, far from merely coexisting alongside more traditional forms, actually disrupt the presumptions of conventional plot.

diction to post-modern theories of play, dissolution, exile and difference. In particular, this theory of the grotesque will focus on the problem of the other as a form of alterity within the self that is inherently ambivalent and that unsettles presumptions of clearly demarcated identity. Ultimately, the grotesque as a form of hybrid identity signifies an openness to difference that articulates the other (and the self) as fundamentally »other«. Kristeva identifies the expression of this radical otherness in the language of poetry. Much of the following chapter will thus explore the implicit grotesquerie of Kristeva's theory of poetic language. [6]

Following this line of inquiry, one may propose that Albert Drach's negotiation of the grotesque in his work makes of him (in Kristevan terms) a revolutionary poet. However, the profile of this figure is itself complex. The chapters that concern themselves with literary analysis will voice just this complexity. In certain texts the gaze of the other informs Drach's aesthetic vision, permeates the indeterminate narrative perspective of his work, and manifests itself also in the universal strangerhood and outsider status of all his characters. Drach's anti-heroes (social outcasts such as Jews, women, criminals etc.) are usually victims of repressive social systems. However, in these texts that debunkingly interrogate images of power the agents representing social repression are exposed as little more than self-appointed defence instances against the threat of difference and the disruption of homogeneity implied by the fringe existence of the expelled other. For the borderline position of this other ensures the recurrent representation to the self of the peripheries that simultaneously demarcate and question identity. Such a perspective has implications for the intransigence of the sovereign self.

It is just this disturbance of otherness from within the confines of rational discourse that articulates a dominant function of the revolutionary poet: the literary use of transgression or *jouissance* as a means of interrogating cultural and political constructions of identity.[7] For Drach the Holocaust survivor, this approach signifies a determination to demystify centripetal representations of power within culture that, given the appropriate political climate, foster the growth of racism. Indeed, the articulation of difference through a language that tries to present difference as external to it is one of the main achievements of Drach's prose. Chapters 4 and 5 explore this aspect of his language which simultaneously enacts and rejects the rigid confines of centralising, ordering structures typical of modernity.[8] It is within this dual functioning of language as manifested in certain

---

[6] Cf. Julia Kristeva: Revolution in Poetic Language. New York: Columbia University Press 1984.

[7] In her critical reception of Kristeva's work, Anna Smith provides a sound general definition of *jouissance*: »Language in its infinite creative aspect causes the subject to experience bliss or jouissance. Jouissance can produce ecstasy and a sense of fainting into language. The subject, dissolved and falling, is ravished by the unending stream of words.« Anna Smith: Julia Kristeva. Readings of Exile and Estrangement. London: Macmillan 1996, p. 14.

[8] Zygmunt Bauman's work on the relationship between order and ambivalence critically explores the centralising tendencies of modernity as a reaction to and product

of Drach's prose works – the simultaneous implementation and transgression of the terms of so-called rational discourse from within these very terms – that we encounter an elevated level of grotesque indeterminacy, a rhetorical grotesque apparent in the decentralising strategy of his prose.

Despite the often distasteful reality that is unmasked by this prose strategy, the epistemological position implied by the dual function of Drach's protocol language may be described in terms of an ideologically optimistic perspective. This is due in large part to the mobile indeterminacy of *jouissance* as a literary strategy. A »metaphor for the infinite«, the latter communicates the de facto openness of cultural systems that present themselves as closed and homogenous.[9] This literary approximation of openness is in turn an indicator of the possibility of change within purportedly fixed social formations.

Drach has claimed that his protocols are vessels of truth. Highlighting the fictitious nature of power discourses through the oppositional aesthetics of a split protocol language conforms to just this optimistic project of revealing the complex truth concerning cultural processes of identification.[10] This literary innovation furthermore allows for an analysis of the politics of (mis)representation, that »peculiar property of language« – exacerbated to truly grotesque levels when in the service of modern institutions of power – to function as a »profound establishment of order in space«.[11] Signifying the latent openness of systems through transgression is thus tantamount to exposing the »beyond« of established order.[12]

In Drach's work, the borderline space of the beyond is presented through grotesque indeterminacy as a suggestible space where nothing remains still. This borderline space represents an ambivalent third dimension to the inside/outside spatial dichotomy. It exposes what Homi Bhabha refers to as the in-between

---

of the modern quest for order: »Modern state and modern intellect alike need chaos – if only to go on creating order. They both thrive on the vanity of their effort.« Zygmunt Bauman: Modernity and Ambivalence. Cambridge: Polity Press 1991, p. 9.

[9]   Smith, Julia Kristeva (note 7), p. 111.

[10] »Die Wirklichkeit und die Wahrheit sind nicht immer dasselbe. Ich bin ein Fanatiker der Wahrheit, der Schriftsteller ist immer ein unbefangener Zeuge.« Eva Schobel: Ich bin ein wütender Weiser. Ein Gespräch mit Albert Drach. In: In Sachen Albert Drach. Sieben Beiträge zum Werk. Mit einem unveröffentlichten Text Albert Drachs. Hg. von Bernhard Fetz. Wien: Wiener Universitäts-Verlag 1995, p. 14–16, here p. 16.

[11] Michel Foucault: The Order of Things. An Archaeology of the Human Sciences. London: Routledge 2000, p. 83.

[12] I find that Bhabha eloquently describes this nebulous postmodern phenomenon of the beyond as a condition of a borderline existence of permanent transition: »The ›beyond‹ is neither a new horizon, nor a leaving behind of the past [...] we find ourselves in the moment of transit where space and time cross to produce complex figures of difference and identity, past and present, inside and outside, inclusion and exclusion. For there is a sense of disorientation, a disturbance of direction, in the ›beyond‹: an exploratory, restless movement caught [...] here and there, on all sides fort/da, hither and thither, back and forth.« See Homi Bhabha: The Location of Culture. London, New York: Routledge 1994, p. 1.

(neither inside nor outside but somewhere on the border) and what Jacques La-can calls the *vel* of signification.[13] For if discourse is to be exposed as the verbal representation (manipulation) of representation processes, i. e. as a construct that gives voice to the unbridgeable gap between signifier and signified, and which thereby forever silences the »vague murmur of similitudes«, then the language that will expose the farce of system is one that focuses on the grotesque moment of deconstructive indeterminacy – in other words, the language of scission.[14] This language which intuits and performs the grotesquely nauseous instance of the dismantling of dichotomously founded hierarchies is a language of undesired separation from the familiar, and dismayed or (if taken from a carnivalesque perspective) gleeful convergence with the other. In short, it is the articulation of the always potential, at times, actual dissolution of homogenous order.

The following question deserves attention, however: how may death and op-timism be reasonably combined in the figure of the revolutionary poet? Death is no straightforward image in Drach's work. Nor is it a simple concept in Kri-steva's theory, largely due to its representation in the conflicting images of stasis and *jouissance*. Similar to Sigmund Freud's understanding of the conservative nature of the drives, Kristeva defines stasis as synonymous with the homogenis-ing tendencies of the signifying process which she locates primarily in »sign, language, identifying family structure«.[15] From this perspective, stasis is an image of conservatism that compares with Freud's theory of the drives.[16]

---

[13] For Bhabha, the in-between is a space in which cultural difference may be articula-ted »[...] beyond narratives of originary and initial subjectivities« (ibid., p. 1). Inter-changeable with his concept of the »beyond« space of transition, the in-between repre-sents »The anti-dialectical movement of the subaltern instance« which »[...] subverts any binary or sublatory ordering of power and sign« (ibid., p. 55). The in-between thus understood maps (and re-maps) the shifting locus of ambivalent selfhood. Meanwhile, the Lacanian *vel* depicts just this upset of binary and originary structures with particu-lar reference to the signifier. Defined by Lacan as »a neither one, nor the other«, the *vel* refers to the lack that accompanies all binary signification. The *vel* may thus also be understood as a »beyond«/»in-between« space in which alterity of self and signifier are evoked. The Four Fundamental Concepts of Psycho-Analysis. Ed. by Jacques-Alain Miller. New York, London: Norton 1981, p. 211.

[14] Foucault, The Order of Things (note 11), p. 70.

[15] Kristeva, Revolution in Poetic Language (note 6), p. 150.

[16] Freud's definition of the drives as ultimately conservative, as opposed to dynamic forces, is similar to Kristeva's above concept of stasis. From a Freudian perspective, the articulation of stasis in the projection of homogeneity onto entities such as family, language structure etc. can be seen as the longing for a return to an idealised earlier state of (non)being akin to death, in metaphysical terms the return to *arche*: »Der kon-servativen Natur der Triebe widerspräche es, wenn das Ziel des Lebens ein noch nie zuvor erreichter Zustand wäre. Es muß vielmehr ein alter, ein Ausgangszustand sein, den das Lebende einmal verlassen hat und zu dem es über alle Umwege der Entwick-lung zurückstrebt [...]. Das Ziel alles Lebens ist der Tod«. Sigmund Freud: Jenseits des Lustprinzips. In: id., Das Ich und das Es. Metapsychologische Schriften. Frankfurt a. M.: Fischer 1999 (Fischer-Taschenbücher; 10442: Psychologie), p. 223.

Stasis thus depicts an economy of death via representations of closure, limitation and immobility. *Jouissance*, on the other hand, is defined by Kristeva as a principle of destruction that »far from setting up an economy of death, abruptly introduces death«.[17] The difference between the two conflicting modes of death would appear to hinge on the element of the abrupt which implies movement, surprise, the unexpected. Whereas the economy of death implies the establishment of an unchanging state of stagnation – death as a norm – the abrupt element of disturbance still functions as a (revolutionary) deviant from this norm. Very generally, *jouissance* may be regarded as a signifier of mobility whilst stasis signifies paralysis.

Drach's more optimistic works employ *jouissance* in order to disrupt closure/stasis of the sociolinguistic system as it is represented in the literary text. In this instance, it would seem that one form of death (*jouissance*) is strategically used to avoid the other (stasis). Thus when Kristeva describes transgression in art as a positively connoted act of murder, she is referring to this anarchic or revolutionary potential of the literary text to rupture stagnant constructs.[18] Likewise, the destructive investment of Drach's prose involves the transgression of existing institutionalised systems, orders and constructs. This literary strategy may be seen as part of a wider discourse on power and powerlessness in which the repressed other avenges itself. *Jouissance* brings about the articulation of the other at the expense of the homogenous, sovereign self: the latter is superseded by the former.

The optimistic content of Drach's protocol language becomes manifest in this alternative articulation of the marginal. The appropriated other whose identity is otherwise determined by a repressive social order transgresses through language ambivalence the confines of this imposition. In such works, otherness is represented as subversion and so disrupts the asymmetrical self/other identity construct. The various manifestations of transgression in Drach's work will thus articulate a politics of subversion that attacks in particular the totalitarian tendencies of an increasingly integrated culture. The iconoclastic modus operandi of the grotesque is of specific interest for such a project; it frustrates binary signification and thereby questions homogenous notions of language and self.

In this way, Drach's language lays bare the structuring and artificial nature of rational discourse. His protocol fashioned novels thus confirm Foucault's claim

---

[17] Kristeva, Revolution in Poetic Language (note 6), p. 144.

[18] The concept of *jouissance* as an act of murder places language »above all as a symbolic system, [...] at the service of the death drive [...], whose endless course conditions and moves through every stasis and thus every structure, in an act of murder« (ibid., p. 119). This pattern highlights just that destructive/regenerative capability of *jouissance* to violently reinvigorate social and aesthetic orders. The revolutionary death drive mentioned here should however be differentiated from the conservative death drive associated with stasis. Whereas the former clearly signifies movement, the latter signifies paralysis. This discussion will be taken up in more detail in chapter 2.

that »discourse is merely representation itself represented by verbal signs«.[19] In other words, the moment of transgression within Drach's prose makes clear the constructedness – and therefore potential collapse – of the politics, prejudices and crass stereotyping that are coextensive with the kind of representative language in the service of systems based on the asymmetrical distribution of power. Through the use of transgression in this destructive/constructive capacity, Drach's work offers us a valuable insight into the mechanisms of power in obscured operation behind the facade of state institutions.

A more disturbing feature of the revolutionary poet emerges in a nuance of this function as bearer of death, however. In my view, the creative/destructive influence of transgression permeates the literary work only if the conservative forces of stagnation (Thanatos/stasis) are disrupted by language fetishism. In other words, *jouissance* relies on a certain pronounced robustness of the transgressive function which avoids through constant disruption of the language system the final and irrevocable disclosure of castration. Thus *jouissance* may be regarded as a performance in language of the ambivalent fetish object which alternatively expresses recognition and denial of the possibility of castration.

Bhabha describes fetishism as a »›play‹ or vacillation between the archaic affirmation of wholeness/similarity [...] and the anxiety associated with lack and difference«.[20] He goes on to remark that the activity of the fetish within discourse derives from the playful differentiation between masking absence/difference and registering the sensed lack. The function of fetishism in discourse thus signals the territory of the in-between: a territory of ambivalence similar to that invoked by the transgressive function of *jouissance*.[21]

However, the fetish object in the case of *jouissance* does not belong to the group of typical peripheral objects described by Freud as characteristic for the fetish.[22] Instead, Kristeva argues that language itself is now the ubiquitously peripheral fetish object which provisionally fills the void »upon which rests the play with the signifier«.[23] Indeed, Foucault's reference to the peculiar property of language to function as the profound establishment of order in space, describes just this denial function of the language fetish. Accordingly, when the literary text makes clear the representative nature of representation and the gap between signifier and signified, it is in fact exposing the linguistic fetish function hard at work in the game of recognition followed swiftly by denial. In this manner, »the fetish becomes a life preserver, temporary and slippery, but nonetheless indispensable«.[24]

---

[19] Foucault, The Order of Things (note 11), p. 81.

[20] »[...] that repetitious scene around the problem of castration«, fetishism is »a form of multiple and contradictory belief in its recognition of difference and disavowal of it« (Bhabha, The Location of Culture [note 12], p. 74–75).

[21] Ibid.

[22] »Fetischismus« in: Freud, Das Ich und das Es (note 16), p. 332.

[23] Julia Kristeva: Powers of Horror. An Essay on Abjection. New York: Columbia University Press 1982 (European Perspectives), p. 37.

[24] Ibid.

Claiming that language is based on fetishist denial, Kristeva probingly asks »is not exactly language our ultimate and inseparable fetish?«[25] Thus understood, the role of writing as the representation of signifying processes incessantly employs language as fetish. However, if the denial function of the signifier in this risky equation should weaken, then the economy of death as stasis (the final and irrevocable recognition of castration) begins to dominate. Castration may be broadly understood in this context as the establishment of a sterile economy of death increasingly lacking the rupture of the transgressive function. In the cultural context, the totalitarian model evidences this economy in social terms: the drive towards uniformity (stagnation or the unleashing of the Death Instinct into the social space) complemented by the reduction of difference (the ambivalent play of the fetishistic signifier).[26]

The texts discussed in chapters 4 and 5 (*IA UND NEIN* and *Das Goggelbuch* respectively) testify to the robustness of the linguistic fetish function in Drach's work. However, the Holocaust text discussed in chapters 6 and 7 (*»Z. Z.« das ist die Zwischenzeit*) highlights an alternative route of the poetic function in Kristeva's sense.[27] In this case, the fetish function of language proves inadequate to stave off the certainty of the coming Final Solution. Instead, the subversiveness of *jouissance* capitulates to the inevitable: the representation of death as absolute negation. In other words, the playfulness of *jouissance* is replaced in the Holocaust text by the now dominant drive of stasis.

That *jouissance* all but disappears from this text signifies a certain fitting destitution of the language that should evoke the unspeakable fact of genocide by calculated and sophisticated means. One could argue that the language of scission is replaced in this text by the economy of death as stasis. Thus the image of an impregnable system is revived by this reduced language primarily as a testimony to the acute entrapment of the Jewish victim of the National Socialist state. Whilst Drach does not entirely abandon his position as incisive critic of repressive discursive structures in the Holocaust texts, he nonetheless switches his focus from the exposure of these structures to their very real consequences for the appropriated Jewish other during the Third Reich. Accordingly, the grotesque is manifested differently in these texts. Its central articulation assumes the shape of the corpse (the castrated self) and with that the spectre of absolute negation. This image contrasts to the notion of death as renewal which informs the other texts and lends a chilling undertone to Drach's assertion that death lurks in all words.

---

[25] Ibid.

[26] For a discussion of the extreme homogenisation of individuals that is characteristic of totalitarian rule and that is argued in terms of the unleashing of stasis into the social space, see Claude Lefort: The Political Forms of Modern Society. Bureaucracy, Democracy, Totalitarianism. Cambridge: Polity Press 1986, p. 306.

[27] Albert Drach: IA UND NEIN. Drei Fälle. München, Wien: Hanser 1992; id., Das Goggelbuch. In: id., Die kleinen Protokolle und das Goggelbuch. München, Wien: Langen-Müller 1965, p. 245–303; id., »Z. Z.« das ist die Zwischenzeit. Ein Protokoll. Ungekürzte Ausg., München: Deutscher Taschenbuch Verlag 1990 (dtv; 12218).

At the heart of the shift in emphasis between stasis and *jouissance* lies Drach's range and subtlety as a grotesque writer. This scope derives mainly from his scripting of the death drives across a range of literary works. The space of ambivalence that arises through transgression signifies a deft flirtation with death that succeeds in upholding the fetish function of language to varying degrees, depending on the subject matter of the text at hand. In the comic texts to be examined (*IA UND NEIN* and *Das Goggelbuch*), this playful function of language is evident in the use of sentence hybrids and hybrid images of identity. The resulting unresolved contradiction in the representation of character along with the indecidability of subject matter account for the grotesque investment of these texts. In such works, Drach craftily manipulates the paralysing terms of an exaggeratedly rational language to illustrate how such emphatic taxonomy paradoxically produces its own irreconcilable ambivalences.

The space of ambivalence or the space of the in-between is the shadowy stage upon which Drach may engage in a deft flirtation with death, emphasising the immanence of death as stasis in the rigidity of protocol prose, yet simultaneously suggesting the non-viability of stasis through the self-transgressive tendency of this very language. For Drach's understanding of truth in art derives from the insight that the vision of a harmonious world may only be fabricated when difference is a casualty of exclusionary practices.[28] Hence the non-viability of stasis in these works: its very origins in the act of expulsion suggest an awareness of potentially disruptive movement that it is at pains to control.

The stasis censured by Drach in his protocol parodies is thus a form of repressive homogeneity that he identifies as consistent with the excluding practice of a potentially totalitarian consciousness. The works that pursue this angle question the signification of totality by demonstrating its obsolescence through a literary language that inadvertently invites the expression of alterity. One could argue that Drach defers stasis as the ideological closure of system, identity and society by evoking through his use of language grotesquerie in particular the ambivalences of the cultural unconscious.[29]

His representation of the Holocaust seems to bypass such concerns, however. Here he is wholly preoccupied with the articulation of inertia, closure and death. The extreme sadness of such a position may be understood as a symptom of traumatic memory that aligns the Holocaust survivor closely with those who did not survive. Death is thus no longer deferred: the productive flirtation

---

[28] Cf. Albert Drach: Essay VII: Stilleben. In: id., Albert Drach: Das 17. Buch, der 17 Essays. Nachlaß Albert Drach, Austrian Literary Archive of the National Library (ÖLA), Wien. This point will be discussed in more detail in chapter 1.3.

[29] Emphasising alterity as the essential fibre of the cultural unconscious, Yuan Yuan states that »the discourse of the unconscious is the discourse of the other« (Yuan Yuan: The Lacanian Subject and Grotesque Desires. Between Oedipal Violation and Narcissistic Closure. In: The American Journal of Psychoanalysis 56 [1996], p. 35–47, here p. 39).

between stasis and *jouissance* breaks down simultaneously with the breakdown of the fetish function in language.

In general, Drach's *Protokolle* can be read in this light as instances of revolutionary poetic language in the Kristevan sense – documentations of instability, flux, *jouissance*, death and creativity. The relativisation of centralising structures opens up the way for the expression of contingency, exile and difference. His literature fulfils the criteria of incisive, multi-perspectivist, post-modern counter-narrative, in which the articulation of difference is diametrically opposed to the narrative of the modern nation and its restrictive tendencies.[30] On the other hand, the protocol in its general pursuit of truth must also communicate the truth of total victimisation. This deviation from the concerns of subversion indicates the representational scope of the protocol form, both as the mouthpiece of insurgent alterity and as the documentation of intense suffering.

1.2 »O Ophelia«: The Encounter with the Cadaver

Where does the complexity of this writer begin? The autobiographical texts »Lunz« and »Martyrium eines Unheiligen« offer some basis for an understanding of Drach's relationship to death and his negotiation of this relationship in his writing.[31] They both refer, albeit with some differences in the narrative detail, to the childhood holiday in Lunz. The former text is narrated in the first person, the latter is a third person narrative in protocol form. In both, the by now (for any Drach scholar) famous encounter with a drowned corpse plays a central role. An assessment of this first confrontation with death will yield a curious contradiction between the subjective desires of the person Albert Drach and the later implications of ambivalence in the writing of *jouissance*. In this contradiction we witness Drach continue his flirtation with death, but this time from a very different, highly personal angle.

To summarise briefly the previous angle taken on Drach's flirtation with death: I have argued that his writing of grotesque indeterminacy is a writing against stasis, against the consolidating, homogenising forces of inertia. For

---

[30] In his discussion of the nation as a particular form of ordering narrative, Timothy Brennan mentions »›the twin threats of disorder and death‹ confronting all societies«, against which the nation, in the formation and perpetuation of its identity through narrative, implements anti-death strategies functioning through a delimitation of both time and place (Timothy Brennan: The National Longing for Form. In: Nation and Narration. Ed. by Homi K. Bhabha. London: Routledge 1990, p. 44–70, here p. 51–52). »This background of spirituality and permanence« is exactly the confining tendency against which Drach revolts, and which he replaces through »the topos of ›exile‹, nationalism's opposite« (ibid., p. 60). For this reason, I find Settele's assertion that Drach avails of conventional literary forms problematic (see note 5).

[31] Albert Drach: Martyrium eines Unheiligen. In: id., Die kleinen Protokolle und das Goggelbuch (note 27), p. 133–185; id., Lunz (note 2). Henceforth cited where appropriate as MU and L in brackets respectively.

Drach this form of writing is not just a literary aesthetic innovation, but serves also as a means of cultural critique that gains particular resonance in the context of the well-trodden path of European totalitarianism.

Nonetheless, when we return to the moment of Drach's personal inauguration as artist, we encounter a different arrangement of impulses. In both of the above-mentioned texts, the event that led to his decision to become an artist and the desire that fuelled this decision are described in some detail. This decision centres on the child Drach's reaction to the drowned corpse recovered from a lake whilst on holidays in Lunz. It stands out as a key event in his personal and artistic development alongside other similar childhood confrontations with mortality.

The dredged-up corpse is given a grotesque description. It becomes clear from Drach's observation that the return to a material state of disintegration goes hand in hand with the loss of individuality, and with that of dignity:

> Das Gesicht des Toten war übermäßig dick, die Nase fehlte und auch an den Lippen waren Stücke angeblich von Karpfen abgefressen. In den Augenhöhlen schien überdies keine Pupille mehr zu stecken. (L 13)

Despite the hasty cover-up of the corpse's face, Drach has witnessed at first hand death's countenance. From this point onwards, his search for an elixir against the power of death commences and proves to be one of the driving forces behind his personal impulse to become an artistic creator:

> Ich aber hatte genug zu sehen, um nicht mehr sterben zu wollen. Mitzi Hansmann allerdings wußte kein Mittel gegen den Tod. Meine Mutter hinwiederum wollte mich glauben machen, daß ich, weil ich bei der Geburt scheintot gewesen, nicht mehr sterben müsse. Aber da ich schon wußte, daß Schein und Sein nicht dasselbe sind, ließ ich es diesmal bei ihrer Aufklärung nicht bewenden. Mein Vater nun, der knapp vor seiner Abreise stand, ließ mich noch wissen, daß Helden und Künstler unsterblich seien. (L 13)

After a series of unsuccessful forays into other art forms, Drach eventually arrives at the creative act of writing, which becomes for him the self-assertive act of the individual in defiance of the greater force of mortality. Keeping the grotesque description of the above-illustrated decaying body in mind, it comes as no surprise that Drach's concept of immortality centres on an intactness of the body that symbolises the integrity of the individual. His concept of immortality through art therefore has metaphysical overtures that differentiate it radically from the, for Drach, far more pedestrian notion of immortality through fame as artist.[32]

The image of the intact and inviolable body signifies a contradictory wish for the stasis, or as Drach himself calls it, the apotheosis of the self. This ideal

---

[32] »Dem Anastasius aber erschien eine durch die Erklärung berufener Kritiker eingeschränkte Unsterblichkeit nicht mehr vertretbar [...]. Er hatte ja nicht im Sinn [...] als unsterblich zu gelten, sondern unsterblich zu sein, das heißt, seine körperliche Existenz durch die Ewigkeit unverlierbar, wenn nicht unversehrt, aufrechtzuerhalten.« (MU 142)

of a homogenous self is the point at which the contradiction between Drach's aesthetic programme and his personal desires becomes clear. Although his literary practice performs to a large extent the deconstruction of absolutism, Drach's childhood ideal of selfhood corresponds to the very image of totality that is later negatively connoted in his work. Thus whilst Drach may ideally have envisaged the apotheosis of himself in the act of writing, the fact is that his work does not convincingly deliver this image. The texts that use *jouissance* as a representational device pulverise the image of complete selfhood into the discontinuity of the grotesque hybrid. Furthermore, the Holocaust texts that use the aesthetic of the corpse as the central image of stasis communicate only the complete negativity of a society in apotheosis. The latter functions in this context not as the signifier of personal omnipotence, but ironically as the signifier of the complete impotence of the self whose entire identity is delineated by the straitjacket stereotype of the reviled Jew. The painful insight into the folly of the childhood wish for omnipotent selfhood arises as a result of this persecution experience during the Holocaust.[33]

Corresponding to this insight emerges the formation of another possible subjectivity, one that is based on the disintegration of the ideal of the sovereign self and that comes to the fore in the portrayals of hybrid identity. Subjectivity is negotiated therefore at the expense of self-apotheosis, because it is precisely in these fictions of the sovereign self (personifications as Drach calls them) that difference disappears.[34]

1.3 *Status Nascendi* versus *Status Quo*: In defence of *Nature Morte*

> Kunst aber kann Aufruhr sein, zu gehorchen
> liegt ihr nicht.   (Albert Drach)

In an unpublished essay »Stilleben«, Drach's preoccupation with the different cultural manifestations of apotheosis and insurgence feeds into his understanding of the revolutionary function of art.[35] The conservative forces of stasis and cul-

---

[33] »Ich aber wollte immer die Ewigkeit für mich und fürchtete das Aufhören der Persönlichkeit. Als Kind glaubte ich, Gott zu sein, und wartete ständig auf meine Apotheose [...]. Man sollte an sich selbst nie einen flüchtigeren Maßstab legen als an alle übrigen. Dann würde die Welt wahrscheinlich nicht aus den Fugen gehen.« Drach, Unsentimentale Reise (note 2), p. 47.

[34] In one of the unpublished essays, Drach refers to such formations of subjectivity both as bureaucratic non-persons and power-crazed fanatics. Albert Drach: Essay I: Die Abschaffung Gottes und dessen Ersatz durch die Behörde. In: id., Das 17. Buch (note 28), p. 4.

[35] Drach, Essay VII: Stilleben (note 28), henceforth cited as S in parentheses with appropriate page numbers.

tural homogeneity find their expression in art works that propagate what Drach critically terms the still life (*Stilleben*) aesthetic. By contrast, he uses the term *nature morte* (strictly speaking merely the French expression for the same tradition of still-life painting) to describe what he understands as the revolutionary qualities of the artwork. *Nature morte* does not shy away from the ugly, disharmonious underside of the world it represents. Unlike the practice of *Stilleben*, it does not respect the integrity of closed, complete structures. Instead, it advocates the introduction of the neglected other of harmony (disharmony or discord) in a bid to expose the falsity of the still life vision. *Stilleben* is for Drach representative of totalitarian practice in art, whereas *nature morte* can be seen as a means of reintroducing difference into aesthetic forms deprived of this plurality.

In Drach's essay, difference is referred to as *Taktlosigkeit* (a lack of tact; in a more abstract sense, it may also be interpreted as a lack of rhythm; S 8). Similar to the abrupt movement of *jouissance*, *nature morte* introduces difference as a form of disruptive movement into the enclosed but fallible still life vacuum. In this manner, the rhythmic discord of *nature morte* evokes the underlying discord of *Stilleben*. For the intrusion of this *Taktlosigkeit* as the other of still life harmony suggests that the self-sufficiency of tranquil systems is not impervious to the disruption of disharmony. After all, these systems are themselves based on the discordant, asymmetrical, expelling practice of separation. The exclusion of ugliness (of difference) from the aesthetic image is symptomatic of the kind of society that, in Drach's words, kills truth (S 7).

The still life aesthetic is thus the mouthpiece of cultural uniformity, identified elsewhere in the unpublished work as consistent with the discourse of bureaucracy.[36] Indeed, Drach's concept of the *Amt* (bureaucracy) functions as a general term for all authoritarian tendencies in modern society and should not therefore be confined merely to the many unflattering images of the Austrian legal system that inform his prose work. Clearly, the still life aesthetic as the appropriate form for the expression of cultural monotony compares well with Kristeva's understanding of stasis as the closure of various structures.

It should moreover be pointed out that Drach's interpretation of the terms *Stilleben* and *nature morte* does not conform to the traditional positioning of the two concepts on the art history map. The Dutch term *Still-leven* originated in Holland around the mid-seventeenth century and was unproblematically assimilated into the art terminology of the Germanic languages. It referred specifically to the painting of objects that do not move. The French language had more trouble finding an equivalent; the term *nature morte* first appears a century later in French academic circles. In contrast to Drach's interpretation, this term was regarded with a certain degree of contempt because it transcends the suggestion that that which is painted in a still life is merely immobile. *Nature morte* suggests beyond this and in blatant disturbance of the *vie tranquille* or *vie silencieuse* (tranquil/silent state of existence) of *Stilleben* that the

---

[36] Cf. Drach, Die Abschaffung Gottes (note 35).

object of the depiction is dead. By virtue of its very name, *nature morte* insinuates the possibility of an anti-aesthetic of untranquility, the disruption of
quiet repose by the strident voice of the ugly (the dead) as it were.[37]

Drach's aesthetic vision reverses this prejudice. He defends the dissimila-
tory tendencies of *nature morte* at the expense of *Stilleben*. In so doing, he is
also questioning the canon of European aesthetic values and its ideal of harmonious beauty as metaphysical truth. The defence of *nature morte* helps to
place Drach within a modern aesthetic tradition of the discordant, the disharmonious, the grotesque. Within this logic of dismemberment, truth takes on the
form of the deformed, the officially ugly or disfigured in the aesthetic work.[38]
In accordance with this, the aesthetic of *nature morte* degrades the represented
whilst *Stilleben* will attempt to elevate it (S 2).

As an aesthetic practice that degrades, *nature morte* should be understood
not only as a logic of decomposition, but also as a signifier of the comic. It
explains why Drach, although concerned with issues of the utmost seriousness,
is also a comic writer. His works rarely miss the opportunity to mockingly
degrade that which is seen to be almighty, powerful and official. Through the
practice of *nature morte* thus, Drach recruits one form of destruction (the vio-
lating *Taktlosigkeit* of *nature morte*) against another, that being the stasis or
paralysis of homogenising systems represented by the still life aesthetic. Although as essayist Drach conceives of these tendencies as opposite aesthetic
developments, as a writer he combines both. The discontinuity of his literary
style testifies to this staccato combination.

The above polarisation of art into two politically loaded aesthetic categories
rearticulates a central concern of Drach's work: the representation of the competing forces of movement versus paralysis, of crisis versus stasis, of the possibility of change versus the maintenance of a hierarchical and unchanging
status quo. As suggested earlier, Drach's poetic language documents elements
of both approaches: the collapse via language transgression of system into
process on the one hand, and on the other, the linguistic simulation of discursive coagulation in the portrayal of society's descent into totalitarianism.

---

[37] Charles Sterling: La Nature Morte de L'Antiquité au XXe Siècle. Paris: Macula
     1985, p. 41–42.
[38] In a recent work, Winfried Menninghaus identifies just this truth ideal of the »disgu-
     sting« as typical of a broader modernist context: »Gerade als das Skandalöse, Unas-
     similierbare, schlechthin Heterogene, als die Transgression der zivilisatorischen
     Verbote, als die (analsadistische) Destruktion der schönen Form und die lachende
     Transzendenz der symbolischen Ordnung avanciert das Ekelhafte in die verwaiste
     Positionen des unverfügbaren ›Realen‹ und der quasi metaphysischen Wahrheit. Das
     Wahre ist das Ekelhafte, das Ekelhafte ist das Wahre, ja das ›Ding an sich‹: auf die-
     sen Satz läuft von Nietzsche über Freud, Kafka, Bataille und Sartre bis Kristeva un-
     versehens eine gewichtige und weithin übersehene Bewegung modernen Denkens
     hinaus.« Winfried Menninghaus: Ekel. Theorie und Geschichte einer starken Emp-
     findung. Frankfurt a. M.: Suhrkamp 1999, p. 20–21.

The essay »Stilleben« is not just a critique of European aesthetic traditions. It is also a thinly disguised attack on the totalising forces of modernity and specifically a personal attack against the failed artist of mediocrity, Hitler himself.[39]

1.4 Positions

> Und wenn Sie die ganze Donau über meinen
> Kopf gießen, ich werde nie ein Christ.
>
> (Albert Drach, sen.)

> Ich aber bin der Ansicht, daß hier in Europa
> die Juden keine andere Rasse sind.
>
> (Albert Drach)

What role does Drach's identity as an Austro-Jew play in his work, and in particular in his writing of difference? Drach's own relationship to Jewry is significant in answering this question, as it helps to further situate him as a writer in a post-modern (more specifically post-colonial) context.

As a reply to the question of his Jewish identity, Drach shows himself to be aware of the moral questionability of philosemitism, and thus advocates the treatment of Jews first and foremost as fellow humans, equally capable of good and bad as any other group of people. He further claims that any feelings he experienced as a Jew are those that arose as a result of his experience as victim during the Third Reich: persecution and the resulting struggle to defend the self against this victimisation.[40] These are not however characteristics of an internal identification with Jewry. Rather they testify to the imposed or external nature of Jewish identity, in Sartre's sense, the proposal that to be a Jew is in fact to be categorised as such within the greater social context.[41]

Zygmunt Bauman and Sander L. Gilman have both referred to what would seem like the inevitability of the internalisation – and in some cases further

---

[39] Drach describes Hitler's paintings as typical of the banal style of the *Stilleben* aesthetic. His failure to be accepted by art academies is seen by Drach as instrumental in the subsequent path he embarked upon: »Denn wie anders würde er zum Führer berufen worden sein [...]?« (S 3)

[40] »Als Jude selbst habe ich eigentlich kein besonders starke Gefühl. Dieses Gefühl, das ich als Jude habe, ist Verfolgung und Abwehr [...]. Nun bin ich allerdings nicht der Ansicht, daß man verteidigen soll, was die Juden Verkehrtes gemacht haben, sondern man muß, wenn man selber Jude ist, viel strenger mit ihnen vorgehen.« Cited in Karlheinz F. Auckenthaler: »Ich habe mich erst als Jude zu fühlen gehabt, als mich der Hitler als einen solchen erklärt hat«. Albert Drachs Beziehung zum Judentum im Leben und Werk. In: Modern Austrian Literature 27 (1994), No. 3/4, p. 51–69, here p. 53.

[41] »Die Erfahrung ist also weit davon entfernt, den Begriff des Juden hervorzubringen, vielmehr ist es dieser, der die Erfahrung beleuchtet; existierte der Jude nicht, der Antisemit würde ihn erfinden.« Jean-Paul Sartre: Überlegungen zur Judenfrage. Hamburg: Rowohlt 1994 (Gesammelte Werke in Einzelausgaben; Politische Schriften 2), p. 12.

projection onto other minority groups – of this imposed identity. Drach's literature certainly lays bare these processes of identity construction. With regard to his autobiographical work, it has been suggested that through his characterisations of persecuted Jews, Drach enacts just this projection of the otherness of the self onto other disadvantaged groups.[42] However, far from being a self-hating Jew, Drach's writing illustrates processes of (auto)stereotyping that are not confined solely to the Jewish question. Whereas characterisations of self-hating Jews appear from time to time throughout his work, these instances are often highly caricatured and critically reflect a more general trend of modernising, uniform societies towards rigid categorisation.[43]

Indeed, Drach's cosmopolitan understanding of Jewish identity as a socially imposed stereotype resulting in the marginalisation of the individual corresponds to theories that propose the *conditio judaica* – as moulded by the ambivalences of the European assimilation drama – as the forerunner to the modern, in some cases post-modern, *conditio humana* of alienation, marginalisation and dispersal of the self.

Drach's universal interpretation of anti-Semitism as an instrument in the victimisation of peoples (and not just Jews) further articulates this desire to make relevant the experience of the Jews in the twentieth century for humanity at large. In this scheme, Jewishness becomes the exemplary instance of a more general mode of existence, this being the experience of processes of stranger-hood, alienation, contingency and otherness.[44]

---

[42] With reference to the first part of Drachs's autobiography »Z. Z.« *das ist die Zwischen-zeit*, Anne Fuchs has – within a broader discussion concerning the complexity of Jewish identity – drawn attention to the further projection of this imposed strangerhood, but as it occurs in the language of gender warfare as opposed to the language of anti-Semitism: »The clinical language of Drach's description mimes a male gaze which is not really driven by desire but by the need to exclude and reject [...]. The ugly woman is a projection of the phobic male who constitutes his own territory through loathing.« Anne Fuchs: Files against the Self. Albert Drach. In: id., A Space of Anxiety. Dislocation and Abjection in Modern German-Jewish Literature. Amsterdam, Atlanta: Rodopi 1999 (Amsterdamer Publikationen zur Sprache und Literatur; 138), p. 123–162, here p. 144–145.

[43] Sander L. Gilman's definition of Jewish self-hatred is, contrary to the specificity of its name, a category widely applicable to general processes of identity construction based on the exclusion of others: »Self-hatred results from outsiders' acceptance of the mirage of themselves generated by their reference group – that group in society which they see as defining them – as a reality.« (Sander L. Gilman: Jewish Self-Hatred: Anti-Semitism and the Hidden Language of the Jews. Baltimore, London: John Hopkins University Press 1986, p. 2) Zygmunt Bauman (Modernity and Ambivalence [note 8], p. 90) emphasises the consequences of this acceptance: »To be a stranger, is to be refused and to surrender the right to self-constitution, self-definition, self-identity. It is to derive one's sense from the relationship with the native, and from the native's examining gaze. It is to forget the skill of making a meaningful pattern out of the inherited ›material‹. It is to surrender one's autonomy, and with that the authority to make one's life meaningful.«

[44] The experience of Jewishness as a projection of strangerhood is also for Drach the arbitrary outlet for the expression of hatred, which, along the same lines as Bauman's

I believe that in defining Jewish identity as the particular instance of a general, socially constructed human condition, Drach displays a certain kinship with those Austro-Jewish writers who have been identified as »ill at ease with national or ethnic categorizations«.[45] His literary strategy of grotesque indeterminacy can, from this perspective, be read as a form of resistance against the force of categorisation, through a language of ambivalence that ruptures »any binary model that defines belonging and not belonging in a culture«.[46]

By taking recourse to universal and generalisable definitions of what it means to be Jewish, Drach transcends other definitions of Austro/German-Jewish writers as the tortured voice of conflicting identities, or simply as exiled outsiders.[47] A fundamental questioning of processes of identity construction persists throughout his work and by no means does it merely confine itself to his many Jewish characters. Instead, Drach constantly raises the instability of cultural identity as an issue of universal concern. In so doing, he relativises the defining and excluding practices of self-appointed, socially dominant groups who take upon themselves the task of setting identity norms.

This renegotiation of cultural boundaries and – through the collapse of binary oppositions – the location of otherness within the frail defences of the sovereign self, places Drach as writer in a post-colonial tradition of the *de*construction of norms of identity construction. His exploration of the ambivalence of identity accounts for the many images of the in-between in his work, the in-between being the space of plurality that emerges once binary oppositions have been transgressed.

Whilst frequently exaggerating the binary representation of the other as excluded outsider, images of otherness in Drach's work are more significantly to be

---

strangerhood and Gilman's self-hatred, has virtually nothing to do with the chosen object of aggression. Cf. Albert Drach: Essay IV: Zur Lösung der Antisemitenfrage. In: id., Das 17. Buch (note 28). This perspective corresponds closely to Theodor W. Adorno's understanding of anti-Semitism: »Nicht erst das antisemitische Ticket ist antisemitisch, sondern die Ticketmentalität überhaupt.« Cf. Max Horkheimer / Theodor W. Adorno: Dialektik der Aufklärung. Philosophische Fragmente. Frankfurt a. M.: Fischer 1991, p. 217. To summarise the general suggestion of the above mentioned arguments, anti-Semitism and the Jewish question are relevant not just with reference to themselves, but for their implications for the power relations of modern culture in general.

[45] Matthias Konzett: The Politics of Recognition in Contemporary Austrian Jewish Literature. In: Monatshefte 90, No. 1 (Spring 1998), p. 71–88, here p. 72.

[46] Ibid., p. 79.

[47] »Die Helden der deutsch-jüdischen Identität werden wegen ihrer Identität verfolgt, und in der Regel löst die Erzählung die Krise nicht. Der Konflikt zwischen verschiedenen Identitäten wie die Erfahrung des Identitätsverlustes machen das Erleben einer doppelten Identität negativ und zerstörerisch.« (Gershon Shaked: Die Macht der Identität. Essays über jüdische Schriftsteller. Königstein/Ts: Jüdischer Verlag bei Athenäum 1986, p. 192) This argument is in my view too one-sided and neglects the area of play that opens up through the experience of double-identity, i. e. it neglects the positive repercussions of identity dispersal. For a discussion of just this positive playfulness see Homi K. Bhabha: Of Mimicry and Man. The Ambivalence of Colonial Discourse. In: The Location of Culture (note 12), p. 85–93.

located in this image of the in-between. It is this image of ambivalence that specifically resists the confines of binary categorisation. Using Homi Bhabha's theory of mimic man in a later section, I will elaborate on the grotesque function of this image as part of deconstructive offensive against fictions of the sovereign self.

It should be pointed out that Drach's portrayal of otherness is not entirely reducible to his identity as assimilated Austro-Jew. Whereas Jewish identity is certainly problematised throughout his work, Drach also concerns himself with various manifestations of the other. To a large extent his treatment of Jewish identity should be regarded as consistent with this framework of inquiry. The anti-heroines of *Untersuchung an Mädeln* and »Vermerk einer Hurenwerdung« (Stella, Esmerelda and Marie respectively) are examples of victimised female others. In »Amtshandlung gegen einen Unsterblichen«, Arthur Rimbaud embodies the artist as other. *Das Goggelbuch* can be described as a comic treatment of the otherness of German identity.[48]

Whether one can argue that this interest in the social constellations of power that produce others derives directly from Drach's experience as persecuted Jew is also unclear. The autobiographical protocols concerning his childhood refer to many different images of Drach as outsider, none of which are linked directly to his assimilated Austro-Jewish status. In fact, his description of childhood days paints the picture of a multi-cultural environment, one in which being culturally or racially different may not have had overt repercussions in the run of the everyday.[49]

In addition to the environment described, the Drach household was, according to Drach, so assimilated that assimilation (during his childhood at any rate) was never a theme of any great significance.[50] Born in Vienna on December 17 1902 to middle-class Jewish parents, Drach ironically belongs to the generation that would provide the flourishing fascism of the 1920s with most of its support – the last generation to be socialised before the First World War.[51] In the above-mentioned autobiographical texts concerned with his youth, this period is not directly historicised. The Great War is thus treated in a marginal way. Drach's alter ego, Anastasius (»Martyrium eines Unheiligen«), is far more concerned with his esoteric search for the way to immortality. Nonetheless, the end of childhood and the end of innocence converge associatively

---

[48] Albert Drach: Untersuchung an Mädeln. Kriminalprotokoll. Ungekürzte Ausg., München: Deutscher Taschenbuch Verlag 1995 (dtv; 12043); id., Vermerk einer Hurenwerdung. In: id., Ironie vom Glück (note 2), p. 69–90; id., Amtshandlung gegen einen Unsterblichen. In: ibid., p. 90–131; id., Das Goggelbuch (note 27).

[49] Cf. MU 153.

[50] »Daß sich die globalen Verhältnisse für Menschen jüdischer Herkunft als katastrophal und lebensbedrohend erweisen würden, konnte Drach in seiner Kindheit und Jugend noch nicht ahnen. Sein Elternhaus war so sehr assimiliert, daß es das Wort Assimilation nicht kennen wollte, weil man sich ganz selbstverständlich dem deutschen Kulturkreis zugehörig fühlte.« (Schobel, Albert Drach [note 3], p. 330–331)

[51] Gerhard Botz: Austria. In: The Social Basis of European Fascist Movements. Ed. by Detlef Mühlberger. London: Croom Helm 1987, p. 242–280, here p. 255.

with the end of the war. Interestingly, this historical cut-off point also converges with a feeling of personal malaise, in Drach's words the vision of futureless-ness that persists strongly throughout his other autobiographical works. This feeling of hopelessness coincides also with his realisation that an intactness of the self in the form of immortality is not realisable.[52]

This juxtaposition of personal and historical events speaks volumes. Drach shows himself to be an author concerned with phases of decline, end-phases, moments of personal and historical rupture. This comes as no surprise when one considers that his generation was one which would witness, in the space of the few decades between 1918–1945, the many political upheavals in Austria, and with that the instability of Austrian (let alone Austro-Jewish) identity.[53]

Drach's father, university-educated, well read and familiar with the cultural and artistic circles of turn-of-the-century Vienna, came from a family of wealthy Jewish farmers in the Bukowina. Drach's mother, presented as the more prac-tical of his parents, came from Vienna and is often portrayed in the role of the overprotective Jewish mother. Drach was the only child of this marriage, his father's second. The first marriage, an intermarriage to a Catholic moreover, produced Drach's older half-sister who maintained the religious identity of her deceased mother. Drach's childhood home seems to have digested this reli-gious diversity with little difficulty. Religion played only a marginal role in the household, yet at the same time there seems to have reigned an open-minded and unconcerned tolerance of the different religious events and holidays.

This non-problematisation of religious identity in the private sphere cannot be said to have been entirely true of Lueger's Vienna of the turn-of-the-century, however. The dominance of anti-Semitic rhetoric in the political discourse of the day would certainly have made highly visible an already existent Jewish »prob-lem«. The politically advantageous public thematisation of the Jewish issue is not surprising when one considers both the hostility of competing cultures within the increasingly unstable Austro-Hungarian empire and the scapegoat role that was refined for the Jews within this context. In addition to the repercussions of

---

[52] »Wie er außerdem begriff, daß seine Kindheit ebenso wie der große Krieg zu Ende ging, sammelte er Zinnsoldaten aller Völker und spielte mit diesen.« (MU 161) »Er hatte die Matura hinter sich gebracht, mußte aus der Wiener Wohnung hinaus [...] verdiente kei-nen Groschen [...]. Dazu verblieben ihm wenig Zukunftsaussichten. Er fand seine er-schienenen Gedichte schlecht und für die Stücke, die er jetzt schrieb, keinen Abnehmer, wiewohl er glaubte, an Selbstmord statt literarische Taten gesetzt zu haben.« (MU 180)

[53] Robert Menasse describes this literary fixation on the sense of apocalypse in specifical-ly Austrian terms: »Es scheint [...] so zu sein, daß es in Österreich einen besonderen Hang zu Endzeiten gibt. Man muß Endzeiten sagen, also den Plural verwenden, weil es eine österreichische Erfahrungstatsache ist, daß am Ende einer Endzeit nie das Ende ist. Die zur Jahrhundertwende geborene Generation etwa hat dies bekanntlich viermal erleben können: Das Ende der Habsburger Monarchie. Das Ende der Ersten Republik. Das Ende des Ständestaates. Das Ende der Ostmark als Bestandteil des Dritten Reiches.« Robert Menasse: Das Land ohne Eigenschaften. Essay zur österreichischen Identität. Frankfurt a. M.: Suhrkamp 1995 (Suhrkamp-Taschenbuch; 2487), p. 10.

this political strategy, there had been an upsurge in anti-Jewish sentiment in Vienna – particularly prevalent in the 1890s – after the liberation of the Jews in 1867 and the resulting rapid increase in the Jewish population of the city between 1869 and 1910.[54]

It has been argued that the exploitation of anti-Semitic rhetoric as a gambit in the political struggle between the Christian Socialists and the Social Democrats is already symptomatic of the selection of the Jews for special treatment in turn-of-the-century Vienna, bearing witness to the mental apartheid which foreshadowed and prepared the way for the fulfilment of the Final Solution.[55] This may well have been the case, yet at the same time Vienna, before 1918 at any rate, as a »multi-contextual space of cultural encounter and hybridity«[56] was an environment which easily »obscured the meaning of Germanness and made ›foreignness‹ less problematic«.[57] Drach's claim that his family were so assimilated as for the topic to be a non-topic is credible in the light of the above general atmosphere, despite the existence of a parallel anti-Semitic rhetoric.

This coexistence of a recognised difference and yet the close identification with Austro-Germanic culture can be explained in socio-historical terms. In contrast to the situation of assimilating Jews in Germany where the pressure to join a single national identity was greater, the cultural hybridity of the Austro-Hungarian empire made it easier for Jews (both of the assimilating middle-class and of those groups who had no intention of assimilating) to assert the sense of a national, or in the case of the Drach family, a liberal bourgeois Jewish identity. In other words, the Drach family history of the turn-of-the-century illustrates how, as Marsha L. Rozenblit has pointed out: »One could easily be

---

[54] »In den Jahren 1869 bis 1880 war die jüdische Bevölkerung von 40 227 (6,10 Prozent der Gesamtbevölkerung) auf 72 588 (10,06 Prozent) angewachsen. Im Jahr 1910 gab es [...] 175 818 Juden (8,63 Prozent) in Wien, wo es fünfzig Jahre davor nur 6 217 (2,16 Prozent) gegeben hatte – eine gewaltige Wachstumsrate.« Robert S. Wistrich: Sozialdemokratie, Antisemitismus und die Wiener Juden. In: Eine zerstörte Kultur. Jüdisches Leben und Antisemitismus in Wien seit dem 19. Jahrhundert. Hg. von Gerhard Botz, Ivar Oxaal und Michael Pollak. Buchloe: Obermeyer 1990, p. 169–180, here p. 172. For further discussion of the role of politics in the development of Austrian anti-Semitism see Peter Pulzer: Spezifische Momente und Spielarten des österreichischen und des Wiener Antisemitismus. In: ibid., p. 121–41.

[55] »Die Vernichtung der Wiener Juden im Dritten Reich zeigte im wesentlichen dieselbe Dynamik der Judenfeindschaft, wie sie in Wien schon vor 1900 angelegt gewesen war.« Gerhard Botz: Die Ausgliederung der Juden aus der Gesellschaft. Das Ende Wiener Judentums unter der NS-Herrschaft (1938–1943). In: Eine zerstörte Kultur (last note), p. 285–311, here p. 310.

[56] Konzett, The Politics of Recognition in Contemporary Austrian Jewish Literature (note 46), p. 74.

[57] Marsha L. Rozenblit: The Jews of Germany and Austria: A Comparative Perspective. In: Austrians and Jews in the Twentieth Century. From Franz Joseph to Waldheim. Ed. by Robert S. Wistrich. New York: St. Martin's Press 1992, p. 1–18, here p. 13.

an Austrian – an essentially supra-national identity not attached to a particular ethnic group – and also remain a Jew.«[58]

When assessing the Drach family's history however, an awareness of Jewish ethnic consciousness becomes apparent. Drach's father born in 1857 in the Bukowina, despite a relatively privileged status, would have belonged to that group of Jews migrating westwards towards Vienna in the latter half of the nineteenth century, a period that witnesses the corresponding rise of anti-Semitism. Despite the suggestion of acceptance within the German national context, incidents such as the seven year wait for permission to marry his first bride along with the fact that intermarriage was forbidden at this time would have made difficult the seamless assumption of an assimilation so complete as to be invisible. Add to this an anecdote from Drach family lore (how Drach's uncle refused to convert as a means of furthering his army career) and it becomes clear that despite their privileged status as assimilated, westernised, middle-class educated Austro-Jews, the Drach family was aware and proud of their ethnic difference.[59]

When considering this double-identity constellation and its corresponding doubling of the individual's spatial location, one can see how Drach would easily fulfil Marcel Reich-Ranicki's description of Jewish identity as simultaneously central and peripheral. It has been pointed out however, that this experience of the ambivalence of identity was not to be found exclusively amongst assimilated Jews, but in fact is present in other non-Jewish authors. The reliability of double-identity as a defining criterion for Jewishness thereby becomes questionable.[60]

It could furthermore be argued that Drach's positing of double-identity as an image of the in-between reflects his cosmopolitan heritage as a Viennese writer. It places him within a literary tradition of Viennese modernism which has been portrayed as not just exemplary for modernism in general, but serves also through the use of ambivalence as an avant-gardist forerunner for para-

---

[58] Ibid., p. 11.

[59] Cf. Schobel, Albert Drach (note 3), p. 333–334.

[60] Marcel Reich-Ranicki's well-known argument posits German/Austro-Jewish writers as outsiders who, through the uniqueness of their peripheral perspective, instigate provocative instances of scepticism: »Innerhalb und schließlich doch außerhalb der Welt stehend, mit der sie sich auseinandersetzten, konnten sie Vertraulichkeit und Intimität mit skeptischer Distanz verbinden: Gerade von der Peripherie her ließ sich das Zentrale oft mit besonderer Deutlichkeit erkennen und darstellen.« Marcel Reich-Ranicki: Über Ruhestörer. Juden in der deutschen Literatur. München: Piper 1973 (Serie Piper; 48), p. 16. However, Hans Otto Horch advocates the treatment of what constitutes the specificity of German-Jewish authors as separate from both the features of double identity and provocation. As he points out, the double identity problematic manifests itself also in non-Jewish writers, and there are reliable examples of German-Jewish writers who, far from upsetting the societal status quo, were in fact best-sellers. Cf. Hans Otto Horch: Heimat und Fremde. Jüdische Schriftsteller und deutsche Literatur oder Probleme einer deutsch-jüdischen Literaturgeschichte. In: Juden als Träger bürgerlicher Kultur in Deutschland. Hg. von Julius H. Schoeps. Stuttgart, Bonn: Burg 1989 (Studien zur Geistesgeschichte; 11), p. 41–65.

digms of post-modernism.[61] Steven Beller has argued that this Viennese liter-ary-cultural tradition reflects a transnational sentiment and therefore owes its origins to a great extent to the late Habsburg era's confrontation with elements of the Jewish Diaspora.[62] This line of argument suggests the inherently Jewish nature of modernism and post-modernism.

Assessing these different currents and influences, Drach can be proposed as a writer whose work displays paradigmatic tendencies of the (post)modern. A certain affinity to the Jewish-Viennese intellectual and literary tradition is undeniable. Whether his use of these paradigms is reducible to his identity as an assimilated Jew remains questionable. It would seem reasonable to suggest that Drach is a literary figure in whom diverse influences collide. His prose work is the expression of just this collision.

1.5 The Child in Flight

Let us return to one last resounding image from the narrated childhood of Albert Drach. It concerns the precise moment in which he discovers his voca-tion as artist of language. The autobiographical short story »Lunz« describes this event in some detail.

Drach and his playmate, Jenny Juch, climb up the hills surrounding the lake in search of adventure. In a remote area they encounter an old woman who offers them refreshments. Both children accept the proffered cake, but Drach at the last minute and in particular when the old woman introduces the theme of death, senses that something is amiss and pulls his friend away in haste. Re-membering the cautionary words of his protective mother, Drach does not dare to eat the cake. For Jenny it is already too late. They run back down the hill to civilisation. Remarkably, whilst in flight, in transition, in fear and in the flux of movement, the child Drach begins to compose verse.[63]

---

[61] Gérard M. Raulet: Vorwort. In: Verabschiedung der (Post-)Moderne? Eine interdis-ziplinäre Debatte. Hg. von Jacques le Rider and Gérard Raulet. Tübingen: Narr 1987 (Deutsche Text-Bibliothek; 7), p. 7–20, here p. 14.

[62] »While there are other traditions and backgrounds which added to Vienna 1900, it was the Jewish experience which was the most prevalent among its central figures and its audience, even when that difference is defined in social and not even ethnic terms.« Steven Beller: Vienna and the Jews 1867–1938. A Cultural History. Cam-bridge: Cambridge University Press 1990, p. 70. Zygmunt Bauman further supports the social implications of this thesis through his concept of universal strangerhood when he argues that the Jewish experience of ambivalence has become a universal norm in the post-modern world: »The sting has been taken out of the assimilation pressure (or of that little that has been left of it) not because of anything the Jews have done but because what happened to the world into which the Jews have been assimilating. This is now a late-modern, or postmodern, world of universal particu-larity.« Cf. Bauman, Modernity and Ambivalence (note 8), p. 161.

[63] »Daraufhin nahm ich Reißaus und riß Jenny mit. Unterwegs aber machte ich trotz-dem Verse, die ich mir merkte.« (L 14)

The constellation of events is striking in terms of its suggestive power. Are we in the nightmare-fairytale world of Hänsel and Gretel, or are we in fact witnessing the re-enactment of the fall of man from the Garden of Eden? If this fall can be described as the further invasion of death of the childhood Lunz idyll, and the paradise lost as a world that has been shifted and shaken up by a knowledge of death, then the restorative function of writing in the face of death emerges clearly.

This restoration is part of an imperfect practice, however. A world unspoiled by the presence of death cannot be entirely regained through a writing practice that takes place in the space of the in-between, a space dominated by *jouissance* that both defers and evokes the possibility of death. Within one year, Jenny is dead. Drach could not save her and his composed lines are a means of improvising survival in the space of transition. The idea that language activity, if not the means through which to gain immortality, at least affords an always temporary survival for the creating individual, is very potent in this instance. It anticipates the function of language for the adult Drach in flight from the Nazis and eloquently confirms Kristeva's general claim that »The writer is a phobic who succeeds in metaphorizing in order to keep from being frightened to death; instead he comes to life again in signs.«[64]

By contrast, the Holocaust texts reveal the treacherousness of the in-between space once the fetish function of language surrenders to Thanatos. Such texts do not signify the above resurrection of the frantically metaphorising phobic writer. Instead, the economy of death takes pride of place in this deadened language as the Holocaust survivor revisits through his own text the scenes of death that are the condition and constant companion of that dubious state, survival.[65]

---

[64] Kristeva, Powers of Horror (note 24), p. 38.

[65] In his analysis of the oral testimonies of Holocaust survivors, Lawrence L. Langer identifies the paradox of survival: »Although nothing could be more final than the deaths recorded there, nothing could be less final either. As a result, the concrete meanings of words like ›survival‹ and ›liberation‹ blur, because they cannot be separated from the doom of those whose ›preoccupation with survival‹ failed.« (Lawrence L. Langer: Holocaust Testimonies. The Ruins of Memory. New Haven, London: Yale University Press 1991, p. 23) For a more detailed discussion of this predicament see chapter 6 of this dissertation.

Chapter 2
The Grotesque: Topography of Transgression, Morphology of Emptiness

2.1 Body Language

The previous chapter introduces a two-pronged understanding of the grotesque that posits it, on the one hand, as saturated by the ambivalences of transgressive *jouissance*. On the other, it is put forward as the index for a state of absolute negation, which is described in terms of stasis or the spectre of death that is final and beyond the regenerative dynamic of transgression. From this dual perspective, the scope of the grotesque covers a dramatic representative range contoured by what Brad Epps has generally termed an »entire thematics of mortality and vitality«.[1] In the case of Drach's particular grotesque scripting, this range is demonstrated in the shift between the more comical works that flirt with and defer death or stasis, and the Holocaust texts that map a certain capitulation to the power of a negation so absolute as to utterly paralyse the individual within the related discourses of totalitarianism and anti-Semitism.

This particular approach argues that the grotesque may be productively expanded upon with reference to psychoanalysis and in particular to drive theory. What is the relationship between the grotesque, psychoanalysis and the drives, however? The area in which all three overlap is that of the subject's corporeality: elaborating subjectivity by placing the body in the context of signifying practices. The grotesque's concern with extremes of the body has been well documented. Indeed, its tendency toward the scatological, its perceived lack of finesse and subtlety may explain why it has been regarded as an emotional (as opposed to intellectual) category and accordingly marginalised within the European canon of aesthetics.[2] Psychoanalysis has attempted the reversal of the

---

[1] Brad Epps: Grotesque Identities. Writing, Death, and the Space of the Subject (Between Michel de Montaigne and Reinaldo Arenas). In: Journal of the Mid-West Modern Languages Association 28 (1995), p. 38–55, here p. 44.

[2] Mikhail Bakhtin's elaboration of the grotesque carnivalesque body is perhaps the strongest articulation of the scatological or »Akte des Körper-Dramas« (acts of the bodily drama) as he terms it. These »acts« are listed as follows: »Essen, Trinken, Ausscheidungen (Kot, Urin, Schweiß, Nasenschleim, Mundschleim), Begattung, Schwangerschaft, Niederkunft, Körperwuchs, Altern, Krankheiten, Tod, Zerfetzung, Zerteilung, Verschlingung durch einen anderen Leib.« Michail M. Bachtin: Literatur und Karneval. Zur Romantheorie und Lachkultur. Frankfurt a. M: Fischer 1996 (Fischer-Taschenbücher; 7434: Fischer Wissenschaft), p. 17. In her analysis of the links between the grotesque and the feminine, Mary Russo draws attention to the physical implications of

mind/body Cartesian dualism that underlies such evaluations by emphasising »the fundamental connectedness of the mind to the body [...], the mapping of the body's interior on its exterior and its exterior on its interior«.[3]

Kristeva's theory of poetic language addresses this embodiment of subjectivity by attaching the linguistic signifier closely to the body. Her concept of *signifiance* claims that the body is indeed signified via drive interference in language. The drives articulate themselves in *signifiance* as »a pattern of psychical marks across the body, thus investing it in a dialectical signifying practice«.[4] This dialectical practice allows for the production of meaning by the drives in excess of consciousness. The Cartesian mind/body dualism is thus to an extent ruptured by this theory of the unconscious that links the body to signifying practices through »the devastating work of the drives«.[5] The excess of *jouissance* on the one hand and the dominance of stasis on the other in the literary text are both manifestations of drive *signifiance* or drive »presence« in the symbolic order of language.

The general direction of the above theory is to emphasise that the body is not only signified via the drives in the symbolic order, but that the mapping of these energy cathexes in *signifiance* – the mapping of a physical as well as psychical space of self-definition – is in fact necessary for the constitution of subjectivity. The body, in other words, is central to any notion of subjectivity in psychoanalysis. As suggested, this renders psychoanalysis of immediate interest for the grotesque which itself appears at first glance to be wholly preoccupied with signifying the body in various postures of distortion.[6]

---

the concept »grotto-esque« with emphasis on the construction of the female body in purely scatological terms: »As bodily metaphor, the grotesque cave tends to look like [...] the cavernous anatomical female body [...]. Blood, tears, vomit, excrement – all the detritus of the body that is separated out and placed with terror and revulsion on the side of the feminine – are down there in that cave of abjection.« Mary Russo: The Female Grotesque. Risk, Excess and Modernity. New York, London: Routledge 1994, p. 1–2. Common to both understandings of the grotesque is an encoding of the body as belonging to the cultural category of the low within a »vertical symbolic hierarchy« (Peter Stallybrass / Allon White: The Politics and Poetics of Transgression. London: Methuen 1986 [University Paperbacks; 922], p. 3) This kind of categorisation of the grotesque as the profane, the low and the unsubtle accounts for its relative marginalisation in European aesthetics. Cf. Wolfgang Kayser: Das Groteske. Seine Gestaltung in Malerei und Dichtung. Oldenburg, Hamburg: Stalling 1957, p. 111, and Philip Thompson: The Grotesque. London: Methuen 1972 (The Critical Idiom; 24), p. 26.

3   Elizabeth Gross: The Body of Signification. In: Abjection, Melancholia, and Love. The Work of Julia Kristeva. Ed. by John Fletcher and Andrew Benjamin. London, New York: Routledge 1990 (Warwick Studies in Philosophy and Literature), p. 80–103, p. 82.

4   Anna Smith: Julia Kristeva. Readings of Exile and Estrangement. London: Macmillan 1996, p. 109-110.

5   Ibid.

6   Yuan Yuan makes this link explicit when he proposes that »Lacanian discourse informs a site of dialogue between theory of the grotesque and practice of the grotesque« (Yuan Yuan: The Lacanian Subject and Grotesque Desires. Between Oedipal Violation and Narcissistic Closure. In: The American Journal of Psychoanalysis 56 [1996], p. 35–47, p. 35). Similarly, Russo identifies *Revolution in Poetic Language* and *Powers of*

Nonetheless, the theory of the drives as the mouthpiece of the body in signification has come under much fire. Anna Smith accuses Kristeva of literalising (and thereby banalising) »the obscurity of Being« with her »biological« theory of poetic language. Similarly, Judith Butler regards Kristeva's concept of the drives and the maternal body that they purportedly articulate as naturalistic and self-defeating.[7] Furthering this critical perspective, Winfried Menninghaus stresses what he sees as the fictional aspect to Kristeva's theory of the drives and by implication poetic language. He makes the point that unless we accept her understanding of the symbolic as a purely negative and repressive order, we cannot accept as credible her theory of poetic language as the subversive (and necessary) disruption of this order.[8]

However, as Kelly Oliver points out, Kristeva does not ultimately advocate through drive interference the irreversible descent into psychosis of the symbolic order. Rather, she »emphasizes the need to steer between stable identities/positions [...] on the one hand, and the complete dissolution of identities on the other«.[9] My understanding of Kristeva's drive theory envisages the above »steering« operation as a symptom of the ongoing negotiations between the energy cathexes of the unconscious and the imaginary projections of the self in the symbolic order, i. e. as a critical borderline position between conscious/unconscious that provides us »with a way to acknowledge processes through which we become invested in fixed representations«.[10] In other words, Kristeva's understanding of the body illustrates the processes through which we become bodies (subjects), providing through drive theory »an elaboration and further detail about the body's imaginary and symbolic status«.[11] The sociopolitical potential of the drives becomes clear here; their rupture of established signifying systems in culture paves the way for a profound critique of the homogenising tendencies of the socio-linguistic totality. Indeed, in some articulations (e. g. the traumatic rupture that constitutes melancholia) drive interfer-

---

Horror as two works that in particular explore the grotesque in its psychoanalytic articulation (Russo, The Female Grotesque [note 2], p. 9–10).

[7] Smith, Julia Kristeva (note 5), p. 107. Judith Butler: The Body Politics of Julia Kristeva. In: Ethics, Politics, and Difference in Julia Kristeva's Writing. Ed. by Kelly Oliver. London, New York: Routledge 1993, p. 164–178, here p. 165.

[8] »Für die Seite der symbolischen Ordnung adoptiert Kristeva eine extrem reduktive, ja repressive Sprachtheorie [...] Sprache wird, [...] zunächst radikal von allen mimetischen, ›poetischen‹ und ›mütterlichen‹ Dimensionen entblößt, damit ihr diese dann von außen als Subversion, ja Zerstörung des ›Symbolischen‹ zustoßen können.« Winfried Menninghaus: Ekel. Theorie und Geschichte einer starken Empfindung. Frankfurt a. M.: Suhrkamp 1999, here p. 548.

[9] Kelly Oliver: Introduction. Julia Kristeva's Outlaw Ethics. In: Ethics, Politics, and Difference in Julia Kristeva's Writing. Ed. by Kelly Oliver. London, New York: Routledge 1993, p. 1–22, here p. 8.

[10] Ibid.

[11] Gross, The Body of Signification (note 3), p. 85.

ence lays the foundations for a radically new ethical relationship between self
and other.[12]

This notwithstanding, Judith Butler criticises Kristeva's theory for its redundancy as a sustainable political practice.[13] However, one must pose the
question as to whether these ongoing negotiations between the drives and the
symbolic subject as they appear in the literary text do not qualify as the intel-
lectual-aesthetic index for a sustained ethico-political practice that necessarily
begins with a priority of flexible thought similar to that put forward by Adorno
in his essay on anti-Semitism.[14] In Kristeva's trajectory, the practice of flexible
thought can be inferred from her postulate concerning the transgression of the
symbolic order for the purpose of its renewal.[15] Clearly, this positive evaluation focuses more strongly on the underlying open-endedness of the symbolic
order and its constant modification by the movement of transgression than on
the outright destruction envisaged by Smith or futile re-absorption under the
hegemony of paternal law understood by Butler.[16]

Jay M. Berstein has recently pointed out that a certain similarity exists between Adorno's critique of identity-thinking and Kristeva's theory of the system/

---

[12] Ewa Ziarek makes this point when she presents the condition of mourning as the nor-
     mal condition of language acquisition, i. e. that the possibility of speaking involves the
     absence of the object. This form of symbolic compensation or linguistic mastery is »pre-
     dicated on the effacement of alterity«, however, as the other/lost object is absorbed into
     the neutrality of the linguistic totality. The melancholy disposition, on the contrary,
     undermines this process of neutralisation because melancholia expresses not just denial
     of the loss, but more significantly »denial of the possibility of recompense for the
     loss«. Ziarek sees this inability to trade the loss of the other for the »symbolic triumph«
     as »an encounter with the other without the intermediary of the third term, understood
     as a paternal signifier, phallus, or the symbolic order« (Ewa Ziarek: Kristeva and Levi-
     nas. Mourning, Ethics, and the Feminine. In: Ethics, Politics, and Difference in Julia
     Kristeva's Writing [note 10], p. 62–78, here 72–73).

[13] Butler, The Body Politics of Julia Kristeva (note 7), p. 166.

[14] Adorno argues that the anti-Semitic mentality that resulted in the Final Solution is a
     product of inflexible thought, i. e. an inability to think beyond aggressive stereo-
     types. In order to prevent this mentality from continuing undisturbed in the post-
     Holocaust world, he suggests negative or flexible thought (the ability to think out-
     side these implicitly violent generalisations) as antidote: »Das wirklich Verrückte
     liegt erst im Unverrückbaren, in der Unfähigkeit des Gedankens zu solcher Negativität,
     in welcher entgegen dem verfestigten Urteil das Denken recht eigentlich besteht.«
     Max Horkheimer / Theodor W. Adorno: Dialektik der Aufklärung. Philosophische
     Fragmente. Frankfurt a. M.: Fischer 1991, p. 204.

[15] Julia Kristeva: Desire in Language. A Semiotic Approach to Literature and Art.
     Oxford: Blackwell 1980, p. 29.

[16] Butler argues that Kristeva offers us only »a strategy of subversion that can never
     become a sustained political practice« because she »reinstates the paternal law at
     the level of the semiotic itself« (Butler, The Body Politics of Julia Kristeva [note 7],
     p. 166). Along the same line of thought, Smith states that »the pleasures of *jouissance*
     and rejection [Kristeva] describes [...] are more often than not destructive and miso-
     gynistic« (Smith, Julia Kristeva [note 5], p. 113).

symbolic order. Both advocate the inclusion – and not the deletion via the violence of a neutralising third term – of the marginal in critical and psychoanalytic theory respectively.[17] Both may be seen in this regard to break with traditional ethical theories that »postulate an autonomous agent whose obligations to the other come from his realization that the other must be the same as himself«.[18] Thus Kristeva's theory of transgression may be regarded as the attempt »to conceive of the relation between subject and other as a relation of difference«.[19] This interest in renegotiating identities and relations along with the attendant obligation to the other suggests that Kristeva's thought – despite what her harshest critics might say – is indeed geared towards a reconception of the ethico-political subject and thereby sets the scene for a political perspective that may be developed in conjunction with the theories of others.[20]

Thus drive theory lends us insight into difference, the otherness of self and the other as disturbingly non-identical with the symbolic subject. In his discussion concerning the aesthetics of disgust, Menninghaus attaches transcendental meaning to this disturbing aspect of the drives. He draws attention to the significance of drive theory for modern literature where the banished and reviled marginal features in an almost sovereign light. A certain truth resides in the apparition of sick and pestilent bodies, he argues during his discussion of Kristeva's theory of abjection. This truth takes the form of the disgust we experience at the interference of the unclean, the disharmonious and the expelled in the representative order of the symbolic. However, the decaying body does not itself embody the moment of truth; rather its disruption of the symbolic world of orderly representation signifies for Menninghaus a break in the construction of reality that in turn heralds the interference of the »Real« (equated here with truth).[21]

Similarly, Smith describes the drives as »an impossible space of fullness outside language«.[22] They are archaic structures that arise in the wake of the sub-

---

[17] Bernstein suggests aspects of Kristeva's psychoanalytic theory as a possibility for enhancing what he sees as Adorno's flawed employment of natural history in explaining »why the domination of identity-thinking should be experienced as damaging«. Further: »A suspicion worth exploring is that Kristeva's works contain the rudiments of a psychoanalytic theory that would match the directions of Adorno's critical theory.« Jay M. Bernstein: Disenchantment and Ethics. Cambridge: Cambridge University Press 2001 (Modern European Philosophy), p. 260.

[18] Oliver, Introduction (note 10), p. 1.

[19] Ibid.

[20] Ewa Ziarek does just this when she welds aspects of Levinasian ethics with Kristevan melancholia. In both of these discourses on alterity, she sees the possibility of an ethical encounter with the other beyond the violence of a neutralising third term (Ziarek, Kristeva and Levinas [note 12], p. 62–78).

[21] »Diese Wahrheit ist nicht die Wahrheit von Aussagen. Sie besteht auch nicht in der Repräsentation eines besonderen Wirklichkeitsausschnitts im Spannungsfeld von Repulsion und Attraktion. Sie impliziert vielmehr einen weitergehenden Anspruch: nämlich im Bruch der Wirklichkeitskonstruktionen das ›Reale‹ selbst durchschlagen zu lassen.« (Menninghaus, Ekel [note 9], p. 546)

[22] Smith, Julia Kristeva (note 5), p. 109.

ject's first attempts to map over the body spatial limits against the assault of
the real. In other words, the drives are both threatening and unrepresentable;
they subconsciously remind the subject of the existence of the Real that cannot
be contained by the signifying practices of the symbolic. This further links the
interference of the Real through the assault of the drives to the experience of
trauma as the subject senses that its identity (the vulnerable spatial limits of its
psychical/physical space in the symbolic relation) is under threat. Hypothetical
though the drives may be thus, they nonetheless provide a compelling (if complex) account of one of the central images of (post)modernism: the breakdown
of homogenous notions of subjectivity as the barrier between subject and object is dissolved.[23]

The psychoanalytical elaboration of subjectivity/corporeality in the above
state of crisis thus thematises the peculiarly vital world of the human psyche
that resists the notional fixity of conscious representations. It articulates a
certain grotesquerie of the self as this self is contradicted, overrun and resisted
by its shadowy underside: the repressed other, that ambassador of the Real,
without whom the self could not have become a symbolic body. This perspective implies that the psychoanalytical theories of the conscious and unconscious portray the human condition as fundamentally grotesque, featuring as
they do an image of the dual self split between the two modes. Both psycho-
analysis and the grotesque thus thematise disturbances of the self and language
as states of permanent scission which express the transgression of culturally
agreed norms. In this respect, the grotesque may be understood as a topography of transgression (psychoanalysis a science thereof), featuring the borderliner self as main protagonist along with the ambivalent language through
which this self emerges.

However, psychoanalysis's concern with the spatially indeterminate body is
linked to its critique of the culturally determinate (and spatially demarcated)
body: the Lacanian Imaginary Anatomy of the symbolic order which is initi-
ated at the mirror stage in the subject's development. The Imaginary Anatomy
could be described as an ideal of flawlessly functioning anality whereby the
self narcissistically perceives itself as an impregnable totality:

> [...] a fantasized image, the complex result of the subject's internalization of the
> specular image and its acceptance of everyday social and familial beliefs about the
> body's organic structure – a product, that is, of cultural and libidinal investments in
> the body.[24]

The critical point here is that the Imaginary Anatomy provides a very different
concept of subjectivity qua corporeality than does the concept of the visceral
body that is constantly ruptured by the drives. We could say that if drive inter-

---

[23] »Auch im Trauma geht es um die Prozessierung einer unassimilierbaren Andersheit,
eines Angriffs auf die eigene Identität, der oft buchstäblich die Gefahr des Todes impliziert.« (Menninghaus, Ekel [note 9], p. 557)

[24] Gross, The Body of Signification (note 3), p. 84.

ference illuminates the processes through which we become invested in fixed representation, the Imaginary Anatomy is one such projection of fixed identity. My contention is that these differing but connected psychoanalytic postulates of the body may be productively linked to broader literary accounts concerning the production of the culturally determinate or indeterminate self. Whilst *jouissance* articulates the indeterminate, grotesquely ambivalent body – the disharmonious other of difference – stasis may be understood as the signal of fixity and totality of identity that refuses to think itself outside the confines of the symbolic order. This notion of stasis goes beyond the rhythmic space of the maternal *chora* in which the component drives of destruction and regeneration (the threat of the real) wrestle for dominance. If the *chora* can be described as a chaotic space in which binary oppositions implode, stasis transcends even the ambivalence of this implosion.[25]

Thus conceptualised, stasis may be understood as the most extreme articulation of the death drives. Distinct from this rather sinister drive manifestation, the *jouissance* drive is ambivalently articulated as destruction/regeneration in the clash of what Gilles Deleuze refers to as the component drives.[26] Whilst *jouissance* is both outcome and symptom of such energy cathexes, stasis does not denote the struggle between life-giving and life-destructive forces. Rather, it opens up a third dimension beyond the death drives which tells of nothingness beyond drive regeneration. It is a space of absolute negation in which resides the »Death Instinct« (the principle of absolute destruction) and which should be distinguished from the death drives as manifested in *jouissance*. For the *jouissance* of destruction »(or, if you will, of the ›death drive‹)«, says Kristeva, attacks »all the stases of the signifying process: sign, language, identifying language structure«.[27] And although *jouissance* is destructive, as she herself states, its offensive against the conservative tendencies (stases) of the symbolic order ensure that it is simultaneously »the very mechanism of reactivation, tension, life«.[28] By contrast, the theory of absolute negation is one of extreme annihilation without provision for resuscitation/reactivation, and as such is a suitable descriptive device for Drach's evocation of a society defined by the rule of absolute destruction. For absolute negation may be equated with the triumph of the above stases in the

---

[25] Kristeva describes the *chora* as a »Curious primacy, where what is repressed cannot really be held down, and where what represses always already borrows its strength and authority from what is apparently very secondary: language«. True to the function of ambivalence, the *chora* becomes most manifest at the site of symbolic prohibition which is »placed on the maternal body (as a defense against autoeroticism and incest taboo)« (Julia Kristeva: Powers of Horror. An Essay on Abjection. New York: Columbia University Press 1982 [European Perspectives], p. 13–14).

[26] Gilles Deleuze: Masochism. Coldness and Cruelty. New York: Zone Books 1989, p. 31.

[27] Julia Kristeva: Revolution in Poetic Language. New York: Columbia University Press 1984, p. 150.

[28] Ibid.

form of what Kristeva elsewhere calls »symbolic cells« or cogs »within a social hierarchy« of systematic organisation.[29]

Far from reading stasis as a drive manifestation of Kristeva's pre-linguistic semiotic *chora* therefore, I am reading it (with reference to Drach's Holocaust accounts) as an index for the over-rationalisation of cultural life and individuality within a specific historical context. In short, stasis may be taken as a manifestation of the Death Instinct in language and social order, one that upholds the law of »confinement«, restriction and paralysis as opposed to transgression and movement. It is the moment of positioning within the symbolic order taken to a pathological extreme which demands the negation of the *chora*.

This is however, a point that firstly deserves analysis within Kristeva's own theoretical framework, and secondly elaboration with the help of Deleuze's reflections on Freudian drive theory. When using Kristevan drive theory as a basis for two very different articulations of the body through two very different discourses, a difficulty arises, in my view, through her insistence on a dual structure of the drives, i. e. the conflation of stasis and *jouissance* in a local struggle that evidences the wider struggle between symbolic and semiotic. In other words, Kristeva never considers the death drive in isolation, but always as part of an ambivalent entity that may well be destructive, but that will nevertheless produce prolifically in the path of its destruction. Whilst the destructive/reconstructive subject of *jouissance* – born of the struggle between semiotic and symbolic – may allow us to expand upon a theory of indeterminate identity, Kristeva does not sufficiently develop her theory of stasis to a level that would enable us to develop a theory of »static« identity (or the culturally determinate body). Kristeva's theory is thus enormously useful for developing the concept of ambivalent identity that is always on the brink of destruction, but falls short somewhat in the task of conceptualising a reverse mode of subjectivity, one that is cold, empty, unproductive and beyond reactivation.

At this point, Deleuze's analysis of sadism in language becomes very useful in taking stasis and re-developing it as a theory of subjectivity reverse to (and not caught up in) *jouissance*. Significantly, his theoretical base expands beyond the concept of the death drives as dualistic and ambivalent. Unlike Kristeva, who understands stasis and the symbolic only insofar as they may be shown to be affected by the semiotic (or vice versa), Deleuze goes beyond this ambivalent dualism of what he terms the death drives and opposes them to a more radical concept of destruction which he calls the Death Instinct. His theory of sadistic language thus derives from a triadic understanding of the drives which he develops from his close reading of Freud's seminal text »Jenseits des Lustprinzips«. Whilst psychoanalysis may start with an understanding of the death drives as a dual structure of Eros/Thanatos, life/death instincts, or in Kristevan terminology *jouissance*/stasis, Deleuze maintains that in order to truly grasp Freud's text »we must make a further and more profound distinction be-

---

[29] Ibid., p. 96.

tween the death or destructive instincts and the Death Instinct«.[30] Whilst the
death instincts are exhibited in the unconscious, he continues, they always
appear in combination with the life instincts »so that destruction, and the negative at work in destruction, always manifests itself as the other face of construction and unification as governed by the pleasure principle«.[31] In this scenario
thus, destruction is not absolute; the combination of life and death instincts
accounts for the endless cycle of destruction, regeneration, renewal etc. One
could argue therefore, that the interference of transgression, *jouissance*, and
the *chora* in the symbolic order, whilst effecting a pulverisation of subject
position, does not effect absolute negation. On the contrary, the dismantling of
subject position is frequently a productive act precisely because it allows the
expression of difference in the ambivalence of self/other hybrids.

The Death Instinct however, argues Deleuze, signifies something quite distinct from the above combinatory life/death instincts. For him, the Death Instinct refers to Thanatos, »the absolute negation« which cannot be given in the
psychic life. Even in the unconscious it is essentially silent: »and yet we must
speak of it for it is a determinable principle, the foundation and even more of
psychic life«.[32] The space of absolute negation as discussed by Deleuze in his
analysis of sadistic language provides a point of departure for a theory of the
grotesque as a morphology of emptiness that reflects both this negation and the
subject who practices it. A more detailed evaluation of the language of negation follows in section 3.3.

The above differentiation of the death drives/Death Instinct underlines the
usefulness of drive theory for the analysis of literature that very deliberately places the body in a variety of socio-political spaces. For literary language that exemplifies aspects of drive theory may be described as a language that grafts the
culturally produced body in whatever articulation (determinate/indeterminate;
insubordinate/obedient) onto the poetic text. As such, this type of »body language« *performs* the socio-political position of the protagonist in question. In
other words, the various positions of the protagonist's (or indeed narrator's)
body function as a major linguistic strategy of the text through which social
attitudes, prejudices and political realities are quite literally performed (brought
into existence) by virtue of the kind of enunciative act in question.[33]

This particular performativity of the body in the literary text can thus say
much about the subject's position within discourses of power/appropriation, or
as the case may be, within the sub-discourse of the marginal. For as Paul Con-

---

[30] Deleuze, Masochism (note 26), p. 31, 30.

[31] Ibid.

[32] Ibid.

[33] Paul Connerton's definition of what constitutes performative discourse clarifies in
this context: »A performative utterance does not provide a description of a certain
action. The utterance of the performative itself constitutes an action of some kind.«
Paul Connerton: How Societies Remember. Cambridge: Cambridge University Press
1989 (Themes in the Social Sciences), p. 58.

nerton remarks »in all cultures, much of the choreography of authority is expressed through the body«.[34] With reference to Drach, the bodies that emerge in the differing narrative strategies of his works are either critical insubordinates that rupture via *jouissance* the social landscape which they refuse to ultimately accept, or they are appropriated linguistic embodiments of apotheosis: in Adorno's sense, personifications of his philosopheme of pure identity as death, their difference or individuality having been assimilated (and therefore effectively negated) by the excising violence of sameness.[35]

Thus psychoanalysis may be viewed as a reasonable way forward for a considered theory of grotesque language, taking linguistically performative images of corporeality as a point of departure for this theory. Gross asks the following question: »In what way does the fact that there are two kinds of body and thus two kinds of subject affect language?«[36] Whilst developing the above theory of grotesque language, section 2.3 and chapter 3 will attempt to address this query. The following section however returns to a more detailed consideration of the images that have dominated the literary-theoretical debate concerning the grotesque: vitality and mortality.

2.2 An Entire Thematics of Mortality and Vitality

The twin images of inert horror and transgressive regeneration have featured strongly in the twentieth century literary theoretical debate concerning the grotesque. For the purpose of better situating the above approach to the grotesque, it is productive to evaluate certain contributions of the main theoreticians, highlighting the limitations of each perspective in order to come to a more balanced and inclusive consensus concerning the uses of each position. My analysis initially focuses on the various stances taken by Wolfgang Kayser, Mikhail Bakhtin and Arnold Heidsieck with regard to the vitality/mortality thematic.[37] In the following section, it then returns to a neglected core image of the grotesque (the grotto) and continues the above discussion of psychoanalysis and the grotesque with reference to this image. Throughout the immediate discussion however, it will becomes clear that the above well-known exponents of the grotesque conceive of subjectivity/corporeality as communicated by the grotesque body in very different ways.

---

[34] Ibid., p. 74.

[35] Bernstein points out that this idea of absolute negativity is elaborated by Adorno as part of his negative theodicy, i. e. as part of the philosophical task »of ›construing‹ of Auschwitz in terms of identity-thinking« (Bernstein, Disenchantment and Ethics [note 17], p. 383).

[36] Gross, The Body of Signification (note 3), p. 101.

[37] Cf. Kayser, Das Groteske (note 2); Bakhtin, Literatur und Karneval (note 2); Arnold Heidsieck: Das Groteske und das Absurde im modernen Drama. Stuttgart: Kohlhammer 1969 (Sprache und Literatur; 53).

Bakhtin's famous critique of Kayser's understanding of the grotesque forms a concise point of departure for this discussion. In this critique, Bakhtin takes umbrage with the angst-filled image of inertia that summarises Kayser's fundamental understanding of the grotesque as an other-worldly phantom figure of death.[38] This terrifying spectacle infiltrates the world of the alienated individual, but is not however presented by Kayser as a product of the social environment. Its origins are instead shrouded in a mystery as great as its insidious manifestation in the vague form of what Kayser loosely calls *Entfremdung* (alienation). The individual who experiences this apparition of death is paralysed into fear and further alienation, a confirmation of total passivity in the face of a threat that cannot be rationally deciphered and thereby demystified. In this angst-ridden world, the grotesque is transmitted in the form of extreme anonymity.[39]

From a psychoanalytical point of view, one could argue that the alienated individual of Kayser's grotesque scenario beholds in the utter emptiness of the terrifying *Es* (a vacuous »it«) the certainty of castration.[40] Indeed, it has been suggested that Kayser's theory of the grotesque is unthinkable without the concept of the unconscious.[41] This particular discursive formation in the debate concerning the grotesque marks »the modern turn towards a more active consideration of the grotesque as an interior event«.[42] However, the move inwards towards »an individualized, interiorized space of fantasy and introspection« brings with it »the attendant risk of social inertia«.[43]

Within the mortality/vitality debate around the grotesque, it would seem that in Kayser's view the grotesque, as a cold and mysterious *Es*, signifies the profound (if unspecified) social and political irrelevance of the alienated individual. A deeply negative evaluation of the general significance of the individual, it thus evokes through the portrayal of powerlessness a death of sorts. It could be argued that in this context inertia, passivity and fear become signifiers of an ubiquitous sense of imminent mortality that is wholly consistent with a society so inert as to resemble a morgue. Clearly, the kind of body and the kind of society

---

[38] »Bei Kayser gibt es weder Zeit noch Wechsel noch Krisen. Es fehlt also alles das, was mit Sonne, Erde, Mensch und Gesellschaft geschieht, wovon und worin die wahre Groteske lebt.« Bakhtin, Literatur und Karneval (note 2), p. 27.

[39] Kayser, Das Groteske (note 2), p. 198: »das Groteske ist die entfremdete Welt.«

[40] »Ins Unheimliche verwandelt erscheint das Menschliche im Wahnsinnigen; wieder ist es, als ob ein ›Es‹, ein fremder, unmenschlicher Geist in die Seele gefahren sei [...] das Groteske ist die Gestaltung des ›Es‹, jenes ›spukhaften‹ Es.« (Ibid., p. 198–199) Bakhtin criticises this very notion of alienation because it may not be deciphered within human terms: »Kayser versteht das ›Es‹ [...] im existentialistischen Sinne. Sein ›Es‹ ist eine fremde, unmenschliche Macht, die über die Welt, die Menschen, ihr Leben und ihre Handlungen regiert.« (Bakhtin, Literatur und Karneval [note 2], p. 27) For the same reason, Heidsieck states: »das Moment totaler Fremdheit ist auf Groteskes gar nicht anwendbar.« (Heidsieck, Das Groteske und das Absurde [note 37], p. 30)

[41] Cf. Russo, The Female Grotesque (note 2), p. 9.

[42] Ibid., p. 7–8.

[43] Ibid.

implied in Kayser's grotesque scenario are defined by stasis. It is precisely this monotonous territory of death that the grotesquely disaffected stiff (the living dead) inhabits. We could thus argue that Kayser's understanding of grotesque subjectivity is based on the image of the corpse which is in turn representative of a politically and socially denigrated mode of atomised subjectivity.[44]

By contrast, Bakhtin's theory of the grotesque marks out an alternative discursive formation (and an alternative understanding of the body) within this debate. For Bakhtin, whose own understanding of the grotesque is based on his insurgent and animated theory of carnival, Kayser's image of the inert goes completely against the true spirit of the grotesque.[45] In Bakhtin's view, the fundamental grotesque image is one of pure vitality that encompasses within its carnivalesque mobility even the prospect of death. Thus whilst Kayser's theory of the grotesque favours the gravity of apocalypse and the accompanying immobility of fear, Bakhtin argues the grotesque in terms of carnival which is regenerative, fearless and transgressive. From the latter perspective, the grotesque is part of a social discourse that is infinite and fearless because« it refuses to settle on any absolute image of power. Indeed, all positions are reversible and open to gleeful deconstruction within the carnivalesque social model. It is precisely this openness that renders the grotesque infinite.

Moreover, Bakhtin rejects the notion that the grotesque world is an alienated world. His model of carnival is profoundly (one could also argue nostalgically) social in that carnival depicts the imaginative uprising of the lower classes as they topple from power the ruling social stratum which is represented in the figure of carnival king. Carnival and the downward thrust of grotesque bodily materialism that characterises it are thus communal exercises that cohere with one another in a social space based on the model of the eternally self-transgressing, cosmic grotesque body. Against the tightly sealed body of Kayser's alienated subject, Bakhtin's version of grotesque corporeality is porous, accessible and therefore not alienated.[46]

---

[44] This sense of powerlessness and lack of autonomy is expressed particularly by the essentially enigmatic nature of the grotesque. Mankind must suffer it without explanation, consolation, or hope for release: »Wer aber bewirkt die Entfremdung der Welt [...]? Wir erreichen erst jetzt die letzte Tiefe des Grauens vor der verwandelten Welt. Denn diese Fragen bleiben ohne Antwort.« (Kayser, Das Groteske [note 2], p. 199)

[45] »Wie bestimmt Kayser die Eigenart der grotesken Gestaltungsweise? An seinen Definitionen verblüfft vor allem der düstere, Furcht und Entsetzen erregende Gesamtton der grotesken Welt, über den hinaus der Autor nichts wahrzunehmen scheint.« (Bakhtin, Literatur und Karneval [note 2], p. 25–26)

[46] Carnival is thus regarded as »das Spiel mit den Symbolen der höchsten Macht« enacted most strongly in the debunking of the carnival king: »Die Erhöhung und Erniedrigung des Karnevalkönigs ist ein ambivalenter Brauch, der [...] die fröhliche Relativität einer jeden Ordnung, Gewalt und Hierarchie ausdrückt.« (Ibid., p. 52, p. 50–51) This toppling of the vertical axis of social hierarchy is further expressed in the eternally disintegrating and developing familiar cosmic grotesque body: »Der Leib der nicht-offiziellen und intimen Rede ist ein befruchtend-befruchteter, gebärend-geborener, verschlingend-verschlungener, ein trinkender, sich entleerender, kranker, sterbender Leib.« (Ibid., p. 19)

Clearly, the human subject is evaluated in a radically different manner here than in Kayser's theory. The principle of movement alone that saturates the regenerative (and generous) grotesque cosmic body suggests an empowered and agentic version of subjectivity, one that can effect social and political change. The refusal to be cowed by the structures of social repression (the carnival king) may be thus read as the refusal to accept alienation (and the *Es*) as shapers of human destiny. In a more abstract formulation, this attitude may be interpreted as the refusal to allow the *finality* of death a determining role in the subject's earthly existence. In other words, the carnivalesque subject positions the spectre of castration within the greater transcendental model of the cosmic body that incessantly reproduces itself, and in so doing constructs a narrative that demystifies death. The carnivalesque subject is thus a committed exponent of vitality as opposed to mortality.[47]

The dynamism of the carnivalesque body may be further explained by the fact that it is a body frequently shaken by spasms of laughter. The laugh accounts for the overcoming of fear within a world that has experienced carnival. The structure of the laugh, so resoundingly absent from Kayser's triste world, introduces a threshold consciousness into the carnivalesque world and so initiates the transgression of existing oppressive structures. Again, the concept of the moving, laughing body suggests that the carnivalesque subject is enriched and empowered by a debunking perspective on the world, refusing to take seriously models of eternal power that claim to be invulnerable to change.[48] The social formations, changes and flux that are conceptualised within the laughing, transgressive and infinite carnival model thus represent »a virile category associated with the ac-

---

[47] A sample of this death-defying narrative: »Vermerken wir schließlich, daß der groteske Leib kosmisch und universal ist. Die dem ganzen Kosmos gemeinsamen Elemente sind in ihm betont: Erde, Wasser, Feuer, Luft. Er hängt unmittelbar mit der Sonne und den Gestirnen zusammen. Er trägt die Tierkreiszeichen in sich. Er spiegelt die kosmische Hierarchie in sich. Dieser Leib kann mit verschiedenen Naturphänomenen verschmelzen: mit den Bergen, Flüssen, Meeren, Inseln, mit dem Festland. Er vermag die ganze Welt zu füllen.« (Ibid., p. 18) It is important to note however, that death never wins in this equation precisely because it is accepted as part of a natural cosmic cycle that is indispensable to life: »In der endlosen Kette des leiblichen Lebens werden jene Teile fixiert, wo ein Glied ins andere übergreift, wo das Leben eines neuen Leibes aus dem Tod eines alten Leibes entsteht.« (Ibid.) By contrast, consider Kayser's insistence on the surreal/supernatural apparition of the grotesque: »Sobald wir die Mächte benennen und ihnen eine Stelle in der kosmischen Ordnung anweisen können, verlöre das Groteske an seinem Wesen.« (Kayser, Das Groteske [note 2], p. 199)

[48] »Im Akt des Karnevalslachens vereinigen sich Tod und Wiedergeburt, Verneinung (Spott) und Bejahung (Triumph). Das ambivalente Lachen des Karnevals ist ein weltanschauliches und universelles Lachen.« (Bakhtin, Literatur und Karneval [note 2], p. 54) By contrast, Kayser: »das Lachen darüber ist nicht frei.« (Kayser, Das Groteske [note 2], p. 48) Also, Heidsieck advances a similar view: »Das Lachen, das sich aus der logischen Struktur des Grotesken ergibt, befreit nicht, es bleibt ›im Halse stecken‹, das es sich der restlosen Perversion menschlicher Freiheit gegenübersteht.« (Heidsieck, Das Groteske und das Absurde [note 37], p. 18)

tive, civic world of the public«.[49] Whilst Kayser's grotesque theory presents an image of the disempowered suffering under the oppressive homogeneity of the *Es*, Bakhtin's notion of constant change as evidenced in the gesture of dethroning allows for the constant decentralisation of power.

Nonetheless, Bakhtin admits that carnival as it has descended to modernity from its peak during the High Middle Ages has survived only in a very diluted form. Traces of carnival may be found in certain literary texts that exemplify the signature carnivalesque threshold consciousness. Such texts are ambivalent, the characters that occupy them are often split and inconsistent with themselves. Hybrid sentence structures along with narrative and character ambivalence testify to what Bakhtin terms the structure of the laugh as a defining principle of these texts.[50] In this manner, the laugh displaces from any position of potential dominance the centripetal tendencies of the text. This is a decentralising process similar to that envisaged by Kristeva in the poetic text – the displacement through transgressive *jouissance* of symbolic structures. Thus the »body language« of *jouissance* may be seen as a descendant both of carnivalesque body language and of the structure of the laugh; whether the concept of life-affirming laughter applies to *jouissance* will be taken up in the next section.[51]

Returning briefly to the psychoanalytic framework, carnival may be generally associated with *jouissance* whilst Kayser's concept of the death-bearing inert as core grotesque image aligns itself with stasis. Death is central to both understandings of the grotesque but whereas Bakhtin subordinates it to the greater regenerative life-force of the cosmos, Kayser's grotesque world appears to accommodate death as a panoramic mono-presence within the stiff

---

[49] Russo, The Female Grotesque (note 2), p. 8. Bakhtin describes this civic world in the terms of the grotesque cosmic body, a macro entity that is constituted by several living, breathing, moving micro parts: »Der Mensch empfindet die Unaufhörbarkeit des Lebens auf dem öffentlichen Festplatz, in der Karnevalsmenge, indem er sich mit fremden Leibern jeden Alters und jeder sozialen Stellung berührt. Er fühlt sich als Glied des ewig wachsenden und sich erneuernden Volkes.« (Bakhtin, Literatur und Karneval [note 2], p. 37)

[50] »Sie [die groteske Lachtradition] lebt fort und kämpft um ihr Bestehen, sowohl in den niederen kanonischen Gattungen (der Komödie, Satire und Fabel), als auch in den nicht-kanonischen Gattungen (im Roman, in einer besonderen Form des Milieu-Dialogs, in den burlesken Gattungen usw.). Sie lebt auch auf der Volksbühne.« (Ibid., p. 46) Bakhtin speaks of such literature as characterised by the »Anatomie des Karnevals« (ibid., p. 64), i. e. the anatomy of disintegration/synecdoche, which in turn may be seen as the reflection of the threshold consciousness, »Schwellenbewußtsein« (ambivalence), of these texts (ibid., p. 75). These two traits evidence the structure of the carnivalesque laugh in the literary text, according to Bakhtin: »Wir sehen gleichsam die Spur des Lachens in der Struktur der dargestellten Wirklichkeit – das Lachen selber hören wir nicht.« (Ibid., p. 67)

[51] Kristeva makes this link clear when she identifies dialogue and carnivalesque phenomena as pointers for »the basis of our time's intellectual structure«. One of the fundamental problems facing semiotics, she adds, is the task of describing this ambivalent logic without denaturing it (Julia Kristeva: Word, Dialogue and Novel. In: id., Desire in Language. A Semiotic Approach to Literature and Art. Oxford: Blackwell 1980, p. 89).

subject and beyond it in the cold confines of the alienated modern world. Bakhtin's difficulty with Kayser's image of the inert could thus be summarised in abstract terms as a protest against his reductionist understanding of death as something to be feared. This is communicated by the *Es* construct which signals the finite (the end-station of mortality) as the defining moment of the grotesque. As shown above, Bakhtin evidently understands the grotesque purely in terms of life that transcends even death (the thematics of vitality), thus it becomes clear as to why Kayser's theory is unacceptable to him.

Beyond Bakhtin's protest however, a further legitimate criticism of Kayser's theory is its lack of specific social analysis. First published in the post-Holocaust decade of the 1950s, his depiction of evil as a vague *Es* that originates from an anonymous place beyond the social order is morally suspect. In a society that has successfully conducted an act of evil as immense as the Final Solution, the kind of naivety implied by Kayser's understanding of evil is untenable. To my mind, this neglect of the social origins of evil is the great weakness of Kayser's theory and not, as Bakhtin suggests, his depiction of the grotesque as an image of inertia. The inert is in fact a perfectly acceptable image of the grotesque when analysing the grotesquerie inherent to totalitarian society.[52]

At this juncture, Arnold Heidsieck's theory of the grotesque becomes useful. One could argue that his fundamental image of the grotesque, the »familiar strange« (*das bekannte Fremde*), expresses to a degree the same sense of alienation put forward by Kayser. However, the considerable difference between the two perspectives lies in Heidsieck's insistence on social analysis. Although he does not specifically discuss the Holocaust, his theory of the grotesque nevertheless derives to a great extent from Adorno's work concerning the grotesque automatisation of the human subject in a society enslaved to the advance of technology and growing consumerism. Thus it would seem that Heidsieck's depiction of the grotesque human/thing anomaly conforms to a certain degree to the personification of inertia described in Kayser's work, the common denominator being the expression of powerlessness in grotesque representation. However, Heidsieck avoids Kayser's naivety by interpreting the grotesque as the product and reflection of social discourses of power, progress and ultimately of dehumanisation.[53]

---

[52] I base this assumption on Zygmunt Bauman's definition of modern culture: »We can say that existence is modern in as far as it is effected and sustained by design, manipulation, management, engineering. The existence is modern in as far as it is administered by resourceful (that is, possessing knowledge, skill and technology), sovereign agencies. Agencies are sovereign in as far as they claim and successfully defend the right to manage and administer existence: the right to define order and, by implication, lay aside chaos, as that left-over that escapes the definition.« (Zygmunt Bauman: Modernity and Ambivalence. Cambridge: Polity Press 1991, p. 7)

[53] Critiquing Kayser, Heidsieck rejects the notion of supernatural alienation as the core image of the grotesque: »wir können die Mächte benennen, die das Schrecklichste vermögen [...] Das von Menschen verübte, und nicht irgendwelche ›dunklen Mächte, die in und hinter unserer Welt lauern‹, sind die realen Gründe der allgemeinen Angst.« (Heidsieck, Das Groteske und das Absurde [note 37], p. 32) He clearly fol-

What kind of »body language« is implied by Heidsieck's image of the human/thing anomaly, however? Does there not exist an element of the carnivalesque in this hybrid form of corporeality – the existence of two conflicting images simultaneously within the one entity – that renders it a transgressive mode more indicative of vitality than of mortality? The answer to this query must be negative when one takes this admittedly contradictory mode of subjectivity as representative of a wider cultural discourse that can only be understood in the overwhelmingly negative terms of death as stasis. For Heidsieck's concept of the human/thing entity is based on Adorno's critique of coldness as the fundamental principle of bourgeois subjectivity. In the essay »Erziehung nach Auschwitz«, Adorno attempts to address the cultural-psychological conditions that made the Final Solution possible. He develops a prototype of the individual who (either passively or actively) allowed the extermination of the Jews.

It is just this prototype that features in Heidsieck's grotesque hybrid.[54] For coldness or indifference to the suffering of fellow humans implies that dignity as a fundamental respect for the moral predicates that apply to human life has been removed from the consciousness of individuals. In the place of this greater »end« or ideal of human life, the »means« of modern technology now assume a dominant position. In other words, technology as the means for the

---

lows Adorno's argument concerning the questionable technological advance of society which made Auschwitz possible: »Man spricht vom drohenden Rückfall in die Barbarei. Aber er droht nicht, sondern Auschwitz war er; Barbarei besteht fort, solange die Bedingungen, die jenen Rückfall zeitigten, wesentlich fortdauern. Das ist das ganze Grauen. Der gesellschaftliche Druck lastet weiter, trotz aller Unsichtbarkeit der Not heute.« (Theodor W. Adorno: Erziehung nach Auschwitz. In: id., »Ob nach Auschwitz noch sich leben lasse«. Ein philosophisches Lesebuch. Hg. von Rolf Tiedemann. Frankfurt a. M: Suhrkamp 1997 [Edition Suhrkamp; N. F. 844], p. 48–63, here p. 48)

[54] Some details of Heidsieck's analysis recall characteristics of the carnivalesque, grotesque body, e. g. »Verzerrung, Mißproportion, Entstellung« are put forward as intrinsically grotesque stylistic features (Heidsieck, Das Groteske und das Absurde [note 37], p. 20). However, within Heidsieck's distinctly non-carnivalesque cultural framework, these strategies of grotesque representation come into play in order to reveal mankind in its modern grotesque, consumerist mode. This mode entails the perversion of human relations as the individual becomes a material thing in the discourse of technological progress: »der Mensch als bloßes Mittel für Menschen« (ibid., p. 18). This materialistic notion of the individual is central to Adorno's concept of a barbaric (if technologically sophisticated) modern society and is, for him, the premise upon which Auschwitz (and its possible repetition) rest. It is, in fact, a prototype of the Massenmensch: »Menschen, die blind in Kollektive sich einordnen, machen sich schon zu etwas wie Material, löschen sich als selbstbestimmte Wesen aus. Dazu paßt die Bereitschaft, andere als amorphe Masse zu behandeln. [...] Hätte ich diesen Typus [...] auf eine Formel zu bringen, [...] so würde ich ihn den Typus des verdinglichten Bewußtseins nennen. Erst haben die Menschen, die so geartet sind, sich selber gewissermaßen den Dingen gleichgemacht. Dann machen sie, wenn es ihnen möglich ist, die anderen den Dingen gleich.« (Adorno, Erziehung nach Auschwitz [note 53], p. 56–57)

self-preservation of the species becomes in the absence of higher ideals also the end of all endeavour. The subject thus loses the »distinctly human shape« it may otherwise have had because, as Bernstein points out in his analysis of Adorno's thought, »life without the applicability of evaluative predicates to it is a kind of death«.[55]

In this social vacuum which tells of deficient libidinal relations between individuals, technology becomes fetishised. Thus Heidsieck's concept of the human/thing is the embodiment of cold subjectivity and a symptom of the grave devaluation of human life that gives rise to it. The spiritual death of this individual situates it closely to the machine which it so reveres. Hence the degradation of life into a kind of death (or meaninglessness); the means (the technological advancement of society and the species) have effectively become the end to the extent that the individual in question too resembles a machine.

One could regard this particular embodiment of the grotesque subject as a detailed and socially grounded (if wholly disaffected) specification of the inexplicably alienated self referred to by Kayser. Whilst in contrast to Kayser's *Es* Heidsieck's techno-self may be logically and socially decipherable, it nonetheless belongs to a greater discourse concerning the disempowerment of the individual within a complex web of cultural values and devaluations. This is the main point of similarity between Kayser's and Heidsieck's respective theories. In contrast to Bakhtin, both portray grotesque art as useful for the representation of powerlessness and appropriation. The main difference between the two is that the individual is allowed a greater degree of critical insight into the causes of grotesque apparitions in Heidsieck's framework.[56]

---

[55] Bernstein, Disenchantment and Ethics (note 17), p. 381. Adorno argues that the prototype of the cold »man of the masses« goes hand in hand with the above described replacement of ends by means: »Die Menschen sind geneigt, die Technik für die Sache selbst, für Selbstzweck, für eine Kraft eigenen Wesens zu halten und darüber zu vergessen, daß sie der verlängerte Arm der Menschen ist. Die Mittel – und Technik ist ein Inbegriff von Mitteln zur Selbsterhaltung der Gattung Mensch – werden fetischisiert, weil sie die Zwecke – ein menschenwürdiges Leben – verdeckt und vom Bewußtsein der Menschen abgeschnitten sind.« (Adorno, Erziehung nach Auschwitz [note 53], p. 59) It is precisely in this distortion that Heidsieck locates the grotesque: »der lebendige Mensch, der ein Selbstzweck sein, um seiner selbst willen sein soll, wird wie beliebiges Material verarbeitet, zum technischen Produkt entstellt.« Its aesthetic representation then takes place by featuring this distortion »in der ganz sichtbaren körperlichen Entstellung des Menschen«. But for Heidsieck the crucial point concerning the grotesque (and in direct opposition to Kayser) lies in the socially critical insight that »der Mensch entstellt sich selbst« (Heidsieck, Das Groteske und das Absurde [note 37], p. 18).

[56] This difference becomes clear in the following citations: »Was einbricht, bleibt unfaßbar, undeutbar, impersonal.« (Kayser, Das Groteske [note 2], p. 199). For Heidsieck however, the grotesque distortion of the individual »so zugespitzt er auch erscheint, bleibt immer faßbar, logisch, auflösbar, weil er doch so offenkundig produziert ist« (Heidsieck, Das Groteske und das Absurde [note 37], p. 37).

In terms of the strand of similarity identified above, the kind of corporeality addressed by Heidsieck is a technological attribute of the corpse: the robot. In other words, Heidsieck's »distorted/displaced« grotesque individual [*entstellter Mensch*] could be seen as the culturally produced and logically identifiable articulation of the *Es*. Certainly, both are highly alienated instances of subjectivity. Without doubt, carnival has no place here, for the body in its robotic articulation is inorganic, closed, and due to its inorganicity, it is more dead even than the corpse. The human/thing anomaly thus also aligns itself with the immobility of stasis. In the above portrayed cultural context, the grotesque as a morphology of emptiness gains a powerful sociological dimension through this particular image. This point clarifies another feature of the society defined by the principle of absolute negation. For stasis or the Death Instinct is characterised not only by the tendency towards paralysis; we could also surmise that this tendency is inseparable from another development, that being the departure from the social space of a certain warm flexibility between individuals – Eros or *jouissance*. Adorno calls this flexibility simply love; the individual who resembles a robot is one incapable of loving others.[57]

Apart from Bakhtin's considerations concerning carnivalesque literature however, none of the three exponents of the grotesque advance a detailed theory of grotesque language.[58] This further grounds the earlier proposal of transposing the different grotesque images of the body onto the text in order to arrive at an approximation of the nature of grotesque language. This involves exploring the drive-based images of mobility (*jouissance*/transgression) and immobility (stasis) as models of highly performative literary language that may be used in the analysis of the text. Moreover, this approach, when extended to a theory of grotesque identity in the text, will also yield certain insights for the understanding of »self as locative system«. The latter refers to a spatial concept of selfhood which is defined very generally by its location in and by culture.[59] Implicit to this perspective is an understanding of identity as produced by highly territorial socio-cultural discourses which are then cleverly *re*-produced by the literary text. An example – albeit troubled – of the literary manifestation of self as locative system is Kristeva's abject deject: an individual

---

[57] »Bei dem Typus, der zur Fetischisierung der Technik neigt, handelt es sich, schlicht gesagt, um Menschen, die nicht lieben können. Das ist nicht sentimental und nicht moralisierend gemeint, sondern bezeichnet die mangelnde libidinöse Beziehung zu anderen Personen. Sie sind durch und durch kalt.« (Adorno, Erziehung nach Auschwitz [note 53], p. 59)

[58] Cf. Michail M. Bakhtin: Die Redevielfalt im Roman. In: id., Die Ästhetik des Wortes. Frankfurt a. M.: Suhrkamp 1979 (Edition Suhrkamp; 967), p. 192–251.

[59] Ciarán Benson develops this idea in a recent work, arguing that »a primary function of the psychological system which is commonly called ›self‹ is to locate or position the person for themselves in relation to others« (Ciarán Benson: The Cultural Psychology of Self. Place, Morality and Art in Human Worlds. London, New York: Routledge 2001, p. 3).

obsessed with the drawing and redrawing of spatial boundaries in a desperate attempt to better locate (define) the self.[60] As shall become clear in section 3.2, the position and function of the body in this kind of literary representation is central to the concept of selfhood (subjectivity/identity) as location. Following this, a tentative definition of the grotesque literary work suggests it as a form of writing that maps locations of the self in the text via linguistically performative techniques of bodily representation. The twin images of interest for this thesis have been identified as vitality and mortality. The various discussions of Drach's work will thus centre on the images of vital bodies and mortal bodies with particular attention to the language through which these bodies are produced.

2.3 Subterranean Spaces

That the grotesque might indeed signify a state of immobility is an idea that, due to the recent dominance of Bakhtinian grotesque materialism, has become somewhat neglected in the theoretical discussion. Brad Epps points this out in an article on the topic of grotesque writing and subjectivity in modern literature. He draws attention to this forgotten grotesque image of death beyond the particular vitality of grotesque transgression. If the ornate intricacies of grotesque adornment may be observed as a play on the artificiality of signification processes, i. e. as a topography of transgression, then the notion of the *grotto*-esque suggests something rather different altogether. Echoing Walter Benjamin, Epps reminds us that the grotesque as etymological descendant of the *grotta* (cave) is in fact »a significant form of ruin and burial«, with death as its »insoluble secret«.[61] Indeed, Benjamin notes that the word grotesque does not derive so much from the *grotta* in the literal sense, but more significantly from the notion of entombment as hiding or »putting out of sight«. This secret storehouse he regards as a place of interment that is characterised by concealment, enigma and mystery.[62]

Epps's mode of argumentation suggests that he too believes that the nature of »the enigmatically mysterious character of the effect of the grotesque« may be convincingly elaborated by aspects of psychoanalytical theory.[63] The following pages thus return to the area of psychoanalysis in an attempt to lay the foundations for a psychoanalytically grounded theory of grotesque language. Curious parallels emerge between a literary category that is on the one hand »as much, if not much more, of the signifier than the signified«, and a theory of identity that posits the self in the role of mobile signifier that continually

---

[60] »The one by whom the abject exists is thus a deject who places (himself), situates (himself), and therefore strays instead of getting his bearings.« (Kristeva, Powers of Horror [note 25], p. 8)

[61] Epps, Grotesque Identities (note 1), p. 42.

[62] Walter Benjamin: The Origin of German Tragic Drama. London: NLB 1977, p. 171.

[63] Ibid.

transgresses the rather less than impregnable barrier between conscious and unconscious.[64] From this point of view, the grotesque could be regarded as a highly appropriate aesthetic receptacle for the portrayal of the divided self as featured in the psychic apparatus.

On the other hand, the *grotta* of concealment in which resides the ultimate mystery of death may be interpreted as a literary symbol of that which initiates the delicately balanced condition of this divided self and then threatens to unbalance it. This is none other than the repressed knowledge of mortality/ castration which, as suggested in chapter 1, receives its most eloquent expression in the personality of the fetishist. The successful fetishist hovers on the borderline space between the knowledge of castration and its denial, remaining in a state of excited anxiety that signifies both the recognition and automatised rejection of potential castration. Clearly, this kind of pleasurable threshold existence between the netherworld of the unconscious and the world of conscious projection may be likened to the borderline existence of the dual self that transgresses and that constantly undergoes transgression. This recalls a point made in the previous chapter where *jouissance* was defined as a functioning fetishism in language. Not only is the self a borderline case of subjectivity thus; the discourse that produces this self also engages in the ambivalent play characteristic for fetishism, i. e. the play between recognition (loss) and denial (compensation).[65]

However, the unsuccessful fetishist will be unable to conceal from itself the nature of the buried secret. The dank space in which fetishism fails could be likened to the *grotta* or the grave as an index for the space of absolute negation in which castration (death) is realised. Understood as the subterranean space of the *grotta*, the grotesque becomes a morphology of emptiness, the signifier of lack with no respite. In other words, the failed fetishist or grotto-esque subject rejects what Ziarek refers to as the language of »mourning«, i. e. he/she refuses the economy of compensation/loss, absence/presence that should, however temporarily, recover the lost (castrated) (m)other in signs.

The position of mourning is, argues Ziarek, a normative stage in the process of language acquisition. Whilst it may suggest a sense of sadness for something irretrievably lost, what it in fact more strongly indicates is the latent aggressivity that surrounds initiation into the symbolic order, made possible

---

[64] Epps, Grotesque Identities (note 1), p. 42.

[65] »Man überblickt jetzt, was der Fetisch leistet und wodurch er gehalten wird. Er bleibt das Zeichen des Triumphes über die Kastrationsdrohung und der Schutz gegen sie.« (Sigmund Freud: Fetischismus. In: id., Das Ich und das Es. Metapsychologische Schriften. Frankfurt a. M.: Fischer 1999 [Fischer-Taschenbücher; 10442: Psychologie], p. 331) Kristeva transposes this complex into the domain of language: »And language, precisely, is based on fetishist denial (›I know that, but just the same,‹ ›the sign is not the thing, but just the same,‹ etc.) and defines us in our essence as speaking beings.« (Kristeva, Powers of Horror [note 25], p. 37)

only by the necessary loss (some would say murder) of the (m)other.[66] However, this loss or »symbolic murder« makes possible the play of compensations and supplements that account for *jouissance*: the attempt to retrieve the (m)other in signs. In this model, loss is experienced as a temporary state of affairs that constantly repeats itself, but that equally may be constantly compensated for in the play of signification. A different economy of language emerges in the case of the failed fetishist however, one which refuses to (or simply cannot) mourn the lost (m)other. This is the economy of melancholia which unlike the economy of mourning, cannot negate the loss of the (m)other through the filling function of the linguistic sign. The language of the failed fetishist approaches thus the discourse of melancholia.[67]

If, as in the case of Kristeva's phobic writer, language is understood as the fetish object par excellence, then all that is needed for entry into that vile space of mortality – the grave/grotto – is a minute disruption in the denial/recognition practice of fetishist speech. In other words, the economy of mourning would have to lose its ability to swiftly replace loss with compensation. This disruption would tip the balance of the psychic apparatus in the uncomfortable direction of incessantly recognising (as opposed to incessantly deferring) castration. Correspondingly, the robustness of the denial impulse recedes as the vital place of the border between loss and compensation is itself ultimately transgressed and the Freudian space »beyond the pleasure principle« – a psychoanalytic variation of the *grotta* – emerges.

As we have seen, in Deleuze's terminology this is the space of absolute negation, a speculative territory in which lurks the Death Instinct. That the component drives (the combination of stasis/*jouissance*) have little effect in this context suggests a striking similarity between the discourse of absolute negation and the discourse of melancholia. For the redundancy of the component drives in the domain of the Death Instinct may be compared to the redundancy of the economy of fetishism/mourning (compensation/loss) in the context of melancholia. With reference to the discussion concerning the body's performativity in literary strategy, one could regard this fatal blip in fetishist speech as a peculiarly hollow enunciative act that, if sustained, begins to »enounce« the corpse. This is an idea that will be explored in greater detail in chapter 6 in the context of both Kristeva's and Deleuze's respective theories. With regard to certain details of the present discussion, Kayser's terrified, alienated individual who beholds the *Es* in every aspect of his/her environment could be seen as

---

[66] Ziarek, Kristeva and Levinas (note 12), p. 72: »Language learning is equivalent to matricide.«

[67] »The signification of melancholia discloses, first of all, an acute awareness of disinheritance, accompanied by a lack of faith in any restoration or recompense for the suffered loss. In this sense, a melancholy person is an atheist, without recourse to a secular or religious economy of salvation. Mourning, on the other hand, provides a way for ›disposing‹ of a loss through an acceptance of the symbolic means of compensation.« (Ibid., p. 71)

one such melancholy embodiment of the failed fetishist. By contrast, Heidsieck's techno-self is spared this kind of final disclosure due to its fetishisation of technology.

However, Freud argues that certain fetish objects are particularly predisposed to the recognition of this space, that is, they are fatally marked by an openness to the shadow of death. Such objects, he says, are manipulated by the fetishist in such a way as to represent castration.[68] As earlier discussed, Adorno seems to suggest that the fetishisation of technology points to a society of individuals all in the throes of emotional/spiritual/intellectual death. With regard to Heidsieck's grotesque scenario of robotic subjectivity thus, one would have to query whether machine as fetish does not to a great degree communicate stasis as opposed to its avoidance through deferral. In other words, are not the machine and the grotesque techno-self, even if fetish object and fetishist alike, marked by this very openness to death? The relation through which they exist – the substitution of the means of human life for the ends – would seem to suggest this.

More significantly however, the risky language of the prolific phobic writer also resembles the above fatally marked fetish object. Correspondingly, Kristeva calls it the language of want »that positions sign, subject, and object« in an attempt to conceal the void or block entry into the *grotta* space. The troubled underside of this want, however, is the sense that the language of want is also a language of fear. The phobic writer who succeeds in hurriedly substituting linguistic signs in the empty spaces that would otherwise deliver the »grave« may thus be regarded as a language fetishist driven largely by the fear of castration. One must ask what kind of language emerges when our »founding status, the fetishism of language« breaks down and starts to insistently embrace, as opposed to deny, the void.[69]

A spatial differentiation of the two grotesque modes is useful in better visualising this kind of language. On the surface proliferates the »convoluted formalism« and »flowering of rhetoric« that are typical of grotesque extravagance, whilst beneath lurks the cave, the grotto, an empty space of death »the sinister, turbulent, and agonizingly fearful dimension [...], the troubling side of all that is the odd, strange, funny, and queer«.[70] Diverse though they may seem, Kristeva makes the minute geographical distance between these two spaces apparent when she further describes the fetishistic language of phobia:

> The one who tries to utter this »not yet a place«, this no-grounds, can obviously only do so backwards, starting from an over-mastery of the linguistic and rhetorical code. But in *the last analysis* he refers to fear – a terrifying, abject referent. We encounter

---

[68] »In anderen [Fällen] zeigt sich die Zwiespältigkeit an dem, was der Fetischist [...] an seinem Fetisch vornimmt. Es ist nicht erschöpfend, wenn man hervorhebt, daß er den Fetisch verehrt; in vielen Fällen behandelt er ihn in einer Weise, die offenbar einer Darstellung der Kastration gleichkommt.« (Freud, Fetischismus [note 65], p. 334)

[69] Kristeva, Powers of Horror (note 25), p. 37–38.

[70] Epps, Grotesque Identities (note 1), p. 41–42.

this discourse in our dreams, or when death brushes us by, depriving us of the assurance mechanical use of speech ordinarily gives us, the assurance of being ourselves, that is, untouchable, unchangeable, immortal.[71]

The above makes clear the relationship that exists between the ornate (the excessive nature of the grotesque) and the empty (the subterranean space). Similar to the motion of Jacques Derrida's endlessly circulating supplement, the ornate surface network of the grotesque refers in a roundabout way to the spectre of lack by deferring it via the ambivalent linguistic sign.[72] This recalls the above recognition/denial relation in the function of the fetish object (or the compensation/loss impulse in the economy of mourning). Epps further strengthens the link between grotesque writing and the language of phobia when he terms the grotesque a »writing of erasure, in certain respects, the most graphic legacy of the grotesque«.[73] Figuring emptiness via the practice of filling the empty void is one of the most fundamental literary means of generating grotesques, he argues. Central to this form of grotesque writing that refers obliquely to the possibility of the *grotta* is »the how and where of writing«: a process of playful deferral through the fetishistic filling of sensed emptiness in and around the border between the surface and the deep.[74] In terms of selfhood as locative system, we here encounter the borderline body that is in constant motion. It is visceral and vital because transgressive, a possible general prototype of marginal and marginalised subjectivity.

The evocation of the Holocaust experience in Drach's work requires a further differentiation of the above theoretical position, however. There is a sense in which these texts figure emptiness not by a policy of playful filling, but by dramatically reducing the play of signification. For figuring emptiness through the process of filling implies that the void is nonetheless repeatedly (if only ever temporarily) concealed. It is my view that in Drach's account of the Holocaust, as readers, we are not spared the thorough disclosure of emptiness. In other words, we are left in no doubt as to the fundamental presence of the grave, and indeed it is the language, bereft of its fetishistic prowess, that both delivers and performs this void. One could define the Holocaust society as a world in which, metaphorically speaking, the *grotta* is no longer concealed, no longer an enigma, but brazenly »out there« in the crass discourse of extermination.

This minute but significant differentiation in grotesque language hinges on the notions of linguistic productivity and unproductivity. As long as the fetish function of language remains active, emptiness may well be referred to, but

---

[71] Kristeva, Powers of Horror (note 25), p. 38 (my emphasis).

[72] »The overabundance of the signifier, its supplementary character, is [...] the result of a finitude, that is to say, the result of a lack which must be supplemented.« (Jacques Derrida: Structure, Sign, and Play in the Discourse of the Human Sciences. In: id., Writing and Difference. London, New York: Routledge 1978, p. 351–370, here p. 367)

[73] Epps, Grotesque Identities (note 1), p. 43.

[74] Ibid., p. 46.

due to the strength of the denial impulse this emptiness does not ultimately determine the tone and texture of the language. In other words, the playful mobility of the signifier *produces* ambivalences, transgressions and a kind of flexibility that points to the pleasurable mode of *jouissance*. Hence the categorisation of these drives as component drives: they combine just the right economy of destruction and regeneration (or emptiness and fullness) to maintain a relation that produces the playful motion of movement and all that it politically or ideologically implies. Again, this language model points to the economy of mourning – the recognition of loss and the attempt to address the void by constantly substituting it with the linguistic sign.[75]

Language that evidences the break-down of the fetish function is the language of what Kristeva in the above quotation refers to as »the final analysis«. This is the language that displays naked fear, no longer held at bay through the linguistic reflex filling gestures of the phobic writer. This is the language that pulls back the curtains on the deadly secret that propels fetishist enterprise (the phallic mother who does not exist), effectively delivering the speech acts of the fetishist into a relation of unproductive immobility that could be described as the discourse of stasis. In other words, language as fetish object no longer produces the surface network of transgression, play and ambivalence that energetically defers negation. And the language that welcomes negation is the discourse of melancholia that by definition rejects the propping, vicarious and compensatory economy of mourning.[76]

Interestingly, this language that evokes (as opposed to defers) the space of absolute negation may also be regarded as a mnemonic device in a theory of memory that perforates the block of amnesia. Freud compares the installation of the fetish to the blocking of memory in the case of traumatic amnesia.[77] For

---

[75] The linguistic position of mourning may from this point of view be compared to what Derrida refers to as the vicariousness of the supplement, i. e. that which gives it away as not quite identical to what it attempts to compensate for/supplement: »the sign which replaces the center, which supplements it, taking the center's place in its absence – this sign is added, occurs as a surplus, as a supplement. The movement of signification adds something, which results in the fact that there is always more, but this addition is a floating one because it comes to perform a vicarious function, to supplement a lack on the part of the signified.« (Derrida, Structure, Sign, and Play in the Discourse of the Human Sciences [note 72], p. 367–368)

[76] Compare the following two positions, the first of which highlights the determination of the fetishist, the second describing the mutation of fetish object into phobic object, i. e. revealing the deadly secret that propels fetishist enterprise: »Um es klarer zu sagen, der Fetisch ist der Ersatz für den Phallus des Weibes (der Mutter), an den das Knäblein geglaubt hat und auf den es [...] nicht verzichten will.« (Freud, Fetischismus [note 65], p. 330) »What is ›nothing‹? The analyst wonders and answers, after »deprivation,‹ ›frustration,‹ ›want,‹ etc.; ›the maternal phallus.‹ [...] the impossible object (the maternal phallus which *is not*).« (Kristeva, Powers of Horror [note 25], p. 42)

[77] »Es liegt nahe zu erwarten, daß zum Ersatz des vermißten weiblichen Phallus solche Organe oder Objekte gewählt werden, die auch sonst als Symbol den Penis vertre-

the self who commemorates the Holocaust experience and faces up to the consequences of brutal decisions taken in the name of survival, it becomes clear that recognising guilt may only be performed by a language that does not stop at the fetish stumbling block, but that goes beyond the ambivalence of the transgressing instance to recover the carefully buried carcass of traumatic memory. Thus the *grotta* may function not only as a symbol of the discourse of extermination, but also as a symbol of commemoration, of »returning to« a place of inconsolable mourning, i.e. the discourse of traumatised memory.[78]

When one takes these two quite diverse dimensions of the grotesque into account, it becomes clear that the drives – stasis and *jouissance* – may be very useful in developing the above spaces of transgression and emptiness in a manner that also convincingly links the grotesque to theories of the split speaking subject. Much of this work is dedicated to the task of imaginatively linking the subterranean grotto space and the fluctuating surface space to images of the self as they arise in Drach's work. On the one hand, language as a topography of transgression is the point of departure for a theory of narrative prose that bears the *stigma indelible* of grotesque interference. Accordingly, the self that is expressed via this language is too grotesque, both self and other simultaneously. In this manner, one may agree with Epps when he states that »the grotesque is [...], a way of drawing and writing the self and (or as) others«.[79]

On the other hand, the metaphor of the grotto, the tomb, the crypt is far more useful for the analysis of language and subjectivity in the Holocaust works than is the motif of transgression. The latter presumes a level of insurgent vitality as existing norms and boundaries are glibly transgressed. This image of vitality does not translate very successfully into the debilitated society depicted by Drach in his autobiographical work. Instead, we are time and again confronted both with the reality of death as anticipated by the entrapped Jew of that historical period and with the memory of death from the surviv-

---

ten. Das mag oft genug stattfinden, ist aber gewiß nicht entscheidend. Bei der Einsetzung des Fetisch scheint vielmehr ein Vorgang eingehalten zu werden, der an das Haltmachen der Erinnerung bei traumatischer Amnesie gemahnt.« (Freud, Fetischismus [note 65], p. 332)

[78] Lawrence L. Langer describes just this survivor predicament in his analysis of Holocaust testimonies: »One of the curses willed by the Nazis to their victims is how deep memory continues to infect their experience of time [...]. Who can find a proper grave for such damaged mosaics of the mind, where they may rest in pieces? Life goes on, but in two temporal directions at once, the future unable to escape the grip of a memory laden with grief.« The »proper grave« would mean a committing to the past for once and for all the experiences that belong there – a final burial, so to speak. However, the paradox of survival dictates that the survivor is buried along with these mosaics, unable to fully forget: »The shadows [...] evoke two adjacent worlds that occasionally intrude on each other but more often imply a life after ›death‹ for which we have no name.« (Lawrence L. Langer: Holocaust Testimonies. The Ruins of Memory. New Haven, London: Yale University Press 1991, p. 34–35)

[79] Epps, Grotesque Identities (note 1), p. 42.

ing/narrating perspective. The usefulness of the grotto image becomes particularly apparent in this dual scripting of the Holocaust experience and the written act of its commemoration. The grave/grotto is an uncannily accurate symbol for memory that does not shy away from the full realisation of what happened back then, and also for the melancholy space in which the guilty survivor finds himself. Furthermore, the grotto as the central language concept in these works also functions as the imaginative space of its modern, historically specific variant: the gas chamber. With reference to the work in question, chapters 6 and 7 will make clear why it is necessary to reconceive of the grotesque in this context as a morphology of emptiness, signifier of »loss, absence, and death«.[80]

---

[80] Ibid., p. 43.

Chapter 3
Grotesque Discourses: Mourning and Melancholia

3.1 Constellation of Cross-Contamination

The above elaborated divide in grotesque representation manifests itself in two quite different textures of literary language. The first could be described as infected by insidious vitality, spasmodic, excessive, monstrous. It is to the determining feature of this form of grotesque language that we now turn: cross-contamination, or the co-existence of two contradictory images within a single entity. A typical rendition of this grotesque image would be the double apparition of man and animal within one body. A particularly crass and unforgiving poke at the vanity of the Imaginary Anatomy, this basic example should alert us to one of the key functions of the grotesque as a topography of transgression: the exposure of the artificiality of defining norms and structures via the deliberate cross-contamination of categories that should not »normally« be welded together.[1]

Articulated thus, the grotesque body is rude because monstrous, incomplete because indeterminate, untidy because ambivalent, and lethal because cross-contaminated. To address Gross's question as to how this type of body and the complex mode of subjectivity it suggests will affect language, it is useful to examine already existing theoretical devices of the post-modern. For one could advance the argument that post-modern theories of signification develop the concept of play and with that a form of signifying vitalism (quite literally »movement in language«) that may be productively transferred to what could well be viewed as the adjacent area of grotesque ambivalence in language.

Through the ploy of cross-contamination, this aspect of grotesque language liquidises the notion of dichotomy, vigorously exposing time and again what Lacan vividly refers to as the »lethal factor« of binary signification. This factor emerges in the wake of binary malfunction when dichotomous categories have been revealed as obsolete. Stripped of the ordering solidity of binary organisa-

---

[1] These kinds of images are well illustrated by some of Franz Kafka's work. Rotpeter, the intellectual ape who is disturbingly more human than his human captors, having completed his metamorphosis from human to animal in all ways except externally, and his inverse opposite Gregor Samsa, the man-turned-beetle who despite his vermin status continues to uphold the civilised behaviour of reflection and contemplation (Franz Kafka: Ein Bericht für eine Akademie und andere Texte zum Rotpeter-Thema. In: id., Die Erzählungen. Hg. von Roger Hermes. Frankfurt a. M.: Fischer 1997, p. 322–337; id., Die Verwandlung. In: ibid., p. 96-161).

tion, the signifier collapses into the in-between zone of cross-contamination where, ironically, permanent ambivalence is the only certainty. There is widespread consensus across writings concerning the grotesque that its core characteristic of ambivalence or unresolvable contradiction derives from the coexistence of two conflicting entities within the one image. This iconoclastic ability of the grotesque to collapse binary oppositions demonstrates the above »lethal factor« of signification, further supporting the argument that postmodern topoi are implicitly grotesque – or indeed that the comic-strange category of the grotesque reflects post-modern strategies of deconstruction.[2]

This tendency of the grotesque to unbind carefully established spaces (and indeed identities) within binary order, to disperse them into complex »surface fields and semiotic networks« clearly demonstrates its affinity with those discursive strategies that mark the predisposition of rational discourse to become disordered from within the terms of a too insistent binary logic.[3] The postmodern landscape is awash with these signifiers of monstrosity. Belonging to this dysfunctional family are, in addition to *différance* and *jouissance*, abjection, mimicry, the Lacanian *vel*, the supplement, the »outside« space of the text, to name but a few. They are all forms of grotesque signification insofar as they frustrate the binary signifier thereby making manifest the knots, contradictions and transgressions that result from within dichotomy. Similar to Der-

---

[2] The »lethal factor« Lacan defines in much the same way as the *vel* of signification, also a configuration of cross-contamination (see chapter 1, note 13). It is »a choice whose properties depend on this, that there is, in the joining, one element that, whatever the choice operating may be, has as its consequence a *neither one, nor the other*« (Jacques Lacan: The Four Fundamental Concepts of Psycho-Analysis. Ed. by Jacques-Alain Miller. New York, London: Norton 1981, p. 211–213). The »lethal factor« which is a form of hybridity could be taken as prototype for grotesque signification as topography of transgression. The paradox of neither one nor the other is reflected in the following views on the grotesque. Typical for the grotesque is »die [...] Verbindung in einem Objekt von verschiedenen Bildern« (Dimitri Tschizewskij: Satire oder Groteske? In: Das Komische. Hg. von Wolfgang Preisendanz und Rainer Warning. München: Fink 1976 [Poetik und Hermeneutik; 7], p. 269–278, here p. 276). Kayser also touches upon this basic structure of paradox when he mentions »die Vermengung für uns getrennten Bereiche« as fundamental to the function of the grotesque (Wolfgang Kayser: Das Groteske. Seine Gestaltung in Malerei und Dichtung. Oldenburg, Hamburg: Stalling 1957, p. 198). Heidsieck speaks generally of »das gesteigert Grauenvolle und Lächerliche in einem« and »die Unvereinbarkeit der beiden Vorstellungen« as intrinsic to grotesque anomaly (Arnold Heidsieck: Das Groteske und das Absurde im modernen Drama. Stuttgart: Kohlhammer 1969 [Sprache und Literatur; 53], p. 17). Bakhtin's concept of carnivalesque *mésalliance* evidences, perhaps most clearly, the structure of cross-contamination: »Der Karneval vereinigt, vermengt und vermählt das Geheiligte mit dem Profanen, das Hohe mit dem niedrigen, das Große mit dem Winzigen, das Weise mit dem Törichten.« (Michail M. Bakhtin: Literatur und Karneval. Zur Romantheorie und Lachkultur. Frankfurt a. M.: Fischer 1996 [Fischer-Taschenbücher; 7434: Fischer Wissenschaft], p. 49)

[3] Mary Russo: The Female Grotesque. Risk, Excess and Modernity. New York, London: Routledge 1994, p. 15.

rida's concept of *différance* which locates the origin of signifying indeterminacy in the forceful rhetoric of a binary logic that attempts in vain to dispel uncertainty, the grotesque signifier draws attention to the inadequacies of taxonomy. From this perspective, grotesqueries are both an inadvertent product and disturbing reflection of purportedly rational order.[4]

As the common denominator of the above-mentioned post-modern modes, the »lethal factor« of ambivalence could be described as a signal of »that uncertain cultural body in which is condensed an intriguing simultaneity or doubleness«.[5] J. J. Cohen notes that this lethal body presents an alternative mode of reading culture purely in terms of its difference. The »genetic uncertainty principle« of this body he describes as a form of monstrousness. The monster – a signifier of terminal difference and disorienting ambivalence – thus comes to represent a mode of cultural discourse that evidences the otherness of self and the indeterminacy of the signifying process. In other words, the monster is an instance of the culturally indeterminate body.[6]

Clearly, the grotesque as topography of transgression is closely linked to this post-modern concept of the monster. »The monster's bones are Derrida's

---

[4] *Différance* Derrida describes as the common ground or irreducible difference of difference (similar to the *vel*) in signification (Jacques Derrida: Structure, Sign, and Play in the Discourse of the Human Sciences. In: id., Writing and Difference. London, New York: Routledge 1978, p. 351–370, here p. 370). For Kristeva however, *différance* has been drained of its potential for producing breaks or gaps in signification, hence her call for the further element of *jouissance*: »The return of the heterogeneous element in the movement of *différance* [...] through [...] the unconscious [...] brings about the revolution of *différance*: expenditure, semantico-syntactic anomaly, erotic excess, social protest, *jouissance*.« (Julia Kristeva: Revolution in Poetic Language. New York: Columbia University Press 1984, p. 144) Bhabha's post-colonial theory of mimicry as a strategy of undoing sovereign identity also makes use of the heterogeneous element, the gap, or the in-between of signification. A discourse of paradox, it is »uttered between the lines as such both against the rules and within them« (Homi Bhabha: Of Mimicry and Man: The Ambivalence of Colonial Discourse. In: id., The Location of Culture. London, New York: Routledge 1994, p. 89). The abject brings this paradox to a crisis point for the monstrous subject who is neither self nor other: »Not me. Not that. But not nothing, either« (Julia Kristeva: Powers of Horror. An Essay on Abjection. New York: Columbia University Press 1982 [European Perspectives], p. 2). Finally, the in-between of the mimic text could be seen as the reflection of Roland Barthes's concept of the outside of the sentence/text in which the »sacred armour of the sentence« (subject/predicate) is ruptured in order to create a space outside or in-between these structures (Roland Barthes: Die Lust am Text. Frankfurt a. M.: Suhrkamp 1974 [Bibliothek Suhrkamp; 378], p. 14). Common to all of the above is a sense of the monstrous, a mixed category which Jeffery Jerome Cohen has identified as a cultural construct. The monster signifies ambivalence that »resists any classification built on hierarchy or a merely binary opposition« (Jeffrey Jerome Cohen: Monster Theory. Reading Culture. Minneapolis, London: University of Minnesota Press 1996, p. 7).

[5] Ibid., p. ix

[6] Ibid., p. 4.

familiar chasm of *différance*« asserts Cohen, »a genetic uncertainty principle, the essence of the monster's vitality«.[7] Similar to the latent lethal factor of the binary signifier, the monster always escapes; it always signifies something other than itself which confirms it as the mouthpiece of the other. Accordingly, the epistemological spaces occupied by the monster are the gap, the in-between, the beyond – spaces of displacement, oscillation and movement. This open-endedness or porosity links the monster to Bakhtin's grotesque carnivalesque body. As in the latter case, it would seem that uncertainty – a sense of the infinite and unrepresentable fullness of the real – breeds vitality.

Certain parallels emerge between a grotesque prototype discussed in the previous section, (the fetishist who constantly resuscitates the self through language by deferring the disclosure of castration with the »filler« of the linguistic sign) and the vitalism of the carnivalesque body. Both are characterised by constant activity/productivity. However, the language fetishist represents a fundamentally worried articulation of this vitality. Uncertainty, whilst productive, is not ultimately celebrated by this potentially phobic individual who senses it as a threat. Within Kristeva's theoretical framework, it is therefore not always possible to speak of *jouissance* (a robust manifestation of language fetishism) in the festive mode particular to carnival. Indeed, the sense that the linguistic acrobatics of the language fetishist are driven by a profound (if repressed) sense of loss has earned *jouissance* the apt title of »bitter carnival«.[8]

The phobic writer could therefore be characterised as a form of grotesque personality that writes the fearfully laughing, bitterly carnivalesque, but highly vital body of itself into language. It is a monstrous body insofar as the phobic senses the disturbing gaps in its physical-psychical make-up. In so doing, it senses the otherness within itself and the prospect that it is an incomplete, self-transgressing hybrid of self and other – the mouthpiece of difference. Cohen argues that the monster's body is pure culture because it constantly transgresses »the manifold boundaries that constitute ›culture‹«, thereby exposing the artificiality of what may appear through other modes of cultural discourse to be divinely ordained.[9]

If this is the case, then the grotesque (the monster) as a topography of transgression becomes a useful *modus legendi* for the understanding of culture as difference. In this respect, it gives voice to the »different« underside of culture

---

[7] Ibid.

[8] Menninghaus points out this difference between Kristeva and Bakhtin in his analysis of abjection: »›Die lachende Apokalypse‹ ist insofern eine Grundfigur in der modernen literarischen Prozessierung des Abjekts. Der groteske Körper im Sinne Bachtins kehrt darin wieder – aber allein als ein stets zugleich verworfener. Der Karneval von Bachtins Rabelais-Buch verliert dadurch seinen ideologischen Optimismus der noch in Exkretion und Tod fortzeugenden Materie und wird zu einem ›bitteren Karneval‹.« (Winfried Menninghaus: Ekel. Theorie und Geschichte einer starken Empfindung. Frankfurt a. M.: Suhrkamp 1999, p. 542)

[9] Cohen, Monster Theory (note 4), p. ix.

that constantly returns from its banished position in the repressed outside of homo-genous order. Once again, the monster signifies a mode of self as locative system that is defined by the borderline between inside and outside, self and other. The monster is a grotesque representation of the marginal, its discontinuous corpore-ality a sign of visceral identity beyond binary definition. And the phobic writer, despite its best self-saving fetishistic-linguistic efforts, is one such manifestation of the monster. To further explore this ambivalent figure, we will now turn to a more detailed analysis of Kristeva's concept of poetic language, for as she re-marks »the subject of poetic language clings to the help that fetishism offers«.[10]

3.2 From System to Process: The Semiotic, the Symbolic and the Thetic

The understanding of binary signification as intrinsically self-transgressing carries implications for the producer of signifiers: the speaking subject. Within a monster culture, that is, within a culture of shifting boundaries, this subject is dislodged from its privileged function of producing meaning, becoming instead an eternally provisional construct within the signifying process. The shift from centre to margin of both signifier and subject alike is coextensive with the dissolution of homoge-nous system into heterogeneous signifying process or practice.[11] One particularly eloquent embodiment of monstrously excessive culture is the revolutionary poet: Kristeva's split speaking subject of enunciation who is put »in process/on trial [*en procès*]« by *significance*.[12] Unlike the transcendental ego, says Kristeva, this subject »does not suppress the semiotic *chora* but instead raises the *chora* to the status of a signifier«.[13] The *chora* as activated by this split mode of subjectivity thus accounts for the heterogeneity of the signifying process – the shift of signifi-cation from finite (symbolic) system to infinite (semiotic) process.

This subject is thus caught between and constituted by the battle between the symbolic – the language of paternal law – and the semiotic, the forgotten side of

---

[10] Kristeva, Revolution in Poetic Language (note 4), p. 115.

[11] System Kristeva defines overwhelmingly by the fixity of a hierarchical structure over which the subject (external to the system) presides. In »an axial position, he is not in-cluded, dissolved, or implicated in the system; instead he hovers above it, subdues it, and is absent from it. Signifying systems alone allow us to deduce that the subject is a fixed point and, conversely, this fact is the sole guarantee of the symbolic system and its logical laws.« (Ibid., p. 94) By contrast, the concept of process/practice she de-scribes as follows: »To have access to the process would [...] be to break through any given *sign* for the subject, and reconstitute the heterogeneous space of its formation. This practice, a continuous passing beyond the limit, which does not close off *signifi-ance* into a system, but instead assumes the infinity of its process, can only come about when, simultaneously, it assumes the laws of this process.« (Ibid., p. 100)

[12] Ibid., p. 91.

[13] Ibid., p. 109.

language. The latter falls outside the confines of the signifying system, rupturing the restrictions of »the symbolic cell« but also characterising the very specificity of the system.[14] This specificity could be illustrated with reference to the linguistic model of mourning: the highly provisional economy of compensation and loss reveals the »system« as borderline construct that constantly substitutes signifiers in a bid to cover up lack. This insight leads Kristeva to surmise that »signification is not the base but the boundary of the signifying process«.[15]

The voice and vessel of two modes simultaneously therefore, the split subject of enunciation is a heterogeneous subject. It indulges in constant transgressions, rupturing the limitations of the symbolic system by confronting it with its »beyond« or expelled other (the *chora*), thereby dissolving the system into process.[16] By rupturing the system of paternal law (the symbolic), this dual speaking subject also spoils the narcissism of the Imaginary Anatomy which posits the body as smoothly contoured, self-sufficient and complete. In its stead emerges the body of difference, or the infinite body of the monster: the genetic uncertainty principle that translates into the grotesque corporeality of self and other simultaneously – the split subject of enunciation.[17]

Again, this hybrid self/other is an infinite, or more accurately, an incomplete mode of subjectivity. Mired in the limitless process of becoming, it is little more than what Kristeva calls a »want-to-be« subject, a mere »scaffold of the process«.[18] It is a mode of subjectivity that evolves from the above-mentioned economy of mourning (compensation/loss). The possibility of symbolic subjectivity is premised on separation from the (m)other; however, this loss paradoxically also ensures the impossibility of homogenous symbolic identity. For in the maternal gap emerges the other as compensation for the loss of the *chora*: »and this other, who is no longer the mother [...] presents itself as the place of the signifier«.[19] Signification may thus never be attributed to a homogenous speaking subject. In fact, true to the economy of compensation/loss »signification exists precisely because there is no subject in signification«.[20] From this point of view, signification can only ever articulate difference – the otherness of self and the self as other. And difference, because it is fundamentally indeterminate, renders the subject an ephemeral phase (as opposed to telos) in the signifying process.[21]

---

[14] Ibid., p. 96.

[15] Ibid., p. 101.

[16] Ibid., p. 113: »what remodels the symbolic order is always the influx of the semiotic. This is particularly evident in poetic language since, for there to be a transgression of the symbolic, there must be an irruption of the drives in the universal signifying order.«

[17] Kristeva emphasises the defensive nature of such narcissistic projections; indeed, language may only be constituted as symbolic »through narcissistic, specular, imaginary investment« which in turn is always vulnerable to »the insistent presence of drive heterogeneity« (Ibid., p. 102).

[18] Ibid., p. 101.

[19] Ibid.

[20] Ibid.

[21] Ibid.

Kristeva's theory of the semiotic and the symbolic articulates thus the cross-contamination of self with other, and retrieves the monstrous speaking subject (the self as other) from exile into the forgotten beyond of the socio-linguistic system (the cultural unconscious). The split subject is then returned to a new non-position that cannot be accommodated by the logic of the symbolic system alone. For this new »position« embraces the instability and ambivalence of language as caught between the semiotic and the symbolic. It entails the subject departing its »»meta‹-position, the series of masks or the semantic layer« of the symbolic order and completing »the complex path of *signifiance*«.[22] In other words, the symbolic subject must step outside its safe haven, »the [...] cell that shelters or stimulates this sealing off of the drives«, into the discontinuity of the process that is by contrast open to the drives.[23] This cross-contamination of the semiotic with the symbolic is the double articulation that Kristeva regards as the fundamental state of poetic language. It is precisely this interference of the semiotic with the symbolic that gives rise to the transgressive dynamic that Kristeva terms *jouissance*.[24]

In order to understand the above as a language of erasure that might be useful for the grotesque however, it is necessary to examine in more detail the contradictory interactions of the semiotic, the symbolic and a third area called the thetic. Firstly, the semiotic designates a pre-linguistic state which »precedes the establishment of the sign; it is not, therefore, cognitive in the sense of being assumed by a knowing already constituted subject«.[25] The semiotic is thus a space in which the subject of the symbolic order has not yet been posited. The split necessary for the forming of symbolic subject/object and signified/signifier dichotomies has not yet taken place. Instead, the totality of the *chora* – the pre-symbolic maternal space in which the phallus as signifier has no place – demarcates the rhythmic space of the semiotic which is filled by drive activity. The semiotic is as such a predominantly feminine location; it is rhythmic, nourishing, vital. It is conceived of as an alternative space to the paternal place of the symbolic order which tries to repress it.[26]

In contrast to the rhythmic space of the *chora*, the symbolic represents the ordering side of the signifying process. It would seem that the semiotic impulse, once beholden to the ordering activity of language, is controlled and regulated by the symbolic: »social organisation, always already symbolic, imprints

---

[22] Ibid., p. 103.

[23] Ibid., p. 96.

[24] *Jouissance* is specifically the representation of the return of that which was rejected »the return of rejection«, i. e. the *chora* in the poetic text (ibid., p. 162). Hence the following definition of the poetic text: »the text is a *practice* of rejection, since practice's key moment is *heterogeneous* contradiction.« (Ibid., p. 187)

[25] Ibid., p. 95.

[26] »The *chora* is not yet a position that represents something for someone (i. e., it is not a sign); nor is it a position (i. e. it is not yet a signifier either); it is however, generated in order to attain to this signifying position.« (Ibid., p. 94)

its constraint in a mediated form which organizes the *chora* [...] through an ordering«.[27] The symbolic system is thus comparable to centralising discourses of order based on ideals of rationality and homogeneity. The heterogeneity represented by the semiotic impulse is something that must either be regulated within the symbolic order, or expelled from it. Fundamental to the initiation of the symbolic then, is either the expulsion of its other (the semiotic) to the margins of the symbolic domain where it languishes as waste, or the assimilation of its other into a regulated (appropriate and appropriated) form of identity as sameness. Both approaches attempt to deny difference and express an equal violence (either neutralising or expelling) towards the other.[28] If we are to understand the symbolic thus – as the seat of rational discourse, order and taxonomic categorisations – then it is at least rhetorically opposed to vitalism of the grotesque kind. In other words, it dislikes the ambivalences that confound its ordering principles, but that are ironically produced by these very principles.[29] Thus one of the primary impulses of the symbolic is to reject or negate this kind of disturbance by expelling the *chora* in order to establish a self-contained, immutable system that, if ordered, is relatively bound to this structure.

The criticisms of Kristeva's general theory outlined in section 2.1 are reflected and condensed with regard to the twin concepts of the semiotic *chora* and its expression through *jouissance* in the poetic text. The feminine in some of Kristeva's writings is often understood in quite violent terms. Smith, in particular, questions *jouissance* as a positive expression of the semiotic *chora*; its transgression of symbolic identity with pre-symbolic, undefined existence in the *chora* presupposes incestuous union with the mother which strangely fails to take into account that »incest remains a real and painful experience«.[30] For Smith, the repeated connection between sexuality and violence is part of a general tendency in the early Kristeva to reinforce »what could be termed male forms of pleasure and fantasy«.[31]

---

[27] Ibid., p. 94.

[28] These two modes of repressing difference are elaborated by Kristeva with reference to a) the Cartesian subject who »draws its position, its isolation within the signifying process, from the reduction of the negative, from the absorption of material discontinuity into affirmation and symbolism«; and b) the necessary formation of social negatives, who in the mode of surplus/waste »must be renounced so that society be formed and social harmony introduced. [...] He [a member of such a caste] is the tamed negative, represented and held in subordination by the potlatch.« (Ibid., p. 94–96) Similar to heterogeneity, the return of rejection and *jouissance*, the term »negativity« also represents difference.

[29] Kristeva's elaboration of the appropriating mechanisms of the symbolic system (the foundation of which is the family unit) makes this paradox clear: »A symbolic cog in a hierarchical totality, a hierarchy within a hierarchy, [...] the symbolic cell reproduces [...] family structures, but having ›swallowed‹ negativity only to experience it as symbolic, it proceeds to dismantle them.« (Ibid., p. 96)

[30] Anna Smith: Julia Kristeva. Readings of Exile and Estrangement. London: Macmillan 1996, p. 112.

[31] Ibid.

However, this insight should not detract from the violence that rejects or negates the *chora* in the first place; the paternal law that expels the feminine to the
status of banished other of the symbolic order. The return of this rejection is
therefore the trespass of the negative other into the system that attempted to
expel it. *Jouissance* as this form of negativity, i. e. as difference that returns, may
(in contrast to violence) be thought of also as »what mediates between self and
other«.[32] Negativity as the return of rejection, along with the depiction of the
chora as the locus of unspoken symbiosis with the other (and not as a violent
incestuous reunion with the mother), may also be regarded as instances of *jouissance* that can have a very positive resonance if linked to an ethical imperative.[33]

The body that is here grafted onto language is one that »even if it exposes
its subject to psychosis, opens literature to a different kind of reality: a place of
negativity and *jouissance*, where everything is put into play.«[34] This is the
language that Smith remarks is literally embodied with the mother tongue.
Through it, the revolutionary poet is enveloped »in an ineluctable process
towards *jouissance*, death, and renewal« as the articulation of semiotic drive
interference in the symbolic inscribes a new map of the body on language.[35]
That this new map of the body utterly perforates the Imaginary Anatomy goes
without saying when one considers that as Kristeva understands the semiotic, it
exists in practice only within the symbolic. If the semiotic may be approximated only through the symbolic forms available to us, then as far as the articulation of the semiotic is concerned, both semiotic and symbolic are inseparable. This fundamental state of cross-contamination implies that the semiotic,
although supposedly separate and external to the symbolic order, is in fact part
of its basic identity. The semiotic is however, dependent on the structures of
the symbolic and its transgressions of these structures for its articulation.[36]

Following Kristeva's argument further, it may also be ascertained that the
symbolic is equally indebted to the semiotic. For the establishment of the symbolic order as symbolic can only come about through separation from (or outright rejection/negation of) the semiotic *chora*. As such, the symbolic is fundamentally dependent on this dynamic of separation for its identity as symbolic. In other words, it is indirectly beholden to the semiotic for its existence.
Kristeva goes as far as to say that all symbolic activity as represented by the

---

[32] Ibid., p. 110.

[33] Kelly Oliver makes the point that Kristeva's concern is »to link the ethical with negativity so that it won't degenerate into either conformity or perversion. Without negativity, ethics is mere conformity. And without ethics, negativity is mere perversion. [...]
By linking ethics and negativity, Kristeva tries to steer between tyranny and delirium.«
(Kelly Oliver: Introduction. Julia Kristeva's Outlaw Ethics. In: Ethics, Politics, and
Difference in Julia Kristeva's Writing. Ed. by Kelly Oliver. London, New York: Routledge 1993, p. 1–22, here p. 1)

[34] Smith, Julia Kristeva (note 31), p. 108.

[35] Ibid., p. 109.

[36] Kristeva, Revolution in Poetic Language (note 4), p. 118: »the semiotic we find in signifying practices always comes to us after the symbolic thesis, after the symbolic break.«

fetish function of the phallic signifier is in fact the expression of this question-able separation from the maternal *chora*, the articulation of an absence for which the phallic signifier attempts to compensate. Thus any recognition of this compensatory function of the phallus will necessitate the distortion of the self-sufficient body of the symbolic order. For in the gaps that are not adequately concealed by the phallic signifier, the debt to the (m)other of the symbolic order must fleetingly be acknowledged.[37]

This insight explains further why one could describe the grotesque as topo-graphy of transgression in terms of the language of erasure. For the combination of semiotic and symbolic in an ongoing struggle of negation (expulsion) and the return of rejection (negativity) is precisely the economy of incessant compensa-tion and loss, excess and erasure that bears witness to the robust fetish function of language.[38] This struggle also expresses the contradictory practice of over-writing and erasure that Epps regards as one of the main features of the gro-tesque.[39] In Kristevan terminology, this highly artificial economy of filling and emptiness is most eloquently expressed by the earlier mentioned non-position of cross-contamination between semiotic and symbolic. This non-position Kristeva calls the thetic, a particularly ambivalent threshold »position« to be found in the moment of scission between symbolic and semiotic.[40] It could be described as one of the epistemological spaces of the monster, a gap or chasm that emerges on the threshold between semiotic and symbolic. As such, it is a particularly

---

[37] Ibid., p. 115: »the very practice of art necessitates reinvesting the maternal *chora* so that it transgresses the symbolic order; and, as a result, this practice easily lends it-self to so-called perverse subjective structures. For all these reasons, the poetic func-tion therefore converges with fetishism.« This is compounded by the earlier state-ment that the phallus is the vacuous signifier par excellence: »In other words, the phallus is not given in the utterance but instead refers outside itself to a precondition that makes enunciation possible (i. e. the semiotic network).« (Ibid., p. 101) Reading these two assertions together, it would seem that the phallus occupies the in-between space of the fetish object that is displaced towards whence it came – the absence (*chora*) that engendered it. Insofar as this is the case, separation from the *chora* has not been completed, and these links, no matter how tenuous, express the fetishist's belief »the mother is phallic« (ibid., p. 115).

[38] The terms »negativity« and »negation« should be kept distinct from one another. Negation »is a mask of the symbolic and/or syntactic function and the first mark of the [...] thetic«, whilst negativity is »an inappropriate term for [...] semiotic move-ment, which moves through the symbolic, produces it, and continues to work on it from within« (ibid., p. 122, 117).

[39] »Writing, at times, is overwritten, excessive, and mannered [...]. Full of fancy and flourish, it seems outlandish and bizarre [...]. It tends then to be read, or rewritten, as something else, as something not quite right, not quite writing [...]. It falls short (of communication, comprehension, meaning) because it goes too far; it is not enough because it is just too much.« (Brad Epps: Grotesque Identities. Writing, Death, and the Space of the Subject (Between Michel de Montaigne and Reinaldo Arenas). In: Journal of the Mid-West Modern Languages Association 28 [1995], p. 38–55, here, p. 38).

[40] Kristeva, Revolution in Poetic Language (note 4), p. 102.

suggestible space that articulates the struggle between ordering and disruptive impulses. The shifting positionality (or »in-between« nature) of the thetic that results from this oscillation testifies to the over-determined fetish function of symbolic discourse. For the substituting function of language fetishism implies the presence of the semiotic within the symbolic, and in this manner it exposes the symbolic's ever more concentrated attempts to compensate for (conceal) its siamese relationship of interdependence with the semiotic.

Simultaneously however, the thetic is also the moment of separation from the semiotic; it is the stage at which the semiotic »assumes the role of a signifier«.[41] Correspondingly, the drives of the semiotic must at this juncture be channelled into the regulating structures of the symbolic order. The thetic thus attempts to regulate a two-way system of unordered drives on the one hand, and projected symbolic positions on the other. Due to the thetic's function as interface between these two opposing but interdependent forces, the linguistic signifier that is posited at this point is always under threat from disruption by the drives. For the thetic position does not actually designate a homogenous ego; it in fact »recalls the very process by which it [the ego] is posited«.[42] In recalling this process, the thetic is »in all its various vacillations [...] displaced towards the stages previous to its positing«.[43]

From this perspective, the language of the symbolic order is never more than the expression of the thetic's defence against the assault of the semiotic. One could also argue that the shadow of *signifiance* in the poetic text testifies to the sense that the thetic never entirely pulled off the seminal act of separation: enough to establish a provisional entity called »subject« certainly, but not enough to guarantee the secure homogeneity of this entity in the face of the continued threat and enactment of further splitting as evidenced by the ambivalence of the symbolic.

Both the revolutionary poet who invites anarchy into language and its phobic relative (the fetishistic arch improviser) are modes of monstrous subjectivity who reside on the apex between the semiotic and symbolic. Neither suppresses the semiotic, but instead raises »it to the status of a signifier which may or may not obey the norms of grammatical locution«.[44] Insofar as this is the case, both manifest a fundamental trait of the semiotic process: the »refusal of the thetic«, that is, the refusal to take up a clear position within the symbolic order.[45]

It would thus seem that the moment of separation from the *chora* is not left behind with the advent of the symbolic. Instead, rupture or scission is constitutive (if contained) elements of language. Far from the ordering ideal it rhetorically represents, the symbolic is, from this point of view, only ever the temporary bind between positions marked out by the thetic. These positions are al-

---

[41] Ibid., p. 117
[42] Ibid.
[43] Ibid.
[44] Ibid., p. 109.
[45] Ibid., p. 104.

ways under threat from the re-enactment of archaic rupture in the form of the return of the repressed. And indeed, what Kristeva terms the »second-degree thetic« testifies to the unconscious performance in artistic practice and poetic language of this primordial drama.[46] The thetic and with it the symbolic are thus best described as essentially borderline instances, provisional markers of identity and position. And the grotesque personalities that inhabit the borderline space are permanently predisposed to semiotic interference in the form of gaps that indicate the existence of the other on the borderline space also.

The semiotic that is raised by the thetic to the state of ambivalent and lethal signifier could be taken as the seminal image of grotesque transgressive language. Neither wholly semiotic nor entirely symbolic, the thetic position is truly an expression of the Lacanian »lethal factor« – a grotesque *vel* of (non)identity and indeterminate signification. The semiotic interference in symbolic signification and the economy of symbolic excess that arises in order to conceal this disturbance is an example of how »the word may be made flesh, given body«.[47] Conversely, the symbolic that attempts to harness the vitalism of the semiotic through the ordering function of language illustrates how »the body may be overrun by words, overwritten«.[48] The disharmonious interrelationship between semiotic and symbolic, between corporeality and language system, articulates thus the peculiar writing of erasure. For if the grotesque is to be understood as a body of writing, then the kind of body we are presented with by the thetic is overwritten only insofar as it narrates deficit and lack – extravagantly, bitterly, at times phobically, but always vitally.

The first of two distinct grotesque subjects emerges in this articulation of the body: the slippery borderliner who occupies several different territories of ambivalence. For the subject *en procès* only emerges within the field of heterogeneous practice and accordingly the human body »caught up within this dynamic [...] is also a process«.[49] The monstrous speaking subject of grotesque vitality is thus a subject-in-process, a spatially dispersed, ambivalent nonentity that may no longer be authorised as the subject of cultural knowledge. Dislodged from its notional position as font of signification, the speaking subject now no longer presides over the paths of meaning that lead from it and which it teleologically directs. Instead, it is dissolved into the murky stream of the signifying process where it loses its centre of gravity, becoming simultaneous with and indistinguishable from the process that grotesquely produces and disembodies it. The vacillations of the thetic interface ensure that this subject may no longer be articulated along the hierarchically organised vertical axis in the cultural production of meaning. Rather, it disperses into a rather fibrous network that is undulatory, fitful and coarse.

---

[46] The second-degree thetic is defined as »a resumption of the functioning characteristic of the semiotic *chora* within the signifying device of language« (ibid., p. 103).

[47] Epps, Grotesque Identities (note 39), p. 38.

[48] Ibid.

[49] Kristeva, Revolution in Poetic Language (note 4), p. 101.

Accordingly, Kristeva remarks that »the essential operation dominating the space of the subject in process/on trial [...] is that of the appending of territories – corporeal, natural, social«.[50] This is an interesting observation, for it further differentiates the subject-in-process from the notion of a homogenous subject of »being«. It suggests that the subject-in-process defines itself primarily by where it is (as opposed to the ontological category of who it is), and moreover that this self-definition must constantly be renewed (because in process) by the constant appendage of new spaces. It is as if the restlessness and incompletion of the thetic rupture continually haunts this subject. Never having departed the no-mans-land of the thetic break, all spatial articulations of selfhood are merely the resurrection of this ubiquitous in-between.

In addition to this, the activity of »appending« is also noteworthy, particularly in terms of the body that comes to be articulated through it. It suggests a relationship to space (and corresponding location of the self within this space) that is horizontal as opposed to vertical. In other words, territories may well be strung together by this subject-in-process, but this annexation of spaces, no matter how intense, will not ultimately reinstate the subject at the top of a vertical hierarchy. This is because the constant annexation of new territories does not amount to a cumulative »heaping« of spaces that might tower upwards towards a lofty position on-high. Rather, these territories are made from unreliable materials; sands that shift and blow away, obscuring boundaries hard fought for, nullifying in effect the typical progressive link that might otherwise exist between acquisition and construction.

The body that emerges in this process and through this relationship to space could be regarded as a culturally specific postural performance that critiques in particular whole systems of metaphoric expression based on the »oppositional concepts ›up‹ and ›down‹«.[51] Clearly, a contemporary version of carnival (perhaps bitter) is implicated here. One of the first casualties of this critique is the notion of identity based on »presence« or the idea of selfhood that completely coincides with itself. With the horizontally articulated subject-in-process, we instead come face to face with absence which should further alert us to the grotesque nature of this subject. For the gap of the thetic, so reminiscent of lack, guarantees the subject-in-process enough space to accommodate uninvited guests. In other words, the subject-on-trial is never wholly consistent with itself but is dual, regularly cohabiting with an unwelcome blood relative: the otherness of self, that scaly siamese other that refuses to detach and that ensures a species of idiosyncratic carnival in the place of hierarchy.[52]

---

[50] Ibid., p. 102.
[51] Paul Connerton: How Societies Remember. Cambridge: Cambridge University Press 1989 (Themes in the Social Sciences), p. 74.
[52] The semiotic process recalls the carnivalesque reversal of the social world which, after the dethroning of the sovereign, ultimately results in the gleeful relativity of all structures (Bakhtin, Literatur und Karneval (note 2), p. 48–52).

3.3 Anaphora of Nothing

I will begin this final section with a short summary of the chapter thus far. Generally speaking, I have argued that the grotesque divides into two distinct images: the topography of transgression and the morphology of emptiness. In the theoretical debate concerning the grotesque, these images may be understood as the subterranean space of the *grotta* on the one hand, and on the other the above surface or horizontal network of carnival. These images I have attempted to develop with reference to psychoanalysis with the aim of arriving at two articulations of the grotesque body and of grotesque discourse. Sections 3.1 and 3.2 dealt with the psychoanalytic expansion of the grotesque image of indeterminacy. To this end, Kristeva's theory of the split subject of thetic enunciation proves very productive. Let us now turn to the grotesque as a morphology of emptiness and the specific characteristics of this discourse, not forgetting of course the crucial issue of who practices it.

If the previous section has dealt with the intricacies of the economy of compensation/loss in the discourse of mourning, then this section now moves towards an entirely different discourse, conducted according to very different rules. Ultimately, this discourse may be likened to the discourse of melancholia which rejects consolation of the linguistic sign, instead communicating the condition of loss without compensation. What central characteristic differentiates these two discursive models from one another?

As argued in section 3.2, the economy of mourning is characterised predominantly by the founding loss of the rejected *chora* which is thereafter manifest as a gap in the structure of the symbolic order. Compensation for the lost *chora* consists in the incessant play of signifiers around this gap. For Kristeva, this play signifies the irruption of the semiotic into the symbolic order that tries to repress it. As we have seen, she has a number of terms for this movement e.g. the return of rejection, *jouissance* etc. Most significant for this section however, is the other term she applies in this context: negativity. As Smith points out, Kristevan negativity is »a *foundational semiotic movement* [...], and refers to the destruction and renewal of drive charges which are *transferred* from the space of the semiotic to the space of the symbolic through *signifiance* as articulation«.[53] It follows on thus, that *jouissance* is the embodiment of negativity (the semiotic *chora*) which appears via transgression in symbolic discourse.[54]

The discourse of melancholia however, is characterised by negation as opposed to negativity. »Unbelieving in language«, the melancholy sufferer cannot

---

[53] Smith, Julia Kristeva (note 31), p. 111. »The sole function of our use of the term ›negativity‹ is to designate the process that exceeds the signifying subject.« The conflict of negativity therefore »registers a *conflictual state* which stresses the heterogeneity of the semiotic function.« (Kristeva, Revolution in Poetic Language [note 4], p. 118–119)

[54] Ibid.

mourn the loss of the *chora* through the play of compensation, and so ends up in a space defined exclusively by an act of final negation – final because there is no possibility of reintroducing the ghost of the *chora* into language via the play of compensation/loss.[55] In the melancholy universe, this final act of negation is suicide which for Kristeva represents little more than »a tragic disguise for massacring another«.[56]

From this point of view, suicide is ultimately an expression of matricide. However, because the maternal object has already been irretrievably lost (put to death) in the melancholy world, and because the depressed individual refuses the solace of linguistic compensation, the hatred for the (m)other becomes directed at the self. One could therefore argue that the melancholy disposition allows the founding act of symbolic negation its most extreme articulation. The act of negation that brings the symbolic subject into existence at the expense of the *chora* brings about – in the economy of melancholia – the demise of this subject. Thus understood, the initiating power of symbolic negation is generally an articulation of Thanatos, a characteristic that becomes particularly clear through the discourse of melancholia. This insight should not surprise us as the subject's initial rite of passage into the symbolic order can only occur when the *chora* has been expelled. Consistent with this view of negation as an expression of the Death Instinct, the discourse of melancholia communicates the irreversibility of loss.[57] Before returning to the melancholy complex, let us address negation in general and the manner in which it becomes apparent in discourse.

Generally speaking, negation is an act of the symbolic order that takes place at the thetic juncture. It is an act of separation from and expulsion of the maternal *chora* at the moment where the subject posits itself as an entity clearly defined by an inside and an outside. The rejected outside is negatively connoted, but as Freud points out, prior to negation (prior to the establishment of the inside/outside dichotomy) the not-yet-subject is indistinguishable from it.[58]

---

[55] Julia Kristeva: Black Sun. Depression and Melancholia. Trans. by Leon S. Roudiez. New York: Columbia University Press 1989 (European Perspectives), p. 14.

[56] Ibid., p. 11.

[57] Kristeva describes this loss in terms of a language inevitably geared towards negation of the self, i. e. one that cannot partake in the economy of compensation/loss: »melancholy persons [...] have lost the meaning – the value – of their mother tongue for want of losing their mother. The dead language they speak, [...] foreshadows their suicide.« (Ibid., p. 53)

[58] »Es soll in mir oder außer mir sein. Das ursprüngliche Lust-Ich will, [...] alles Gute sich introjizieren, alles Schlechte von sich werfen. Das Schlechte, das dem Ich Fremde, das Außenbefindliche, ist ihm zunächst identisch.« (Sigmund Freud: Die Verneinung. In: id., Das Ich und das Es. Metapsychologische Schriften. Frankfurt a. M.: Fischer 1999 [Fischer-Taschenbücher; 10442: Psychologie], p. 322–323) The subject's inability to complete the process of separation (negation) leads to what Kristeva terms the condition of abjection; the identification of self with the bad object. Thus ensues a state of permanent negativity as the abject subject repeatedly attempts to exorcise the »negative« (identification with the *chora*) that prevents it

Negation, in other words, negates negativity, i. e. it negates the space of symbiosis with the *chora* in order to establish the boundary between (good) self and (bad) (m)other. This process is both the precondition for and reverse image of the process described in the previous section where negativity constantly overrides the act of expulsion, irrupting through the weak thetic position into the symbolic order. Is it possible to conceive of a rather more barricaded thetic position than Kristeva envisages however, and if so, how must relations be rearranged in order to ensure its domination?

Section 2.1 pointed out that in order to develop a theory of grotesque language that addresses the spectre of absolute negation (the *grotta*/grave), it is necessary to go beyond Kristeva's theory of *jouissance*. Clearly, Kristeva is most interested in reintroducing the maternal function into the paternal order, a project that emphasises the latent power of the negative, i. e. that which was expelled in order to establish the symbolic function. Now however, we turn to the particular violence of negation – the triumph of the symbolic function over the expelled – in order to develop a theory of discourse devoid of *jouissance*.

Deleuze's theory of sadism in language provides an excellent point of departure to this end.[59] Whereas Kristeva concentrates on the return of the rejected *chora* in a thetic relation defined by ambivalence, Deleuze isolates the negating power of the paternal metaphor and focuses on its articulation in sadistic discourse. One could therefore say that whilst Kristeva's theory of the *chora* in poetic language depends to an extent on a faulty phallic signifier, Deleuze's analysis of sadistic language by contrast recognises the maternal function only as negated victim of symbolic triumph. Following this, three main characteristics of the sadist's discourse reveal it to be a sophisticated system of concentrated, repeated and accelerated negation. Firstly, we encounter the primacy of the paternal metaphor: »Sadism is in every sense an active negation of the mother and an exaltation of the father.«[60] Secondly, linked to this matricidal drive is a complementary destructive relation to the fetish object (in the context of the current debate, language). In other words, the sadist goes beyond the fear experienced by the phobic subject who senses (but tries to block) the fact of the castrated mother. Instead, the sadist enters a relation of open aggressivity through the mode of negation. This subject does not content itself with merely sensing and deferring the spectre of absolute negation (castration), but actively pursues negation which may be witnessed most clearly in the violence directed at the maternal metaphor.[61]

---

from becoming a fully-fledged subject of the symbolic order: »I abject *myself* within the same motion through which ›I‹ claim to establish *myself*.« (Kristeva, Powers of Horror [note 4], p. 3) The melancholy individual by contrast, refuses this form of abject *jouissance* (which could be seen as a mode of living with negativity), preferring instead the final negation of suicide.

[59] Gilles Deleuze: Masochism. Coldness and Cruelty. New York: Zone Books 1989

[60] Ibid., p. 60.

[61] »To say that the destruction of the fetish implies a belief in the fetish [...] is to indulge in meaningless generalities. The destruction of the fetish is a measure of the

A third feature of this discourse, as indicated above, is its concentrated repetition of negation. Again, this must be differentiated from the nature of repetition discussed in the previous section. Deleuze makes this distinction quite clear in his extended discussion of the Death Instinct. In sadistic discourse, he argues, we encounter Thanatos beyond Eros, »beyond the ground, the abyss of the groundless; beyond the repetition that links, the repetition that erases and destroys.«[62] The »repetition that links« could be taken to be the constant (if provisional) constitution of temporary binds between positions of the semiotic process discussed in the last section. In other words, it is a repetition consistent with the movement of negativity – linking the expelled *chora* to the expelling symbolic order. The »repetition that destroys« however, demonstrates a form of negating violence that Deleuze elsewhere describes in terms of »pure negation as a totalizing Idea«, the »Idea« being an abstract ideal of paternal dominance.[63]

The repetition that destroys thus evokes through persistent negation the »Idea« of totalising violence that eradicates difference in the form of the maternal *chora*. In other words, the demonstration of violence that Deleuze identifies in sadistic discourse is a direct result of repeatedly enacting the scene of maternal annihilation, of negating difference in order to more effectively project the paternal »Idea« of negation into experience. As discussed in 2.1, this totalising »Idea« takes the form of stasis/Thanatos without the playful disruption of *jouissance*/Eros (the component drives). In other words, the »Idea« could be understood as an abstract and sterile caricature of the main symbolic principle: negation. This leads Deleuze to argue that sadism is in essence a speculative (because it aspires to a level of abstraction) and analytical (because it practices negation/separation) method of apprehending the Death Instinct.[64] It is the task of the sadist to demonstrate in localised practice precisely this idea of absolute negation.[65]

---

speed with which projection [of negation] takes place, and of the way in which the dream [of the phallic mother] as such is eliminated.« (Ibid., p. 73, elaboration in parentheses added M. C.)

[62] Ibid., p. 114.

[63] Ibid., p. 26–27.

[64] Ibid., p. 35.

[65] Deleuze identifies the »Idea« with a level of impersonal violence that is produced by paternal reason and that, if practised locally in the lived world, implies the greater abstraction of apocalypse or universal negation. The sadist is the practitioner of this concrete instance of universal negation. Translated into real terms thus, the »Idea« »requires for its realization that real characters should experience actual pain« (ibid.). The perversion of reason to justify the infliction of suffering on others goes to the heart of sadistic enterprise. The sadist is therefore not interested in eroticism: »He is interested in something else, namely to demonstrate that reasoning itself is a form of violence, and that he is on the side of violence, however calm and logical he may be.« (Ibid., p. 18–19) Along these lines, Lacan has argued that the Sadian exposure of the monstrosity of the Idea may be understood as a critique (or caricature) of the Kantian Idea of pure reason. Cf. Jacques Lacan: Kant avec Sade. In: id., Écrits. Paris: Seuil 1966, p. 765–790.

Yet how does the sadist access this idea of absolute negation which as a speculative »Idea« of total destruction cannot be given in experience? The answer is relatively simple; the sadist must at all times follow a behavioural programme of destruction aimed at removing Eros from the drive equation. This he does by inflicting acts of violence on his victims. It is precisely this reduction of Eros and corresponding shift in drive balance that characterise the new arrangement of relations which ensures a strongly guarded, if aggressive and cold thetic position. Freud puts this very succinctly in his article on negation. *Bejahung* (affirmation) of the negative (m)other is for him an act of Eros, whilst *Verneinung* (negation) – a consequence of expulsion of the (m)other – is representative of the drive to destruction (Thanatos). The separation of Eros and Thanatos in this rather extreme scenario he describes in the following terms:

> Die allgemeine Verneinungslust, [...] ist wahrscheinlich als Anzeichen der *Triebentmischung durch Abzug der libidinösen Komponenten* zu verstehen.[66]

According to Freud's logic thus, if Eros – the pleasurable mode of negativity – is no longer encountered in conjunction with Thanatos, then pure negation is the end result of this process of separating the drives. In other words, once the component drives are separated, Thanatos or the Death Instinct proves to be more powerful than Eros. This »purification« of the drives (*Triebentmischung*) accounts for what Deleuze calls the asceticism or apathy particular to sadistic discourse. Once negativity has been outlawed by the symbolic order, the element of the (inter)personal as represented by self/other relations in the model of *jouissance*/Eros disappears and the coldly impersonal nature of sadism emerges.[67]

Again, we may return to Adorno's earlier discussed cold bourgeois subject to elaborate on Deleuze's figure of the sadist who clearly cannot empathise with the victims of his sadistic behaviour. Adorno's cold subject is very similar to Deleuze's sadist; both are figures that function best in a vacuum devoid of Eros. This coldness Deleuze describes as a form of convenient apathy: convenient because it allows the detached demonstration – through repeated acts of cruelty – of absolute negation, »a form of thinking out the Death Instinct (pure negation) in a demonstrative form«.[68] Deleuze's depraved figure of the sadist could also be viewed as the logical development of Heidsieck's grotesque automaton who substitutes the ends for the means (see section 2.2). If the end of all sadistic behaviour is the destruction of others, then the means of sadistic practice (the repeated demonstration of negation) are indistinguishable from this end (the speculative principle of absolute negation).

---

[66] Freud, Die Verneinung (note 58), p. 324, my emphasis.

[67] »The ›apathy‹ of the sadist is essentially directed against feeling: all feelings, even and especially that of doing evil, are condemned on the grounds that they bring about a dangerous dissipation which prevents the condensation of energy and its precipitation into the pure element of [the] impersonal.« (Deleuze, Masochism [note 59], p. 51)

[68] Ibid., p. 31.

The above summary of Deleuze's theory poses the question as to where melancholia may be situated in relation to sadistic discourse. For although the two may practice negation without the interruption of negativity, they are far from interchangeable. Mechanically similar, they are nevertheless worlds apart in terms of affect. The melancholy world is one of pure sadness without the release of mourning whilst the sadist, as we have seen above, is a caricature of the non-affective intellectual function of negation.[69]

However, melancholia and sadism may also be differentiated by the level and direction of their destructive intent. Let us clarify this further. Were one, for the sake of argument, to envisage the adjacent (but distinct) discourses of phobia, sadism, and melancholia upon a progressive (or regressive) route, the following is how they might appear. Phobic discourse is tainted by what Kristeva describes as the anaphoric dimension of the sign, an »indexing value, pointing to something else, to some non-thing«.[70] Thus whilst the vertiginous linguistic skill of the phobic subject might normally propel it »at top speed over an untouched and untouchable abyss«, it is nonetheless aware of maternal castration (the untouchable abyss).[71] In this manner, phobic language continually evidences the flaw of fetishistic signification: an inconvenient slippage in the compensation/loss process. This flaw could be described as a slowing down before hurriedly bridging (and not necessarily falling into) the abyss of castration.

For this reason, Kristeva eloquently maintains that phobic discourse shows up time and again »*the hallucination of nothing*«, a metaphor that is, she continues, the anaphora (or repetition) of nothing: »the maternal phallus, which *is not*«.[72] In contrast to the sadistic repetition of nothing however, »nothing« is at the phobic stage still a hallucination (a sensed lack) and not a demonstration (a void actively sought). More significantly, it is a hallucination that is feared and therefore swiftly repressed through the play of signifiers. We are within the economy of mourning yet, hence Kristeva's diagnosis of phobic discourse as »the hollowing out of anguish in the face of nothing«.[73]

Sadistic discourse does not avoid the abyss however, but is actively geared towards entering it. In other words, sadism does not attempt to conceal the anaphora of nothing through the play of signification, but in fact desires through repeated matricide the reality of female castration. Unsurprisingly then, the

---

[69] Freud identifies the negating function as the beginnings of an intellectual process that transcends and transforms the play of the drives (Freud, Die Verneinung [note 58], p. 324). Kristeva goes one step further by describing the subject of this intellectualisation process as a homogenous entity, the reverse mode of subjectivity to the heterogeneous subject of negativity: »thought absorbs negation within the thetic position of its bearer [porteur], the subject who is always identical to himself.« (Kristeva, Revolution in Poetic Language [note 4], p. 120)

[70] Kristeva, Powers of Horror (note 4), p. 42.

[71] Ibid., p. 41.

[72] Ibid., p. 42.

[73] Ibid., p. 43.

victim par excellence of sadism is, as noted by Deleuze, the mother. Sadism is thus several notches of extremity further down the route of depraved discourse than is phobia. However, both are closely connected. Kristeva locates the origins of phobia in failed separation from the *chora*. At the same time, this half-constituted self cannot fuse with the *chora* and so is left hanging in a no mans land of undirected drive energy. Its first experience is the aggressivity that arises from these unconnected drives. However, this aggression is sublimated into fear by a process that Kristeva terms »syntactical passivation«: the switching of the self from agent (subject) of aggression to the target object position.[74]

Behind all expressions of phobia thus is the anger of an aggressive subject. Deleuze's theory of sadism could be viewed as the reversal of syntactic passivation, the determined positioning of self in the role of aggressor who, unlike the phobic subject, has overcome its fear of absolute destruction. Hence the sadist's openly violent approach to the fetish function of discourse and by implication, the secret of female castration it conceals.

Finally, melancholia (although an expression of entirely disaffected grief) contains perhaps the most extreme expression of destruction. Just as Deleuze argues that sadism demonstrates the negating power of the Death Instinct, so too does Kristeva argue that melancholia is determined by Thanatos. Another point of similarity is the assertion that melancholia is experienced by subjects who cannot endure Eros.[75] The sadist who practices violence on the bodies of others also displays an equal intolerance of Eros.

Whilst sadism is aimed at the destruction of the (m)other however, melancholia refers to a stage after this act of negation. In the melancholy universe the (m)other is no longer apparent, not even as a victim of sadistic-aggressive matricide. One could say that this act of negation has already taken place. Coupled with the melancholy individual's inability to linguistically trade on this loss, it would seem that the fetish function of language is redundant and with that, the *grotta* space has been entered. The melancholy sufferer could be viewed as a prior sadist who, having reached the space of absolute negation – characterised by complete emptiness and absence of all possible victims – has no real option but to direct its aggression at itself. Hence the shift from matricide to suicide in the melancholy universe. The spectre of nothingness has progressed from mere hallucination in the phobic relation to an aggressive demonstration in the sadistic relation (on the bodies of others, notably); but in the melancholy world, this hallucination becomes a lived reality, and moreover one that is experienced on one's own body.

The above aligning of these three types of discourse must not be taken as a given, of course. The melancholy sufferer, for example, does not have to be a graduate from the school of sadism; nor is sadism the inevitable outcome of phobia gone askew. However, the possible path of regression outlined above

---

[74] Ibid., p. 40.
[75] Kristeva, Black Sun (note 55), p. 20.

traces the discursive descent from the surface network of grotesque ambivalence (the topography of transgression) into the grotto space (the morphology of emptiness). In the context of Drach's Holocaust work, this shift may also be read as consistent with the enforced production of culturally determinate (obedient) bodies. For a point of comparison can be drawn between the product of successful negation processes (the Imaginary Anatomy or the conservative self of symbolic projection) and Deleuze's sadistic self who successfully safeguards the boundary between self/other through matricide.

In contrast to the subversive body described in the previous section, the body that emerges as a cold morphology of emptiness articulates the rigidity of hierarchical organisation. For the safeguarding of self/other demarcations within the sadistic relation amounts to perpetuating the asymmetrical power constellation of victim/perpetrator. The bodies produced by this demarcation appear in rigid symbolic cells that affirm the vertical distribution of identities within the symbolic order. Purged of difference, the overriding characteristic of these bodies is the lack of movement implied by the absence of the *jouissance* dynamic. Hence the image of the sadistic stiff who perpetuates the values of the totalising »Idea«: the creation through negating violence of a static sociolinguistic totality.

However, the grotesque body of sadistic-melancholy discourse also narrates the other mode of stasis: from the perspective of the Holocaust survivor, the trauma of imprisonment, victimisation and the limbo of survival that are symbolised most clearly by Drach's evocation of the melancholy *grotta* space. Chapters 6 and 7 focus on this complex. The coming chapters 4 and 5 now focus on images of ambivalence in Drach's prose work, with particular attention to his development of the protocol as a literary form.

Chapter 4
Floating Documents

4.1 The Protokoll: Epic of the In-Between

The previous chapters have followed a dual argument that polarises psycho-analysis, the grotesque and Drach's prosework into two distinct modes: the Death Instinct and the *grotta* image respectively which in turn provide an interesting reading of the Holocaust (auto)biography on the one hand, and on the other *jouissance* and the grotesque borderline topography which feature in other proseworks. I concluded that these two lines of development, whilst related, ultimately articulate two quite distinct discourses: the discourse of melancholia/sadism and the discourse of mourning (compensation/loss). I now turn to Drach's shorter prose works where aspects of Kristevan poetic language, the grotesque as topography of transgression, and the problem of ambivalent identity will become evident. Chapters 4 and 5 are therefore concerned with prose-works belonging to this group whilst chapters 6 and 7 will return to the discussion of melancholia/sadism with reference to the Holocaust autobiography. The concept of the protocol as a floating document of ambivalent characterisation, loose utterances and thetic instability thus focuses the discussion of Drach's prose within the framework of mourning. The Holocaust work as protocol requires further differentiation which will be taken up in chapter 7.

The development of the protocol as novel is one of Drach's main and most original contributions to the literary avantgarde. With few exceptions, his best known texts all bear the title (or subtitle) of »protocol« or »report«.[1] The protocol appears as a concept for the first time in 1929 in the unpublished introduction to the collection *Die kleinen Protokolle*, which at that time bore the rather more sentimental title of *Bildnisse der Erfolglosen, ein Wiener Lied aus unserer Zeit* (Portraits of the Unsuccessful, a Viennese Ballad for our Time). These small protocols portray various situations of the socially disadvantaged in Vienna and its surrounding area. Drach states clearly the purpose of the protocol at this point: the interests of objective narrative. His choice of narrative style thus excludes a sense of the lyrical or the dramatic, which as he states in the unpublished introduction, explains the lack of dialogue in these works. Instead, he is interested in exposing protagonists as victims of a social

---

[1]   Of Drach's six novels, only two are not declared protocols: the futuristic novel *»O Catilina«. Ein Lust- und Schaudertraum* (München, Wien: Hanser 1995) and the diary-styled *Das Beileid. Nach Teilen eines Tagebuchs* (Graz, Wien: Droschl 1993).

milieu that conspires against them and from which it is ultimately impossible to escape.[2]

This early understanding of the protocol continues into Drach's later works where he is also clearly dedicated to voicing the underdog's plight. However, his understanding of objectivity undergoes a clear metamorphosis in the following decade and during his exile in France. As can be seen from certain unpublished manuscripts concerning the novel *Das große Protokoll gegen Zwetschkenbaum*, in these later years the protocol evolves into a clearly unobjective, biased literary form in which the author decisively pursues a policy of »writing against« the title heroes. This shift from the uncompromising stance of unbiased objectivity to a more subjective approach may be explained by Drach's personal circumstances at that time. He was already in exile by 1939 when he began to produce the *Zwetschkenbaum* manuscript. Eva Schobel points out that, from this point onwards, Drach starts to systematically place his main characters (who are always victims) in the position of wrongdoer also, a reflection perhaps on survival politics of the enforced position in which Drach found himself at that time.[3] A letter to the Rowohlt publishing house dated December 13 1959, concerning the *Zwetschkenbaum* manuscript, documents this transition from the drive for total objectivity to measured partisanship. Central to this conceptual shift is Drach's understanding of the protocol as a form of epic prose which ironically involves the above policy of »writing against« the hero.[4]

What does the act of »writing against« entail? As there is no such thing as unintentional art in epic form, Drach tells us in the above letter, he decides ultimately to write in favour of the hero, usually the victim of social injustice. However, writing for this character may only occur, somewhat ironically, by writing against the tradition of heroic epic. In other words, the hero of Drach's protocol-epics is often exposed in various postures of cowardice, dubiousness, and at times outright caprice. Drach's protagonists are therefore not so much epic heroes as epic anti-heroes. Their actions are intended to reflect the social situation which produces them and against which they battle. Because the social milieu itself is quite complex, Drach takes the above contradictory approach of writing against the character (and therefore against the network of power relations in which the victim is enmeshed) in order to write for the character – if not entirely to exonerate them, at least to contextualise their behav-

---

[2]   Albert Drach: Eigenhaendige Literarische Einfuehrung. In: id., Bildnisse der Erfolglosen, ein Wiener Lied aus unserer Zeit. Nachlaß Albert Drach, Austrian Literary Archive of the Austrian National Library, Wien, dated July 31 1929.

[3]   Eva Schobel: Albert Drach. Ein lebenslanger Versuch zu überleben. In: Albert Drach. Hg. von Gerhard Fuchs und Günther A. Höfler. Wien, Graz: Droschl 1995, p. 329–375, here p. 344–345. Cf. id., Unerbittlich, zynisch, zärtlich. Albert Drachs eigene Auswahl seiner kleinen Protokolle und Erzählungen. In: Süddeutsche Zeitung, December 17/18 1994, p. 4.

[4]   NLAD, Austrian Literary Archive of the Austrian National Library, Vienna.

iour. Drach tells us that this strategy is intended to provoke the reader into criticism of the status quo.[5]

Writing in favour of the character may thus only come about through paradoxical representation. The reader becomes familiar with the epic anti-hero in a veiled manner; he is fleshed out by the protocolled utterances of all the different characters who encounter him in the protocol. This is usually a far from flattering representation because the protocolled utterances of other characters are always coloured by prejudice. In this vein, Drach claims that the purest form of epic is the protocol that documents all utterances concerning the hero, whether for or against him. Moreover, this »pure epic« will not stop at gathering the sum total of all statements, but will more significantly document the way in which utterances are delivered, misunderstood, misconstrued and deliberately manipulated along the path towards the establishment of so-called facts.[6]

This strategy of »writing against« the hero thus serves two purposes: to show up the unattractive truth about social reality through a strategy of textual contradiction, and in so doing to encourage the reader to begin to see, through this minefield of contradiction, the web of injustice (the protocol and the society it represents) in which the anti-hero is entangled.

Whilst Drach's use of the term epic should ultimately be understood as his literary term of choice for prose narrative, it nonetheless contains a criticism of the modern novel's portrayal of subjective, interior landscapes. Drach appears to have regarded epic and protocol-novel as interchangeable terms. Epic he defines with reference to Homeric epic: its plot-driven action and the clear line of development undergone by its principal characters throughout the course of events. This character development, it should be noted, is presented externally through the channels of action taken by the character. It is not rendered through sentimental forays into the psychological or spiritual progress of the inner life of the individual. In direct contrast to the protocol-epic is the modern novel which for Drach delivers just this introspective articulation of subjectivity. A »novel« that omits the above epic trait of exterior representation does not qualify as a novel at all, according to Drach.[7]

---

[5] Schobel, Albert Drach (note 3), p. 344.
[6] Albert Drach: Wurmfortsatz: Zum Protokoll »Wie man Zwetschkenbaum steinigt«, NLAD, p. 322.
[7] In reply to the question concerning the novel of the twentieth century in which plot development and clear resolution of plot seem to be secondary concerns, Drach unequivocally states: »dann ist der Roman auch verloren gegangen. Denn ein Roman ohne Entwicklung ist nichts. Wenn Sie die Versromane, die ›Ilias‹ und die ›Odysee‹, anschauen, dann sehen Sie, es muß etwas geschehen, es muß sich etwas entwickeln, es muß aus jemand etwas werden. Das ist der Roman. Was anderes ist der Versuch einer Prosaumschreibung.« (Peter Huemer: Albert Drach im Gespräch, 9. 1. 1992 Österreich 1. In: Prozesse 2. Mitteilungsblatt der Internationalen Albert Drach-Gesellschaft 1998, p. 14–26, here p.22). Cf. Wendelin Schmidt-Dengler: Wider die verzuckerten Helden: Ein Gespräch mit Albert Drach. In: Albert Drach (note 3), p. 9–27, p. 12–13.

The above features of the protocol – writing against, pure epic, exteriority of character representation – are part of a considered literary programme that Drach terms the aesthetics of unsentimentality. Narrative distance as a form of writing against pathos is in fact part of an oppositional strategy which aims ultimately at the provocation of reader sympathy for the hero, but significantly through the aesthetics of unsentimentality. In the distant tone of the protocol narrative thus, we encounter elements of subjectivity; the authorial desire to reveal truth about the world through a strategy of paradox along with the pseudo-objectivity of the protocol narrator which is in fact none other than a narrow-minded subjectivity loaded with social and racial prejudice. From this point of view, it becomes difficult to talk of narrative distance in Drach's work as anything other than an *Inszenierung* (a performance or production) of distance, as André Fischer has pointed out in his discussion of *Unsentimentale Reise*.[8]

What body is produced by the aesthetics of unsentimentality? The above concept of pure epic along with the representative strategy of paradox are consistent with certain key features of the grotesque as a topography of transgression. Central to the notion of pure epic is in fact the notion of a lack that must be constantly overwritten. In keeping with this notion of lack, the subject of the protocol rarely speaks for itself. Usually a character from the social sphere of the disempowered, these personalities are marked by vocal absence from the verbal constructs that mould and shape them. These disadvantaged persons assume shape, form and personality for the main part through the words, narratives and judgements of many others, a literary strategy which itself performs the power of bureaucratic structures to create victims through documentation. The protocol as such could be described as a sea of words that quite literally swims around a troublesome spot that requires constant redefinition.

Pure epic thus appears to conform to the discursive economy of lack/compensation. In the highly formal tone of bureaucratic language however, com-

---

8   Despite his criticism of the novel as an emotional piece of propaganda in favour of the hero, the following citation reveals Drach's understanding of narrative distance as a calculated closeness. To the claim that there is no emotional involvement allowed through his epic style Drach replies: »Nein, das ist nicht richtig [...]. Im Gegenteil, die emotionale Beteiligung soll durch Opposition zu diesem Stil entstehen und zwar in dem Sinn, daß etwas durchsichtig gemacht wird durch den Stil [...]. Die emotionale Beteiligung [wird nur] durch einen wirklichen Roman bewirkt, den es vor mir nicht gegeben hat. Denn was bisher als Roman ausgegeben wurde, ist eine Propagandaschrift für den Helden, und bei mir ist das nicht der Fall. Es ist das Protokoll, das gegen ihn genauso schreibt wie gegen alle anderen, und es nimmt ihn viel stärker noch her. Am Schluß aber bleibt alles Sympathie für ihn übrig, das heißt, er überlebt seine Widersacher, er überlebt sich selbst, er überlebt sein Schicksal. Die Emotion wird nicht gewonnen im Wege der Sentimentalität, sondern durch die Unsentimentalität.« (Huemer, Albert Drach im Gespräch [note 7], p. 21) For a further discussion of the role of unsentimentality in Drach's work see André Fischer: Inszenierte Naivität. Zur ästhetischen Simulation von Geschichte bei Günther Grass, Albert Drach und Walter Kempowski. München: Fink 1992 (Theorie und Geschichte der Literatur und der schönen Künste; 85), p. 214–267.

pensation is parodied into excess which in turn reflects the indeterminacy of the protocolling enunciative act with regard to its protocolled subject. For there is a pronounced sense in which the subject who is created by the protocol and against whom the protocol is written embodies the ambivalent language of the *Amt*. Drach's epic style thus suggests a mode of characterisation that is conceptualised around a linguistic image of the grotesquely incomplete and self-transgressing body. Writing against the anti-hero amounts to writing against the structures that produce him/her. From this point of view, the representation of the transgressive grotesque body that is hopelessly overwritten functions ultimately as a critique of the *Amt* more so than the protagonist.

Consistent with this, Drach's outcast anti-heroes are presented in an unflattering light which reflects more the negative bias of those who see and report them than any kind of inner life of the character. In a certain sense then Drach's use of epic, despite his insistence on concrete, plot-driven action, can be seen as an epic documentation of the distorting (because subjective) channels of reported speech, a kind of language epic. It is at this point that Drach's epic diverges completely from the Homeric epic which he takes as a reference point. Not only is the site of heroic action usurped by the »action« of incidentally documented utterances in Drach's protocol-epic. If one regards epic in the classical sense as a narrative form concerned with voicing collective identity, then Drach's use of the term epic to describe a prosework of sliding utterances becomes quite ironic. For it is in the gaps that open up between these utterances (the in-between) that the subject in process emerges and difference is voiced.[9]

If Drach's protocol style is at all epic, then predominantly as an epic parody of epic grandeur. Whereas Homeric epic narrates heroic events of national relevance, Drach's comic epic stresses the accidental nature of most large scale events, not to mention the monumental, but in the annals of historiography highly contingent stupidity that lurks behind decisions. Presenting Hitler's failed attempt as artist as the main reason for his transition to politics is one such illustration of Drach's view of the arbitrary, highly subjective, banal and incidental way in which history occurs.[10] These are the irregular details that never make it into the linear, teleological narrative of the nation as an object of epic discourse. As a means of drawing attention to the marginal, non-heroic history of European

---

[9] Georg Lukács defines epic as given to the expression of such immanent phenomena as family, love, state (Georg Lukács: Die Theorie des Romans. Ein geschichtsphilosophischer Versuch über die Formen der großen Epik. 2., um ein Vorwort vermehrte Aufl., Berlin: Luchterhand 1963, p. 26). Homi Bhabha terms this kind of discourse pedagogical which represents a view of the nation's imagined community as homogenous and authorised as such by a »pre-given or constituted origin *in the past*«. Drach's protocols diverge from this tradition – they are in fact comparable to a form of discourse Bhabha calls the performative which presents people not within what could be termed the epic symbolic cells of nation, family etc., but as »›subjects‹ of a process of signification« (Homi Bhabha: The Location of Culture. London, New York: Routledge 1994, p. 144–145).

[10] Cf. Schmidt-Dengler, Ein Gespräch mit Albert Drach (note 7), p. 18–19.

culture in the twentieth century, Drach inverts the lofty tone of classical epic and replaces it with an exploration of the insidiously ubiquitous meandering trail of error, incident, coincidence and accident. In this sense, his protocols are epics of the epic stupidity that gives rise to prejudice, stereotyping and enmity.

By including all utterances of the different characters who encounter the individual against whom the protocol is written, Drach wishes to effect the epic documentation of social prejudice, how it arises and how it is kept in circulation. In this way the protocol becomes the epic of a politically loaded language trail that slides its way half accidentally, half arbitrarily, but mostly hatefully from capricious mouth to capricious mouth, from there into the protocol itself, where these images should crystallise. However, they do not as a result of the ambivalence of the narrative voice. Instead, attention is drawn to the *process* by which these stereotypes emerge and the problematics of identity that give rise to such fear of the other in the first place. As such, Drach's version of the epic as protocol moves away from eurocentric notions of occidental greatness. Self-delusional idiocy and the ambivalent self as other take the place of this outmoded image.[11]

Moreover, Drach's concept of the protocol as the epic of accidentally converging, snaking language trails suggests the multi-perspectivist nature of the protocol. The strategy of writing against the anti-hero involves the reporting through indirect speech of the subjective impressions of arbitrary individuals concerning the hero. However, these subjective impressions undergo further pulverisation through the enunciative act of the narrating self. This kind of third (or even fourth) remove narration results in the increased dispersal of the anti-hero through the focalisations of unreliable others. The protocol thus emerges through this process as a specimen of ceaselessly embedded narrative with, at best, a dimly recognisable a priori and no truly identifiable motiviation. In this regard, the protocol is a floating document of incidental utterances, semi-posited characters and plot that seems to lead nowhere. This sense of indeterminacy is further exacerbated by the split and poorly embedding narrative of the protocolling instance, a sure sign of the slippage that takes place through the fetish function of language. One could say that the protocol floats (is badly posited) because the *Amt* must, like the phobic writer, constantly revive and determine itself through a prolific spewing of the linguistic sign. Taking this into account, the protocol is a literary form wracked with instances of thetic instability, a text that raises the semiotic continually despite (or as a result of) its exaggerated staging of symbolic discourse.

It is not just as the unwieldy document of sliding utterances that the protocol may be termed an epic of the in-between. The poorly posited narrative

---

[11] The epic as the documentation of the forgotten, marginal and non-heroic side of history corresponds to Drach's notion of pure epic. Drach's understanding of world events in terms of banal error based on »protokollierten Mißverständnissen« explains why he sees stupidity as the greatest evil of all, certainly worthy of epic representation: »Das Schlimmste auf der Welt ist die Dummheit. Die Bosheit ist nur eine Form der Dummheit.« (Huemer, Albert Drach im Gespräch [note 7], p. 19)

instance that is outstandingly inept at embedding the protocol is the epitome of the grotesque transgressing body – the in-between of identity. Structurally therefore, similarities arise between the incomplete but overwritten body and location of the anti-hero, and the invisible but busily overwriting body of the narrator. Both are borderline instances of subjectivity; the former lives between the lines of what is asserted about him whilst the latter is divided from the onslaught as a result of the policy of simultaneously writing for and against the anti-hero. Of the two the narrator presents perhaps the more complex mode of subjectivity. On the one hand, we have the protocolling instance who gathers and documents the scattered utterances of others, but not before he slyly invests them, already heavily loaded with judgement usually of the negative kind, with his own prejudices. On the other hand, we have what could be called the implicit author who arises through the terms of the narrative language, but who debunks the representatives of this language and so engages in a subtle and indirect defence of the appropriated others of this discourse.[12]

Thus the gesture of writing against the anti-hero does not just confine itself to writing against the victimised other. The narrative instance in Drach's prose also writes against itself, effaces and erases itself, debunks and decentralises its appropriating drive. In this act of »writing against« we encounter certain aspects of Kristevan poetic language. Taking the narrative space as the locus for such comically spiteful warfare, it becomes clear why a grotesquerie of the dismembered subject is one of the most fundamental images of Drach's work.

Before proceeding to the analysis of *UND*, let us place Drach's protocol generally within the theoretical framework of chapter 3. With reference to the discussion in 3.3, the protocol could be regarded as a mimicry of the language of negation. A written product of the cellular cogs that construct the bureaucratic organisation of the symbolic order, the very notion of the court or police protocol suggests official formality and etiquette, a conformity to the rules of exclusion and separation that establish symbolic hierarchy. The protocol in this specific sense is the written counterpart of the Imaginary Anatomy discussed in chapters 2 and 3. In other words, the protocol would seem at first glance to perform images of the culturally determinate body, that mode of subjectivity that reflects and

---

[12] The implied author we understand as a phenomenon of the text distinct from the author, Albert Drach, but also to a certain degree distinct from the narrator as protocolling instance. As such, the narrator is dislodged from any pretensions as the ultimate authority of the text through the space of the implied author who »emerges from our overall reading of the positions, values, and opinions espoused by the narrative text as a whole, reconstructed by that reading as the semiotically necessary authorial *stance* demanded by this particular text. These opinions and values may or may not be the same as those of the real author.« (Patrick O'Neill: Fictions of Discourse. Reading Narrative Theory. Toronto, London: University of Toronto Press 1994 [Theory, Culture], p. 66) Drach's notion of contradiction as a means of reaching the reader both cognitively and emotionally is compatible with this definition of the implied author as a potential text-space or indirect point of orientation for the implied reader.

reproduces the vertical, classifactory body of »binary extremism«.[13] If this is the case, one could argue that the protocol is generally a form of sadistic literary discourse that perpetuates the rigid categorisations of victim/perpetrator, self/other etc. This perspective will be immensely useful for a reading of the Holocaust autobiography which communicates the image of a severely disciplined society. However, in the protocols to be discussed in chapters 4 and 5, the convoluted formalism of protocol language functions as a tool in its own dismantling process.

Mimic men, vagabonds, criminals, strangers, outcasts, madmen and shunned women, all articulations of the culturally indeterminate other, abound in these protocols. These figures are all embodiments of the subversive cultural body, the borderline others that are produced by the indeterminate thetic position of the protocolling voice. The body of *jouissance* is therefore not solely located in these protocol protagonists. The supposedly objective reporting instance itself is constantly exposed as a splitting, unstable, indeterminate space where a disintegrating grotesquerie of the speaking self takes place. Thus whilst the laboured objectivity of the protocol might initially suggest stasis of language, in the protocol analysis of *UND* it will become clear that this stasis is uprooted constantly by poetic negativity. Despite its bureaucratic, factual tone, the protocol functions in this regard as a vessel for Drach's *nature morte* aesthetic, the exhaustive staging of disintegration in process. In the protocol as topography of transgression, the appearance of stasis in whatever form is always pulverised by *jouissance*, the body of negativity. One could say therefore, that in these protocol-parodies the body of negation (stasis) is overwritten by the body of negativity (*jouissance*) as the subversive apparition of the self/other hybrid disrupts the projection of an Imaginary Anatomy. It is just this perforation of subjectivity through grotesque overwriting that occurs in the protocol *UND* to which we now turn.

4.2 Outside the Text: Creating the Catachrestic Space

> Als Schriftsteller gilt, nicht wer sein Denken, seine Leidenschaft oder seine Imagination in Sätzen ausdrückt, sondern wer in Sätzen denkt: ein SATZDENKER (das heißt: nicht ganz ein Denker und nicht ganz ein Satzbilder).
>
> (Roland Barthes)

The short protocol *UND* offers us a clear example of how the poetic text, as Kristeva puts it, retraces the path of its own production.[14] This entails the realisation of language transgression, the raising of the semiotic through poetic

---

[13] Peter Stallybrass / Allon White: The Politics and Poetics of Transgression. London: Methuen 1986 (University Paperbacks; 922), p. 26.

[14] Albert Drach: *UND*. Protokoll einen Richter treffend. In: id., IA UND NEIN. Drei Fälle. München, Wien: Hanser 1992, p. 37–61. Henceforth cited in main text as *UND* in parenthesis with appropriate page numbers.

negativity (the rejection of rejection) and the resulting erosion of the thetic position. As we shall see, there are some highly specific ways in which Drach achieves this. For the moment however, suffice it to propose that the connective »und« is, as far as this text is concerned, the locus of thetic instability. This epic in short form not only candidly thematises Drach's concept of the parodic epic telling of epic asininity and the corresponding slide into the seeming triviality of the in-between. The basic premise of the text evidences also the operational tactics of the rhetorical grotesque, foregrounding the issues of language ambivalence, the ideological fixity of the phenomena »system« or »structure« along with the threat posed to these by language and conceptual cross-contamination, i. e. grotesque indeterminacy. In other words, a case can be made for »und«, the bland and harmless connective, as the epitome of the grotesque fetishistic signifier, linguistic depository of excess, place of lack, reminder of the language internal problematic of ambivalence.

Through the example of *UND*, it will also become clear that grotesque indeterminacy as the transgression of system designates the »outside« of the system, the cultural space outside the sentence, as Roland Barthes calls it, which is also the space for the articulation of marginality, the contingent, the difference of others as it were. This *jouissance* or disruption of the system is expressed for Barthes in the »atopical« nature of the text, that is in the tendency of the text to enact the dissolution of system. The signification of such a text is to be found in this very process of dissolution which betrays the text in the process of production. In other words, the signification of the text outside itself *is* dissolution, *is* transgression, *is jouissance*, an instance of movement beyond the ideological fixity of the system.[15]

Barthes's notions of the atopical text and the sentence outside itself are complementary to Kristeva's depiction of the poetic text. In particular, her concepts of the threshold thetic position, semiotic negativity and the transgression of the system for the purpose of its renewal portray this outside space. For the outside of the text or sentence, as Barthes understands it, does not imply that the text has an inside, but that its status is that of the outside without inside (the

---

[15] Barthes makes clear that the outside space of the sentence is to be distinguished from any ontological understanding of a spontaneously existing, language-anterior origin: »dieser *Nicht-Satz* war keineswegs etwas, das nicht die Kraft gehabt hätte, zum Satz zu werden, das vor dem Satz gewesen wäre; es war: was auf ewige unnahbare Weise *außerhalb des Satzes* ist.« (Roland Barthes: Die Lust am Text. Frankfurt a. M.: Suhrkamp 1974 [Bibliothek Suhrkamp; 378], p. 74) Cf. Bhabha: »The non-sentence is not before (either as the past or a priori) or inside (either as depth or presence) but outside (both spatially and temporally ex-centric, interruptive, in-between, on the borderlines, turning inside outside).« (Bhabha, The Location of Culture [note 9], p. 182) The atopical nature of the text refers to the process of text production which, similar to Kristeva's understanding of the semiotic process, conceives of text as language that transgresses itself. The atopical text is for Barthes (as for Kristeva the poetic text) an alternative to the oppressive language of system (Barthes, Die Lust am Text [above], p. 46).

marginal or the contingent in other words), without a metaphysical presence, or as Kristeva would put it without the transcendence of a phenomenological speaking subject. Thus the binary opposition of inside/outside does not hold, as the outside becomes the grey area of ambivalence beyond symbolic language, the system and the sentence. Both theories reflect the post-structuralist attempt to think language without presence. In particular, Barthes's concept of language outside the sentence will be helpful for the coming analysis of the grotesquerie of Drach's prose style.

In proposing the connective »und« as the articulation of this space, it is also implied that the entire text is torn and outside itself despite its appearance as a protocol littered throughout by the over-precision and seeming accuracy of what Barthes terms the »lexicographic artefacts« of the symbolic order.[16]

In many ways, this is a key text in understanding Drach's use of language. By problematising the issue of language connectives around the subordination and coordination of thought into certain narrative structures, he is not only engaging in an incisive critique of cultural, political and institutional hierarchy, but also in the issue of the fictions of such constellations as the narrative products of certain social formations. The subversive moment of language however, its »outside«, is of key interest here and centres around the ambivalence of the word »und«.

Three »cases« form the small volume *IA UND NEIN. Drei Fälle* published by Hanser in 1992 in honour of the author's ninetieth birthday.[17] Written during the previous fifteen years, the thematic material of the stories engages with and critiques the corrupt politics of contemporary Austrian society; the survival of anti-Semitism long after the fall of the Third Reich; the persistence of misogyny despite the widespread Feminism of the 1970s; the apocalyptic reflection of man's self-destructive folly in the post-nuclear war, radioactive bunker wasteland depicted in *IA*; the tenacity of totalitarian world views as exemplified by the Austrian judicial system in the protocol *UND*.

On the face of it the three stories, although rhetorically linked in the half sentence of the title, have little in common. *IA* tells the eerie futuristic story of the human race.[18] In the grotesque setting of an Austrian bunker, the only post-nuclear survivors of the human race are presented to us: sixteen elderly men, the youngest of whom is sixty three and a seventeenth person, a wailing female infant (its only cry are the two sounds of »Ia«) abandoned by its mother at the door of the bunker. The following pages are taken up by the protocolled discussion concerning the urgent reproduction of the human race and the parts to be played in this vile, paedophilic drama by the female child (the only surviv-

---

[16] Ibid., p. 42.

[17] Cf. Peter Mohr: Spät entdeckter Individualist. Schriftsteller Albert Drach feiert seinen 90. Geburtstag. In: Main-Echo, December 17 1992.

[18] Albert Drach: *IA*. In: id., IA UND NEIN (note 14), p. 5–36. Henceforth cited as *IA* in parenthesis with appropriate page numbers.

ing female on planet earth) and the sixteen male elders. The patriarchs have the word, and they also determine the »word« of the infant. It is a cry of affirmation to their plans, they decide, and then turn to the task of selecting the most suitable among them for the act of copulation. Misogynistic, paedophilic, pornographic and grotesque, yet all delivered in the detachedly summarising coldness of protocol objectivity, this protocol joins the many other Drach prose-works in which women's bodies are the epitome of abject waste, rag dolls used and abused, but that nonetheless reflect the degradation of the agents that visit violence upon them.[19]

NEIN, the last of the three cases, tells the story of M. M., the successful bureaucrat who has internalised the monologic system of the *Amt* so much so as to be indistinguishable from it. He is a kind of grotesque half-man/half-machine, not too far removed from Arnold Heidsieck's concept of the grotesque automatised (non)individual.[20]

We encounter one of Drach's most beloved themes in this story: the complexity of identity, its constructedness, malleability and artificiality. Clearly, the question of identity is here inseparably linked to the notionally unimpeachable right of bureaucratic authorities to name, categorise and effectively label the world around them into the *mise-en-scène* of their desire. The result of this attempt to deep-freeze identity is borne out by the story. Is M. M. really the Jewish Jakob Weißschopf, as repeatedly suggested to him, or is he the foundling child Max Mayer named after his adoptive parents, the Aryan and successful official who has followed in the footsteps of his foster father, or is he Meier, offspring of a remote Jewish grandfather? No definitive conclusion is reached. M. M. remains in the half-darkness of identity, yet his answer to the last claim that he is of the Jewish clan Meier is unequivocal rejection: »Nein«.[21]

The fiction of identity as it emerges on scraps of paper, by word of mouth, through chance meeting or sudden memory is offset against the blank of M. M.'s mind. His amnesia corresponds to the blind spot of the society that has created him, an orphan child with no clear or certain origins except for what the authorities, his adoptive parents or incidental ghostlike figures from a forgotten

---

[19] »Immerhin sei das Kind sehr klein, und man sollte nicht warten, bis es ganz herangewachsen und mannbar geworden sei.« (Ibid., p. 10) This deliberate representation of women's bodies as waste is a constant motif in the Holocaust trilogy, the main theme of the later novel *Untersuchung an Mädeln. Kriminalprotokoll* (Ungekürzte Ausg., München: Deutscher Taschenbuch Verlag 1995 [dtv; 12043]), and a dominant image in the Sadian styled futuristic novel »*O Catilina*« (note 1). For a discussion of Drach's treatment of the female body, see Anne Fuchs: Files against the Self. Albert Drach. In: id., A Space of Anxiety. Dislocation and Abjection in Modern German-Jewish Literature. Amsterdam, Atlanta: Rodopi 1999 (Amsterdamer Publikationen zur Sprache und Literatur; 138), p. 123–162.

[20] Albert Drach: NEIN. In: id., IA UND NEIN (note 14), p. 63–99.

[21] »Das alles bedachte M. M. oder der nun völlig in Frage Gestellte, denn er wußte nun zwar vielleicht, woher er kam, aber gewiß nicht, wohin er ging. Und er sagte nur ein Wort, und das war Nein.« (Ibid., p. 99)

past manage disharmoniously to paste together. The shadowiness of his beginnings as contrasted to his rejection of this ambiguity – »Nein« – mirrors none
other than the false ontology upon which concepts of the Eurocentric, sovereign self are premised (after all we are dealing with the specifically central
European, Germanic-Jewish identity complex here), and the whiplash reflex of
denial – »Nein« – emitted from the mouth of the amnesiac M. M. mimics the
determination of socially dominant groups that goes into the forgetting of the
obscure origins of symbolic identity.[22]

Within the volume under discussion, *NEIN* can be read as part of a dialogue
concerning the dubious origins of the species »subject« set in motion by the
repulsive scenario in the bunker of *IA*. Given that the renewed origin of the
species founds here on the twin taboos of rape and paedophilia, not to mention
what could be construed as the simulation of the violent ejection of the not-yet-
subject from the domain of the *chora* (the infant of *IA* is flung by its mother
into the arms of patriarchs, discursive personifications of the symbolic order),
it is no wonder that M. M. in the later story recruits the force of rejection to
more determinedly forget what he does not cognitively know, but may apprehend: the beginnings of the lofty sovereign self as violent, repressive and based
on the necessary taming and subordination of either the (in the case of *IA*)
female other, or (in the case of *NEIN*) the Jewish other. A false fixity that is all
too easily disturbed by the casually circulating trail of papers and accidentally
mumbled words proving, disproving, muddling and contradicting claims to
identity. As is displayed in works such as *Unsentimentale Reise* and *Das Goggelbuch*, scraps of paper can produce only scraps of identity which are in any
case partial, transitory, easily lost and always open to interpretation. In an
abstract sense, these disturbing floating documents and utterances can be understood, particularly in the story *NEIN*, as disruptive instances of semiotic
memory, which threaten to upend the posited but fictional subject M. M., an
instance of semiotic cross-contamination in the symbolic as it were. »Nein«,
the utterance, thus becomes the mark of a renewed symbolic position: »I am
because I am not«, so to speak. »Ia«, the calamitous cry of the child »all by
herself« becomes, on the other hand, the affect-laden mourning for the lost
chora, the abject mother of the semiotic.[23] It is thus all the more ironic that this

---

[22] The opening passage of *NEIN* could be read as a parody of the efforts of positing
symbolic identity, exacerbated by the historical context which is clearly the Third
Reich: »Am Anfang steht, was am Anfang von dem bemerkt wird, um den es geht,
oder was zu dieser Zeit von denen entdeckt wird, die über ihn berichten. Bei M. M.
sind die Dinge so, daß er von sich aus nichts weiß und nur getuschelt wurde, daß er ein
Findelkind gewesen, und das zu einer Zeit da jeder seinen Stammbaum haben mußte,
um sein Recht auf Leben auszuweisen. Er selber aber kannte sich in Papieren nicht aus
und behielt nur das im Gedächtnis, was er dringend brauchte.« (Ibid., p. 65)

[23] Kristeva defines abjection as »the culminating form of that experience of the subject to
which it is revealed that all its objects are based merely on the inaugural loss that laid
the foundations of its own being«. The loss experienced by the child »all by him-

sound which designates the semiotic space before or beside symbolic language should be interpreted by the patriarchs as symbolic affirmation and affirmation of the symbolic. Thus the blind spot of the symbolic is again evoked by Drach through this domination of the other by the symbolic subject, a necessary process in the perpetuation of symbolic hierarchy.

How seriously should we treat these floating documents? No one more than Albert Drach can know the value and the horror of paperwork that claims to fix the individual. Having survived the Holocaust due in no small measure to his crafty manipulation of papers concerning his membership of the *Israelitische Kultus Gemeinde* (Drach translated the initials I. K. G. as standing for *Im Katholischen Glauben* for the benefit of an unsuspecting French official, thereby narrowly escaping deportation),[24] it is hardly surprising that paperwork in the form of the protocol not only features as the framework of most of his prose work, but that in addition to this, floating documents often arise within the protocols as embedded sliding texts that comically reflect through their circulating movement the false a priori of the embedding text: the protocol. As well as functioning as the documentation of accidental verbal utterances thus, the protocol also conspicuously follows the trail of written utterances, sometimes to the point of preposterousness, as will be seen in the next chapter in the case of *Das Goggelbuch*.[25]

It can be said of all of Drach's prose work that the floating document functions as the signifier of fragmentary, half or partial identity. The sum total of amalgamated utterances and written evidence never amounts to anything conclusive. Instead, we are confronted by the endless circularity of the protocol. This underlying indecisiveness of the protocol, its complete ambivalence, can also be read in terms of the ornate surface network of grotesque excess. As such, it is a product of the supplementary grotesque signifier that, due to its predisposition towards the semiotic, constantly exceeds the terms of symbolic signification so apparent in the rhetorical pose of the protocol.

---

self« who has »swallowed up his parents too soon« is emptiness in the place of maternal love (Julia Kristeva: Powers of Horror. An Essay on Abjection. New York: Columbia University Press 1982 [European Perspectives], p. 5–6). The wailing infant in *IA* is one such instance of the abandoned abject child whilst its desperate mother may be read as a personification of the abject *chora*: »Immerhin schickten sich darin fünfzehn versammelte Herren an, die Stunde Null des Jahres Null festlich und feierlich zu begehen, als sich der Diener Armin Krachtowil durch das Haustelefon anmeldete, es habe soeben eine nackte Frau ohne jedweden Beistand auf der obersten Stufe zu seiner Portierloge einen Säugling geworfen. Das Kind, das die Worte *Ia* ausgestoßen habe, sei durch einen plötzlich geöffneten [...] Türschlitz hereingekommen, die Mutter aber, es im Stiche lassend, in der Nacht verschwunden, mangels Kleidung und Wäsche nur unter Mitnahme der Nachgeburt.« (*IA* 7)

[24] Albert Drach: Unsentimentale Reise. Ein Bericht. Ungekürzte Ausg., München: Deutscher Taschenbuch Verlag 1988 (dtv; 11226), p. 226–227.

[25] Similar to *NEIN*, *Das Goggelbuch* parodies the obligatory research into Aryan ancestry demanded by the Nazi Racial Laws of 1933 (in: In: Albert Drach: Die kleinen Protokolle und das Goggelbuch. München, Wien: Langen-Müller 1965, p. 245–303).

Through its transgression of itself as a floating document between failed fixity and resulting supplementarity, the protocol thus stipulates a space outside or beyond itself, a catachrestic space of the in-between where utterances are out of synch with what would seem to be their referents and where the text is primarily characterised by a split between propositions and their meaning. Such texts are marked by an empty garrulousness as signifiers are spewed forth into a space with no clear signified. As these partial signifiers come to resemble a make-shift text, they are seen to function precisely through this tendency to miss the mark, positing the wrong theme or beating around the bush, thereby ensuring that all words bearing the tone of thematic self-importance signify a false image. Out of time with and lagging behind itself, and also as the mark of the ambivalence of the signifier/signified structure of the sign, this language is to be located in the space beyond the text, the outside of the text. This space is defined through its orchestrated misuse of words and sentences, a catachrestic space.[26]

Such is the situation in the protocol *UND*. Circularity and inconclusiveness of plot would seem to be the order of the day as the entire motivation of the plot is based on what logically appears to be a complete non sequitur. Alois Balduin Huntzinger, the judge against whom the protocol is written, has disappeared with no prior warning to his housekeeper, the devoted Antonia Muckenhuber (Mucki). The motivation for the protocol would seem to be Mucki's desire to locate the whereabouts of her employer, for whom it is suggested, despite the pretence of objectivity in the protocol tone, she harbours rather more than strictly professional feelings.[27] What ensues is an unusual protocol. It documents Mucki's reconstruction of the judge's past life, his habits in the present up to his disappearance, and the path of his career within the Austrian judicial system. Helping her in this task is the ex-policeman, Sebastian Besserwisser, with whom, it is implied by the intrusive tone of the protocol, Mucki has a certain understanding. Thus we are confronted by a species of police protocol, set in motion by a lowly and ignorant servant (Huntzinger's colleagues, we are informed, knew of his departure and had already made arrangements for his replacement in the courts) and which records the efforts of the »unofficial policeman«, Besserwisser, to come up with a picture of the judge that may shed some light on his present whereabouts.[28]

---

[26] Bhabha defines the catachrestic space within the postcolonial context as follows. It is a space in which »words or concepts [are] wrested from their proper meaning, ›a concept metaphor without an adequate referent‹ that perverts its embedded context« (Bhabha, The Location of Culture [note 9], p. 183).

[27] »Auskünfte von anderen Personen waren nicht zu erlangen, da der Richter privat mit niemandem Umgang gepflogen hatte, auch Frauenbesuche während der ganzen Dienstzeit der Muckenhuber niemals erfolgt waren. Ihre Besorgnis wuchs immerhin, als er einerseits nicht zurückkam und andererseits von ihm auch keine Nachricht über seinen Verbleib einlangte.« (*UND* 41)

[28] »Bei diesen von einer rechtskundigen Person aus eigenem Antrieb angestellten Erhebungen ging ihr freilich ein früherer Polizist an die Hand, der mit ihr in einem gewissen Vertrauensverhältnis stand.« (Ibid., p. 41)

However, the first detail concerning Huntzinger mentioned in the introductory sentence of the protocol emerges from a scrap of paper discovered by Mucki in the judge's desk during her initial search for an explanation of his absence. Of all conjunctions, we are told by this particular floating document, Huntzinger hates the connective »und« the most because it unreflectingly tacks concepts together in a manner that deprives them of hierarchical organisation. In other words, the judge would seem to be a stickler for the pecking order of a certain kind, that being binary, oppositional and hierarchically asymmetrical. »Und« as the neutral linking space of main clauses does not introduce the subordination necessary for such a structure. Instead it confuses issues that should be kept apart and that should remain within the hierarchy described above.[29]

Such structuration demonstrates a strategy of hierarchical subordination which, as we shall see, is one of the trick features of this protocol. When Barthes describes the sentence as hierarchical, implying subordination, dependency, the ideological precedence of one idea over others, he is in fact describing the sentence in its hypotactic, finite closure. Hypotaxis describes the syntactic relationship between dependent and independent constructions. In the protocol *UND*, this particular syntactic logic is inseparable from the issue of judicial power. It is the sentence prototype of the finite system that has not burst its banks, thus maintaining a hold on the mechanisms of subordinating power. How the protocol presents the syntax of hypotaxis remains to be seen. The judge however, approves of and can only work within a conceptual system that is based on the hypotactic assembling of language.[30]

Returning to the document discovered in the judge's study: the exceptional nature of such a statement by so laconic an individual provides the motivation for Muckenhuber to go to the police. Thus the search is set in motion and although the impetus behind it is to establish the whereabouts of the judge, the floating scrap of paper is strategically, if somewhat superfluously it would seem, placed at the beginning of the protocol. For Huntzinger's absence from most of the framework action of the protocol is outdone only by the absence of any further reference to his strange dislike of the connective »und«.

---

[29] »Auf der Polizeistelle konnte man damit auch nicht viel anfangen, doch wandte man sich an das Präsidium bzw. die Personalabteilung der Dienststelle des angeblich Verschollenen, welche nur die Auskunft gab, sie sei von der Abwesenheit ihres Richters in Kenntnis, habe auch sofort für einen Ersatz gesorgt.« (*UND* 40)

[30] Definition of hypotaxis taken from J. A. Cuddon: A Dictionary of Literary Terms and Literary Theory. 4th Edition, revised by C. E. Preston. Oxford: Blackwell 1998, p. 407. Barthes reflects on the implications of hierarchical subordination in the sentence: »Der *Satz* ist hierarchisch: er impliziert Abhängigkeit, Unterordnung, innere Ausrichtung. Von daher seine Abgeschlossenheit: wie kann eine Hierarchie offenbleiben?« (Barthes, Die Lust am Text [above], p. 75) Mikhail Bakhtin's theory of carnival and dialogue, both of which are open, ambivalent and infinite, is the antithesis to this closed, monologic form of the sentence. Cf. Michail M. Bakhtin: Die Ästhetik des Wortes. Frankfurt a. M.: Suhrkamp 1979 (Edition Suhrkamp; 967).

Apart from the image we receive of him in Besserwisser's reconstruction, Huntzinger remains absent from the protocol as an agent of the framing plot until the very end when he suddenly reappears at his study desk and promptly asks for Mucki's hand. She believes that she has a certain understanding with Besserwisser and therefore refuses the offer. Huntzinger fires her, Besserwisser abandons her and she loses her life running across the road after him. For Huntzinger however, life resumes its normal pattern as he returns to work the next day after his break.[31]

Where had he been? Apparently on his way to his fiancée who unfortunately was killed in a trite and incidental manner on her way to meet him. This we know not from the mouth of Huntzinger himself, but from yet another floating document espied accidentally by Besserwisser, a newspaper announcement in which a judge, but not specifically Huntzinger, is mentioned.[32] Nonetheless, his timely reappearance at home shortly thereafter and his proposal to his housekeeper would seem elliptically to suggest that the person in the announcement was in fact himself. Typically however, the protocol categorically states nothing and we are left to flounder in inconclusive circularity.

The above forms the framework plot of the protocol. The reconstructions within this framework action do not particularly correspond to, flesh out or develop it. If anything, they refer to the internal disparity of the protocol, the lag between signifier and signified. However, the reconstructions follow a fairly chronological sequence. Firstly, we are given a description from Muckenhuber as to the habits and character of the judge, then a corresponding assessment from his colleagues. What emerges from these statements is the image of a taciturn loner, rarely coaxed into speech but nevertheless mechanically diligent in his function as judge. An isolated individual, he maintains distance from all relationships, does not get involved in politics and can only be observed at times to be subtly smirking on the job.[33]

---

[31] »Da er nun einmal die Absicht zu heiraten habe, biete er ihr seine Hand an. Das gewesene Mädchen aber faßte sich rasch und erklärte, auch es habe inzwischen einen Ersatzmann gefunden, den es vermutlich in nächster Zeit heiraten werde. Daher kündige es sein Dienstverhältnis zum nächsten Termin. [...] [Der Richter] legte ihr nahe, wenn sie es so eilig habe, auf die Einhaltung der Kündigungsfrist zu verzichten und noch in dieser Nacht ihrem offenbaren Bewerber zu folgen. Dieser [...] half ihr bei der Einsammlung [...] ihrer Habseligkeiten, ohne daß er die Absicht gehabt hätte, sie in seiner Wohnung aufzunehmen. [...] Er versuchte ihr dies im Abgehen noch schonend beizubringen und verließ vor ihr die Wohnung. Sie lief ihm nach, ohne den Verkehr zu achten [...]. Bei dieser Gelegenheit wurde sie von einem Kombiwagen erfaßt und fand den Tod.« (*UND* 60–61)

[32] »Mit vielsagendem Blick zeigte der Polizist diese Notiz der von ihm geliebten und so treu bedienten Wirtschaftsführerin und bemerkte, ihr Dienstgeber werde nie zurückkommen.« (*UND* 59)

[33] »Aus diesen kleinen Schilderungen schloß der früher diensthabende Polizist bereits, daß es sich bei dem nicht mehr Anwesenden um einen Menschen gehandelt haben müsse, der [...] schon durch fehlende Geselligkeit sich den Sonderstatus eines Ein-

Secondly, there is a reconstruction of his childhood through which we find out that he was born in 1935, orphaned young and taken in by kindly neighbours, the Krachtowils. In a manner characteristic for the superficial, anecdotal tone of the protocol we are informed, by the by, of the random deaths of his parents, his mother during the war, and his father absurdly afterwards, victim of a chance mine languishing unnoticed in his garden. Incidents from Huntzinger's adoptive childhood in the Krachtowil household portray him as a cold and cynical person, anti-Semitic and misogynistic.[34] As he moves from this phase of his adolescence into the next, a certain gristly symmetry of the plot becomes apparent. Shortly after he absconds from the Krachtowil family, the pregnant corpse of Herr Krachtowil's only daughter is found in a shallow stream. The conundrum as to whether she accidentally drowned or was murdered and her body then dumped is again typically foregrounded by the protocol, but left open to interpretation as the text glides unproblematically on to the telling of the next episode.[35]

The next phase of his life finds Huntzinger again in his function as the foundling protégé of an older gent who supports his studies, but who is then also suspiciously found dead on the street after the final school examination celebrations of his ward. Even more suspiciously, the savings book of the elderly man is missing, never to be recovered. Equally missing is Huntzinger who moves to another city to begin his studies. Relatives of the deceased (a niece, Ursula Wildwasser and her husband) who have caught wind of the existence of this absent savings book set about tracking down Huntzinger, but after depositing their deaf-mute daughter, Walpurga, with a miracle-worker doctor they both drown in »wild waters« off the coast of Italy. Needless to say, Huntzinger's unfortunate fiancée, who also dies in transit (but by train), is strongly suggested (but not confirmed of course) by the protocol to be the same Walpurga. Apparently she had just been cured of her illness before she was killed.[36]

Thirdly, the protocol documents three different cases over which Huntzinger presided as judge of the Supreme Court. His activity as judge seems to follow the course of increasing the hostility of the arguing parties, using details of court protocol to avoid deciding in favour of plaintiff or defendant so that

---

zelgängers zu sichern bestrebt gewesen war. In der Tat hatten vorsichtige Umfragen [...] bei seinen Kollegen [...] ergeben, daß er außer einem haüfig auch bei Parteien des Gerichtes angelegten Lächeln [...] kaum außeramtliches für seine Umwelt bereit hatte.« (*UND* 42–43)

[34] During this time which covers World War II, Huntzinger makes himself noticed for anti-Semitic remarks passed whilst a Jew, who was in hiding, is beaten to death. In addition, Frau Krachtowil is attacked and raped by a soldier whilst Huntzinger looks on. He afterwards remarks that she ought to have given in earlier in order to reduce the extent of damage (she remains mentally disturbed for the rest of her life). (Ibid., p. 46–47)

[35] »Gelegentlich nachfolgender Obduktion konnte zwar festgestellt werden, daß sie nicht durch erweisliche Gewaltanwendung in das nicht sehr tiefe Wasser gelangt, wohl aber vor ihrem Ableben im vierten Monat schwanger gewesen war.« (Ibid., p. 48)

[36] Ibid., p. 49–51, p. 59.

nobody wins, and nullifying cases that manifest minor deviations from legal norms. Emphasised by this activity is the complete superfluousness and irrelevance of judicial maxims for the reality lived out by the people involved, a concrete institutional instance of the incompatibility of abstract, finite systems with the materiality of the infinite process.[37]

Finally the judge returns, Besserwisser makes himself scarce and Mucki is killed on the run, like so many others before her.

The suggestive constellation of movement, language and death is present in this final scene. It reflects the Wildwassers' deaths in transit and furthermore evokes Drach's archetype of the child in flight. However, far from language functioning as a means of survival through the deferral of death, here in Huntzinger's monologic world, attempts at the linguistic assertion of the self seem to end in disaster for certain characters. For if Mucki had never set in motion this (for her) disastrous investigation along with its written documentation in the form of the protocol, the chain reaction of certain events would never have arisen and she would surely still be alive.

The return of the silent judge at the end of the protocol, his successful survival as contrasted to the frequent demise of others would seem to suggest that the plot of *UND* articulates the absolute negation Deleuze associates with the Death Instinct. Were one to view this protocol as a sample of language fetishism, then clearly the plot appears to state that the text fails the task of deferring stasis. Mucki's death in particular bears out this irony. However, this is tantamount to proposing that in *UND* the body of *jouissance* is effectively extinguished by absolute negation. This would be an incorrect reading of the text.

In Huntzinger we certainly witness the closure of the anal-sadistic stiff, an image of the body that articulates negation. A virtual mute, he appears at first glance to be immune to any unsettling revelations that could arise through engaging in discourse. This characterisation of Huntzinger as an enemy of language is supported by his cynical view of speakers in court:

> Und schließlich schlinge sich ihr eigenes Wort und was da noch sonst geschwätzt werde, wie ein Strick um ihren Hals, aus dem sie nicht mehr herauskönnten.
>
> (*UND* 53)

This refusal to engage in discourse – a form of silent negation – is complemented by his »negation« (albeit associative) of the individuals who cross his path. It is his ill-fortune however, that the infinite body of poetic negativity should be performed by the written word »und«, and that this body of language should ultimately overwrite his own. For the written word, as borne out by the

---

[37] »Wiederum war es Huntzinger, der die Sache bekam, um die Entscheidung auszuarbeiten. Er benötigte zur Erledigung des Aktes eine Anzahl von Monaten, dann aber kam er auf die fehlende Unterschrift auf dem Widerruf des Vergleiches und erklärte das ganze darauffolgende Verfahren für nichtig, so daß die Partei, die den Prozeß sonst gewonnen hätte, völlig im Nachteil war, die andere aber den Hauptteil ihrer Kosten nicht ersetzt bekommen konnte.« (Ibid., p. 58)

protocol that documents his life, proves to be no less reliable than the spoken word of which Huntzinger is so sceptical. If the other characters are put *en procès*, so too is he. Yet how does this come about? The plot simply does not seem to enlighten us in this regard. A tight-lipped judge marked by his absence and the trail of corpses that erupts in his wake, an unreliable ex-policeman, a desperate housekeeper, the account of a meagre, mean life spent in isolation and absenteeism, the platitudinous infamy of an indifferent legal system; none of it appears to add up. What is the point of this protocol? Against whom is it written?

Reading the text on the level of plot and event yields few answers, partly because of the absurd nature of the occurrences themselves, partly because the protocol in its function as objective summary of reported utterances and events refuses to evaluate (at any rate openly) the goings-on of this bizarre world. The reader clearly must look elsewhere to understand the mechanisms of this text. My suggestion is that through an examination of the syntactic organisation of the protocol certain possible inroads into the text yield themselves and go some length to provide highly interesting readings of *UND*. As disturbances in syntactic completion (disturbances of the language system) are a central issue here, let us return briefly to some details of Kristeva's theory of poetic language

Reconsidering this theory as a negativity that permeates and rejects the language of symbolic negation, it becomes clear that this counter movement of rejection in the thetically unstable text manifests itself in discordant syntax, through which, for Kristeva »the ex-position of the thetic« reveals itself.[38] The threshold position of the thetic as the not-yet but would-be symbolic subject spliced between the poorly repressed force of the semiotic and the positing attempts of the symbolic is borne out, in the eloquent words of Bhabha, by »the agonism between the sentence of predicative syntax and the discontinuous subject of discourse«.[39] In Kristevan terminology, this agonism is described as the lack that becomes apparent as a result of the irregular relationship between the enunciating or positing moment of the subject in process, and the stasis of denotation or the posited. In short, the agonism of the sentence results from the constant struggle of the component drives around the thetic position. The positing motion of the would-be-subject takes place in the enunciative process of the verb/predicate whilst denotation is staged in the noun/subject. For Kristeva, the subject and predicate split makes clear the division of the thetic. Denotation is the locus of the ideal static invariant of the phenomenological subject whereas enunciation represents the process, the struggle of the subject between constitution and annihilation.

Jouissance and transgression of the system characterise the process of enunciation. It is through this retracing of the discontinuous path of production that discourse, defined by Kristeva as the »sensuous certainty« of rejection, is in-

---

[38] Julia Kristeva: Revolution in Poetic Language. New York: Columbia University Press 1984, p. 106.
[39] Bhabha, The Location of Culture (note 9), p. 180–181.

troduced by the poetic text.[40] The warring facets of the sentence which facilitate the emergence of this discourse, the posited and the positing, represent the two faces of the thetic break. The poetic text as Kristeva understands it will frustrate denotation through the disruption of enunciation that brings with it the reversal of symbolic rejection. This reversal of rejection, or the redistribution of the *chora* through the terms of the symbolic signifying chain distinguishes the discourse of poetic language. The exposure of the process therefore, goes hand in hand with the *ex*-position of the thetic through poetic discourse, as temporarily claimed thetic positions are forced out of their weak denotated havens only to create new equally (in terms of the poetic text) untenable positions, ex-positions. This »shattering of conceptual unity« manifests itself through »rhythms, logical distortions [...] paragrams, and syntactic inventions [...], all of which register within the signifier, the passage beyond its boundary«.[41]

The consequences of this disturbance are manifold. One of these is the frustration of the syntagm as the return of rejection breaks up the linearity of the signifying chain. The redistribution of the signifying chain through this erosion of the denotating function of the thetic break results in the infinitisation of the system as it mutates into process. Localized examples of this, to name but a few, are the absence of the subject from syntax as it is displaced through the thetic break, syntactic ellipsis, ad infinitum linking.[42] In short, syntactic destruction emerges in different forms as a result of disturbances around the thetic position, and it would seem that precedence is given to a metonymic disturbance of language in many of these cases. As the subject disappears, reappears, disappears, becoming as Kristeva puts it »the consequence of non-recoverable deletion«, the possibilities for play along the distorted chain of signification grow and multiply.[43]

The opening sentence of the text *UND* bears many traits of the above described syntactic disturbances. It prototypically asserts the curious glitch that severs the protocol throughout and that could be construed as evidence of thetic erosion:

> *Von allen Bindewörtern war dem* von daheim ohne Angabe von Gründen schon drei Tage ferngebliebenen *Richter Alois Balduin Huntzinger das Wort »und« am widerwärtigsten.*   (*UND* 39, my emphasis)

The main clause of this sentence tells us that Huntzinger dislikes the word »und« whilst the extended participle, here compressed into a descriptive adjectival clause, informs us that he has been missing without explanation for three days. Remaining with this single sentence for the present, it is a perfect example of how the syntagm is frustrated. Instead of opting for the relatively straightforward structure of main clause/sub clause which would more clearly indicate

---

[40] Kristeva, Revolution in Poetic Language (note 38), p. 187.

[41] Ibid., p. 185.

[42] »The disturbance of sentential completion or syntactic ellipsis lead to an infinitization of logical (syntactic) applications [...]. The sentence is not suppressed, it is infinitized.« (Ibid., p. 108–109)

[43] Ibid., p. 108.

the hierarchical distribution of information and thus the subject matter of the protocol, the text absorbs this implied subordinate clause into the main sentence. Whilst the extended participle still occupies the secondary position consistent with the status of a subordinate clause, the absence of a subordinating connective, at least formally, puts it on a par with the content of the italicised sentence. In effect it is now a legitimate, if only descriptive, part of the main clause.

This structure of coordination (as opposed to subordination) does not really hold however, as a subversive subordination manifests itself upon closer inspection. The point of the main clause (that Huntzinger harbours a particular aversion to a certain word) gets lost in the busy detail of the compressed adjectival description. Such a tactic is typical for Drach's mocking parody of rational language. It could be described as a strategy of deliberate, circumlocutory diversion resulting in confusion of the main point of the protocol and frustrating the presumptions of teleological discourse so apparent in the staged chronology of the remaining text.

It is also an example of the return of rejection in and through the terms of symbolic language. Poetic negativity is not necessarily identifiable within the individual words, but in the paradigmatic piling effect of the adjectival clause which in turn frustrates the flow of the main syntagm. Furthermore, this rather elliptical cross contamination of the semiotic with the symbolic points to the space of the non-sentence, that ambivalent space outside the sentence that arises in this instance as a result of the incongruity of the sentence with its adjectival participle. Cross contamination can be understood in this context as an instance of latent language grotesquerie, or as Bhabha puts it »that menacing sense in which the non-sentence is contiguous with the sentence, near but different, not simply its anarchic disruption«.[44]

Through the precise, pompous, meticulously constructed formal terms of the syntax emerges an actual economy of excess as the reader is left to combat with the indecidability of the purpose of the protocol. This ambivalence is achieved through the incongruity of the overall sentence content, or more exactly its unexplained welding on grammatical and, bearing in mind the presumptuous tone of the protocol, rhetorical levels. For any logical or causal connection between Huntzinger's odd tic and the fact of his disappearance is thereafter missing. The two pieces of information are squashed together in an unwieldy manner *as if* they were logically linked in some way.

To paraphrase Henri Bergson, the comic structure of this sentence is to be found in just this unresolved interference of two separate systems in the one phrase, signifier of the absentmindedness of the text. For Bakhtin, this absentmindedness or indecidability of two utterances in the one phrase results in what he calls the hybrid sentence, largely characterised by the ambivalence of the narrative voice. Without wishing to examine the narrative voice at this point, suffice it to say that on the basis of such sentence structure, the protocolling instance of

---

[44] Bhabha, The Location of Culture (note 9), p. 182.

the text betrays the main feature of the comic hero as defined by Bergson: his confusion and inability to orientate himself sufficiently, his mental displacedness or cognitive deficiency. Remaining on the level of sentence structure for the present, Bakhtin's hybrid sentence along with Bergson's interference of different systems, both fundamentally following the transgressive structure of the grotesque (indeterminacy and ambivalence), are compatible with Barthes's theory of the outside of the sentence. The infinitisation of the sentence through the transgression of its structure is the common feature of these theories.[45]

The protocol at hand never progresses beyond the initial glitch of incommensurability as the juxtaposition of incompatible information remains unresolved for the remainder of the text. If the two assertions have anything to do with one another, this is not spelled out and it becomes the task of the reader to bridge the elliptic gap in the opening structure of the narrative. Thus it would seem that we have at hand a self-effacing text that, apart from opening up the area of the non-sentence, thematises in the introductory sentence the non-viability of its premise, that being clear and accurate, purposeful narrative.

The teleological aim of the text, we are told in due course, is the location of the judge, or at least finding an explanation as to why he left so suddenly. As such, the text rhetorically, at least, goes along with the chronological presumptions of cause and effect relations, but as is announced by non-completion of the first sentence where the burden of the adjectival clause displaces any attempt at linear narrative, this logical hierarchisation of information gets confused in the formulaic demands of protocol language, leading to the slide into a rather comic adjacency of facts.

Put another way, the formal structure of this first sentence is revealed by the rest of the text to be an instance of complete non-sense, as the priority position given to the information of the main clause dissolves inconsequentially into a nothingness that is simply ignored from this point on. That the subject of this sentence (the word »und«) is hereafter superseded by the content of the extended participle would seem to point to a certain inadequacy of denotation, to the flimsiness of the posited grammatical subject of the sentence as it were. The ensuing thematic indeterminacy of the text, its diverting, trivial mode of narration can be seen in this light as the attributes of the thetic insecurity of this subject. Thus the text reveals its atopical nature as the latter attributes can be regarded as part of an enunciative discourse on the constitutive process of the subject.

---

[45] This infinitisation is referred to by Bergson as »the reciprocal interference of series« (Henri Bergson / George Meredith: Laughter. Essays on Comedy. New York: Doubleday 1956, p. 123). Similarly, Bakhtin describes the hybrid sentence as the collision of two language consciences or systems in the one phrase: »Wir nennen diejenige Äußerung eine hybride Konstruktion, die ihren grammatischen (syntaktischen) und kompositorischen Merkmalen nach zu einem einzigen Sprecher gehört, in der sich in Wirklichkeit aber zwei Äußerungen, zwei Redeweisen, zwei Stile, zwei ›Sprachen‹, zwei Horizonte von Sinn und Wertung vermischen.« (Bakhtin, Die Ästhetik des Wortes [note 30], p. 195)

That the text, after the first paragraph, never returns to the subject of the main clause of this sentence is consistent with this policy of adjacency. Is the protocol thereby suggesting that the remainder of its narrative is in fact beside the point, or missing the point entirely? Is the entire investigation on the wrong trail? By locating the main justification for its written existence on the in-between of this first sentence (the judge's disappearance), the protocol strongly suggests that it is, as a narrative form, the breeding ground of contingency, that in metonymically sidestepping what is possibly the real issue – the language problematic posed by the word »und« – it in fact blithely pushes itself into the status of complete superfluousness, concerning itself with the irrelevant, and in so doing sentencing itself to a condition of unmitigated excess.

Recalling Derrida's notion of the supplementary nature of the excessive signifier, the text can be regarded in its structure of unconnected contiguity as a thoroughgoing instance of supplementarity. The signifier that supplements is the sign of an excess that in turn refers back to a lack that must be compensated for or supplemented.[46] If we regard the protocol *UND* from this perspective, it appears as a hollow supplementary shell, marked by the incongruity of title and text, and the absence of any direct problematisation of the connective »und«. The entire text can be seen from this angle as compensating for its lack of referent through ever more exhaustive (and confusing) recourse to the structure of purposeful, linear narrative. The more it indulges this strategy, the more excessive, burlesque and ridiculous it becomes. The whole text takes on the appearance of a castle in the air, or a house of cards whose a priori is the place of lack as expressed in the conspicuously missing reference to the word »und«. Attempts to establish an ordered narrative thus end in the circularity of supplementary movement which, bearing in mind Wolfgang Iser's depiction of the comic as a self-cancelling, self-toppling phenomenon (*Kipp-Phänomen*), is evidence of yet another comic paradigm in this text.[47]

In the relentless play on the missing a priori, we encounter the linguistic economy of mourning that, far from communicating sadness, parodies the compensation of signifiers into a ridiculous excess which draws attention to the lack upon which it is premised. The lag between signifier and signified is carried to the extreme in the supplementary space of excessive compensation. Never getting to the point (or any point for that matter), the text embodies the temporality of delay or dragging. The temporal space of the in-between is one of procrastination or supplementarity. Catachresis as the displacement of words is the linguistic result of this procrastination between signifier and signified. Following this line of argument, it is no wonder that the language of ex-

---

[46] Jacques Derrida: Structure, Sign, and Play in the Discourse of the Human Sciences. In: id., Writing and Difference. London, New York: Routledge 1978, p. 351–370, here p. 365.

[47] Wolfgang Iser: Das Komische – ein Kipp-Phänomen. In: Das Komische. Hg. von Wolfgang Preisendanz und Rainer Warning. München: Fink 1976 (Poetik und Hermeneutik; 7), p. 398–402.

cess, as also the language of lack and catachrestic displacement, goes hand in hand with the narrative of trivial events. Missing the point, the protocol must necessarily find itself in the in-between of narration following what would seem like a pointless policy of parenthesis. This turgid and wordy dragging of the text, its aimless excess is exemplified by the style of the following sentence:

> Auch das Sterben des Onkels bedurfte nachträglicher Aufklärung bezüglich dessen Herbeiführung.   (*UND* 51)

Naturally enough, the explanation of the death of Huntzinger's second foster father never emerges and the complex construction of this sentence joins the economy of waste that runs through the protocol as a whole.

This contiguity of information is the main reason for the monotonous tone of irrelevance, triviality and incidentalness that enshrouds all events relayed in the protocol. It goes some length to explain why a string of tragedies can leave one so indifferent, for one of the main effects of this structure of contiguity is to stress the highly inconsequential nature of events, their arbitrary appearance for a moment, and their subsequent dissolution into forgetfulness as the text proceeds to narration of the next unconnected event. In this manner, we are rushed from one undigested horrific event to the next tragedy. The murder of an innocent Jew is followed by the rape of Frau Krachtowil; this is then followed by the drowning of the pregnant Amalasunta, the unexplained gutter death of the old pensioner, the drowning of his niece and her husband, the death of her daughter in a train, and finally Mucki's death. In between these happenings, there is absolutely no reflection.

One could say therefore, that a strategy of the non-integration of information is announced in the opening sentence. It is a tactic of unconnectedness that is manifested by the text in several ways. This unconnectedness is also a key to understanding the manner in which rhetorical grotesquerie functions in the text. The syntactic structure of hypotaxis as it permeates the whole text is out of step with itself because in fact the logic of the text, the way in which facts, events and persons are strung together is one of unconnected coordination, the logic of parataxis as it were. What is more, the opening sentence suggests through its uncoordinated syntax (after all it is an example of the juxtaposition of clauses minus a subordinating connective) that this strategy of parataxis, despite the proliferation of connectives and hypotactic structures throughout, is the most productive way in which to read the text.

Parataxis as the coordination of clauses without conjunctions is the opposite of hypotaxis. It normally relies on the middle ground of a clear ellipsis between coordinated statements to convey the message of a text.[48] However, the protocol drags the gap between hypotactic affectation and paratactic coordination to such an extent that it becomes very difficult, in the meandering business of the style,

---

[48] Definition of parataxis taken from *A Dictionary of Literary Terms and Literary Theory* (note 30), p. 638–639.

to define the nature and message of the missing link. Hence the thematic non sequitur of the text and the descent into the non-teleological intermittent.

Language grotesquerie arises as a result of this interference of hypotaxis and parataxis. The confusion of these two strategies is evidence of sentential non-completion: the inability of the sentence to close itself. This admixture of style and logic refers back to the cross-contamination of the symbolic, through its own terms, by the semiotic. For it is suggested through the exaggerated use of increasingly meandering subordinate clauses that hypotaxis fails to effectively link narrative, instead ending up as a form of paratactic episodic narration, paradoxically marked by excessive connectives.

It cannot be claimed however, that parataxis *is* the semiotic per se. Both parataxis and hypotaxis are forms of combination that occur in the symbolic positing of the sentence. As an elliptical mode of combination, parataxis could be seen as more predisposed to the articulation of the in-between of the thetic position than is hypotaxis. As a structure based on subordination, hypotaxis could be construed as having a more pronounced relation to the centrality of system and the ideal of the posited symbolic subject that goes hand in hand with this.[49] With its economy of elliptical suggestiveness, parataxis is on the other hand less resistant to the semiotic precisely because ellipsis, which signals the intermittent absence of the subject, also evokes an image of the subject as never quite present, posited or complete, but infinitely *en procès*. A combination of hypotaxis and parataxis that is designed to frustrate the former can therefore only lead to a more pronounced sense of the weakness of the thetic threshold in the positing of the symbolic subject. This combination in the sentence is thus an excellent example of how the Imaginary Anatomy of the symbolic order is debunked by a language that performs *jouissance*. By flattening out sentence structure into a confused contingency, Drach simulates in language the complementary flattening of the vertical body of authority – the unary subject of the symbolic order.

Let us take a closer look at this cross-contamination or rhetorical grotesquerie as it appears in the text. In examining the following extract, certain features of the text outside itself become apparent:

> Ihrer Meinung nach konnte seine Meldung bei der Dienstbehörde *doch wohl* nur dazu gedient haben, in Amtsdingen reinen Tisch zu machen, *was* aber seine Privatsphäre betraf, es seiner engeren Umgebung zu überlassen, Mutmaßungen sonderbarster Art anzustellen. *Daher* setzte die sonst nicht als neugierig verschriene Hilfskraft eines nicht geselligen Menschen und Richters verschiedene Stellen in Bewegung, *um* jetzt, wo ihr Arbeitsfeld nahezu wegfiel, *obwohl* sie für ihre Dienste auf längere Sicht im voraus bezahlt war, *doch* etwas zur Aufklärung des Sach-

---

[49] Citing Kristeva's assertion that all ideological activity is presented in a closed form, Barthes surmises the following: »jede abgeschlossene Aussage läuft Gefahr, ideologisch zu sein. Tatsächlich ist es das Abschließungsvermögen, das die Satzbeherrschung definiert und die Agenten des *Satzes* wie eine teuer erworbene, errungene höchste Meisterschaft auszeichnet.« (Barthes, Die Lust am Text [note 30], p. 75)

> verhaltes zu leisten *und so* den Aufenthalt des bei seiner Dienststelle gehörig ab-
> gemeldeten, *aber* ihr gegenüber verschollenen Richters herauszubringen. (*UND* 41)

The above italicised proliferation of connectives and modal particles points to
a laborious, hypotactic structure of syntax – in Kristeva's terminology an example of ad infinitum linking – and ironically detracts from its formal pose as an
objective explanatory mode of discourse.[50] Instead, the protocol employs these
connectives to create a sense of trivial conjecture, (*Mutmaßungen sonderbar-
ster Art*), which has much more to do with Muckenhuber's characterisation
than to do with the judge's disappearance. This betrays the pseudo-objective
motivation of the narrative position which Bakhtin identifies in the very mimicking function of such connectives.[51] For the protocol is here concerned
with judging Muckenhuber, thus quashing any unquestionable claim to objectivity that might be suggested by the anonymity of the narrative voice. In this
sense, the protocol is written against Muckenhuber.

However, by judging the housekeeper the protocol also diagnoses itself as
an unobjective and prejudiced piece of intrusive conjecture, much more interested in nosily exercising the art of supposition than in clarifying the »main«
issue at hand: the disappearance of the judge. Thus the official tone conveyed
in the structuring function of the connectives gives itself away as a purely
rhetorical gesture, a motion of protocol language here recruited only in order to
detract from and therefore justify the attack on Muckenhuber's character. The
protocol therefore overwrites itself by doubling back on its rhetorical premise
(the interests of objective reporting) and the above proliferation of speculative
connectives is just one example of this transgression. In these connectives that
seem to seep over the boundaries of protocol requirement, we again encounter
the body of *jouissance* (the semiotic device) beginning to overwrite the text of
symbolic discourse. The following paragraph continues this invasion of Mucki's
private life with an increase in the intensity of the above pseudo-objective,
judgmental language:

> Bei diesen von einer rechtsunkundigen Person aus eigenem Antrieb angestellten Erhe-
> bungen ging ihr freilich ein früherer Polizist an die Hand, der mit ihr in einem gewis-
> sen Vertrauensverhältnis stand, das *möglicherweise* versprach, sich auf hautnahe Ge-
> gebenheiten auszudehnen, *denn* die Mucki (Muckenhuber) war durchaus nicht übel
> anzusehen, *wenn* sie auch die erste Jugend hinter ihr hatte. *Möglicherweise* mochte sie
> sich auch Hoffnungen gemacht haben, einmal anders denn als bloße Wirtschaftsführe-
> rin in das Leben des Richters einzudringen, wiewohl dieser *wahrscheinlich* von sich
> aus zu einer solchen Vorstellung wenig Anlaß gegeben hatte.   (*UND* 41–42)

The first sentence of this extract exemplifies a syntactic similarity with the
opening sentence of the protocol. The same delaying tactic is applied in the
extended participle as we find out that Mucki is ignorant in legal matters and
that her desire to find a private reason for the disappearance of the judge is the

---

[50] Kristeva, Revolution in Poetic Language (note 38), p. 109.
[51] Bakhtin, Die Ästhetik des Wortes (note 30), p. 196.

main motivation of the protocol. This is also painstakingly put across in the first extract, where the final sentence reminds us in its parenthetical way that the mystery of Huntzinger's whereabouts is only a mystery for Muckenhuber. Further judgement of her search is apparent in the above use of the verb *eindringen* (to penetrate). The protocol summarises her activity as an invasion of the private life of the judge but the irony of this judgement cannot be lost as it encapsulates exactly what the protocol itself is doing: invading Muckenhuber's life, speculating on her relations with the opposite sex, and going as far as to claim to have a good idea of how she views the judge, i. e. as a potential husband. That the protocol should openly state that her view of the judge represents an intrusion leads one to conclude that she is regarded by the narrative position as a social climber, a pathetic barely semi-attractive spinster, classically left on the shelf and with little prospect of improved social status except through a liaison with her employer.

However, by drawing attention to this the protocol in effect focuses on the arbitrary motivation of the entire investigation and so reflects the subjective bias of the report. The language of hypothesis (*möglicherweise*; *wahrscheinlich* etc.) both emphasises this and indicates another undefined, judgmental presence in the protocol which can be located around the narrative position. Far from dealing with the supposed matter at hand, this discontinuity of the narrative position is interested in directing our attention to what it presents as the scheming calculations of a servant. Just as Muckenhuber searches for a link to the judge, so does the text introduce a series of hypothetical links that lead away from any clear purpose. This policy of pseudo-linking is in many ways the linguistic reflection of the inability of individuals to connect with others, the protocol as much a product of Mucki's isolation as of Huntzinger's. This is in turn a reflection of the social structure in which both are embedded. For it is clear that a strong element of social prejudice is present in the use of the verb »to penetrate« to describe the attempts of a working class woman to haul herself up the ladder into the middle classes which implies, consistent with Huntzinger's language perspective, that social structure should not be transgressed and individuals should remain in their allotted category. Again, this is a subtle articulation of the cellular structure of the symbolic order which propagates the authoritative body of the Imaginary Anatomy. However, this body of stasis is once more ironically overwritten by the body of *jouissance*, for *IA UND NEIN* with its cast of orphaned children and twisted surrogate families is a volume that constantly thematises the breakdown of social structure through the disintegration of the family unit. In this discontinuous fashion, the protocol indirectly tells us what kind of subject is at hand throughout its pages: a decentralised, heterogeneous, partial self who as locative system may be found on the borderline territory implied by the »und« problematic – the in-between or the outside space of the sentence.

Let us examine this space further. The protocol style as exemplified by the above extracts operates through the logic of paradox which arises through the conflict of rhetorical connection and logical dispersal. In other words, the conflict takes place on the axis between hypotaxis and parataxis. Whereas the proliferation of connectives in the first extract points to (at least formally) hypotactic organisation, this very emphasis on connectives suggests traces of Roman Jakobson's similarity disorder which points to the erosion of the subject of the sentence. In *UND*, this disorder is manifested both by the ambivalence of the narrative position that simultaneously writes against itself, Muckenhuber and Huntzinger, and also by the indecidability surrounding the nature of the thematic material. If we paraphrase some of the subordinate clauses of the first extract, this thematic hesitancy becomes clear, for what exactly is the issue at hand: the fact that the housekeeper has been paid quite a bit in advance, the fact that she is not normally curious, the fact that her employer is unsociable, or the fact that she is the only one in the dark about his disappearance? Again, nothing is directly explained and we are left to infer elliptically from this string of juxtaposed (despite subordination) clauses what the nature of the subject matter might be. Thus whilst this scenario may not present quite the diminished skeleton sentence observed by Jakobson in the most extreme cases of similarity disorder, it nonetheless communicates the general difficulty of producing sentences with an identified subject experienced by sufferers of this disorder. [52]

This shiftiness with regard to thematic consolidation is suggestive of just that process which Kristeva calls the ex-position of the thetic. In the current context then, Jakobson's similarity disorder is further evidence of the semiotic device at work in the symbolic order. A text that simply slides from one theme to the next is the locus of a language that cannot pull off the pretence of effective positing, let alone any positing itself. In this sense, the glib movement from sentence to sentence (or clause to clause) renders each last sentence quite literally an *ex*-position of the thetic, as this position remains poorly explained and badly linked within the overall context of the protocol. Such sentences are in effect outside the text. As they relentlessly make up the body of the text, the whole protocol can be diagnosed as fatalistically outside itself. In other words, it talks about anything and everything except that which it inadvertently and indirectly thematises despite itself: language and the problem of narrative as represented in the word »und«.

---

[52] Similarity disorder is one type of aphasic speech in which »the grammatical subject of the sentence tends to be vague (represented by ›thing‹ or ›it‹), elliptical or nonexistant, while words naturally combined with each other by grammatical agreement or government, and words with an inherent reference to the context, like pronouns and adverbs, tend to survive« (David Lodge: The Modes of Modern Writing. Metaphor, Metonymy, and the Typology of Modern Literature. London, New York: Arnold 1997, p. 75). At its most critical, this type of aphasia results in a depleted language: »Es bleibt bei diesem Aphasietyp in seinem kritischen Stadium also nur ein Skelett, die Verbindungsglieder der Kommunikation, übrig.« (Roman Jakobson: Zwei Seiten der Sprache und zwei Typen aphatischer Störungen. In: id., Aufsätze zur Linguistik und Poetik. Hg. von Wolfgang Raible. München: Nymphenburger 1974 [Sammlung Dialog; 71], p. 117–140, here p. 124)

The effect of juxtaposition-despite-subordination furthermore reveals that the formal sentence structure of hypotaxis is in fact ruled by the paratactic logic of unconnection. This paradox accounts for language ambivalence in the protocol *UND* and is a feature typical of Drach's protocol style in general. In the absence of a definite theme, language, the shunned subject matter of the text's opening paragraph, becomes the focus of attention as the protocol increasingly seems to be engaging in a broken discourse about its own complexity.

Another means of emphasising the theme of unconnectedness can be observed in the depiction of the judge. If we were to regard Huntzinger himself not as a character, but following Bakhtin as a parodied personification of a particular language image, it becomes clear that this radical unconnectedness of the text is most articulately rendered in the isolated life of the judge.[53] He emerges as the epitome of monologic isolation in his function as silent, unforthcoming individual. His occupation as judge further reveals his closure towards any form of dialogic discussion. In upholding the ideology of binary opposition through his refusal to resolve cases in the courts, he shows himself to be committed to the perpetuation of reigning hierarchical structures of power which subordinate the individuals involved:

> Er hatte zwar die Gesetze, so viele auf ihn zukamen, nach Möglichkeit und Tunlichkeit in sich aufgenommen. Einem tieferen Sinn ging er nicht nach [...] Wenn er allerdings das Referat bekam, war kaum mehr von einem Vergleich zwischen den Prozeßführenden die Rede. Es war, als ob der Haß oder Gegensatz, der zwischen ihnen von Anfang bestand, sich in seinem Beisein nur steigerte, ja selbst dort, wo nur verschiedene Meinungen aufeinander zukamen und die Möglichkeit einer gültigen Beilegung von Anfang an bestand, sich, sowie er das Referat führte, die Abstände zwischen Klägern und Beklagten vermehrten und keine Einigung mehr zuließen. (*UND* 43–44)

The Austrian legal system, as is borne out by the summary of the three cases over which Huntzinger presided, allows the judge to practice this policy of implicitly totalitarian despotism. By acting in this manner, Huntzinger remains consistent with the law which suggests that the practice of justice is premised on the subjective whims of the individual who, even more perversely, is actually working within the parameters of the law and so cannot easily be accused of personally obstructing the course of justice. In other words, the Austrian legal system as presented by Drach is structured in such a manner as to uncritically facilitate the personality of the ruling judge. It is a case of random bad luck if he/she happens to be an enemy of ambivalence.

As the faithful product of this system, Huntzinger can be no other than a closed, finite entity, silent and shut off from discussion of any kind, equally

---

[53] »Für die Gattung des Romans ist nicht das Bild des Helden an und für sich charakteristisch, sondern vielmehr das Bild einer Sprache. Um aber zum künstlerischen Bild zu werden, muß die Sprache zur Rede im sprechenden Mund werden, wobei sie sich mit dem Bild des sprechenden Menschen verbindet.« (Bakhtin, Die Ästhetik des Wortes [note 30], p. 223–224)

impenetrable in his private and public life, the result of an ideological stasis that manifests itself most in his refusal to tempt dialogue through language and the erosion of fixed concepts that might arise in the wake of any ambivalence. The means of the survival of systems irrelevant for the perplexity of everyday living is indicated here. It is based on a radical reduction and abstraction from the reality of the society in which such systems have taken root, an attempt to enact the violent conceptual simplification of the finite system onto the infinite complexity of life's open-ended narrative.[54] Could Drach, through his parody of this language representative, Huntzinger, be commenting on the obsolete nature of safe, straightforward narration for a world that has grotesquely surpassed itself and the corresponding need for a trickier strategy of narration, one that gets across an adequate sense of the perplexity of living in the modern world? Certainly the protocol, through its different uses of transgression, would seem to express just this concern.[55]

For if we examine the exact nature of Huntzinger's problem with the word »und«, it becomes clear that the text confronts us in a roundabout, elliptical way with the problem of language and power, the clash between system and process, or more exactly the tendency of system to reveal aspects of the transgressive language process that force a critical reassessment of the central location of the system:

> Er [Huntzinger] gab auch für diese Meinungsäußerung nachfolgend eine besondere Begründung an, nämlich die, daß das verbindende »und« Nennungen, Behauptungen, Bezeichnungen in einen Zusammenhang brächte, der in Wahrheit gar nicht bestünde, ja oft dazu diente, die Unterschiede zwischen einander Entgegengesetztem im Vortäuschungswege aufzuweichen oder geradezu auszugleichen.   (*UND* 39)

---

54 Alfred J. Noll points this out in an article on Drach's general representation of the Austrian legal system. He further argues that Huntzinger's dislike of the word »und« derives from the aggressively reductionist approach of this system: »Alles zielt auf Entscheidung. Entscheidungen aber bedürfen gesicherter Prämissen, Kriterien, etc., jedenfalls aber: abgeklärter Sachverhalte. Das ist im wirklichen Leben nicht zu haben. Dort regiert das Tentative, Versuchsweise, Korrigier- und Abänderbare. Die richterliche Abneigung gegen das ›und‹ resultiert aus dem auf Entscheidung zielenden Zwang, die Komplexität des Lebens entscheidungsorientiert zu reduzieren.« (Alfred J. Noll: Die böse Justiz: Enttäuschungsreflexion bei Albert Drach. Eine Notiz. In: In Sachen Albert Drach. Sieben Beiträge zum Werk. Mit einem unveröffentlichten Text Albert Drachs. Hg. von Bernhard Fetz. Wien: Wiener Universitäts-Verlag 1995, p. 71–85, here p. 75)

55 Walter Benjamin's well-known essay on the epic narrator raises the issue of the narrative challenge posed by the conditions of modern life. In contrast to the wise epic storyteller of the Hellenic past who could guide his community through narrative, the modern day narrator is confused and uncertain: »Einen Roman schreiben heißt, in der Darstellung des menschlichen Lebens das Inkommensurable auf die Spitze treiben. Mitten in der Fülle des Lebens und durch die Darstellung dieser Fülle bekundet der Roman die tiefe Ratlosigkeit des Lebenden.« (Walter Benjamin: Der Erzähler. Betrachtungen zum Werk Nikolai Lesskows. In: id., Illuminationen. Ausgewählte Schriften. Hg. von Siegfried Unseld. Frankfurt a. M.: Suhrkamp 1969, p. 409–436, here p. 413–414)

Such a dislike for the willy nilly connecting potential of »und« goes hand in hand with the image of a life spent in disconnection. The judge shows himself to be an enemy of the ambivalence that ensues once the hierarchy of binary opposition is broken down by the levelling, juxtaposing, innocently adjacent implications of this rather too neutral connective. The resulting context of all-encompassing contingency is exactly the reality concept that Huntzinger believes to be false. How utterly ironic that the judge should inhabit a text that demonstrates just this *jouissance* of the contingent, the constant ex-position of the thetic. The only true context for Huntzinger is one in which the centrality of a monologic world order is upheld and where there can be no doubt as to the order of things in this rigid hierarchy. And because he represents the greater body of the Austrian legal system, this problem does not simply confine itself to Huntzinger's individual case, but can be taken as a diagnosis of the asymmetrical power relations that exist between those who, like Huntzinger, know how this system works, and those who do not.[56]

At a further level of abstraction, the judge's dislike of the pulverising force of »und« – particularly expressed in the ability of the word to facilitate the transgression of opposites (their breakdown in effect) and the blurring of borders between concepts – can be understood in terms of symbolic rejection of semiotic ambivalence, similar in gesture to the explosive »Nein« of M. M. However, this dislike which borders on the neurotic belies an all too uncomfortable awareness of potential language and conceptual ambivalence. More precisely, in person and through his practice as a judge Huntzinger can be regarded as the personification of a neurotic, denotating instance of the thetic break, hell bent on the ideal of finite denotation, yet acutely aware of the potential indeterminacy, perplexity, incongruity – in a word grotesquerie – of existence, his own and by implication the system of which he is the representative. That this complex is centred around the most bland (but perhaps the most democratic) of all connectives makes of »und« a space of transgression, *jouissance* and contingency. In this sense, it typifies the beyond of the system, or as Barthes calls it that ambivalent space outside the sentence. In Kristevan terms, it is an enunciating moment of thetic instability, a point along the signifying chain that manifests traces of semiotic disturbance. It also hypothetically opens up the political aspect of the carnivalesque, as Bakhtin would describe it the moment where the carnival king is toppled and the gleeful relativity of carnivalesque *mésalliance* takes his place. For the danger of the paratactic logic implicit in the word »und« is that any image can be tacked onto any image and

---

[56] »Dieser Rahmen läßt es für niemanden zu, ›sein Recht‹ oder gar ›Gerechtigkeit‹ zu begehren. Die beteiligten Personen sind Unterworfene [...] einer alle Lebensbereiche bis ins Intimste hinein erfassenden juristischen Weltsicht. Diese erweist sich gerade deshalb als gewalttätig, weil sie einzelne Aspekte dieser konkreten Lebensbereiche aus ihren lebensgeschichtlichen Zusammenhängen herauslöst, verabsolutiert und im artifiziellen Verfahren juristischer Bearbeitung nach Kriterien bewertet, die im Chaos des Alltagsleben keinen Sinn machen.« (Noll, Die böse Justiz [note 54], p. 77)

that just this kind of linking will sooner or later result in the transgressive counter-logic of carnivalesque anarchy.

However, the great irony of the text is that the language problematic of the connective »und«, the implied breakdown of rational discourse in and through its own terms, is exactly the language through which the protocol is narrated. Huntzinger's fear of binary breakdown is realised by the text through the confusion of hypotactic structure and paratactic logic. As we have seen, this results in the space outside the sentence, a space beyond binary signification. The last laugh is to a great extent on the judge who believes that the protocol represents a permanence of utterance that cannot be reneged upon or transgressed:

> Im einen Falle habe er seinem Schriftführer gegenüber erklärt, das Wichtigste im Prozeß sei das Protokoll, dadurch wären sowohl die Rechtsuchenden als auch die Zeugen und was sonst noch vor Gericht erscheine, gebunden, auch wenn sie nicht das gemeint, was sie zum Ausdruck gebracht hätten.   (*UND* 53)

The use of reported speech above creates a distance all the more ironic between the judge and the text that posits him because the protocol is, if anything, an exercise in ambivalence and the unreliability of supposedly posited utterances, quite far removed from Huntzinger's ideal. The protocol is thus not just writing against the judge, it is also wryly writing against itself as it depicts the above obsolete image of itself. In this sense, it is no wonder that the protocol can be defined as a text outside itself. In order to critically observe itself, it must transgress itself, in a sense cancelling itself out as it comes to resemble the text of the in-between. For the language used by Drach in his protocols, although deriving from the portentous language of court protocol, also introduces a new dimension to this language: the self-critical, shadowy side of rational language.[57]

To complicate matters further, as we have seen, the proliferation of connectives and ad infinitum linking of the text serve ironically to erode context by frustrating the syntagm of clear and directed narrative, dispersing it into tangential anecdote and superfluous conjecture. This implies that the protocol language exemplifies aspects of another form of language aphasia: contiguity disorder.[58] In other words, the erosion of context is not compensated for by a

---

[57] For this reason, I disagree with Gerhard Melzer's general diagnosis of Drach's protocol style: »Wie Drachs Figuren in den Bahnen ihrer ewigen Unerlöstheit kreisen, so bleibt die Sprache im Bann ihrer obrigkeitlichen Grammatik.« (Gerhard Melzer: Endzeit ohne Ende. Albert Drachs jüngstes Buch, »Ia Und Nein«. In: Neue Zürcher Zeitung, February 2 1993, p. 17)

[58] Whilst *UND* is not written in the »telegram style« typical for contiguity disorder, it nonetheless displays disruptions of coordination and subordination, and a general wordiness [*Wortanhäufung*] that Jakobson identifies in this disorder (Jakobson, Zwei Seiten der Sprache und zwei Typen aphatischer Störungen [note 52], p. 130). As Lodge points out, Jakobson's theory of the two types of aphasia does not demand that both should appear in isolation in literary language: »it is a theory of dominance of one quality over another, not of mutually exclusive qualities.« (Lodge, The Modes of Modern Writing [note 52], p. 80)

strengthening of context. The context too is outside and beyond itself. Action takes place in diverse locations over an extended time period and the actors must necessarily be replaced because they all seem hastily to meet their end. Most absurd of all in this regard however, is the non sequitur of the entire plot. It is very difficult to sensibly contextualise the story because its justification is so flimsy. This of course reflects back onto the vacuum of the narrating instance or rather the disturbance of similarity disorder.

In *UND*, similarity and contiguity disorder are thus two sides of one general problem: the inability of the narrative to identify itself in an undivided voice (to be recognisable as a representative of the symbolic order), and the related inability of this non-subject to locate itself in one context/territory. In this combination of the two disorders, we encounter the grotesque self of the topography of transgression: the abject deject who incessantly acquires and discards territories, and through whom the body is articulated as a horizontal, metonymic construct. And behind the careful front that Huntzinger presents to the world lurks the shadow of the language phobic, the language consciousness that knows of and fears castration because, in the judges's case, it senses the suggestibility of the word »und«. Thus Huntzinger's fear of this most ordinary of ordinary words translates into a deep-rooted fear of what language badly conceals: the want or loss as Kristeva puts it, upon which all signification is premised. In this way, »und« could be described as the linguistic fetish object par excellence.

In this general erosion of coherence, we witness a comic critique of modern bourgeois culture, a critique of who speaks (who has the power to determine reality), what is spoken about (by implication what is silenced), where the socially authoritative voice comes from, and how it comes to occupy this place of authority.[59] The protocol questions the presumptions of power and structure as it presents itself, through the logic of unconnection and episodic juxtaposition as always in a state of incompletion, production and dispersal. That the rational discourse of institutions should produce this effect of disintegration relegates images of power to the status of floating entities that can be disturbed from within their own terms. In other words, the ambivalence of the concept »system« is thematised by the protocol's self-diagnosis: it languishes outside itself contrary to the image of closure it seeks to portray.

---

[59] This insight is taken from Adorno's theory of epic naivety. He introduces the concept of epic naivety (the unreflected fixation of the narrator on the narrative object) as itself the result of a sceptical intelligence. Adorno argues that in this very gesture of narrative fixation on the object lies an eminently sceptical awareness of a missing a priori, an acute insight into the estrangement of signifier from signified. Epic naivety is therefore anything but naive and may function as a critique of enlightened bourgeois reason, as within Adorno's theoretical framework it is understood as a language written against the conceptual manipulation of rational narrative (Theodor W. Adorno: Über epische Naivität. In: id., Noten zur Literatur. Frankfurt a. M.: Suhrkamp 1958, p. 50–60).

Although Huntzinger remains in the mode of a closed image, the protocol language ridicules him as it presents everything around him to be in a process of disintegration. Ultimately thus, he is not portrayed as a finite entity. It is far more the case that he represents a point in the process of constituting the subject: the automatised reflex of symbolic positing. Whereas he might maintain this position, the text anticipates its collapse through the transgressive language of the protocol.

By seeking out an alternative location for the narration of the text in the outside of the text, Drach can be seen as an author concerned with the problem of narrating in the complex conditions of the modern world. The protocol as it has been presented in this chapter is both diagnosis and symptom of cultural hybridity, in other words it is the expression of the perplexity and discontinuity of the world and also the concession that this discontinuity, if squashed into continuous narrative, will ultimately transgress the terms of this narrative mode. What emerges is an increased sense of the protocol as an alternative narrative form interested in exploring the alternative sites of the contingent and the in-between.

Chapter 5
Ex-centrics, Evil Eyes and Missing Persons:
The Optics of Mimicry in *Das Goggelbuch*

5.1 Grotesque Surplus: Mimic Man

One could argue that the cross-contamination of parataxis and hypotaxis in the protocol *UND* is a signifier of that ›genetic uncertainty principle‹ that was identified in 3.1 as the monster's body. Using J. J. Cohen's concept of the monstrous body of difference as the signifier of pure culture, I proposed the monster as a general personification of the grotesque body as topography of transgression.[1] Other articulations of this monster were identified in the personalities of the language phobic and the paranoid language fetishist. As we have seen, Huntzinger most certainly fulfils the criteria of the monster. A language phobic, his attempts to realise language stasis through the cogs of the legal system are pitted against his unease with regard to the ambivalence he senses to be inseparable from language.

Despite this language awareness, I identified in Huntzinger an anal-sadistic, closed and static caricature of the corporeality of the Imaginary relation. The protocol narrative logic ultimately transgresses this finite body however, and Huntzinger who in any case was absent for most of the narrative, is shown to occupy the monster's location: the gap, the beyond and the in-between. However, this insight is delivered more by the self-reflective level of the narrative than by any local descriptions of the judge's body. In other words, Huntzinger embodies the genetic uncertainty principle of the monster most clearly when he is regarded as a Bakhtinian language personification.

In this chapter, I now turn to representations of the body of difference that whilst produced by the ambivalent narrative style of protocol language, are also articulated very clearly through personified apparitions of the monster. The main character in this analysis is Homi Bhabha's mimic man who as a double articulation of selfhood embodies the genetic uncertainty principle of the monster. Bhabha's concept of mimic man focuses on the British colonial expansion into India; however, his discussion of »the white man's artifice inscribed on the black man's body« is easily transferred to the construction of the Jewish other that arises as a subtext of *Das Goggelbuch*.[2] In this work, one could

---

[1] Monster Theory. Reading Culture. Ed. by Jeffrey Jerome Cohen. Minneapolis, London: University of Minnesota Press 1996, p. 4.

[2] Homi Bhabha: The Location of Culture. London, New York: Routledge 1994, p. 45. Albert Drach: Das Goggelbuch. In: id., Die kleinen Protokolle und das Goggelbuch.

easily speak of mimic man as a product of the Aryan artifice being inscribed on the Jewish body. *Das Goggelbuch* in particular confirms Drach as a post-colonial writer albeit with a difference, for he sets his bizarre tale within the geographical terrain of the European continent.

In this text, we witness how Drach ruptures »any binary model that defines belonging and not belonging to a culture«.[3] The function of the protocol as a floating document of in-between language writing solidly against the myth of Eurocentricity emerges strongly here. Drach does this by evoking »the phantasmic space of possession that no one subject can singly or fixedly occupy, and therefore permits the dream of the inversion of roles«.[4] *Das Goggelbuch* articulates the dream of this inversion in a reverse manner as a nightmare, however. Through this, Drach may be regarded as warning his readers about the corrupting propensity of power. In many ways, *Das Goggelbuch* functions as both a vision of European power structures gone wrong and a fantasy or counter-simulation of destabilising these very structures. Before proceeding to the text analysis however, let us contemplate the post-colonial monster of mimic man and his language (the discourse of mimicry) in a little more detail.

Mimicry's complexity originates from its status as two simultaneously conflicting forces. It is at first glance a discourse of colonial power, an authoritarian discourse of othering that »›appropriates‹ the Other as it visualizes power«.[5] It expresses on the one hand »the desire for a reformed, recognizable Other«.[6] As such, it is representative of the modern Western culture of rationalization and civilization, a culture that expounds »normative knowledges of the priority of race, writing, history«.[7] On the other hand, colonial discourse is a discourse which through the self-produced strategy of mimicry conducts a self-commentating examination of the above civilizing project, for »in ›normalizing‹ the colonial state or subject«, argues Bhabha, »the dream of Post-Enlightenment civility alienates its own language of liberty and produces another knowledge of its norms«.[8] In other words, the discourse that implements power as it appropriates the other also simultaneously questions and destabilises its own authority in the moment of appropriation.

This disavowal of colonial authority from within colonial discourse itself occurs as a result of the split project of mimicry. The constant feature of mimicry is its duality. Mimicry is Bhabha's conceptualisation of the ambivalence of colonial discourse. Taking the example of post-Enlightenment English colonialism, Bhabha argues that this discourse »often speaks in a tongue that is

München, Wien: Langen-Müller 1965, p. 245–303. Henceforth cited as *Goggelbuch* with appropriate page numbers

3 Matthias Konzett. The Politics of Recognition in Contemporary Austrian Jewish Literature. In: Monatshefte 90, No. 1 (Spring 1998), p. 71–88, here p. 79.

4 Bhabha, The Location of Culture (note 2), p. 44.

5 Ibid., p. 86.

6 Ibid.

7 Ibid., p. 91.

8 Ibid., p. 86.

forked, not false«.[9] As such, mimicry is the sign of a double articulation, i. e. the creation of a series of appropriate others, which on the one hand denies difference and is sanctioned by the colonial power, but on the other hand also demands the sign of the inappropriate other, the contradictory raising of the sign of indelible difference. It is the misfortune and the doing of the colonial power that both of these partial objects should reside in the one image: that of the anomalous other, mimic man.

Mimic man is the ideal of the colonial subject gone wrong. Originally, he is the middle man between the colonial power and the mass of governed colonial subjects. He is educated in the English tradition, the colonial ideal of »a class of persons Indian in blood and colour, but English in tastes, in opinions, in morals and in intellect«.[10] However, the reality of mimic man is somewhat different. He is in fact the anomalous product, reflection and creation of an anomalous mode of discourse. The production of this anomaly is dependent on a strategic limitation or internal prohibition of colonial discourse. The desire for the appropriate other is highly conflictual; the other should simultaneously reflect the colonial authority in a suitably flattering and affirming light. In this fashion, the colonial subject should be »almost the same« as the power that civilizes him. However, the moment of prohibition arises at this point; the colonial subject must affirm the identity of colonial power as power, and so the colonised, as subservient subject, cannot be the exact mimesis of colonial authority.

This cross-classificatory demand produces the anomaly of mimic man, i. e. the colonial subject who is »*almost the same, but not quite*«. Bhabha argues that »the very emergence of the ›colonial‹ is dependent for its representation« on this strategic limitation »*within* the authoritative discourse itself«.[11] The moment of prohibition – the stipulation of *not quite* – thus externalises the internal disturbance of colonial discourse. It does this in the production of discursive excess or slippage. This moment of excess can be located in the »not quite/not white« feature of mimic man, a condition of colonisation »in which to be Anglicized, is emphatically not to be English«.[12]

This slippage is the sign of the ambivalence of colonial discourse. Mimic man is the personification of the excess of colonial discourse, a waste product that uncovers colonial discourse's compulsion to self-transgression. As a cross-classificatory category, mimic man in fact exposes the exhaustion of the normative categories of knowledge usually expounded by colonial discourse. Mimic man can do this because as an anomalous image, the mimic figure is non-classifiable according to dichotomous structures based on opposition. For the image of the mimic colonial subject contains the countenance of the colonial authority, but this countenance is intertwined with the marring features of the other. It is self and other at the same time. It is a grotesque figure of cross-contamination.

---

[9] Ibid., p. 85.
[10] Ibid., p. 87.
[11] Ibid., p. 86.
[12] Ibid., p. 87.

This mimic figure of a grotesque doubling crystallises the mechanism of transgression. The transgression personified by mimic man produces that »other« knowledge of colonial discourse. In other words, colonial identity and the discourse of power that aims to perpetuate it are rearticulated through mimicry in terms of an otherness which transgresses the homogeneity of the system that produced this mimicry. Ultimately, this homogeneity is rendered redundant, as mimic otherness »does not merely ›rupture‹ the discourse, but becomes transformed into an uncertainty which fixes the colonial as ›partial‹ presence«.[13] This uncertainty, originating in the authoritative discourse, then projected onto the construct or discursive representation of the other, finds its way back to the colonial authority in the moment of disavowal. This is the moment where the imperfect creation of mimic man, the carrier of virtual or partial identity, i. e. *split* identity (neither self nor other), is registered in the discourse of the colonial as »the effect of a flawed colonial mimesis«.[14] The anomalous gaze of mimic man – a combination of the appropriate and the inappropriate – is a reversal of the colonial scopic drive, a »process by which the look of surveillance returns as the displacing gaze of the disciplined, where the observer becomes the observed and ›partial‹ representation rearticulates the whole notion of identity and alienates it from essence«.[15]

In other words, the colonial subject mimic man is none other than the articulation of the colonial power's self-alienation, its insurgent acknowledgement of its own existence as a construct, a partial presence. The colonial subject in the form of mimic man mimes the colonial power's forms of authority and in so doing deauthorises them. To put it another way, the status of mimic man as a construct of virtual identity reflects back to the colonial power its corresponding status as partial or incomplete entity. Its position as a centralising discourse of power is thus revealed as a self-appointed position, a result of discursive strategies and not the divinely ordained position of racial superiority that it would ideally be. Colonial identity as authority, played out and reflected in the discursive space afforded by mimic man, is revealed as an »identity effect«, a mimicry or farce of identity.[16]

Far from the smooth extension of the sovereign, civilised self into cultures of lack, the mimicry or ambivalence of colonial discourse is in fact the expression of the conflictual, contradictory and rupturing elements of a discourse that attempts in vain to produce the ideal of the homogenous, essentialist self. Mimicry is in fact testimony to the illusory nature of this ideal and the articulation – in the various different metonymies of presence expressed in the proliferation of appropriate and inappropriate others – of a lack at the heart of colonial discourse. This lack is the menace of mimicry, »its double vision which in

---

[13] Ibid., p. 86.
[14] Ibid., p. 87.
[15] Ibid., p. 89.
[16] Ibid., p. 90.

disclosing the ambivalence of colonial discourse also disrupts its authority«.[17] For »mimicry conceals no identity or presence behind its mask«.[18]

In concrete terms, this menacing double gaze of mimicry rearticulates the identity of colonial authority, now revealed as virtual, »in terms of its otherness, that which it disavows«.[19] The colonial other is thus none other than a version of the lacking self and the construct of a split and self-analysing discourse that acknowledges this. This acknowledgement, the other scene of colonial power, is expressed for Bhabha in the narcissistic and paranoid tendencies of colonial discourse.[20]

It is my argument that the above complex can be read in terms of a grotesquerie of language. Taking recourse to the Kristevan concepts of semiotic and symbolic, I will try to demonstrate how colonial (or other) discourses of power are in fact discourses of transgression and cross-contamination. Firstly, the enunciative modality of the colonial authority can be read as an extreme instance of the thetic, i. e. the ambivalent moment where identity is both established and pulverized through the aggressive assertion of difference. In the case of the thetic, this is the moment of departure from the semiotic *chora* and the corresponding moment of the inauguration of the symbolic. In the case of the colonial power, this is the moment where the latter positions itself both hierarchically above and apart from the other as a discourse of regulatory and normative knowledge.

However, taking into consideration the contradictory and bilateral nature of the relationship between the assertion of colonial power and the creation of appropriate others, the hierarchical construct of power is revealed as just that: a construct. That the project of power assertion is dependent for its perpetuation on the image of a static other implies the bilateral and intrinsically cross-contaminatory nature of the relationship between the established self and the projected other. As illustrated above, this bilateral moment is most clearly articulated in the other's returned gaze of surveillance, the moment where the authoritative gaze outwards is sent back to the self in an inappropriate form, a grotesque form. For the gaze of the self has been acquired by the other, but not in the manner of a simple switching of positions. Instead, the arbitrariness of such positionality is revealed through the uncertainty registered by the colonial power in the moment where it sees its strategies mimicked in the gaze of the other.

In this scenario, the whole concept of position in the dichotomously asymmetrical relation of self/other is questioned. The legitimisation of such a structure of power is thus also questioned. This bilateral moment – the reciprocal movement of cross-contamination where the other, in a grotesque parody, acquires features of the self – is a central deconstructive moment of grotesque discourse. It illustrates the potential of grotesque discourse as a critique of dis-

---

[17] Ibid., p. 88.
[18] Ibid.
[19] Ibid., p. 91.
[20] Cf. ibid.

courses of power. This critique is necessarily conducted from within the language of power itself. Through its transgressive disrespect of boundaries of power and identity, the grotesque however manages to create, in the figures of anomaly that it produces, alternative and ambivalent categories that decentralise the former homogenous constructs of language, power and identity.

Following this line of argumentation, it would seem that any disruption in the image of the other will result in the destabilisation of colonial power. As illustrated above, mimicry is the symptom of this confused picture of the self which is in turn externalised in the confused picture of the mimic colonial subject, then bilaterally redelivered to the displaced gaze of the colonial power. As a threshold modality which takes into account the presence of both the semiotic and symbolic in language even as it attempts to assert order, the thetic is afflicted by the same double gaze as the trope of mimicry. For even as it tries to instigate the practice of positionality through separation from the semiotic – a foundation of symbolic activity – it remains in a strangely antithetical manner »displaced towards the stages previous to its positing«,[21] i. e. towards semiotic stages which threaten to pulverize the very notion of position. This is due to none other than the transformative, positing function of the thetic itself. In other words, the semiotic, although apparently absent from symbolic functioning, is in fact incorporated into the linguistic signifier through the altering aspect of the thetic. This aspect could be described as »the thetic break's inability to remain simply [...] a division within a signifying homogeneity«.[22] Instead, in a manner that goes against the presumptions of the symbolic order, the thetic is »a heterogeneous division, an irruption of the semiotic *chora*«, which »prevents the ›other‹ from being posited as an identifiable syntactic term«.[23] Through the unstable division of the thetic, the other »has become heterogeneous and will not remain fixed in place«.[24] As such, the symbolic signifier »indebted in this manner to semiotic functioning tends to return to it«.[25] And if we are to accept the view of the signifier as other, then the symbolic order is from the moment of its inception also an ambivalent discourse in which the other of the symbolic, the semiotic, is partially present. The thetic is the attempt to regulate the semiotic in the symbolic, but the ambivalence of the thetic position allows for the intrusion of the semiotic in the symbolic as a pulverising force.

Viewed within the Kristevan theoretical framework, the enunciative modality of colonial discourse – the modality of mimicry – is a thetic modality of transgression. In other words, it attempts to assert positions of superiority and inferiority through which it can operate, but its awareness of its dependency on the other for the fulfilment of this project results in the challenge or refusal of this

---

[21] Julia Kristeva: Revolution in Poetic Language. New York: Columbia University Press 1984, p. 117.

[22] Ibid., p. 108.

[23] Ibid.

[24] Ibid.

[25] Ibid., p. 117.

very position, i. e. the refusal of the thetic. This refusal is usually brought about by the raising of the semiotic. As illustrated above, the thetic, already beholden to the semiotic, is structurally predisposed to raising the semiotic even as it disavows the latter. It could be argued that the anomaly of mimic man represents most clearly this refusal of the thetic. The effect of a flawed colonial mimesis is thus, as a sign of discursive rupture and disturbance, an instance of the semiotic in the symbolic. It is the moment where the homogenous discourse of power is reminded of its split and heterogeneous status of lack or incompleteness.

One could argue therefore, that the »subject« of colonial discourse (the inappropriate other who subverts the authoritative gaze) is neither subject nor object. Almost (but not quite) white, it resides in an in-between discursive space between subject and object position. This anomalous subject is thus very similar to Kristeva's abject personality, an insufficiently posited »subject« who is marked by the lack of »a definable object«.[26] Indeed, Bhabha argues that the desire of mimicry reveals this same abject lack of an identifiable object or »that impossibility of the Other« as he calls it.[27] It is with regard to this indecidability of the »other« object that mimicry may also be confirmed as part of the discourse of mourning (compensation/loss) discussed in chapter 3. It is a discourse that is marked therefore, by a very active fetish function, for as Bhabha notes, mimicry may not have an object, but it has substitute objects which he terms strategic objects or »metonym[ies] of presence«.[28]

The notion of strategic objects follows the same pattern of the linguistic signifier as a temporary (strategic) filler in the play of constant compensations. »Mimicry, like the fetish, is a part object«, states Bhabha, one which »mimes the forms of authority at the point at which it deauthorizes them«.[29] Thus the mocking game of mimicry may suddenly mutate into menace precisely because it is structured in the same manner as the fetish object that both defers and raises the spectre of castration. For the »impossible object« of the mimic other reflects to the appropriating self its impossible status as self. Just as the fetish object is the result of a demand for confirmation of self through denial of (female)castration, so is mimicry the product of interdictory desire: »the demand for identity and stasis – and the counter-pressure of [...] change, difference«.[30]

Discourse as fetish which fails to discern adequately between subject and object expresses precisely the metonymy of presence articulated in the gaze of mimic man. Mimic man is thus little more than the abject reflection of the discursive body of the colonial authority as slippery fetish. In this way, mimicry uncovers the partial identity of the symbolic subject, here the voice of the colonial authority. The speaking subject (the colonial authority) is a divided speak-

---

[26] Julia Kristeva: Powers of Horror. An Essay on Abjection. New York: Columbia University Press 1982 (European Perspectives), p. 1.

[27] Bhabha, The Location of Culture (note 2), p. 89.

[28] Ibid.

[29] Ibid., p. 91.

[30] Ibid., p. 86.

ing subject, whose split identity is revealed in the ruptured reflection of the self in the form of mimic man. This figure has the ability to transgress the norms of colonial discourse revealing the latter as instances of empty rhetoric which »violate the rational, enlightened claims of its enunciatory modality«.[31] Thus the modality itself is split between the post-Enlightenment rhetoric of civility and liberty and the language of racial discrimination. As a discourse »uttered between the lines and as such both against the rules and within them«, it has the potential to renew itself through play.[32]

Colonial discourse is thus not a closed system of homogenous, centralised power; rather it bears all the features of a *process* that decentralises itself, and so questions the assumptions of power and dichotomy on which it is based. In this way, it »liberates marginal elements and shatters the unity of man's being through which he extends his sovereignty«.[33] This shattered unity takes on the physique of a body constantly between existence and dismemberment, a hybrid of self and other »that bears the mark of splitting in the Other place from which it comes«.[34] The body of mimicry is therefore a post-colonial specification of the body of negativity/*jouissance*. It is to the particulars of this bodily articulation and how it overwrites the »phobic myth of the undifferentiated whole white body« that I now turn.[35]

5.2 Representing the In-Between: The Secret Art of Invisibility

Das Goggelbuch continues the protocol practice of ambivalence identified in *UND*. Slipperiness of reference and rhetorical grotesquerie are features of this work that may also be described as a text outside itself. However, the offensive of ambivalence in *Das Goggelbuch* is clearly directed at the phallocentric myth of origins with particular attention to the construction of Eurocentric identity. As such, the text conducts an interrogation of the self and its relationship to the other. This it does by means of the mirror device which not only features as a prop in the story but is also parodically reflected in the mise-en-abyme structure of the entire narrative. Not only does the text subvert through the use of this optical device the interrelated issues of who sees (who appropriates), who is seen (who is appropriated), what is visible (present) and by contrast what remains invisible (absent), the mirror as the paradoxical intersection of reflecting surface and reflected depth also addresses the fiction of profundity associated with a Eurocentric understanding of identity. The fictitious recess of the mirror that is translated into the prose strategy of deferral in *Das Goggelbuch* thus becomes the signifier of narcissistic crisis as the aggressivity of the metonymic

---

[31] Ibid., p. 91.
[32] Ibid.
[33] Ibid., p. 89.
[34] Ibid., p. 45.
[35] Ibid., p. 92.

relation fractures the imaginary locus of identity: the desired seamless identification with the other as self that Lacan situates in the Imaginary relation and
that Bhabha refers to as »the transitive desire for a direct object of self-
reflection« in the scopic drive of the Eurocentric self.[36]

One could thus propose *Das Goggelbuch* in the first instance as a sample of
the mimic text that, by telescoping the ambivalent grotesquerie of the observing/
observed self (mimic man no less), comically questions what Bhabha terms the
appropriating metaphor of vision complicit with a Western metaphysic of man.[37]
Secondly, whilst the framing and framed action of *Das Goggelbuch* may not be
set in the extra-European location of the colony, it nonetheless deserves attention
as a text that manifests several fundamental features of the post-colonial work.
Perhaps it is more accurate to describe *Das Goggelbuch* as an autoethnographic
text that re-presents the periphery of the Eurocentric self from the unsettlingly
intimate perspective of the intra-European Jewish other, itself a product of the
former. This perspective is primarily evident in the comic discourse concerning
the master/slave relation which attempts to break down the binary divide of this
couple, thereby opening up the area of the ambivalent post-colonial encounter:
the contact zone of self and other. This zone is not only to be located in the
metonymic relation of the mirror paradox, it is also staged in the dream-like encounter of an observing consciousness with another observing consciousness that
effectively disrupts the unilateral fantasy of colonial scopic desire.[38]

Elements of the autoethnographic text are also evident in the occasional but
very deliberate references to anti-Semitism throughout the text within the text
(also – and confusingly – entitled *Das Goggelbuch*).[39] Most significantly however, the business of re-presenting the periphery via the autoethnographic text of

---

[36] Ibid., p. 47. Lacan's use of the concept *Gestalt* makes clear the fictitious nature of the
specular image: »The total form of the body by which the subject anticipates in a mirage the maturation of his power is given to him only as *Gestalt*, that is to say, in an exteriority in which this form is certainly more constituent than constituted, but in which
it appears above all else in a contrasting size [...] that fixes it [...] in contrast with the
turbulent movements that the subject feels are animating him.« (Jacques Lacan: The
Mirror Stage as formative of the function of the I. In: id., Écrits. A Selection. London:
Tavistock 1977, p. 2)

[37] Cf. Bhabha, The Location of Culture (note 2), p. 42.

[38] »If ethnographic texts are a means by which Europeans represent to themselves their
(usually subjugated) others, then autoethnographic texts are those the others construct in
response to or dialogue with those [...] representations.« (Mary Louise Pratt: Imperial
Eyes. Travel Writing and Transculturation. London, New York: Routledge 1992, p. 7)

[39] One of the most striking of these references is the plundering of a Jewish ghetto in a
small town just outside Osnabrück: »Da gibt es viel Schreiens und Weinens im Juden-
viertel, als man die Alten an den Bärten zerrt, die Jungen genicksüber wie junge Kat-
zen auf die Straßen wirft. Den Weibern tut man, was man gerade kann, und zu dem
man Lust hat. Die besten dienen der allgemeinen Ergetzung und die schlechten für den
gesammelten Holzstoß.« (*Goggelbuch* 262). The text within the text is henceforth referred to in the main text in inverted commas as »Das Goggelbuch« whilst the text as a
whole is referred to as *Das Goggelbuch*.

the subordinated is announced in the opening sentence. The motivation for the entire work is premised on the search for documented proof of Aryan ancestry. Thus the post-colonial aspect of *Das Goggelbuch* may be understood from within the field of Jewish assimilation in twentieth century Europe as Drach, in the manner of the autoethnographic writer, engages with and critiques the terms of Eurocentric representation from his ambivalent position as Austro-Jewish other.

One of the most striking characteristics of the autoethnographic mimic text is its alternative articulation of identity as difference. This it does by focusing its attention on the duplicity of colonial or Eurocentric discourse, that is, by allowing the tongue that is forked (but not false) to twist itself into a self-disseminating ambivalence that opens up the impossible space of the in-between (the peripheral contact zone of self and other) as the only possible space of enunciation.[40] Replacing the vertically constituted subject of resemblance in the mimic text is its nightmare other that, true to the mode of mimicry, spoils the continuity of resemblance (the familiar) with the intrusion of the unfamiliar. Hence Bhabha's claim that mimicry is at once resemblance and menace. In theoretical terms, this other is not necessarily a person but a structure of difference that (in the case of *Das Goggelbuch*) laughingly negates the notion of primordial identity.

Difference thereby displaces the vanity of smug self-reflection, disrupting what Bhabha calls the analogical relation of resemblance. This latter relation prioritises a signifying limit of space that posits the privileged status of the image. The »profound geological dimension of the sign«[41] that is premised on the above analogical relation of resemblance between signifier and signified thus creates the illusion of a conceptual space prior to signification. This space is none other than the primary space of the a priori, the origin of the self before language and its conceptual permanence in image. For as Foucault points out, the indispensable fulcrum of the analogical relation is none other than man whose image radiates out into the universe that gratifyingly returns to him the familiar vista of the self in all objects, all relations and all spaces.[42]

---

[40] Pratt points out the duplicity or mimic characteristic of the autoethnographic text when she states that »autoethnography involves partial collaboration with and appropriation of the idioms of the conqueror«. (Pratt, Imperial Eyes [note 38], p. 7)

[41] Bhabha, The Location of Culture (note 2), p. 48.

[42] Foucault argues that the form of similitude represented by analogy »makes possible the marvellous confrontation of resemblances across space [...]. Its power is immense, for the similitudes of which it treats are not the visible, substantial ones between things themselves; they need only be the more subtle resemblances of relations. Disencumbered thus, it can extend from a single given point, to an endless number of relationships.« The central point, which is saturated with analogies, is man. His physical shape is rediscovered constantly in the natural, cosmological and geological spaces which are in turn organised according to the »up« and »down« bodily experiences of verticality: »Upright between the surfaces of the universe, [man] stands in relation to the firmament [...]; but he is also the fulcrum upon which all these relations turn, so that we find them again, their similarity unimpaired, in the analogy of the human animal to the earth it inhabits [...]. Man's body is always the possible half

Similarly, Lacan remarks that the specular stage of psychoanalysis (the Imaginary projection of self into the unary signifier) is matched by the Cartesian mode of philosophical contemplation. Both may be seen as consistent with the analogical relation which could, in psychoanalytical terms, be described as narcissism or »that form of vision that is satisfied with itself in imagining itself as consciousness«.[43] This view is echoed in essay XI of Drach's series. Here he takes umbrage with the egocentricity of the Cartesian subject, *der Ich-mensch*, as he terms it. This entity exists solely unto and for itself, argues Drach. According to its consciousness, it is the sum of all things in the world. Others come into play only insofar as the self can project its surplus (its negativity) onto these others thereby understanding, creating and organising them in the negative image of the self.[44] Whilst Drach may have shown himself to be highly suspicious of syntactical organisation in the previous chapter, equally he now reveals himself as a stinging image sceptic. At the heart of these related forms of scepticism is an earnest critique of ideological (mis)conceptions of the self, of others and of the language that represents both.

As antidote to these misconceptions, the mimic text of ambivalent discourse upsets the analogic relation through the strategic confusion of the metaphoric and metonymic poles in the cultural production of meaning. In *Das Goggelbuch*, we thus encounter the nauseous but carnivalesque lurch from the metaphoric understanding of the self as already posited in the extra-linguistic space of the image (the signified) to the horizontal axis of metonymy which, through the play of displacement and deferral, absence and presence, articulates image as always spatially split. »The image is at once a metaphoric substitution, an illusion of presence, and by that same token a metonym, a sign of its absence and loss«, remarks Bhabha, further clarifying the cleft in the image between the metaphoric and metonymic poles of articulation.[45] Thus image is the site of ambivalence, the figure of a double that simply cannot be contained by the analogic relation.

In the slide between metaphor and metonymy, we therefore encounter the priority of the disappearing/reappearing signifier as the articulatory principle of a discourse that, in its slippery way, presents image/identity as provisional instances in the flux of the identification process. From this perspective, Bhabha argues that image can only ever be an appurtenance to identity but never its finished product.[46] In other words, image is part of the drive for identification that, as an ongoing process, always remains to greater or lesser degrees within the realm

---

of a universal atlas.« (Michel Foucault: The Order of Things. An Archaeology of the Human Sciences. London: Routledge 2000, p. 21–22)

[43] Jacques Lacan: The Four Fundamental Concepts of Psycho-Analysis. Ed. by Jacques-Alain Miller. New York, London: Norton 1981, p. 75.

[44] Albert Drach: Sprache als Verständigungsmittel sowie zur Erzeugung von Missverständnissen. In: id., Das 17. Buch der 17 Essays, Nachlaß Albert Drach, Austrian Literary Archive of the Austrian National Library, Wien, p. 5.

[45] Bhabha, The Location of Culture (note 2), p. 50.

[46] Cf. ibid., p. 51.

of indecidability: the in-between. The desire for identity is thus both represented in and frustrated by the struggle for identification which is itself marked by the deferral of identity. This transfiguration of identity in difference marks out the unstable territory of the grotesque self whose ambivalent desires of imaginary projection are both incommensurable with and deformed by the discourse of slippage that breaks up the image of self unified and consistent with the appropriated (and appropriate) other.

In the case of *Das Goggelbuch*, the slide from identity to identification, the strategic confusion of the metaphoric and metonymic poles, and the revelation of the otherness of the self all occur in the double space of inscription which is paradoxically communicated by the mirror device. That the »feint of writing« should be represented by the mirror in this text suggests that its surface is at once the site for the emergence and disappearance of the partial mimic subject. In short, the mirror's surface no longer signals the deep »glassy metaphorics of [...] mimetic [...] narratives«.[47] Instead, it now assumes the tattered texture of metonymic slippage, the sense that what is made present in the reflection is in fact but an absence, the virtual or partial presence of the mimic self. Thus is the mirror posed at the complex juncture of the metonymic and the metaphoric poles (the intersection of reflecting surface and reflected depth) where it becomes apparent that the relationship of language to image is one of infinite incompatibility.

Foucault summarises this relationship of indefinable slippage, the surplus or deficit of meaning that disrupts the bilateral relation of signifier to signified, when he remarks that what we see never resides in what we say, just as what we say cannot be adequately substituted by image.[48] In other words, both language and image are governed by a mediating order that displaces on the one hand the conceptual immediacy implied by the field of vision, and on the other, the linguistic realm of metaphorical substitution that appears to be closely affiliated to image. The incompatibility of language and image derives from the sequential order of syntax that fragments the perceived wholeness of image, translating the simultaneity of the seen into what Bhabha refers to as »the tethered shadow of deferral and displacement«.[49] Likewise, language itself is forever tardy in its attempts to capture image which betrays a bias towards the metonymic axis of articulation. Following Foucault, the space approximated by language is defined by the sequential elements of syntax and therefore becomes manifest only as the in-between of sequence, the surplus or deficit that is the tethered shadow of the sequential relation.

In the last chapter, this space was presented as that of catachresis. However, in the related discussion pertaining to the grotesquerie of the self, the temporal lag of the catachrestic space (the tardiness of the signifier) translates into the »aphanisis« or tardiness of the self. In other words, the grotesque self of the

---

[47] Ibid., p. 48.
[48] Foucault, The Order of Things (note 42), p. 9.
[49] Bhabha, The Location of Culture (note 2), p. 45.

mimic/mirror relation is defined largely by the fading of the self implicit in the »not quite« addendum of the Eurocentric scopic drive. This fading effect is best described by the Lacanian term »aphanisis« which denotes the cross-contamination of self-alienation in the space of the other that is truly grotesque. »Aphanisis« may thus be regarded as an endemic disturbance of subject position (a variant of thetic instability) that is generated by the partial structure of the signifier. If the cultural production of a predominantly Eurocentric meaning is premised on the narcissistic establishment of the self, then this endeavour is doomed by the aphanisic structure of the signifier. For the self is dependent on the place of the other for its emergence as self in the specular stage of the Imaginary relation. However, this elsewhere location of the self condemns it to disappearance as soon as it emerges in the place of the other, i. e. the place of the signifier. »Aphanisis« thus becomes the eclipse of the self in the process of emergence by the disappearance of the self as it projects into an other. That the whole of the signifying chain of self and other is based on the disorientation of absence/presence crystallises in this aphanisis that exposes the vanity of subject position by highlighting the absurdity of being eclipsed by an other that is itself also disappearing.[50]

In *Das Goggelbuch*, this grotesquerie of the self is largely communicated by the mirror's metamorphosis into a site of dual identity that contradictorily »gives voice« to the psychic gap or narcissistic wound of mimic slippage (»not quite«) which in language becomes the shadowy space tethered to the sequential relation. Just as the catachrestic gap frustrated the syntagm, the refracted image of self in the fictitious recess of the mirror prevents the »phrase of identity« being spoken.[51] In other words, the seeing subject fails to perceive an other or an object that would sublimate into a convincing fictitious unity the complexity of cultural difference. The act of seeing encounters instead the psychic gap, the narcissistic wound or deferral of aphanisis that characterises the »not quite« demand. The seeing subject sees only this gap, the internalised difference of otherness in the self that splits the observing subject. In short, the seeing subject, itself poorly posited, virtual and partial sees only the invisibility of the other and by that same token the invisible self.

Seeing invisibility however is not seeing nothing. It is in fact the viewing of the in-between space of the self and of signification, the appraisal of the self/other anomaly (the otherness of the self) that becomes visible once representation has been freed from the analogic relation of resemblance that impedes it. For as Bhabha points out, there is no identity behind the mask of mimicry. Thus the

---

[50] »[...] the subject appears first in the Other, in so far as the first signifier, the unary signifier, emerges in the field of the Other and represents the subject for another signifier, which other signifier has its effect the *aphanisis* of the subject. Hence the division of the subject – when the subject appears somewhere as meaning, he is manifested elsewhere as ›fading‹, as disappearance.« (Lacan, The Four Fundamental Concepts of Psycho-Analysis [note 43], p. 218)

[51] Bhabha, The Location of Culture (note 2), p. 47.

visible as the fictitious depth of the posited self dissolves into invisibility as the invisible, the struggle of identification, emerges in the aphanisic rupture of the analogical relation. The presence implied by the metaphoric axis of the sign falls away as the missing person (the other self) of the psychic gap appears in the vague adumbration of aphanisis. Seeing the self becomes the act of seeing a missing person, the »I« that is permanently displaced and elsewhere. Seeing the self as other in short amounts to recognising difference not just in the decentralised reflection, but significantly also in the privileged vantage point of the observer.

It is around this position of thetic instability that Bhabha locates the overriding metonymy of the post-colonial text: the substitution of the narrating/seeing »I« for the partial eye of mimic man, the displacing returned gaze of the inappropriate other that violates the signifying limit of the self. Not only does the part (the eye) replace the whole (»I«) in an act of fragmentation, the replacing part is, as Bhabha says, partial. In other words, it is the signifier of further fragmentation, the gaze that can see only the scission, the fissures and the frontiers of the self. The evil eye of the partial gaze is the displaced and displacing perspective that sees invisibility. In this manner, the evil eye is blind to the reflections of the »I«, seeing and being seen only by missing persons in a subtext of distorted, discontinuous images that pulverise, ridicule and mock the conceptual unity of the self.[52]

Seeing invisibility is thus tantamount to beholding the self as monster, that embodiment of culture as difference. In *Das Goggelbuch*, the mirror is the object that delivers the monstrous image. Due to the distortions it reveals, one could regard the mirror as a signifier of the fetishistic body of negativity that overwrites the phobic myth of the whole, white body. The narrative logic of *Das Goggelbuch* thus follows a pattern similar to that in *UND* as the body of symbolic negation once again dissolves into the body of semiotic negativity.

However, the mirror is not just a symbol for the disembodied subject of mimic articulation. It is also a parody par excellence of the fetish object. It reveals the gaps in the subject's make-up, thereby allowing it to witness in horror the nightmare of potential castration. Yet it also withdraws the subject from the »looking game« at just the moment where swift demise seems unavoidable: the very end of the text when the main protagonist, Goggel, finally meets his master. The mirror thus functions as a main site of fetishistic revelation and deferral in *Das Goggelbuch* – a topography of transgression as it were – one of the metonymies of presence that Bhabha identifies as so central to the strategic enunciation of mimic discourse.

---

[52] »The familiar space of the Other (in the process of identification) develops a graphic [...] cultural specificity in the splitting of the postcolonial or migrant subject. In the place of that ›I‹ [...] there emerges the challenge to see what is invisible, the look that cannot ›see me‹, a certain problem of the object of the gaze that constitutes a problematic referent for the language of the Self. The elision of the eye insists [...] that the phrase of identity cannot be spoken, except by putting the eye/I in the impossible position of enunciation.« (Ibid., p. 47)

5.3 Fallible Frames

Das Goggelbuch documents just this bias towards the metonymic in the cultural production of meaning and the accompanying interrogation of Eurocentric identity. Another prototype of the poorly embedded floating document, it is populated by missing persons constantly in motion. The structure of the mise-en-abyme suggests narrative invisibility, the sneaking suspicion that narrative perspective is focalised through the duality of evil partial eyes. Thus one could suggest that the interrogation of identity takes place through the interrogation of visibility, both of the seeing (narrating) and seen (narrated) instances of subjectivity. Moreover, there is the question of myriad narrative frames that seem to assume the refracting function of the transfigured mirror of metonymy that reflects, and indeed multiplies, difference.

Firstly however, a summary of the bizarre sequence of events which make up *Das Goggelbuch*. The introductory sentence, no less than twenty-three lines in length, forms the initial frame for the entire text. Within this thicket of language, it eventually becomes clear that the framing action is situated in the twentieth century, certainly after the Nazi ascent to power and most likely directly in the wake of the Nuremberg Laws. The action centres upon the person of Klaus Xaver Johann Guckelhupf who is currently researching his proof of Aryan ancestry. Bhabha's notion of a western (specifically Germanic in this case) metaphor of vision that is naively premised on the transparent visibility of the self is thematised by this character's very name: *Guckelhupf* (Peep-Hop).[53] Already the kind of habitual blindness that goes with the Eurocentric epiphany of the self is suggested by the hopping/skipping appendix of this name. Throughout his paperwork journey into the origins of his ancestry what does Guckelhupf see and what does he conveniently edit or skip? Furthermore, the plethora of first names seems to imply a certain indecidability of the self that can be neither contained by the telescoping action implied in the surname, nor by the proper nouns that try to capture the individual.

He eventually comes to the origin of his species in the form of »Das Goggelbuch«, a report left behind by the German servant Xaver Johann Gottgetreu Goggel, Guckelhupf's earliest identifiable forefather. Thus ends Guckelhupf's search at the dawn of the early modern age in the founding figure of the subordinated. The text then shifts into the text within the text (the ancient report entitled »Das Goggelbuch« within the literary text of *Das Goggelbuch*) and begins a summary of Goggel's misadventures several centuries previously. To complicate matters further, the report from the early modern era itself is a mise-en-abyme. It begins with Goggel's detailed self-appraisal in front of his

---

[53] The translation of Guckelhupf's name as »Peep-Hop« is based on the interpretation of »Guckel« as a play on the Viennese colloquial expression for eyes: »Guckerln«. See Peter Wehle: Sprechen Sie Wienerisch? Von Adaxl bis Zwutschkerl. Erw. und bearb. Neuausg., Wien: Ueberreuter 1980, p. 153.

mirror before setting out to Osnabrück in order to start a new life in the service of his master, Herr von Hahnentritt. Before he embarks on his journey, he smashes his mirror in a bid to rid himself of his lowly reflection. Goggel has ambitious aspirations for himself we learn, most of which centre around the eventual usurping of his employer's role as master.[54] He then commences his journey which is anything but straightforward. Only after several years of meandering around the European map does he make it to Osnabrück and actually come face to face with his master. Just as Herr von Hahnentritt discloses his identity as the devil who has stealthily directed the course of Goggel's strange journey, the horrified Goggel finds himself suddenly whipped back to his room where he still stands in front of his mirror which evidently is still unsmashed. No time has lapsed, everything is just as it was, thus it would seem that the mirror experience was both visionary and imaginary.[55] Nonetheless, within the narrative structure of the report the mirror experience forms a second text that returns to the frame of the report but not to the initial frame of Guckelhupf's search.

The narrative complexity does not resolve itself in the recognition of the mise-en-abyme, however. The opening marathon sentence tells us that Goggel's report, when it is happened upon by Guckelhupf, has already been modified by three notaries and a geographer who must also have discovered it during similar paperwork excavation trips. Goggel's voice is thus mediated by at least four others by the time it reaches Guckelhupf. By the time it reaches the reader, it has been further altered by Guckelhupf's account and again by the anonymous narrative voice which implies towards the end of the text that it could only roughly relate the contents of Goggel's report, modified as it has been by the voices of protocolling notaries. There is no further reference to the mysterious geographer. Whilst the notaries are mentioned for their ordering of the report, his contribution remains rather more obscure.[56]

One could argue that this kind of text arrangement imparts the post-colonial subversiveness of *Das Goggelbuch*. Briefly leaving aside the particular theme of mimic optics, *Das Goggelbuch* in all its confusing metalepses epitomises

---

54 »Siegfried unähnlich, aber doch dem Volk der Nibelungen angehörend, [...] be-
    schließt er, von Haus aus nicht zu erben bestimmt, der Bestimmung langsam und
    beharrlich ein anderes Bett zu graben [...]. Ein Diener könne auch immerhin die
    Sprosse des Herrn erklettern.« (*Goggelbuch* 246–247)

55 »[...] er [wird] im Winde mittels Teufelsgefährt sogleich in seine Wohnung gebracht,
    woselbst er sich alsbald, Grimassen schneidend, wieder vor seinem Spiegel findet.
    Dieser ist noch immer ganz [...]. So ist es ihm klar, daß er sein Zimmer niemals ver-
    lassen hat. Offenbar hat er alles nur im Spiegel gesehen, der ja unzerschlagen ge-
    blieben.« (Ibid., p. 303)

56 »Nach dieser Erläuterung seiner Beschaffenheit und Person, welche der Diener Gog-
    gel wahrscheinlich der Nachwelt nur in groben Zügen vermittelt, die seine Mitteilun-
    gen protokollierenden Notare aber in ausführlichere Ordnung gebracht haben dürfen,
    schränkt Herr von Hahnentritt immerhin ein, daß Goggel, [...] die zwei Dukaten auch
    verdiene.« (Ibid., p. 302–303)

the floating document of the post-colonial text. In other words, it replaces the monumental text of history with the accidental, incidental and marginal *»objet trouvé«* status of the mimic text that is written in between and against the lines of the official historical document.[57] Bhabha points out that mimic men are »parodists of history«.[58] In *Das Goggelbuch*, we encounter one such parody of history that premises itself on the myth of superior (Aryan) origins. Trawling back into his past, Guckelhupf can only come up with the lowly dim-witted but cunning servant Goggel whose physiognomy suggests that he is not too far removed from the Neanderthal dwellers of caves. Bhabha suggests that alongside the book, the Eurocentric body as a further staple artefact of history too undergoes a metamorphosis into something not quite so central. This fragmentation of the body is evidenced in the text by just that erasure of »I« into »eye« mentioned above. This elision of the posited subject of the symbolic order »I« into the bit-part of the body »eye« expresses just that shift from the vertical axis of presence/metaphor in the understanding of self to the horizontal axis of metonymy. The passage concerning Goggel's self-appraisal in the mirror communicates just this overwriting of the whole, white body as the distorted body of mimic man begins to emerge. In the following extract, it is clear that the text shows him to be almost Aryan, but not quite:

> Sein Antlitz sei von einer stumpfen Beschaffenheit, daher nicht als Waffe (Schneide oder Spitze), wohl aber als Schutz oder Schild zu gebrauchen. Die gut eingehöhlten, rostbraunen Augen seien bereit, einen in deren Reichweite eingetretenen, fangbaren Gegenstand zu umklammern und sich nicht so leicht wieder entwinden zu lassen. Die tückisch niedere Stirn mache den Kopf widerspenstig gegen das freche Eindringen frische Gedanken begünstigender, natürlicher Luftzüge, aber ebenso unnachgiebig gegen Aufgeben eines einmal eingenommenen Standpunkts. Das dunkelblonde Haar zeige zwar nicht den Anreiz der Sonnenfarbe, [...] halte aber das gute Mittel der Unauffälligkeit. Der stämmig dicke Nacken samt breit angelegtem Halse bekenne gleich dem untersetzten, ein wenig abgebogenen Gestelle den Ehrenstolz eines, der sich auf krummen Wegen nicht unterkriegen lasse. Der breite Busen und der noch in der Knospe befangene Bauch zeigten durch ihre Buchtung beide mit Deutlichkeit Stoßkraft und kämpferische Gesinnung ihres Inhabers. Hände und Füße, hart und groß, die einen anzupacken, die zweiten sich anzusetzen und bewiesen darüber hinaus Erziehung zur Arbeit durch Notwendigkeit und Herkunft. (*Goggelbuch* 246)

It is clear that although Goggel may at this point still be under the illusion of himself as an Aryan subject descended from the Nibelungs, the text has other ideas, and sets them in motion by putting the above self-appraisal through the unforgiving »feint of writing«. For the narrative perspective systematically finds fault with all of Goggel's features. His countenance is dull and blunt we learn, ill-suited for the kind of warrior heroics one would associate with the Nibelung race. His hair, the colour of dirty dishwater it is implied, is »not quite« blonde. Furthermore, his eyes (not quite blue) are a rusty brown, fur-

---

[57] Cf. Bhabha, The Location of Culture (note 2), p. 92.
[58] Ibid., p. 88.

rowed deep into the heavy brow of the primitive thinker. Far from the long limbed race he claims to be a descendant of, everything about Goggel's physique is blunt, short, stocky and inelegant. And though the narrating instance might identify in the thickset neck the stubborn earnestness of one who will not be corrupted, the following sentences contradict this assertion by suggesting that this personality is already corrupt by its dim readiness to violence.

One could argue that in this passage we witness the fetish function of language hard at play. For »the myth of historical origination – racial purity, cultural priority« comes under attack here in the form of the Aryan-Germanic stereotype.[59] The »limited form of otherness« that Bhabha terms the stereotype is reflected back to the want-to-be Aryan subject who is then found to be lacking.[60] By wickedly listing off Goggel's deviations from Aryan norms, the text collapses the »metaphoric or masking function of the fetish« and directs attention towards the metonymic »figuring of lack«, alluding to a form of identity that is predicated as much »on anxiety and defence« as it is on mastery.[61] The figuring of lack as featured in Goggel's physical shortcomings thus amounts to a list of mini-castrations that critique almost item for item the criteria for ideal Aryan personhood.

Nonetheless, the text does not state this criticism directly. In fact, its laborious use of the subjunctive implies that it is objectively reporting Guckelhupf's findings in »Das Goggelbuch«. We should not be fooled by this pseudo-objective position, however. For the ambivalent narrative voice makes fun of the demand for identity as stasis or stereotype by focusing on the several deviations of Goggel the want-to-be. As such, the narrative voice represents the »ironic compromise« between stasis and difference that results in mimicry.[62] And Goggel, the German who is not quite Aryan, emerges in this introductory passage as mimic man, the mythological wholeness of his inherited white body castrated in the unreliable fetish object of the mirror. What becomes clear in this mimic sidelining of the character Goggel thus, is a corresponding sidelining of Eurocentric myth. Both communicate a refusal of the Aryan-Germanic thesis as the subject incessantly transgresses its position before the mirror of European history, which itself is exposed as an expanding subtext of marginality, »an insurgent counter-appeal«.[63]

This strategy of transgression identified in the not quite German is reflected in the strategy of metalepsis (the transgression of narrative frame) announced by the impossible spiral of the opening sentence. It is fitting that a floating document such as *Das Goggelbuch* should be introduced by this perforated sentence that, similar to certain key constructions in *UND*, slides very easily

---

[59] Ibid., p. 74.
[60] Ibid., p. 77f.
[61] Ibid., p. 75–77.
[62] Ibid., p. 86.
[63] Ibid., p. 91.

outside itself. More relevant to the discussion of mimicry however, is the questioning of the frame that takes place in this sentence. As Bhabha points out, »the problem of identity returns as a persistent questioning of the frame« in the post-colonial text which introduces »the space of representation, where the image [...] is confronted with its difference, its Other«.[64] Identity is thus repeatedly negated in the post-colonial text as the seeing subject is split by the evil eye, a descendent of the Lacanian gaze that posits the observing/appropriating »master« subjects as observed/appropriated *speculum mundi* of an other's gaze. In other words, what Lacan describes as the »lethal factor« of the signifier's structure (the »elsewhere« and »other« indeterminacy of the signifier) comes into play in this disturbing reciprocity of the returned gaze (the evil eye), as the gap between eye and »I«, between the rim or the joining of the seen and the imagined substance of the given-to-be-seen, becomes apparent.[65] One could say that the frame of representation as part of an imposed analogic order that is premised on the dual desire to possess and to determine the world becomes visible in this moment of insight.

In the mimic text, the frame makes visible the above site of interdiction/ prohibition of the colonial gaze, the juncture at which the appropriated should be the same, but not quite. Thus the frame that can so easily be transgressed renders the invisible (the traces of mimic slippage and the fading inconsistencies of the subject) visible. That the frame emerges from the structure of the signifier is clear in this »petrification« of the subject as the inside-out bias of its vision is turned on its head in a movement that makes the subject the other of an other subject.[66] Lacan defines the signifier as »that which represents a subject for another signifier«, effectively laying the foundation for Bhabha's theory of colonial partial identity.[67] This realisation of one's relative and provisional identity exposes the ambivalence of colonial desire, the complex de-

---

[64] Ibid., p. 46.

[65] »The gaze is presented to us only in the form of a strange contingency, symbolic of what we find on the horizon, as the thrust of our experience, namely, the lack that constitutes castration anxiety.« (Lacan, The Four Fundamental Concepts of Psycho-Analysis [note 43], p. 72–73)

[66] Lacan views the formula *I see myself seeing myself* as correlative with the Cartesian cogito by which the subject apprehends itself as thought. It is this illusion – consciousness *seeing itself seeing itself* – that centres the seeing subject in a privileged (if ultimately untenable) position of knowledge and that forms the inside-out structure of the gaze (ibid., p. 80–82). By contrast, »the gaze in question is certainly the presence of others as such [...] does this mean that originally it is in the relation of subject to subject, in the function of the existence of others looking at me, that we apprehend what the gaze really is?« (ibid., p. 84). The movement of petrification goes hand in hand with the contingency of the gaze. It is the movement of the signifier (the gaze of the other) that reduces the subject in question to the status of signifier (an other caught in someone else's gaze) (ibid., p. 207).

[67] Ibid., p. 207. See Lacan's discussion of mimicry in ibid., p. 73–74. He comes to the conclusion that it is primarily a visual phenomenon.

mand that my other should resemble and confirm me but should also be different (other) to me (and therefore question the notion of me). At the heart of this predominantly scopic ambivalence – Lacan refers to this as the »belong-to-me« aspect of representation – lies a castration anxiety as the partial subject becomes aware of its invisibility, its signifier status.[68] For the other that slides outside the confines of appropriated otherness is a deadly reminder to the seeing subject of what Lacan terms the »factitious fact«, that is the disappearance and reappearance of the phallic signifier.[69] In post-colonial terms, this facticity of the signifier is similar to the inappropriate otherness of mimicry. Just this vanishing/reappearing movement of petrification describes the fading effect of aphanisis, the condition that applies to all subjects who are apprehended at birth in the field of the other.

Aphanisic petrification in *Das Goggelbuch* is initially suggested by the fading effect of the subclauses that transgress and perforate the main clause (italicised below) of the framing sentence:

> *Bei Ermittlung seines Ahnennachweises*, den Klaus Xaver Johann Guckelhupf, öffentlicher Notar, emsig und ehrlich zusammenzustellen im Begriffe stand und der ihn zunächst auf eine lange Reihe gleich und ähnlich benamster, zumeist dem Notarsstande angehöriger Blutsvorgänger führte, mit Ausnahme eines aus der Art gefallenen, der neben den noch bestehenden Erdteilen Eurasien, Afrika, Australien, Amerika und Antarktis auch noch das versunkene Eiland Atlantis anführte, das sich bisweilen neben die noch nicht untergegangenen als siebentes in unser Bewußtsein einschiebt, *kam schließlich der Nachforscher auf den letzterweislichen Urzeuger zurück*, der nicht einmal ein phantastischer Geograph oder Erdkundler gewesen, sondern kurzweg ein deutscher Diener mit dem einfachen Namen Xaver Johann Gottgetreu Goggel, der außerdem über sein Dasein in früher Neuzeit einen Bericht hinterlassen hatte, dessen Ursprünglichkeit auch noch durch die Bearbeitung dreier Notare und eines Erdkundlers seine nackte Haut zeigte, wie auch immer, wenn in Folianten gepreßt, die reine Einheit der Seele eines deutschen Dieners mit seinem Gotte, über den er trotz seinem Stande und seiner Zeit nicht allzulange nach Erfindung des Schießpulvers gehörig nachgedacht hat, sich urtümlich bekundet.   (*Goggelbuch* 245, my emphasis)

There is no mention of a mirror at this stage, yet the text is clearly thematising in a very roundabout way the issue of self-perception. From the vantage point of the twentieth century, an industrious search is launched into the distant past in pursuit of the origins of the Aryan self. That this search is an act of appalling *méconaissance* or scotoma (Lacan's optical term for the narcissistic illusion) is relentlessly evidenced in the meandering structure of the subclauses.[70] On the one hand, the text lists what could be understood as stereotypical traits of the stalwart German character, among them industriousness (*emsig*), honesty (*ehrlich*), the transparent/bare skin of the individual who shows himself as he

---

[68] Ibid., p. 81.
[69] Ibid., p. 70.
[70] Ibid., p. 83.

is (*nackte Haut*; *sich urtümlich bekundet*), and pious devotion or the simple unity of the German servant's soul with his God (*die reine Einheit der Seele eines deutschen Dieners mit seinem Gotte*).

On the other hand however, the immediacy of this wholesome and consistent understanding of self that unproblematically spans several centuries is continually pulverised by »the endless mill of speech« in which it is described.[71] The reader must rummage around the sentence to locate the practically invisible main clause that seems to be just as obscure as the textual source of Aryan identity mentioned in it. The twenty-three or so lines that comprise this sentence thus account for the »feint of writing« that is typical of the post-colonial offensive against images of the sovereign self. In the manner typical of aphanisis, each statement of a certain characteristic that would seem to suggest the presence and visibility of a solid Germanic self is slyly followed by an indirect but incisive reminder of the partial nature of this subject.

The petrification assault on the subject (the root of Aryan identity) that vaguely appears in the main clause only to be eclipsed in a tumult of myriad subclauses thus encapsulates the appearing/disappearing momentum of aphanisis. Any hopes for a narcissistic confirmation of the self in the forefathers of the past are decimated by the suggestion of otherness implied by the syntactical spaces of the subclauses, each of which seems to contradict (if not transgress) both frame and assertion of the previous clause. We are told by the first subordinate clause that Guckelhupf's search is conducted in an industrious, honest fashion and that he initially encounters self-affirming notary forefathers (he is also a notary) in the texts that he unearths. However, the second subordinate clause introduces the face of the other, the exception of one forefather who deviates from the norms of the family tree (*mit Ausnahme eines aus der Art ausgefallenen*), the mysterious geographer no less, who henceforth goes missing from the text.

Why this disappearance, one must ask oneself. A Jewish geographer perhaps, who must at all costs be deleted from the genealogical records? Is this vanishing an uncommented actualisation of Guckelhupf's peep-hopping editing prowess, his reluctance to fully see the traces of his own invisibility? The politically loaded language that describes this exception of profession in the incongruous terms of a deviation from the Guckelhupf *species* suggests also a racial (and racist understanding of) deviation. However, this subtle suggestion is not confirmed and one must draw the conclusion that this deliberate deletion is part of a prose strategy that creates gaps into which the implied reader may step and ponder in dialogue with the text.

It would thus seem that the dependable nature of Guckelhupf's notary ancestors is mentioned only to be eclipsed in the manner of aphanisis by the inconsistency of the geographer exception who, like the partial signifier that eclipses the self-seeking subject, himself disappears from the text. A sense of

---

[71] Michel Foucault: The History of Sexuality. The Will to Knowledge. London: Penguin Books 1998, p. 21.

uneasy ambiguity is therefore cast over the industriously executed search. Indeed, it would seem that these subclauses, as they proliferate and multiply like a nervous habit, communicate the pressure brought to bear on citizens of the Third Reich to seek and find a pure (if ironically prescribed) Aryan origin of the self. This pressure translates into the textual petrification of the ambivalent self who senses the possibility of castration (lack) at the heart of its quest for a conformist identity. The uneasiness of the petrified self can be identified in the jitteriness of the endless parenthesis that posits implicitly racist stereotypes, only to immediately erase (and therefore question) them.

Clearly, this kind of sentence structure refers back to a split narrative perspective that guides the text into aphanisis. The indecidability that is apparent from one clause to the next as the direction in focalisation continually shifts could be described as a kind of narrative ventriloquism. Just as the main clause is buried deep within the opening sentence, the location of the narrative voice remains obscure. The erasure of one subordinate clause by the next makes verbal the battling exchange between the voice that asserts identity and the voice that questions it. Narrative position thus too engages in an intense and unrelenting pulverisation of the »given-to-be-seen«.[72] Its hasty skidding action from one perspective to the next is reminiscent of the visual (and aural) flexibility of the carnivalesque text, not to mention the transgression of representative frames that is also typical of the threshold consciousness of carnival.[73]

That the text within the text does not ultimately return to the introductory frame of the twentieth century reinforces the sense of the above-mentioned narrative gap into which the reader may step. The open-endedness of this poorly embedded structure is a form of sentential non-completion that is typical for the text outside itself. In this case however, it is the frame that remains incomplete. The entire text (and not just the meandering opening sentence) is thus perforated, open-ended and, in the manner of carnival, potentially infinite. Indeed, it could be argued that the vagueness of the narrative position arises from the manoeuvres of a particularly wily implied author who orchestrates interpretative gaps for the reader. From this perspective, the entire text becomes the dialogic terrain of implied author and implied reader, a meta-textual strategy that subtly evokes the contact zone between self and other in a dialogue that relativises both.

This fundamentally dialogic prose strategy of ventriloquism structures the optical organisation of the entire text to follow: the peep-hopping (appearing/disappearing) of aphanisis that represents the spectacle of invisibility as the phallocentric »I« of Germanic origin dissolves into the incessantly roving evil eye of dual mimic vision. The seeking instance suggested by the Guckelhupf construct is thus little more than a personification of the petrified self that must contemplate the possibility of its illegitimate origins and under Hitler suffer the

---

[72] Lacan, The Four Fundamental Concepts of Psycho-Analysis (note 43), p. 74.
[73] Michail M. Bakhtin: Literatur und Karneval. Zur Romantheorie und Lachkultur. Frankfurt a. M: Fischer 1996 (Fischer-Taschenbücher; 7434: Fischer Wissenschaft), p. 75.

consequences: the certainty of castration in the form of extermination. A burlesque triumvirate of petrified positions that alternatively fear (edit) but inadvertently entertain castration links Guckelhupf to the ambivalent narrative voice(s)
and further to the equally dubious originary point: Goggel himself. It is little
wonder that the framing sentence should thematise the absence of identity as a
problem of the present when one considers that Guckelhupf's last identifiable
forefather is himself an aphanisic fader, a missing person who, as shall be demonstrated, merges almost invisibly with several other characters. The text thus
conducts its interrogation of identity via the interrogation of visibility by exposing the facticity of both the seeing (narrating) and seen (narrated) instances. In
this set-up, no single position seems to enjoy the upper hand of unilateral scopic
vision. Position (both narrated and narrating) is divided and transgressive, rendering all apparitions of subjectivity the other of an other's gaze.

Thus is the search for a past Aryan likeness of the present self antagonised by
the feint of language through which this search must necessarily be conducted.
The several references to the reports and volumes that form Guckelhupf's trail of
enquiry frustrate the elsewhere fatally posited notions of primordial identity. The
second onslaught of subclauses, which arrives immediately after the main clause
is (technically) completed, mercilessly pits narcissistic image of self (*Ursprüng-
lichkeit*; *nackte Haut*; *zeigen*; *reine Einheit der Seele*; *sich urtümlich bekunden*)
within and against the fragmenting effect of language (*einen Bericht hinterlas-
sen*; *die Bearbeitung dreier Notare und eines Erdkundlers*; *wenn auch in Folian-
ten gepreßt*). The function of the frame may be observed at work here as image
is confronted by its other: the difference and indecidability of identity that seems
to be a condition of language in general and of the signifier in particular. The
image of primordial identity is thus made the subject of scrutiny for an »other«
assessing and observing partial subject who, between the loose narrative nodes
of Guckelhupf and narrative perspective, registers the questionable founds of the
Germanic self.

This observing instance that effectively perforates the framing sentence (and
hence the frontier of the entire text) is the partial mimic signifier in action. It is in
effect the structure of alternative identity (inappropriate otherness or difference)
that is mimicry. It is also an approximation of the contact zone of mimic interdic-
tion that reverses the unilateral gaze of colonial scopic desire. However, whilst
the displacing returned gaze of the inappropriate other is here represented via
both ventriloquist unreliability and Guckelhupf's treacherous search for himself
in the age-old signifiers of dusty volumes, the »not quite« of inappropriate identity is specifically represented by the vacuous figure of the notionally Jewish
geographer and his preoccupation with the lost empire of Atlantis. Just as the
geographer forefather is a missing person whose mention nonetheless provisionally eclipses the emergence of the notary ancestors, so may his interest in the
legend of Atlantis be interpreted as a reminder of the mythical status of Eurocentric identity. Within the debate of the opening sentence the brief appearance of
Atlantis takes on a tone of foreboding. Firstly, Atlantis has always been lost in

the watery depths of an undetermined ocean. Secondly, its existence remains a speculative matter, the subject of text and debate but never ultimately proven.[74] Thirdly, *Das Goggelbuch* seems to suggest that a similar lost and irretrievable fate awaits the other significant land-masses of the world. Within the context of the Third Reich, this may be understood as the articulation of an apocalyptic cultural pessimism.

However, the juxtaposition of the mythical, speculative and lost Atlantis next to the rest of the world may also be read as a subtle diagnosis of the fictitious and highly narrated myth of cultural superiority. The dark downwards position of the drowned Atlantis suggests the fall of man from a position of illegitimately grasped ascendancy. That the Aryan myth of the Nazi vision is specifically targeted here should come as no surprise in a text that mentions the *Ahnennachweis* (proof of ancestry) in its first breath. The implication is that this font of Nordic purity like the missing, invisible and invented city of Atlantis is never quite within grasp but always elsewhere. The scopic drive of the Germanic self that seeks out its Aryan blueprint in the texts of bygone times encounters thus the returned gaze of lack in the otherness of the written word, configured here in the twin spectres of castration: the geographer and the lost empire of Atlantis.

Clearly, this sentence reveals a mode of syntactical organisation similar to that discussed in the previous chapter. It too seems to flaunt the paradox of paratactic logic masquerading as exaggerated hypotaxis. If this is the case, then the grammatical organisation of the sentence is also signalling to the reader that its message is to be found in the many contingent clauses and not in the main clause. In other words, the movement of petrification, the slide into contingency, deferral and displacement brings forth the shadow of the sequential relation that according to Bhabha is its tethered other. This at first glance invisible shadow heralds the beginnings of absence: the catachresis of the sign and the aphanisis of the self. It is thus entirely consistent that the geographer and Atlantis should appear (and fade) in the contingency of subclauses. The text suggests in its incidental way moreover, that both are afterthoughts appearing occasionally on the fringes of our consciousness. Whose consciousness, one would be justified in asking. One that regards itself as visually articulated? One that narcissistically sees itself seeing itself with no »other« interruptions? As if to completely refute this possibility, Guckelhupf himself is tainted by the shadowy face of his »other« ancestor. For he too is mentioned in this opening frame only to forever disappear in much the same manner as the geographer.

The deviant (geographer) and the conformist (notary) – two sides of one ill-posited self that incessantly eclipse each other and thereby disrupt the analogical

---

[74] One of the earliest references to Atlantis is in Plato's *Timaeus*. It features as a distant land situated »beyond the pillars of Herakles« in which there lived »a confederation of kings, of great and marvellous power« who ruled far and wide. »One grievous day and night befell them« and the earth swallowed up all warriors, »and the island of Atlantis in like manner was swallowed up by the sea and vanished« (Plato: Timaeus. London: Heinemann 1966, p. 42–43).

relation of resemblance. Again, we encounter the structure of difference that is mimic man, the articulation of the self along a metonymic axis that, similar to the tethered shadow of the sequential relation, is accompanied at all times by its disturbing other. Between the vague positions of Guckelhupf and the geographer, Guckelhupf and Goggel, Guckelhupf and the narrator, the contact zone of mimic prohibition appears and fades. The Eurocentric self emerges here in all its ambivalent ex-centricity as flickering aphanisis. In the moment where it attempts to investigate its origin it sees only its invisibility. This opening sentence suggests that the self is generated in the likeness of difference, that is, in the likeness of the factitious fact, the phallic signifier that disappears and reappears in a game that produces mimic man.

5.4 Aphanisic Faders

The representation of character in the text within the text »Das Goggelbuch« clearly personifies the notion of identity as mimic construct. This is not just true for Goggel himself but for the many characters he encounters on his wayward trip around Europe. The presumption of clearly demarcated subjectivity implied by Goggel's desire to become a master is refuted in the portrayal of intertwining characters that inevitably fade only to unexpectedly reappear throughout his story. In effect, these characters externalise the different elements of subservience and majesty that clamour for space within the Goggel construct. By no means does this imply that the sixteenth century Europe portrayed can be reduced to the outer reflection of an individual schizophrenic state, however. Similar to Guckelhupf, Goggel is not so much an individual subject as a discursive construct through which a debate on power, subservience and authenticity is conducted.

This debate illuminates the extent to which Goggel is inconsistent with the image of identity through which he perceives himself. An indentured other (servant), he wishes to be »the same« as the master figure who in the function of appropriator appears to assign all positions on the hierarchical scale. This desire signifies two aspects of Goggel's character. Firstly, it indicates the uncritical acceptance of a social stereotype that categorises the world according to the master/slave binary opposition. He is thus articulated as an unthinking member of the masses who understands society in terms of this radically asymmetrical and implicitly racist stereotype. Secondly, in a text that clearly cites the primitive law of the survival of the fittest, the desire to be the master of others suggests the profile of a tyrant in the making.[75]

---

[75] »[Goggel] denkt [...] besser fressen als gefressen werden und handelt, wie er denkt« (*Goggelbuch* 293). This mentality is objectified (and parodied) in Goggel's treatment of his dog, Wonnemund: »Abgehend äußert er sich noch zu seinem räudigen Rüden, welcher Wonnemund heißt, er sei ein zumeist läufiges Luder [...]. Mithin verabfolge er ihm einen Tritt. Aber er tut dies vielleicht, weil der Hund unter ihm steht, wie er selbst den Tritten seines Herrn ausgesetzt bleibt.« (Ibid., p. 247–248)

With these nuances in mind, Goggel's portrayal is one of complete mediocrity and dullness of intellect, underscored by a mulish determination to lord it
over the others of his society. In social reality an inferior, Goggel is nonetheless convinced that as a descendent of the Nibelungs he is truly a member of
the master race. As such, he must only bide his time until the truth of his identity is actualised in social terms. This racist understanding of identity derives
from a mythological notion of past tribal greatness that is waiting to rise again.
For Goggel, identity is the straightforward position of superiority over others
justified by a glorious past that is, according to myth, teleologically driven
towards an equally glorious future.[76]

Ostensibly a figure from the late sixteenth century, one would be justified in
asking whether Goggel, in terms of his cultural-psychological make-up, is not
a devoted citizen of the Third Reich. Upon closer reading of the text, there is
no doubt that he and many other characters exemplify elements of the narcissistic, paranoid and ultimately unenlightened personality type identified by
Adorno as the lynchpin of Nazi society. One must ask oneself whether the
potentially tyrannical, ambitious but fatally stupid aspects of the Goggel character do not combine to present us with what is intended as a parody of the
Hitler prototype: a mediocre character with grandiose visions of himself based
on a crude understanding of fictional texts from the past.[77]

However, in this desire to become a master, Goggel is constantly confronted
by the inconsistent »not quite« element of his personality that time and again
displays his identity through the image of difference. This »not quite« interruption is signified by the slippage of stereotypes that prove to be less fixed than implied by his simplistic understanding of society and the positioning of its members. Despite his best efforts to emulate the master figure, Goggel is doomed to
scrutiny under the gaze of the evil eye, destined to be a missing person and
riddled by aphanisis. The more he endeavours to usurp the master role (in Goggel's unperceptive eyes a vision of power-oriented homogeneity), the more severely he is »petrified« by a series of adventures that precipitate his experience

---

[76] »Seiner Meinung nach sei Siegfried ein Nibelunge erst geworden durch Beraubung
und Ermordung des früheren Inhabers seines späteren Hortes [...] Ein Diener könne
auch immerhin die Sprosse seines Herrn erklettern, [...] bis [...] Nibelungenhort und
-namen schließlich in die Dienerschürze glitten.« (Ibid., p. 247)

[77] Adorno's profile of the paranoid individual of the fascist state could be understood
as a pathological corruption of the analogical relation: »Indem der Paranoiker die
Außenwelt nur perzipiert, wie es seinen blinden Zwecken entspricht, vermag er immer nur sein zur abstrakten Sucht entäußertes Selbst zu wiederholen. Das nackte
Schema der Macht als solcher, gleich überwältigend gegen andere wie gegen das eigene mit sich zerfallene Ich, ergreift, was sich ihm bietet, und fügt es, ganz gleich-
gültig gegen seine Eigenart, in sein mythisches Gewebe ein. Die Geschlossenheit
des Immergleichen wird zum Surrogat von Allmacht. Es ist, als hätte die Schlange,
die den ersten Menschen sagte: ihr werdet sein wie Gott, im Paranoiker ihr Verspre-
chen eingelöst.« (Max Horkheimer / Theodor W. Adorno: Dialektik der Aufklärung.
Philosophische Fragmente. Frankfurt a. M.: Fischer 1991, p. 199–200)

of mimicry. His grandiose ideals of selfhood are continually disrupted by the seedy reality of his person and his social standing. He seems destined always to be returned to the place he so scorns: the position of abject other, reviled and despised by all.[78]

Nothing remains in place on the greasy vertical pole of cultural identity in »Das Goggelbuch« it would seem. Clearly, the positions that constitute this hierarchy (tyrannical master, gormless middle-man and reviled other) represent a pastiche of Nazi discourse bluntly reconfigured in a seemingly arbitrary sixteenth century context. The carnivalesque slide of positions experienced by the main protagonist challenges the Nazi world view of Aryan superiority. Goggel's petrification thus takes the form of carnivalesque rough and tumble as his character, contrary to his lofty expectations, is only ever partially articulated. In this manner, Drach again expresses identity as a structure of difference that stealthily undermines the uniform positions that conform to the Nazi organisation of society The fudging of the subject's frontiers in the Goggel hybrid conducts at the level of character an interrogation of identity and frames similar to that conducted at the level of the text's general structure. If an image of identity may at all be observed therefore, then it is the non-image of invisibility that questions the presumption of irrefutable presence at the heart of Goggel's self-understanding.

Within the dual historical framework of the entire text which elliptically connects early modern Europe to Nazi Germany, *Das Goggelbuch* thus examines the origins of the Eurocentric personality with particular attention to the Aryan construct of selfhood. Moreover, it suggests that the question of the lofty origins of this self is not primarily a matter of past history, but more a concern of present readings of the past that are dangerously selective, conveniently myopic and under the influence of ideologies contemporary to Nazi society. This perspective is clearly elaborated in the bizarre constellation of phantom readers of the past that structures the different frames of the text. The reader is challenged by the mise-en-abyme of interpreting/looking positions that come to light via Goggel and Guckelhupf. For Guckelhupf is introduced to us in the mode of reading Goggel's journal who himself is engaged in an active, if dangerously simplified, reading of texts that construct his cultural past. Both would appear to be practitioners of the peep-hopping optical mode. The overall impression is one of half-digested legends of the past that are regurgitated in a certain manner by inhabitants of the present (whether early modern Europe or Nazi Germany) with the express purpose of justifying contemporary actions.

Through these different portrayals of selective misreading and wilful *méconnaissance* of difference, this text also functions as a commentary on the negative consequences of stupidity. Drach's dialogic invitation to the reader discussed in the previous section may thus be interpreted as an argument for independent

---

[78] Kristeva describes the life of the abject individual as one defined by exclusion. This is the case for Goggel who never truly penetrates the upper echelons of social organisation (Kristeva, Powers of Horror [note 26], p. 6).

thought, a warning that the individual should be at all times critically aware of its cultural baggage. Stupidity is represented by the Goggel/Guckelhupf protagonists who unthinkingly follow the dictates of their respective societies. An important subtext of *Das Goggelbuch* is thus the responsibility involved in the act of reading the past and thereby coming to certain understandings of the self in the present. In this way, Drach presents his reader with a model of the Germanic self derived not so much from a detailed understanding of the past as from a crude reading of the past from the perspective of the Nazi present.

One could furthermore argue that the aphanisic offensive against the main protagonist represents an alternative model of critical self-contemplation which, in the contemporary context, writes against the amnesiac whitewashing of Austria's recent Nazi past. Goggel's absurd trip on the merry-go-round of identity functions in this way as a subtle writing against forgetting. In this desire to awaken from false complacency the inhabitants of the Austria that Drach describes as a nation of informers and whistleblowers, one may well recognise the contained outrage of the Nazi victim survivor who, upon return from exile, encounters levels of anti-Semitism similar to those experienced in the pre-war years.[79]

Set in the early modern Europe of the Eighty Years War between the Dutch and the Spanish, Goggel's adventures begin roughly in 1574 ending in 1581 shortly after the victory of Utrecht. The Great Age of European Discovery is well established, the Spanish and Portuguese having colonised parts of Africa, Asia and the Americas. However, the backdrop of the Eighty Years War in this text hints at the victory of the Dutch over the Spanish in the next century and their ascendancy to the much desired position of Europe's greatest seafaring nation.[80]

Drach's choice of early modern Europe for a veiled discussion of Nazi and post-Nazi society makes sense when one considers that his portrayal of the

---

[79] Albert Drach: Martyrium eines Unheiligen, in: id., Die kleinen Protokolle und das Goggelbuch (note 2), p. 133–185, here p. 172. For a discussion of the politics of Austrian memory, see Lutz Musner: Memory and Globalization. Austria's Recycling of the Nazi Past and its European Echoes. In: New German Critique 80 (2000), p. 77–92. Musner states that the Austrian postwar coalitions favoured a politics of amnesia with regard to the Nazi past and that this whitewashing further reflects one of the central myths of postwar Austrian identity: that of self-victimisation resulting in the refusal to take full responsibility for collaboration with the Nazis. This politics of remembering has not entirely disappeared; Musner notes the continuance of the myth of self-victimisation in Kurt Waldheim's indignation and more recently in Haider's defence of the SS and the Wehrmacht (p. 83).

[80] When Goggel first arrives in Osnabrück, the Dutch are canvassing for volunteers in the war against Spain (Goggelbuch 263). Later, he signs up with the Spanish army and then switches sides to the Dutch, participating in the victory at Utrecht (ibid., p. 297). This latter historical event situates the story in the period between 1574 and 1581; the seven northern provinces of the Netherlands grouped together in 1579 and formed the Union of Utrecht against Spain. In 1581, they declared themselves independent of Spanish Succession (Brockhaus-Enzyklopädie in 24 Bänden. 19., völlig neu bearb. Aufl., Mannheim: Brockhaus 1986–1995, vol. 23 [1994], p. 20).

domestic battle for ascendancy notably concerns the most powerful European colonial nations of that time. By framing early modern Europe within the Nazi context, Drach implies that the anti-Semitic society of Guckelhupf's era is the inevitable outcome of a continent accustomed to conquering and appropriating others. That Guckelhupf casts his eyes backwards from the brink of another war in the twentieth century suggests a continuum of European violence that has developed unhindered since the Middle Ages and before. The laconic reference to the invention of gunpowder in the opening sentence backs this up; Goggel existed not too long after this landmark discovery. One cannot help but feel that from the atomic perspective of twentieth century warfare, a slippery slope towards self destruction was activated by the German monk who is reputed to have invented gunpowder in the fourteenth century. Again Drach presents European history, somewhat fatally one might argue, through a caricature of the paranoid Eurocentric personality that at times bears an uncanny resemblance to the anti-Semite of Nazi society.[81]

Within this context, it is unsurprising that any traces of Renaissance thought are twisted to suit the ends of the would-be master personality. This is evident in Goggel's position as he sets out to enter the service of his master. We are told that he is not born to the aristocracy but nevertheless intends to carve out his own path to power. His desire is to succeed to the position of master and the perceived centre of power by cunning and trickery. In a parody of the warring nations through which he travels and of which he is only vaguely aware, he intends to become a master, not by learning or self-improvement as would befit a Renaissance man, but quite simply and in keeping with the war discourse of his time by ousting his master at an opportune moment and usurping his role:

> Ein Diener könne auch immerhin die Sprosse des Herrn erklettern, wenn jener diesem lange die Leiter halte, dabei unmerklich schüttle, bis, freilich in zunächst geringfügigen, aber zuletzt sehr fühlbaren Brocken, die sich, spät wieder aufgeweicht, zu einem stattlichen Laib wiederknetet, Nibelungenhort und -namen schließlich in die Dienerschürze glitten. (*Goggelbuch* 247)

Behind Goggel's ambition lurks one indisputable truth: that the only position worth occupying in the early modern Europe of discovery, colonial expansion and wars on the home front is emphatically that of the master. These European events that are inadvertently mentioned by the text appear to be caricatured in the ridiculous figure of Goggel and his above burning desire for ascendancy. Translated into the twentieth century context, this desire assumes the ominous overtures of the Nazi vision of an Aryan master race. Bearing this in mind, it can again be argued that in the bizarre world of Goggel we encounter certain traits of Nazi society, overlain by the more parochial concerns of Goggel's character certainly, but nevertheless present as a cloaked premonition for the more or less discerning eyes of those descendants who may read Goggel's journal.

---

[81] The monk in question was a certain B. Schwarz. He discovered gunpowder in Europe in 1320, but it had been discovered earlier in China (ibid., vol 19, p. 344).

The counter-narrative of aphanisis utterly ridicules these assumptions of identity in a number of ways, however. Firstly, there is the bizarre map of Europe that is articulated by Goggel's trip. He sets out from his homestead in an unspecified location somewhere to the north-east of Lüneburg. His goal is Osnabrück and the residence of Herr von Hahnentritt. He follows a meandering trail through the towns of Lüneburg and Braunschweig before he reaches Osnabrück. However, he is a wanted criminal by the time he arrives at his destination. Taken prisoner and put on trial, he becomes a member of a chain gang that travels in bondage to Spain. Spending seven years in Seville, Goggel eventually returns to Osnabrück via Straßburg and Paris.

Despite his best intentions to scale the heights of the social hierarchy, the downwards direction of Goggel's journey delivers him continually into the doldrums. This is communicated by the first noteworthy event on his trip. Hitching a lift on a farmer's wagon, his journey is halted by three highwaymen disguised as carnival fools. Stealing the vehicle, they take farmer and wife hostage as Goggel is left behind to continue his trip on foot:

> Damit ist dem Tüchtigen die Bahn wiederfreigegeben, der sich holpernd heidenwärts nach dem fernen Osnabrück in Marsch setzt.   (*Goggelbuch* 250)

Significantly, Goggel's goal has receded somewhat after this mishap. The text also hints that he will have to traverse some moors in order to get to Osnabrück. Thus the straightforward trip that should have brought him to his destination is already coming apart at the seams, and the moors towards which Goggel stumbles (*holpernd*), symbolise the orientational difficulties he will soon (and thereafter constantly) encounter. For shortly after his second tryst with the fool thieves in the carnival celebrations of Lüneburg, Goggel embarks on his journey across this vague, unpunctuated terrain. However, in order to understand the significance of this strange phase of his outlandish journey, a short summary of events in Lüneburg is necessary.

Shortly after the first attack, Goggel falls asleep on a rubbish heap and is discovered by a bearded man who carries him off to the nearest village. All inhabitants believe him to be royalty because of his fine livery. Goggel goes along with the ruse, both enjoying and abusing the mayor's hospitality; in a fit of temper, he smashes a valuable Chinese vase. Thus it would seem that he metamorphoses all too easily into the role of tyrant; his fine garments and the adulation of undiscerning others seduce him into the identity of master. Indeed, when he leaves this village in the mayor's carriage, the stumbling steps of the disoriented Goggel seem very distant.[82]

Just as rapidly as his fortunes seemed to change for the better, on arrival in Lüneburg they immediately take a turn for the worse. For his fantasy throning undergoes a carnivalesque reversal when the selfsame fools happen upon him in the street, kick him into the gutter and force him to‚drink out of the sewer.

---

[82] »Fürst Goggel jedoch begehrt Gespann und Gefährt und Geschirr bis über die Heide nebst dreien Knechten zu seinem leiblichen Schutz.« (*Goggelbuch* 253)

Not only does this incident have all the classic ingredients of a Bakhtinian topp-ling of the carnival king, it also contains the rather familiar details of grotesque bodily materialism. The overall downward thrust of Goggel's ill-fated, south-bound European trip is condensed in the indignity of the fool's kick which sends him flying into the dirt. The gutter image also connects with the carniva-lesque »low« location of the rubbish heap upon which Goggel collapsed before being raised to the status of a prince.[83]

The kicking index is itself worthy of contemplation. It is the one action that remains constant throughout the tale, as Goggel time and again asserts his au-thority by kicking his faithful hound, Wonnemund. It is a slap-stick gesture that occurs in rotation, for as we have seen Goggel is also not immune from the kick-ing action of others. Beyond carnival however, the kicking motif may be read as the caricatured performance of the culturally determinate body: the body of negation. It is the comic symbol of a violent assertion of the self over the appro-priated other and so enounces the vertical body of authority that is demarcated between the poles of »high« and »low«. This form of subjectivity articulates the master's body, nowhere more clearly signaled than in the name of Goggel's master, Herr von Hahnen*tritt*. From the top down thus, this society is defined by an aggressive attitude towards the other, violently excluding it (kicking it out of vision), but by the same token appropriating/situating it in this very act. For this reason, the kicking index may be read as a parody of thetic positioning as the other is appropriated/negated into a »safe« symbolic cell.

However, the authoritarian kicking reflex is overwritten by the body of negativ-ity implied by the constant carnivalesque transgression of position. Consistent with this, Goggel's carnivalesque degradation in the sewer is swiftly followed by an-other rethroning episode. He finds an inn and is promptly mistaken by the owners for an individual of some importance. Again, his livery is the essential ingredient in this misunderstanding and again, the prospect of power turns Goggel into a brute; he rapes the landlord's daughters and then resumes his journey in a coach for which he has no intention of paying.[84] This is the point at which he comes to the moors. Significantly, the trip takes on a dream-like quality in this space:

---

[83] Goggel's degradation in the sewer is conducted through an act of the grotesque bodily drama: »Goggel fällt davon in die Gosse und leckt an derselben, wiewohl diese von er-lustigten Narren sogleich mit ihrem gelassenen Wasser erweitert wird.« (Ibid., p. 254). His confrontation with the fools thus reinforces the carnivalesque law concerning as-cendancy: »Durch die Krönung und die Erhöhung schimmert von Anfang an die Er-niedrigung hindurch.« (Bakhtin, Literatur und Karneval [note 73], p. 51)

[84] Drach uses this episode to further critique the categorisation of society into the domi-nated and the dominating: »Sie wimmert wie eine gequetschte Katze, und er läßt es gerne gelten, denn die Liebe ist ein Gemetzel für den deutschen Mann, und wehe der Unterliegenden. Doch wiederholt er seine Gunst an der anderen und läßt auch sie noch einmal solche Wonne kosten. Dann geht er ohne Dank.« (*Goggelbuch* 256) Goggel fulfils in this situation several criteria of Adorno's unlightened post-Auschwitz indivi-dual. His behaviour expounds the basic anthropological traits fundamental to this per-sonality: the ideal of hardness/severity (Ideal der Härte) and coldness (Theodor W.

> Das Gefährt läßt er sich von einem Buben holen und jagt den mit dem Hund, als er
> auf den Groschen wartet. Und so guten Werks wohlgemüt, läßt er sich über die Heide
> fahren, wiegt sich in neuen Träumen, doch wechselt ihm lustiges Rülpsen mit häßli-
> chem Husten. Aber wie die breite Heide noch im Zwielicht liegt, überholt ihn ein
> schlankes Gespann mit drei Narren drin. [...] Der mittlere Herr, den er leider schon
> kennt (es muß der Narrenkönig gewesen sein, der ihn auch zum Pfütschenschlecken
> veranlaßt hat), springt vom Bock, heißt Goggels Fuhrwerk anhalten, verlangt den
> Knechten den Flinten ab, die sie willig liefern. Somit befiehlt er Goggeln, abzustei-
> gen, weil ja ein Diener nicht in Karossen fahre, der Narrenkönig aber schon. Goggel
> staunt seinen Entlarver an.   (*Goggelbuch* 256)

In this manner, yet another dethroning is effected and Goggel finds himself in
the same position as several stages earlier on his journey: on foot, a few coins
poorer and on the lower end of the social hierarchy. The identity of his discov-
erer remains a mystery to him, but for Goggel the impression takes hold that
this figure sees through him and will frustrate his plans wherever possible.[85]
How should we read the fool king? This is a point that I will return to later, for
it is insufficient to read this figure as a solo apparition.

It would seem however, that the pattern of Goggel's journey takes on the
rhythm of constant carnival as he skids about the vertical pole of social organisation. That Drach puts him through these moves communicates a central concern of the text. Position is presented as a matter of chance, fortune, cheating
and opportunism. This insight matters little in a society that evaluates individuals according not even to position per se, but to the appearance of position
as communicated by dress or behaviour. Drach thereby profiles a public who
understands power only in the most superficial of ways. The mayor's gormless
acceptance of Goggel the impersonator into his home is one such example of
this semi-literacy.[86] Against this backdrop, the fool-king as Goggel's discov-
erer (*Entlarver*) seems to be the only individual versed in the workings of
power. As a power sceptic, it is no accident that he is a representative of carnival.

Alone on the moor, Goggel now seriously begins to doubt that he will ever
arrive at his destination:

> Sowie er aber geht, wird die Heide immer breiter und weiter mit jedem Schritt, und
> er weiß bereits, daß er nicht ankommt.   (*Goggelbuch* 257)

   Adorno: Erziehung nach Auschwitz. In: id., »Ob nach Auschwitz noch sich leben
   lasse«. Ein philosophisches Lesebuch. Hg. von Rolf Tiedemann. Frankfurt a. M.:
   Suhrkamp 1997 [Edition Suhrkamp; N. F. 844], p. 48–63, here p. 56–60)

[85] »Und im Zuge dieses Grübelns geht ihm ein schwaches Licht auf, dieser Mann
   müsse mehr von ihm wissen als er selber vermeine [...] dieser sei ein Schnüffler und
   gefährlich und ihm über, denn er treffe seine Schwächen.« (*Goggelbuch* 257)

[86] This mindless devotion to his lord emerges as the defining principle of the mayor's
   life and behaviour towards the other: »Der Bürgermeister [...] betont, nicht immer
   im Dorf gewesen zu sein, Kriege gegen Türken und Juden ausgefochten zu haben,
   den letzteren sein Weib, jetzt Agnes, früher Chanah, abgewonnen habend, nun auf
   ererbtes und erzinstes Gut zurückgezogen, nur noch den Segnungen seines Fürsten
   lebend.« (Ibid., p. 253)

One could argue that the above wayward direction of the trip is condensed in the vagueness of the moor and that this space of misfortune between Lüneburg and Braunschweig constitutes a deconstructive gap, not just in Goggel himself, but in the geographical terrain he travels through on his journey. In effect, the manner in which Europe is mapped in »Das Goggelbuch« communicates lack of centre and lack of orientation. Thus even the territorial mapping that is evident in the tale performs the body of mimicry. For if one were to consider Goggel's ultimate goal of usurping the master position in the social order as an articulation of the vertical symbolic hierarchy, then the above descriptions of geographical space and spatial location signify the transgression of this hierarchy. It is not just the character Goggel who undergoes constant metamorphoses in this instance; the geographical body of Europe is shown through Goggel's journey to be on a downward trend.

Beyond this sense of inevitable descent however, the defining spatial location of »Das Goggelbuch« is the edge of the moor (*am Heidebeginn*). A borderline area between the inhabited world and the twilight world of space without demarcation, it is the territorial embodiment of mimic man. It represents the spatial experience of mimic man: the shift from verticality to the horizontal. In other words, the moor is an in-between space that disrupts the verticality of Goggel's upwardly mobile journey. Furthermore, there is a sense in which the moor space functions as a latent motif for all other locations on the trip. The carnivalesque coronations and degradations experienced in the more clearly defined urban centre of Lüneburg bear this out. For there is no reason why Goggel, if we are to take him as mimic man, should ever escape the in-between. Kristeva argues that the essential activity of the subject-in-process is the appending of territories.[87] If we understand mimic man as a manifestation of semiotic interference in the symbolic, then Goggel on his journey is constantly appending (and losing) territories, be they imaginary positions on the social ladder, rooms in inns or prison cells, jobs and possessions.[88] The dizzying carnivalesque rotation along with the reversal of the kicking index are signifiers of this activity as one position is exchanged for the other.

Most significantly of all, the moor is also a space in which aphanisis takes place. Gloomily lit and unmarked, it is an appropriate setting for the disappearance of self and the encounter with the other. One could regard the carnival fool as just this other who interrupts Goggel's journey and returns him to a position of ambivalence. Thus Goggel fades from the »not quite« supremacy of the carnival king to an undefined entity on the moor. In the manner typical for aphanisis however, no sooner has Goggel been reduced to this indetermi-

---

[87] Kristeva, Revolution in Poetic Language (note 21), p. 102.

[88] Goggel loses Wonnemund for the seven years he spends in Spain (*Goggelbuch* 274–275). Likewise, he loses Emma and all his possessions in a poker game just outside Osnabrück (ibid., p. 261). In Spain, he goes from the service of de Tenorio to the service of de Manara (ibid., p. 282). Back in Holland, he switches from the Spanish army to the Dutch (ibid., p. 296–297).

nate state than the instigator of this metamorphosis (the carnival fool other) disappears in the fog. Goggel has been eclipsed by an apparition of the other that is itself disappearing and is left to grumble aloud to himself in the dark.[89] In this way, the text articulates the fool as another facet of the mimic personality. If we were to regard Goggel as the aspect of mimic man that continually experiences the disorientation of the returned gaze of the other, then the fool functions as that aspect that turns to menace: the set of evil eyes that keep the myopic Goggel in their field of vision and force him to constantly experience the fading of his symbolic post, »I«.

This suspicion is borne out by the grand finale meeting with Herr von Hahnentritt at the end of the text. He admits to engineering Goggel's trip from the start and reveals that he was indeed the carnival fool. Thus the figures of master and fool are conflated in the baron's personality and Goggel as mimic man emerges in the in-between of this hybrid. For this reason, the fool represents part of a grotesque hybrid and cannot therefore be contemplated in isolation. Hahnentritt's words convey the exact nature of who he is: an embodiment of the psychic gap or lack that constitutes the ambivalent subject of mimic man. Thus Goggel is not and never has been an apprentice of the master. Because the »master« himself embodies the in-between space of mimicry, Goggel has only ever been an apprentice mimic man:

> Er [Hahnentritt] sei der Irrtum im Weltgeschehen, die Fehlerquelle in der allgemeinen Ordnung, die Verwirrung der verankerten Gedanken sowie die der lose herumschwimmenden, der Zufall, der die Schlüsse in Frage stelle.   (*Goggelbuch* 302)

The above tells us that the vertical structure of power is a purely ideological construct. In practice, the position of ascendancy is subject to the same inconsistencies as those who revere or fear it. The general field of characterisation in the text bears this out. At the top of the social order sits Goggel's invisible master, Herr von Hahnentritt. The fact that Goggel never finds him (in the last minute it is in fact Goggel who is found by von Hahnentritt's chief servant) implies that the ideological space of the master is for the main part empty. If it is at all occupied, then only briefly by ambitious upwardly mobile impersonators like Goggel. In the text, this space never appears to be fully inhabited by a reliable point of presence that would, in accordance with the analogical relation, organise all others in its likeness. Thus the absence of the master figure introduces the structure of difference as a defining principle of Goggel's world. The search for a phallocentric figure such as the master yields only vague and transient approximations of identity as the factitious fact of phallic ambivalence frustrates the ideal of presence. Goggel's quest for himself in the authoritative figure of the master patriarch is in this way burdened by absence from the outset.

On the same level as the German lord are the two Spanish Don Juans who also remain largely invisible to the Goggel who serves in their respective house-

---

[89] »[...] trotzdem und mit Inbegrimm bewegt er sich hinter der guten Karosse, die bald im Nebel verschwindet. Seine Gedanken schleifen und zerren ihn. (ibid.).

holds over a period of seven years.[90] Thus the master figure partially appears in multiple guises, but due to its disappearing prowess, it avoids what was in the last chapter termed denotation in the signified. Instead, it proliferates as a signifier of constantly eclipsing presence and absence that connotes only the difference of a figure that is initially envisaged by the impressionable Goggel as a fully posited point of identity. The facelessness of Herr von Hahnentritt is perhaps the most profound signifier of this absence. However, this anonymity connects von Hahnentritt (and by association the two Don Juans) to the masked fool who also never reveals his identity to Goggel. This connection of the culturally »high« to the culturally »low« constitutes a transgression that further explains the lack of a master signifier that would order the vertical pole of social organisation somewhat more effectively.

The aphanisis of the symbolic subject is communicated in other ways, however. Indeed, the aphanisis of apparel is one of the chief signifiers of invisibility in »Das Goggelbuch«. If one were to understand costume as an outer boundary of personhood, a skin of sorts, then what emerges through the semiotics of attire in this tale is an image of the thin-skinned body. Through clothing, Goggel fades from one identity to another as an in-between contact zone opens up between one character and the next. When one considers that in the first instance identity is organised according to a vertical pole of increasing subordination, this type of fading comes to represent a deconstructive politics of mimicry through which the master position in particular is articulated as completely inauthentic. The subtext that critiques Nazism becomes clear in this regard as Drach highlights how those who ascend to positions of power are little more than cheats, thieves and impersonators.

An episode in Seville whilst in the service of Don Juan de Manara highlights just this slipperiness of the master figure through the discourse of clothing. Goggel watches in horror as de Manara metamorphoses into a duplicate of himself purely by dressing in Goggel's servant robe:

> Im Saal angekommen, [...] wird nun auch Goggel alsbald seines Gewandes beraubt, und zwar von den Damen [...]. Don Juan verlangt den Damen dieses Kleid ab, zieht sich dann einen Augenblick zurück und kehrt als Goggel wieder, so zwar, daß er nicht nur dessen Gewandung anhat, sondern auch sein Gesicht auf Goggelart verstellt. (*Goggelbuch* 285).

Even de Manara's face has grotesquely become Goggel's. Perhaps for the first time Goggel here clearly beholds the invisibility of the master figure that is eclipsed by an impersonation of himself, the servant figure. The invisibility of

---

[90] This absence of the master is communicated by the facelessness of Goggel's first superior in Spain, Don Juan de Tenorio: »Mitnichten erhält er seinen Oberherrn selbst zu Gesicht, noch wird er zu Diensten verwendet, die ihm Monsieur Sganarell in Aussicht gestellt [...]. Vergebens wartet er anderer Anordnungen zu ihm angekündigtem Wohlgefallen seines Herrn, der für ihn auch weiterhin unsichtbar bleibt.« (ibid., p. 275)

the master figure as displayed by de Manara's impersonation thus shows Goggel a disturbing image of his own invisibility. This is a double blow for the main protagonist who has thus far mulishly presumed (if not experienced) the fixity of the self. Instead, he now beholds the ambivalent fading point of both stereotypes (master/slave) which implies that he briefly regards the world through the cracked goggles of the evil eye. In a text that largely narrates wilful stupidity, misreading and myopia, this scene represents a rare case of literacy as the emptiness of Goggel's goals becomes clear even to him. For it is implied that once enslaved to the myth of mastery, one no longer truly inhabits one's own body. Rather, it has been appropriated by another. However true to amnesiac type, Goggel suppresses the implications of this insight and thereafter reverts to his want-to-be self.[91]

Goggel's trial in Osnabrück is a reverse enactment of the above scene. He is accused of many crimes, one of which is the theft of von Hahnentritt's livery. It is thus implied that Goggel has tried to »steal« his position of increased stature in the social hierarchy. Whilst the text suggests that those in positions of actual power like von Hahnentritt are little more than impersonators, it also suggests that these figures are highly intolerant of others who may also want to cheat their way to the top. Goggel is accordingly found guilty, but not before he is also accused of being the masked carnival fool/thief. To this end, he must try on the fool's robe in court which fits him like a second skin. Thus Goggel once again slides into the identity of fool. That de Manara, via the servant's robe, so easily slides into Goggel's identity links him as master figure to the figure of the fool. Thus the simple and rather bland garment of the robe reiterates in the semiotics of clothing the borderline space identified in the spatial semiotics of the moor. The fool, the servant and the master are not separate entities but partial selves that articulate the ambivalence of mimic man through the trompe l'œil effect of the robes.[92]

Further confirming the terminal absence of the master figure are the chief servants of each aristocrat: Emerandus Ungefähr, Monsieur Sganarell and Leporello. The latter figure is the least complex. He mainly personifies the cowering subservience that constitutes much of Goggel's character. However, the name Ungefähr (*Thereabouts*) announces the general state of personhood in »Das Goggelbuch« where like de Manara and Goggel, characters fade into one another despite their positioning on the vertical axis of social organisation. It is also significant that the character closest to the absent Hahnentritt is presented through his

---

[91] His savage beating of Wonnemund, the innkeeper's daughter Emma and his one son shortly after leaving Seville confirms this regression (ibid., p. 300).

[92] Das Narrengewand, das ihm wie angegossen passen müsse, legen sie auf dem Tisch. Täter sei entwischt, hier sei der Täter. Goggel [...] beteuert den Narren in diesem Gewand gesehen zu haben, und wird hierauf vom Richter scharf befragt, warum er ihn dann nicht gestellt und der Wache übergeben. Goggel erklärt, es sei das über seine Kraft gewesen, worauf er das Gewand probieren muß und sich zeigt, daß es nirgends Falten wirft und auf seinen Leib geradezu geschnitten sei.« (Ibid., p. 268)

name as the personification of ambiguity. Paralleling Hahnentritt's single appearance at the end of the tale, Ungefähr only shows up twice throughout the course of the narrative. This constellation of increasing stature that correlates with increasing absence suggests that the closer one appears to approximate the sovereign position, the more blurred and less visible it becomes.[93]

Sganarell too personifies just this predicament of the fading »I«. The French chief servant of Don Juan de Tenorio, the intricacies of Sganarell's personality confirm the vagueness suggested by Ungefähr's name. Goggel first encounters Sganarell at the Schelde river estuary. He had been expecting to meet the carnival fool here whose parting words as he disappeared into the fog on the heath instructed Goggel to meet him here. In this manner, the text yet again suggests (but does not confirm) that Sganarell is the fool in disguise. Goggel has had no intention of coming this far, but arrested, put on trial and banished to the chain gang, he has ended up at this meeting point. At the river's estuary, an aristocratic looking man approaches Goggel and asks him to join the de Tenorio household in a servant capacity. Goggel believes he beholds the master, but in fact this person is Sganarell who is merely a high-ranking servant. Under Sganarell's guidance Goggel boards a galley ship for Spain and, never having located Hahnentritt in Osnabrück, now enters the service of a different master (*Goggelbuch* 271–272).

This may seem like a relatively straightforward episode. However, Sganarell presents an interesting point of ambivalent characterisation. His personality does not confine itself to the frontiers laid down by elevated indenture. Instead, the text subtly implies via the semiotics of clothing that the oppositional personalities of Goggel and the Spanish lord de Tenorio are pulverised in the ambivalent personality of Sganarell. For the latter functions as an obscurely convoluted articulation of partial identity in which no single »I« (whether master or slave) orders the others according to its scopic desire. Rather, Sganarell is portrayed through the deconstructive device of the evil eye which envisages only the overlap or the »not quite« inconsistency of identity frontiers.

Even though Goggel is situated on a far lower rung of the social ladder, he and Sganarell are initially linked by their desire to usurp the master role. This is clear when Sganarell claims to control the de Tenorio household, but is even more evident in his opportunism after de Tenorio's death. Sganarell literally appoints himself the master of de Tenorio's domain, claiming always secretly to have been a member of the aristocracy. Clearly, Goggel is witnessing the enactment of his own visions for himself in this farcical self-appointment. Thus when Goggel imagines himself in the master's garb enjoying the fruits of sovereignty, he is really imagining himself as an impostor. Through Sganarell it becomes clear

---

[93] Leperello, Goggel's cowardly alter ego, runs like a hare when de Manara disappears (presumed murdered) (ibid., p. 289). Ungefähr appears for the first time as a witness in Goggel's trial in Osnabrück; he accuses Goggel of stealing the Hahnentritt livery. Seven years later, he reappears in Osnabrück to finally bring Goggel to Hahnentritt, (ibid., p. 267 and 301 respectively).

that the role of master is little more than the role of an impersonator, a mimic other who decides to control the flow of power if the opportunity presents itself (*Goggelbuch* 272–281).

The journey to Spain on the galley ship presents a theatre of optical tricks that facilitates the renewed rise of Goggel. Convinced that he will suffer at the hands of the head whip, Goggel – who has just revisited the sewer position through his membership of the chain gang – feels powerless to defend himself. However, Sganarell fixes him with a steely gaze and from this Goggel takes courage:

> [...] ein eisiger Blick [stärkt] ihn aus den Augen des Herrn Sganarell. Er entnimmt diesem, was noch nicht unterwegs geschmolzen ist, und gibt dasselbe dem obersten Auspeitscher weiter. Sowie es ihm gelungen ist, vermöge dieser übernommenen und zum Teil weitergegebenen Äußerung eines gebieterischen Auges sich in Sicherheit zu bringen, schaut er auch über die Gefangenen hinweg wie über Blöcke und Klötze, meistert die Quelle seiner Mißgerüche, speit nicht mehr und vermag das Boot herrenmäßig zu lenken.   (*Goggelbuch* 274)

One could argue that this passage narrates the return of »I«, the whole and omniscient body of the symbolic order. Sganarell's iron gaze thus signifies a comic re-positing of Goggel in this order; it is his masterful look that gives Goggel renewed shape and reminds him of ascendancy. Thus Goggel temporarily departs the unchartered territory of his wayward journey and finds himself back on track. He »masters« the rudder of the boat and »masterfully« steers it towards Spain. However, the manner in which this metamorphosis is narrated tells us that Goggel is again merely slipping into a role. Furthermore, by impersonating Sganarell's authoritative gaze, he in fact impersonates the gaze of an impersonator. Nonetheless, impersonation is enough to gain command of the boat and also to demarcate clearly the self from those others who a short time previously had been Goggel's equals in the chain gang.

The nature of the look is, however, bilateral. Part appropriated (*übernommen*) and part passed along (*weitergegeben*), it represents in fact a temporary imitation of power that articulates the master subject as a pure identity effect. Thus whilst Goggel may believe that he is once again rooted in his position as want-to-be-master, the arrangement of eyes, glances and looks articulates both himself and Sganarell through the gaze of mimicry. For Sganarell is no master; his authoritarian look is mimicked from some other source. Once again, Goggel is mimicking a mimic man and both emerge in this scenario as partial subjects.

Sganarell's reappearance in disguise at the end of the tale further undermines his bid to take over the master position. Since Goggel last saw him in Seville, he has become the landlord of a Parisian bordello where all guests and employees are incognito. He appears in a uniform of golden brocade which immediately evokes the many liveries worn by Goggel over the years (*Goggelbuch* 298–299). Thus the golden brocade which (like the masterful look) should signify aristocracy instead signifies Sganarell's brotherhood with the underdog Goggel. Despite his visions of himself in the elevated role of the master, Sganarell ends up in the degraded position of high-class pimp. In this way, he clearly mimics Don Juan de Tenorio and Don Juan de Manara who, as implied by their names, have insatiable sexual appetites.[94] Yet this mimic instance of head servant as master is continually eclipsed by Sganarell's association through his ornate garment with the master's other: Goggel the lowly servant. The tendency of the master position to be eclipsed by the indentured other, that itself incessantly disappears into the master figure, is thus communicated through the contact zone of the ambiguous golden livery. Sganarell functions as an aphanisic fader through this very garment. Similar to Goggel, his naive projection into the glory promised by an ornate uniform delivers not the experience of self-affirming omnipresence, but a clouded vision of the otherness of self.

The concept of the master position is further criticised in the representation of sexual practice as the only consistent activity of the aristocracy. De Tenorio and de Manara are driven by carnal urges and gluttonous excess whilst Sganarell recreates in his Parisian bordello the orgies that characterised the master's domain in Spain. Goggel in his impersonator role as master further parodies what the text presents as the sovereign practice of sexual violence when he rapes the daughters of the innkeeper on the first leg of his journey. The subtext of such practice suggests that the appropriation and abuse of others' bodies is a necessary trapping of the master status. Moreover, Goggel's lowly reflection of the prime activity of both Spanish lords confers a certain inauthenticity on their respective positions. If it is so easy for Goggel to impersonate power through sexual brutality, then it becomes possible that de Tenorio and de Manara too began their master apprenticeship as gormless Goggels, assuming and perfecting the various gestures of power along the way. The authority of this position is further undermined by the text which one minute presents Goggel as a tyrannical rapist, and the next as the appropriated other in the chain gang.[95]

That Goggel is put through these extremes of experience should come as no surprise, however. The opening pages of the text present him through the complex layering of his garments as an inherently split character. He is wearing the Hahnentritt livery under a protective hair coat, we learn. Clearly, the hair coat (or hair shirt) may be interpreted as the signifier of the humiliations to come. Goggel wears it in order to disguise the livery underneath and so put off any lurking highwaymen along the way. However, the hair coat has a tendency to gape, leading to diverse situations in which Goggel is indeed mugged or more

---

[94] One of Goggel's main duties in the de Tenorio household is the procuring of virgins for his master's purposes whilst de Manara stages mass orgies in his residence (ibid., p. 272 and p. 283–284 respectively).

[95] As a member of the chain gang, Goggel is articulated as the lowest of the low: »Sein Bart ist ihm bis über die Brust gewachsen. Die Mädchen bewerfen die Bande mit Stroh und ihn besonders mit faulen Äpfeln [...]. Allgemein findet man ihn als den häßlichsten überall heraus [...]. So ist er weiter ein unguter Anblick für die Straßengänger, die sich bald um ihn stauen, bald ihn beiseite lassen wie ein Aas, das an Pest, Typhus, Aussatz, Cholera oder aus einem ähnlichen Anlaß verreckt gewesen. (ibid., p. 271–272)

agreeably mistaken for a prince. As we have seen, the latter scenarios are very short-lived, always marked by Goggel's transformation into a brute and swiftly followed by humiliating carnivalesque-style degradations.[96]

However, the finely tasselled livery which is constantly mistaken for the master's garb also signifies the degradation implied by the hair coat. This is not clear at first as Goggel dreamily regards his liveried self in the mirror before he departs to Osnabrück. To his mind, the livery confirms his membership of the Nibelung race. It marks the beginning of his ascent to glory, wealth and power. The text tells a different tale, however. Goggel's experiences suggest that the uniform signifies little else but a position of indenture on the vertical pole of social hierarchy. This is communicated by the mysterious circumstances surrounding the arrival of the uniform on Goggel's doorstep. Delivered by anonymous hand, Goggel has seen neither Hahnentritt nor Ungefähr before deciding to join their household. This being the case, he can have no concrete idea of what to expect in Osnabrück. A nebulous area of uncertainty thus disturbs the teleological expectations of his decision, a fact that is reflected in the misty landscapes and lengthy detours that frustrate his journey.[97]

Finding money in the concealed pocket of the uniform, he wonders if it belongs to someone else. However, he is distracted by its golden allure and glibly slips into this anonymous garment of questionable origin and dubious ownership, effectively signing away any remnant of autonomy. In so doing, he steps into the prescribed identity of the mindless follower, allowing himself to be led by forces he does not want to see and therefore cannot control. The livery thus becomes a hair shirt in its own right. In this respect, it is the clothing counterpart of uncritical thought and represents a parody of the Nazi man of the masses. Thus the desire to be a master is paradoxically undermined by the willingness to be led. Goggel's foolishness lies in his vulnerability to the seduction of appearances and his carelessness in questioning the situations that mysteriously propel him towards what transpire to be ever receding goals.

In contrast to the uncomfortable scene of metamorphosis in de Manara's castle, this opening situation thematises Goggel's illiteracy concerning his cultural environment. By questioning nothing, he refuses to consider the potential dangers of his actions and in so doing divests himself of all cognitive responsibility for what may come. The *méconnaissance* that influences his narcissistic self-vision in the mirror thus corresponds to the inability to critically assess

---

[96] »Seine Reise hat die Anmeldung zum Dienst bei Herrn Baron Eugen von Hahnentritt zum Ziel, dessen brokatbestickte Livree er bereits unter dem härenen Mantel trägt, der diese und ihn selbst gegen das Faschingsschneegestöber schützen soll.« (Ibid., p. 249)

[97] »Nach Untersuchung seiner Jacke – die goldenen Tressen an der Livree zeugen von Pflanz und Wohlstand – finden sich darin eingenäht zwei Dukaten in Gold, das ist die Anzahlung. Oder mag dieselben wer anderer drin vergessen haben? Kaum anzunehmen, denn der Rock ist gut gebürstet und sauber ausgelaugt [...]. Nur schade, daß Goggel niemals wen anderen als den Sendboten des Verwalters, nicht letzteren selbst, schon gar nicht den Herrn und obersten Befehler in Person zu Gesicht bekam.« (Ibid., p. 248)

situations. This prototype of the deliberately obtuse is enhanced by his selective reading of the Nibelung legend.

The livery does not confine itself to parodied representations of the followers of the Nazi regime, however. By donning a strange garment, Goggel is unwittingly committing himself to an experience of otherness that will paradoxically contest his assumptions of German identity. For Goggel, German identity is interchangeable with the image of Nibelung superiority and therefore consistent with the general position of master. As he understands it, by entering the service of one such master he is signalling his membership of the master race. However, as it is not known to whom this uniform belongs or from whence it came, a gap of absence comparable to that evoked by the faceless Hahnentritt emerges in the fabric of the livery. When he dresses himself as a servant, Goggel thus commits himself to the split identity of the notionally uniform individual who is frequently disrupted by an indeterminate otherness.

This paradox is already at work even as Goggel narcissistically envisages himself in the mirror. His self-appraisal is conducted according to the vertical phrase of identity that sees its point of origin in the mythological person of King Siegfried. However, the racist ideology that is apparent in this scopic desire is completely contradicted by Goggel's unreflected but accurate insight into the identity mechanisms of his society. Appearance is all important it emerges. The chances of the individual's progress are maximised by affiliating oneself to a powerful figure and then openly communicating this position by wearing the appropriate uniform. Identity is thus articulated as a question of costume that can easily be shed, upgraded or downgraded. This very insight ridicules concepts of superior identity based on biological racism and the mythology that supports it.

This understanding is most clearly articulated in the first subterfuge of his journey when he allows Mayor and Mayoress Knippelrind to receive him as a prince. Fr. Agnes Knippelrind entertains him with her own verse compositions, but in the same breath the text informs us that she was once a Jewess called Chanah until she was hunted down by her present husband and »liberated« into matrimony with him. She fulfils all requirements for the appearance of successful assimilation. She has changed her name, acquired the German language, and as Mayoress has ascended to a position of some standing within her provincial community. Her outer appearance thus articulates her identity as a female member of the lower German bourgeoisie.

The text tells a different tale, however. By thematising her background at all, it portrays her difference as an impostor who is almost the same, but not quite. Her strangerhood is communicated mainly through the suggestion that her command of the German language is not quite native (*Goggelbuch* 252). However, the complete irony of the situation only emerges when one considers that Fr. Agnes (Chanah) reads her less than idiomatic verse to the servant Goggel who masquerades as royalty. A member of the Nibelung folk, he is nonetheless »not quite« the King Siegfried he so admires, as is borne out by the several humiliations to come. The text thus highlights that both German and Jew are foreign to the positions that they mimic. In other words, the anti-Semitic society that punishes the Jews for their perceived impersonation of German identity is shown to derive its principles of identity from the very notion of impersonation.[98]

In this manner, Goggel's livery may be taken to represent the »not quite« point of aphanisic fading. It is the signifier of terminally incomplete identity. Through the revealing and concealing function of this garment, Goggel converges with a degraded form of the master (Sganarell) which is unsurprising as degradation is the only form in which the master figure appears in »Das Goggelbuch«. Equally, the livery which momentarily elevates him to the identity of prince ironically conjoins him with the specific figure of Jewish strangerhood. Whilst the livery may signify on the one hand the uniform identity of totalitarian subjects in the Nazi state, on the other hand it may be understood as the ultimate apparel of mimic man. This is implied by the above portrayed ambivalent merging of Jew and Germanic master through the common image of impersonation. The mechanisms of colonial ambivalence become clear in this space of mimicry. As a matter of appearance, impersonation and disguise, identity is completely alienated from essence and usually a matter of trompe l'œil. Most ironic of all however, is the implication that the desire for a narcissistic image of the self in fact facilitates the pulverisation of the self into mimic man.

This paradox is announced by the smashing of the mirror which marks Goggel's departure from his home. Clearly, the smashed fragments contrast to the introductory mirror vignette which suggests that seeing the reflection of the self often involves the imaginary distortion of self-aggrandisement, a form of self-evasion that compares to the act of not looking at all. The unsmashed mirror thus signifies the refusal to see the invisibility of the self, as the narcissistic projection into the other (the unary signifier) of the reflection appears to enact itself.

More subtle is the suggestion that Goggel's model of selfhood in the legendary figure of King Siegfried precipitates the experience of aphanisis. For the latter possessed an invisible/camouflage helmet (*Tarnhelm*), the suggestion of a vanishing point in the originary myth of Germanic identity that henceforth becomes the dominant image of subjectivity in the text.[99] With this in mind, it is little wonder that clothing functions as one of the chief signifiers of mimicry. Moreover, Goggel unwittingly externalises the narcissistic concern of invisibility

---

[98] »Des Bürgermeisters Gespons Agnes, seinerzeit von diesem bei einer Judenhatz erjagt und später ertauft, zuletzt auch gefreit, liest Ihrer Durchlaucht, dem Goggel, viele deutsche Reime vor, die sie in Feierzeit und zu ihres Wahlvolks Ehren ineinander verfilzt.« (ibid., p. 252) The verb *verfilzen* (to become matted) in particular communicates her strangerhood in the German language.

[99] The helmet is featured in the third scene of *Das Rheingold*. Not only does it cause its owners to disappear, they may also change physical form. See Richard Wagner: Das Rheingold. Der Ring des Nibelungen. Kompletter Text und Erläuterung zum vollen Verständnis des Werkes. Hg. von Kurt Pahlen. München: Goldmann/Schott 1982 (Goldmann-Taschenbuch; 33072: Goldmann/Schott: Opern der Welt), p. 83–109.

into his own world (and into the text) as a visible wound when he smashes the mirror. This is the point at which one could argue that the Lacanian gaze openly announces itself »in its pulsatile, dazzling and spread out function«.[100] In other words, Goggel devoid of mirror can no longer indulge the narcissistic scotoma. He mistakenly believes that he is ridding himself of his lowly servant appearance by smashing the object that reflects himself in this light. Instead, he is launching himself on an irreversible journey of ambivalence in which the quest for the omnipotent self is frustrated by the interruptions of invisibility.

Most telling however, is the text's statement that Goggel, by smashing the mirror, renders it incapable of further contradiction.

> Mit dieser hochfahrenden Hoffnung Seifenblasen von sich pfeifend, greift Goggel nach dem strafenden Stein, der dem gegenwärtigen Spiegel zugunsten des künftigen unrecht gibt, indem er denselben in eine Lage versetzt, aus der er eines Wider-spruchs nicht mehr fähig ist   (*Goggelbuch* 247)

What was the nature of the initial contradiction? Clearly, the text thematises here the illusion of wholeness that is delivered to the less discerning observers of self in the deceptive vertical depths of the mirror. By smashing it, Goggel forces the mirror (and any further reflections of the self) into a metonymy of minute and fragmented pieces, none of which thereafter amount to an image of wholeness. The smashing of the mirror is therefore a central event in »Das Goggelbuch«. It undoubtedly demonstrates the dissolution of the Goggel »I« into the evil eyes of the split (smashed) self, implying that Goggel's quest for himself is, like Guckelhupf's, certain to fail before it has ever begun. The smashed mirror thus refuses to gratify the grandiose scopic desire of Goggel's self-delusion.

The broken glass is also significant in that it provides yet another perforated frame for a vision or dream experience that occurs in the text within the text. After venting his dissatisfaction on the mirror, Goggel sets out on his quest to find himself in the image of the phantom phallus, his master. However, the closing paragraphs of the text tell us that the intervening seven narrated years of inevitable bad luck were part of a dream. If these years occurred only in Goggel's imagination, then what are we to understand by them?

Keeping in mind the troublesome optics of the text, a convincing explanation lies in the understanding of Goggel's dream/vision in the mirror of his mind as an encounter with the invisibility of the self and therefore an exercise of the mimic gaze. In essence, Goggel's dream narrates in many parodic forms the encounter of master with that other of himself, the slave. By smashing the mirror, Goggel provokes this encounter, or as Lacan would say, he provokes the gaze.[101] In other words, he inadvertently exposes the contact zone between self and other that arises in the narcissistic gap and that dislodges the self from any imagined position of superiority. Whilst the dream may narrate at local

---

[100] Lacan, The Four Fundamental Concepts of Psycho-Analysis (note 43), p. 89.
[101] Ibid., p. 75.

level the meandering everyday of the quest for the self, its point of departure in the metonymic relation of the smashed mirror tells another tale.

Goggel's several encounters with others thus demonstrate the nature of the encounter implied in the smashed mirror. This encounter is none other than what Lacan terms the *tuché*, a dream-like confrontation that occurs by chance when one is asleep. Paradoxically, the *tuché* is a form of rude awakening that reminds the individual of its status as an object of the gaze of others.[102] From this point of view, Goggel's self-appraisal through the goggles of narcissism is tantamount to the myopic sleep of the Imaginary, whilst his smashing of the mirror and subsequent rite of passage through the shards of the looking glass may be described as the tychic point of awakening, i. e. an uncomfortable insight into processes of identity constitution. It is precisely this notion of the tychic encounter that associates the mirror's surface with the moor space, for both articulate the confrontation with the otherness of self.

The dream/vision within the text within the text may also be regarded as a parody of memory processes. The sudden moment of smashing glass represents the disturbing return of the repressed. The story that then unfolds does not shy away from the uglier acts of the individual who is narrated both in his capacity as victim and tyrant. That Goggel decides to get rid of the mirror when he awakens out of his trance suggests that he desperately wants to forget both images: the self as the appropriated servant other of evil forces (the obedient man of the masses who is capable of great cruelty), and the self in the position of Jewish victim of this evil. Throwing out the mirror is tantamount to whitewashing the past. In this way, Goggel represents a mode of dealing with the recent Nazi past of contemporary Austrian society which involves deleting from memory the identities of victim and victimiser.[103]

However, whilst the narrative ends with this representation of deliberate amnesia, the incomplete frame of the text within the text suggests that the debate concerning Austria's role in the Third Reich should not end in the blind spot of memory. Instead, it becomes the task of the reader/rememberer to read in between and against the lines of the whitewashed past in order to establish contexts that may implicate or enlighten the remembering individual.

---

[102] Ibid., p. 69.

[103] This argument concerning Austria's dealing with the Nazi past is put forward by Alexandra Millner: »Hätten Goggels Nachfahren die Lektüre des ›Goggelbuchs‹ ernst genug genommen, das Allegorische des Lesens erkannt, wäre der Verlauf der Geschichte ein anderer gewesen. Albert Drach scheint uns zu warnen: Der Text als Spiegel darf nicht dasselbe Schicksal erfahren, er soll uns durch die Unabgeschlossenheit der Erzählung zur Auseinadersetzung mit dessen Inhalt zwingen.« (Alexandra Millner. Spiegeltexte. Das Spiegelmotiv in der deutschsprachigen Gegenwartsliteratur dargestellt an Texten von Elfriede Jelinek, Adolf Muschg, Thomas Bernhard und Albert Drach. [PhD] Wien 1999, p. 185)

Chapter 6
»Z. Z.« das ist die Zwischenzeit: Paralysis of the Powerless

6.1 Diverging Paths: A Theoretical Re-evaluation

The analyses of *UND* and *Das Goggelbuch* in the previous two chapters have explored manifestations of the grotesque as a topography of transgression in the shorter prose works of Albert Drach. These final two chapters now return to the other image of the grotesque discussed in chapters 2 and 3: the morphology of emptiness as a leading motif in the first part of the Holocaust trilogy, *»Z. Z.« das ist die Zwischenzeit*.[1] The body of *jouissance* that was identified both in the rhetorical grotesquerie of catachresis in *UND* and in the hybrid subject of aphanisis in *Das Goggelbuch* now recedes as the body language of negation becomes the main articulation of corporeality in this work. For *»Z. Z.«* exposes the difficulty of arguing a text concerned with the pre-Holocaust period of 1935 to 1938 through the theoretical terminology of liberating *jouissance*, anti-establishment ambivalence or rhetorical grotesquerie. Accordingly, the ornate surface network of grotesque play – the *jouissance* of signifiers in the discursive economy of compensation/loss – makes way for what was identified in chapter 3 as the interrelated economies of sadism and melancholia. In this manner, Drach evokes the space of absolute negation which I have described as the space of the *grotta*/grave.

If *UND* and *Das Goggelbuch* both narrated the transgression of the body of negation by the body of semiotic negativity, *»Z. Z.«* now narrates the precedence of the former. For the body of negation is performed by Drach's depiction of totalitarian society, the rigidity of symbolic cells that entrap, appropriate and incapacitate the Jewish other. Identity, the body and the location of the subject are therefore all presented in a manner quite distinct from what was found to be the case in the last two chapters. Far from the carnivalesque body of transgressive *jouissance*, the dominant mode of corporeality in *»Z. Z.«* could be generally described as a kind of sadistic stasis. For although this work covers only the period from 1935 to 1938, it nonetheless communicates the logic of extermination which may be compared to the destructive drive of the sadist. Following Adorno, J. M. Bernstein identifies the essence of this logic in »the expropriation of death« from the victims doomed to die. In other words, even death as a site of individuality is

---

[1] Albert Drach: »Z. Z.« das ist die Zwischenzeit. Ein Protokoll. Ungekürzte Ausg., München: Deutscher Taschenbuch Verlag 1990 (dtv; 12218). Henceforth cited as *Z. Z.* with appropriate page numbers.

voided by the administrative nature of death in the concentration camps. Thus the categorial syntax which conceives of death as belonging to a life and which links process (life) to result (death) is radically ruptured by the logic of extermination. Here, death – »the poorest possession left to the individual« – is expropriated and »the result overtakes the process itself, leaving it without result«.[2]

This is the kind of society that we encounter in »Z. Z.« It is a world in which the categorial distinction between life and death is lifted and the victim self is accordingly reduced to a meaningless organism. In other words, though the body is left alive, the humanity of the individual is removed. The most fundamental image of the body of negation in this work is thus the corpse which in turn communicates the »literal process of reification« experienced by the entrapped Austro-Jewish protagonist.[3] If *jouissance* may be described as a mode of transgressive flexibility that resists such processes of reification, then stasis communicates the stiffening of negated, disempowered bodies in the space of absolute negation (the *grotta*) that transcends even the borderline location of cross-contamination. In »Z. Z.« therefore, the grotesque is no longer predominantly articulated through the signifiers of mobility such as ambivalence and transgression. Rather, we must look to the conservative element of the death drives (stasis/Thanatos) in order to locate grotesque functioning in this novel.

This latter concept of stasis takes the form in Drach's literature of the excluding, separating activity of totalitarian consciousness. One could therefore argue that the negating and negated body of this society (the bodies of victim and victimiser) both derive from the primacy of the pathological paternal metaphor Deleuze identifies in sadistic discourse.[4] Drach's aesthetic choice for the representation of this morgue society is the still life image in prose, a form of grotesquerie that functions both as the aesthetic mouthpiece of the dead and as the visual form of apotheosis. Broadly speaking, the grotesque can be understood in this protocol as the writing of death vis-à-vis the still life aesthetic. This chapter will sketch in detail the inexorable persistence of stasis in representations of discourse and the body as the still life aesthetic begins to dominate the text.

Taking this into account, the grotesque potential of the still life (a genre originally known for its exclusion of the human subject) becomes more evident. For surely the use of the still life aesthetic is most appropriate in a novel that narrates the treatment of individuals as objects for consumption. In this way, we are confronted with a grotesquerie of normalised dehumanisation that is contained in the bourgeois aesthetic of the still life. In line with this, Drach closely associates the concept of the still life with the institution of the *Amt*, so much so that within this work it can also be viewed from a broader perspective as the aesthetic reflection of totalitarian culture. In »Z. Z.« however, Drach puts

---

[2]   Jay M. Bernstein: Disenchantment and Ethics. Cambridge: Cambridge University Press 2001 (Modern European Philosophy), p. 379.
[3]   Ibid., p. 380.
[4]   Gilles Deleuze: Masochism. Coldness and Cruelty. New York: Zone Books 1989, p. 60.

this aesthetic to work as an aid in the literary depiction of totalitarian society and its product, the subordinated subject.[5]

This shift from the representation of bodies in various stages of (de)construction to the representation of paralysed corporeality reflects the reduction of the fetishistic play of the signifier discussed in the final section of chapter 3. As argued there, it is this destructive attitude towards the fetish that characterises sadistic discourse. In chapter 1, stasis was presented as consistent with the notion of individual death as final apotheosis that is avoided through the artistic act of language composition/fetishism. In Drach's work, the child in flight is one such embodiment of the deferral of death as the end of all movement (stasis) through the act of writing. Language activity understood in terms of this deferral brings about an exploration of the self that in the process of constitution is only ever partially and inadequately posited. Here the self is articulated between metaphor and metonymy as simultaneously present and absent, a structure of subjectivity that Bhabha identifies as ultimately in the mode of fetish.[6] As we have seen in the previous chapters, this is for the main part a positively connoted existential mode in Drach's work, dismantling as it does the fictitious claims of the sovereign self and exposing stasis as a non-viable projection of homogenised identity. This overwriting of the symbolic self through the transgressive mode of *jouissance* exposes images of stasis as farce.

However, the limitations of this argument become apparent when faced with a text such as »Z. Z.«. In a narrative that has one eye cocked towards the inevitability of the approaching concentration camps and that talks incessantly of death, the writing of apotheosis gains the upper hand. This sense of absolute negation is constantly evoked through the images of stasis, paralysis and entrapment that litter the pages of the work. Reading this text, it would seem that Drach's flirtation with death no longer possesses the restorative function of deferring the inevitability of stasis through language fetishism. Instead, the ability to suspend stasis is now superseded by the dominance of apotheosis. In other words, the sadistic attitude of destruction towards the fetish function of language (compen-

---

[5] Mark Seltzer argues that the conflation of the portrait and the still life collapses the differences between persons and things, resulting in »the representation of persons as objects for consumption«. Consumption is furthermore a form of self-making and self-possession that links the still life representation to what he terms »the bourgeois style of appropriation«. The still life thus reflects certain fundaments of capitalist culture: »the precarious difference between person and thing« is articulated in this representation »as the difference between consuming and being consumed« (Mark Seltzer: Bodies and Machines. New York, London: Routledge 1992, p. 139–141). This view corresponds to the view put forward by Drach in his essay »Stilleben« where the still life is regarded as the aesthetic vehicle for the representation of the bureaucratic-totalitarian appropriation of culture, i. e. as in Seltzer's argument, the still life form embodies to a degree the power relations of consumerist cultures that are based on the possession/appropriation of not just material things, but others (Albert Drach: Das 17. Buch der 17 Essays, Nachlaß Albert Drach, Austrian Literary Archive of the Austrian National Library, Wien).
[6] Homi Bhabha: The Location of Culture. London, New York: Routledge 1994, p. 77.

sation/loss) becomes the general discursive strategy of this novel. This logically implies a dramatic reduction in the ambivalent space of the in-between, a change that is evident in the portrayal of historical circumstance at the time.

Contrary to earlier images of the in-between, the between image of time in this novel (*die Zwischenzeit*) effectively negates the general portrayal of ambivalence. This is due to the complete lack of space that the between image almost always portrays. One cannot help but feel that all protagonists are stuck in the still life of a negative historical period where lack of space and lack of movement are dominant attributes of the between time. As with many discourses in this novel, the discourse of timelessness/spacelessness is woven into the discourse concerning sexuality and the female other. In keeping with the dominance of stasis, the motif of the sex ghetto (to be handled in the final chapter) is one of many that disclose the shift of representation from the agility of ambivalence into the immutability of the still life. The misogynist undertones that repeatedly deliver the sex ghetto (a variation of the *grotta* space) link the above images of spacelessness/timelessness to the greater disciplinary discourse of anti-Semitism of that time. The conflation of prejudiced or sexist/racial discourses with the discourse of anti-Semitism is an undeniable feature of this novel.

Thus the dominant mode of narrative language in this text is that of stasis, and if the reader encounters conflations of stasis and *jouissance*, the latter is more often than not subordinated to the former. This would suggest a constellation similar to the Freudian theory of the Death Instinct in which Eros ultimately becomes a functional strategy and effect of Thanatos, in turn suggesting the inherently conservative nature of the pleasure principle. Again, this constellation also points to the sadistic principle underlying the narrative, for Deleuze's understanding of sadistic discourse is based on Freud's isolation of the Death Instinct as the dominant principle of psychic life.[7] From this perspective, »sex« never signifies Eros. In a society of diminished libidinal relations, sex always embodies the darker principle of violence towards the other, an enunciation of Bernstein's ruptured categorial syntax through which life (the process) becomes death (the result). There are some remarkable representations of just this destructive economy of the Death Instinct in »Z. Z.«, as Drach reveals time and again through the signifier »sex« the operational tactics of totalitarianism.

The repetition of static images thus communicates a certain concession of defeat of the subversive marginal in an increasingly uniform society. The reader is confronted in many different forms by the aesthetics of the inert as Drach paints a disturbing picture of the far-reaching consequences of totalitarian culture. Far from the ambivalence of identity usually portrayed in the protocol, we are now confronted with the human product of subjection whose behaviour expresses a politics of obedience consistent with this culture.

---

[7] Deleuze, Masochism (note 4), p. 30 and Sigmund Freud: Jenseits des Lustprinzips. In: id., Freud, Sigmund: Das Ich und das Es. Metapsychologische Schriften. Frankfurt a. M.: Fischer 1999 (Fischer-Taschenbücher; 10442: Psychologie), p. 223. See also 2.1 of this work.

The amnesiac style of the floating protocol that cannot decide on the subject matter of its enquiry is in this case exchanged for a writing of stasis which both commemorates and performs the normalised violence of the time. However, Drach not only writes against the violence of this historical period; by exposing the ruthless behaviour of his alter ego, the son, he also writes against himself. To an extent, this harsh representation of himself as violent womaniser and selfish child is in fact elucidated by the protocol policy of »writing against« the protagonist in order to »write for« him. Certainly, Drach paints a subtly comprehensive picture of himself losing resistance whilst becoming more deeply entrenched in the power discourses of the time. This is the aspect of the narrative perspective that »knows«, that has been through the Holocaust experience and that has had time to reflect on the influences of the between time.

The older Drach who remembers and writes in order to commemorate the complexities of a time all too conveniently oversimplified in the annals of Austrian historiography could be associated with this aspect of the narrative voice.[8] There are no excuses made for what could be regarded as the criminal behaviour of the protagonist as the son is presented always in the mode of doing or acting mostly without thought for the welfare of others. From this perspective, the society of *»Z. Z.«* prognosticates the bloody survival politics of the extermination camps even if the latter are not as yet a concrete reality of the 1935 to 1938 everyday. The aforementioned »knowing« perspective that commemorates the depraved self becomes a melancholy subtext of the novel as the overt portrayal of cruelty dominates in the narrative. These twin possibilities will be examined in greater detail in the final chapter.

At the same time, the text is dominated by a second more openly dominant narrative perspective that also writes against the son, not in order to expose him as a self-oriented wrongdoer, but to appropriate and expose him as Jew. This is the perspective that represents the values of totalitarian culture and that ensnares all protagonists in the still life order of the *Amt*. In this instance, we can no longer talk solely of the author Drach who writes against his earlier self. Instead, the son is also narrated through a controlling panoptic perspective that appropriates him as undesirable other and watches his reaction to this. In *»Z. Z.«*, we thus encounter a reversal of the optical metaphorics examined in *Das Goggelbuch*. This reversal is consistent with the shift from the representation of inappropriate bodies (mimic men) to the representation of appropriated bodies.

The son's reaction to this form of expulsion takes the form of a self-fulfilling prophecy as he increasingly grows into the identity of the criminal. His delinquent development culminates in the final tragedy of the matricide. Thus the delinquent figure of the son is presented as a murderer of sorts, the confession of matricide being the point towards which the narrative inexorably gravitates.

However, if the individual matricide is regarded as a symbol for the more general societal hostility towards the maternal space of the semiotic *chora* (most

---

[8]   Cf. Lutz Musner: Memory and Globalization. Austria's Recycling of the Nazi Past and Its European Echoes. In: New German Critique 80 (2000), p. 77–92.

apparent in the treatment of the Jewish and female others), then the son's behaviour can be read as a form of compliance with dominant societal norms. The question becomes one as to whether delinquency is no longer a deviation from the norm, but in a time of legalised crime a reflection and affirmation of the norm. Thus the complex son character emerges at contradictory but interdependent discursive sites. On the one hand, there is no doubt that he is the expelled and despised other of the anti-Semitic state; on the other, he is the obedient subject of this state, adopting its racial values particularly in his treatment of the female other.

He has thus to a certain extent fallen into the trap of Jewish self-hatred. Exiled by the dominant social group, he nonetheless assimilates its values and projects them onto another other. In the pattern of a vicious circle, the one form of censure (the racist appropriation of the son as Jewish other) along with its consequences (auto-stereotyping or Jewish self-hatred) inevitably leads to the other form of censure: writing against the past self from the vantage point of the more experienced but troubled survivor. There is no real way out of this disastrous circle which could be described as a pattern of guilty memory particular to the Jewish survivor of the Holocaust trauma. The circular trap of »othering« perspectives in the between time thereby mirrors the memory trap inhabited by the survivor and accounts for Drach's conviction that the between time is not just a memory, but an existential landscape – the parallel universe of the dead – that continues into the society of postwar Austria.[9]

»Z. Z.« covers the period of the Schuschnigg dictatorship up until the Nazi annexation of Austria in March 1938.[10] In terms of Drach's personal story

---

[9]   The kind of splitting of the subject that occurs in Jewish self-hatred is comparable to a form of memory that Lawrence L. Langer terms tainted memory. Here, the remembering self remembers the »self-ish« actions undertaken in the name of survival, which like Jewish self-hatred involves detachment »from any internal system of belief« and a kind of cancelling out of the self, »a totally paradoxical killing of the self by the self in order to keep the self alive« (Lawrence L. Langer: Holocaust Testimonies. The Ruins of Memory. New Haven, London: Yale University Press 1991, p. 124 and p. 131 respectively). The tainted self could be regarded as the product of an intensification of the mechanism central to Jewish self-hatred: the »self-abnegation« of minorities that is necessary for survival within dominant societal groups (Sander L. Gilman: Jewish Self-Hatred: Anti-Semitism and the Hidden Language of the Jews. Baltimore, London: John Hopkins University Press 1986, p. 1). Drach's use of the term *Zwischenzeit* to depict not just the historical epoch of 1935–1938 but also the amnesiac postwar society of Austria becomes clear when he describes an anti-Semitic episode of denunciation: »Der Assistenzarzt hinwiederum kam dieser Denunziation wegen in noch späterer Zeit mit fünf Jahren Kerker davon, als Österreich zwar wieder bestand, sich aber nur höchst ungern der Zwischenzeit erinnerte. *Vor diesem Teil der Zwischenzeit aber*, nämlich während des Ablaufs der in dieser protokollarischen Darstellung vorgestellten Epoche, bot sich immerhin eine junge Nonne [...] zur Blutspendung an.« (Z. Z. 190–191, my emphasis)

[10] Drach situates the narrative in this historical period in the early stages of the novel when he mentions the »weak dictator« (Kurt Schuschnigg) who came to power after the murder during a national socialist takeover attempt of the previous chancellor, Engelbert Dollfuß (ibid., p. 31). Cf. Gerhard Botz: Der 13. März 38 und die Anschluß-

during this time, the novel begins with the death of his father on 19 May 1935 and ends in Yugoslavia with the apprehension of his mother's death. He has left her behind in Vienna in order to embark more expediently on the first stage of a ten year exile which is to last from 1938 to 1948. Beginning with the onset of rigor mortis in the paternal corpse and ending with the symbolic murder of the mother through the prohibited adulterous activity of the son, the novel's circularity thus delimits a poetics of the dead and dying. These twin images seem to demarcate the aesthetic territory of stasis as the dominant mode, effectively freeze-framing the text in a still life of parental loss and death.

Structurally, this is reminiscent of the circular, non-linear narrative that is typical of Drach. Starting with the death of one parent, an entire novel later we are still hovering around a corpse, that of the murdered mother. Thus death clearly marks out the boundaries of the novel. Bearing this in mind, it is no surprise that »Z. Z.« diverges as a protocol from the concept of the eternally provisional, poorly embedded protocol text previously discussed. Further supporting the impression of a static aesthetics is the limited difference between the above two images of death. This »difference«, which is really little more than an intensification of elements already present in the opening scene, is to be located in the son's regressive »development«. At the beginning of the novel, his strangeness arises from his inability to grieve conventionally at the deathbed of his father. By the end, this disaffection has escalated to the extent that he betrays a promise and so to his own mind, brings about the death of his mother.[11]

In many ways, the narrative space between one death and the other confronts the reader with the account of a deviant and questionable rite of passage from childhood to adulthood, one that is imbued with regression and frustration. These latter modes of existence can be explained in part with reference to the title of the novel itself. The between time particular to Austria of 1935 to 1938 is presented as suspended from historical reality whilst it is at the same time a product of this reality. External historical events are conveyed in the parenthetical, incidental manner typical of Drach as the romantic pursuits of the main protagonist seem to assume precedence of plot. This notwithstanding, it can be argued that social and historical stasis is illustrated indirectly through the figure of the main protagonist and his particular complexes. It is a time of chronic social infirmity as the sickness of passivity spreads throughout the entire social body. There are constant references to the inevitability of approaching disaster, culminating in the annexation of 1938, yet resignation is the order of the day as individuals seem to lack the power to do anything to prevent this.[12]

---

bewegung. Selbstaufgabe, Okkupation und Selbstfindung Österreichs 1918–1945. Wien: Verlag der SPÖ 1981.

[11] The framing sentences of the novel bear this out: »Auf dem besonders flachen Lager gegen die Terrasse [...] lag der einschlägige Tote im Beisein seines Sohnes.« (Z. Z. 7) Further: »Da wußte er plötzlich, daß er seine Mutter ermordet hatte.« (Ibid., p. 347)

[12] »Im Zusammenhang mit diesen Ideengängen, die ihn damals beschäftigt hatten, überprüfte der Sohn sein bisheriges Zwischendasein auf seine Grundlage hin und kam zu folgendem Ergebnis: Er war [...] hauptsächlich mit zwecklosen Dingen beschäftigt

In terms of the son's story, the rite of passage to an autonomous existence is blocked by the stases of the between time, a time of paralysis, a reduced time inhabited by diminished, disempowered half-individuals. Instead, the main protagonist is condemned to a ghostlike existence of aimless repetition that is conveyed through the proliferation of unsatisfactory sexual adventures narrated in the novel. The poetics of death becomes synonymous with the representation through repetition of entrapment as both images evoke the impression of captivity within and subjection to externally imposed projections of inflexibility. In Deleuze's words, this is precisely the repetition that evokes the idea of absolute negation which typifies all activity in the sadistic universe. It is distinct from the repetition that temporarily binds positions in the more flexible economy of compensation/loss.[13] For this reason, it becomes difficult in the case of »Z. Z.« to identify the poetic subject as constantly pulverised through the ex-position of the thetic. It seems much more the case that this particular protocol shows how the subject is assigned a number of inflexible, socially crafted positions within discourse, positions moreover, that are consistent with the totalitarian vision of society.

It is therefore necessary to move away from the Kristevan notion of discourse as *jouissance* with regard to this work. Although the novel is bursting with sexual escapades of one form or another, they are not part of an ambivalent discourse that articulates the disturbing but erotic return of the forgotten (m)other. On the contrary, these incidents can be aligned with hostile discourses of othering that aim to conquer through the exclusion of undesirables. This explains why the novel, which consists mainly of these sexual conquests, in fact narrates the reduction of difference. For the main part, this particular protocol focuses on the image of identity fixity as a form of death (the death of difference) through apotheosis. In theoretical terms, apotheosis represents not only the negating impulse of the symbolic system that is signified by the expulsion/appropriation of the other and that provides an interesting reading of the pathology of the totalitarian state. It also represents the establishment of a discursive field that is marked out by highly regulated modes of »subjectivity«. If as Foucault says, regularity »specifies an effective field of appearance«, then the discursive field of apotheosis (totalitarianism) is characterised by the regularity of rigidity (expulsion/negation).[14]

---

gewesen, wobei die Bekanntschaft von Menschen vorgezogen wurde, die in keiner Weise nützlich sein konnten. Seine sogenannten Liebesabenteuer hatten meist die Begegnung mit Wundern zum Gegenstand, aus denen er nichts machen konnte und die auch nie zu einer körperlichen Einigung führten. Statt dessen suchte oder fand er diese Befriedigung, die in Wirklichkeit keine war, mit Gestalten, die er sich statt dieser Wunder unterschob.« (Ibid., p. 145)

[13] Deleuze, Masochism (note 4), p. 115.

[14] Foucault emphasises that regularity should not be understood as the opposite of irregular or deviant statements such as the pathological. Regularity designates »for every verbal performance (extraordinary, or banal), the set of conditions in which

This text does not raise the semiotic in order to pulverise symbolic positing; nor does it excavate the inconsistencies of the thetic position. On the contrary, it narrates the disappearance of the semiotic and the subsequent coagulation of the symbolic into a fixed hierarchy of demarcated positions. Again, this shift in relations communicates the anal-sadistic tendencies of the symbolic order, for as above noted, the sadistic universe is defined by the aggrandissement of the paternal metaphor and the annihilation of the maternal. In »Z. Z.«, we therefore encounter the resurrection of the vertical body of cultural authority which was the target of mimicry in *Das Goggelbuch*: the body of negation.

The sense that the semiotic subject of enunciation may not be the most productive concept through which to read the text by no means heralds the return to a phenomenological subject of speech, however.[15] Instead, Foucault's concept of the discursively produced, subjected subject provides a means for describing both the apotheosis of the individual and of the society that produces it. From this perspective, individual apotheosis is always the effect of society's closure, its ability to prescribe identity and assign position. At the same time however, this theory also accounts for the self-alienation of the main character who is expected to fulfil several socially produced identities simultaneously. Similar to the concept of poetic language as bearer of death, there is a sense in which the son is absent from the various externally imposed signifiers of symbolic identity that he is obliged to fulfil. However, unlike the poetic subject, the son is for the main part too apathetic to effect transgression of these socially imposed roles. In other words, he is largely incapable of autonomous behaviour and so remains entrapped in the confines of a pathological patriarchy.[16]

If one were to exchange the Kristevan sentence of non-completion for Foucault's theory of the statement, then reading »Z. Z.« becomes a reading of overwhelming power structures that mobilise the subject and leave it virtually no room for manoeuvre. General features of the statement are for Foucault its production and manipulation by men along with its status of being what he terms »in the true«, an effect of political power that may decide versions of truth as part of a propaganda exercise. Most notably however, Foucault claims that »if one can speak of a statement, it is because a sentence (a proposition) figures at a definite point with a specific position, in an enunciative network

---

the enunciative function operates«. In the totalitarian context, this regularity could be described as the repeated practice of negation of others (Michel Foucault: The Archaeology of Knowledge. London: Routledge 1995, p. 144).

[15] Kristeva's theory of the split speaking subject of semiosis is conceived against the background of phenomenological speaking subjects she identifies in other linguistic theories (Julia Kristeva: The System and the Speaking Subject. In: id., The Kristeva Reader. Ed. by Toril Moi. New York: Columbia University Press 1986, p. 24–34).

[16] This reading derives from Foucault's analysis of the disciplined society that produces a distinctive political anatomy of »subjected and practised bodies« (Michel Foucault: Discipline and Punish. The Birth of the Prison. London: Penguin Books 1991 [Penguin Social Sciences], p. 138).

that extends beyond it«.[17] Thus assigning subject position becomes the definitive function of the statement. As such, it is an ordering principle that defines and delimits subject position similar to the Kristevan concept of denotation as exemplified by her understanding of the predicate function.[18] In this fashion, the statement is the reverse image of the sentence outside itself.

This understanding of the statement is most relevant for *»Z. Z.«*. If one were to assume that the main statement of the novel is one of stasis, then it becomes highly interesting to identify the different enunciative manifestations of this particular statement as they occur in the narrative. How is subject position assigned for instance? Who assigns? What form does the discursive field of rigidity assume in the novel? The following section will address these queries.

6.2 Writing Apotheosis

The key to understanding manifestations of stasis as statement is through observation of the different discursive situations portrayed in the protocol. These discursive sites range from the medical to the judicial and the familial, not to mention the discourse of tourism along with the semiotics of sex. In terms of narrative structure, these portrayals form a succession of still-life tableaux that suggest the enclosure of the subject within discursive structures. The subject and the possibility of subjective experience as personal or private are furthermore delimited by the partitioning function of this discourse.[19]

The exteriority of this kind of representation accounts to a great extent for the highly impersonal tone through which the protocol relates private matters. Protagonists are accordingly presented as the products of power relations particular to the historical period. We are therefore confronted by the dispersion of the subject as it emerges at several different discursive sites (judicial, racist, romantic etc.) but the latter, when observed in an increasingly totalitarian context, tend to articulate a certain homogenisation of the discursively produced entity, the disciplined subject.[20] This homogenisation coupled with the official tone of the protocol effects a complete indifference to the private/public opposi-

---

[17] Foucault, Archaeology of Knowledge (note 14), p. 99.

[18] Julia Kristeva: Revolution in Poetic Language. New York: Columbia University Press 1984, p. 106–108.

[19] Foucault identifies partitioning as one technique of the disciplinary society in the project of surveillance/location of individuals at all times: »It was a procedure, therefore, aimed at knowing, mastering and using.« (Foucault, Discipline and Punish [note 15], p. 143)

[20] The son is a solicitor whose experiences in the legal system documented in the novel uniformly communicate the powerlessness of the individual within this bureaucratic machine, e. g. (*Z. Z.* 69–70). His romantic pursuits are to an extent symptomatic of the racist discourse of the time; he is aware that if the government changes, he will not as a Jew be allowed to practise (ibid., p. 55). His energies are thus invested in the mostly unsuccessful pursuit of women.

tion. What might normally be termed »private« affairs are shown to be the rightful property of the bureaucratic perspective which is itself the mouthpiece of that totalitarian culture machine identified by Drach as the *Amt*. Equally, public matters such as the rise of Hitler are presented as issues which invade and define the individual.[21]

A number of key incidents in the text impart this sense of imprisonment within societal formations and the discourses that both constitute and convey the former. The three discursive milieux to be analysed thematise different aspects of this complex: firstly the assigning mechanisms communicated by the still life representation, secondly the dominant model of power in the between time, and finally the anomaly of travel as an expression of non-movement.

The opening paragraph of the novel immediately problematises the issue of discourse as construct that disempowers the individual. More specifically perhaps, the excerpt thematises how discourse produces images of the disempowered. We are confronted with the image of the son by the side of the paternal corpse in the pose of mourning. How the text communicates that this pose is a discursively produced instance is a matter of reading juxtapositions:

> Auf dem besonders flachen Lager gegen die Terrasse, über welche Singvögel *aus symbolischen oder aus Gründen der Gewöhnung* herangeflogen kamen, wobei nur drei oder vier gewissermaßen als Abgesandte, möglicherweise auch wegen größerer Kühnheit aus eigenem Antrieb ins Zimmer flatterten, lag der einschlägige Tote im Beisein seines Sohnes noch nicht aufgebahrt, sondern erst in jenem Zustand, in dem die Haut und die Nägel zu sterben begannen, was ein Knistern verursachte, als ob sich die ausglühende Leiche solche Verständigungsmöglichkeit vorbehalten hatte. (*Z. Z.* 7, my emphasis)

The juxtaposition of birds of song in flight with the image of the stiffening corpse seems rather incongruous. However, the narrative reflection on the signifying capacity of these creatures has a function other than that of raising the trivial at an inappropriate moment. Drach indicates to us through the apparently incidental tone of the italicised parenthesis (»for symbolic or habitual reasons«) that there are always a number of discursive options for the execution and interpretation of behaviour. Here the possible modes outlined are those of lyrical language or the banal discourse of the habitual everyday. By

---

[21] This is made clear by the implication that the son's dreams of romantic adventure will be frustrated by the political situation in Austria at the time: »Kaum aber hatte er sich das Erreichen des bisher von ihm nicht Erreichten als erforderlich vorgestellt, als sich bereits seine sehr erleichterten Gedankengänge, viel schwerer angeschirrt, in die Gegenrichtung in Trab setzten. Er sah Ziffern eines unausgeglichenen Kontos in einer ohnehin unguten Gegenwart unter einem schwachen Diktatur [...]. Nach der Art der Schullehrer, die der Sohn um so wenig ehrte, je subalterner sie waren, stand dieser Mann [...] vor einer Tafel, an der er den österreichischen Weg erklärte, und setzte dabei einzelne Ziffern jenen hinzu, die bereits das unausgeglichene Konto anlangten, welches den Sohn betreffen sollte.« (Ibid., p. 31)

outlining these possibilities, Drach thematises the production of behavioural positions in and through different discursive types thereby suggesting a certain lack of authenticity as a constitutive feature of social behaviour in general.

This incidental parenthesis also announces the shape of subjectivity to come in the novel. From the perspective of one who lives in the Austria soon to be annexed by the Nazis, and who will increasingly experience appropriation as Jewish other, this circuitous diagnosis of »subjective« motivation as determined by discourses greater than the subject suggests a prototype of personal passivity that will vary little for the remainder of the novel. The momentary speculation furthermore conveys a sense of utter indifference to the question of choosing between different discursive modes. Or rather, the question of choice at all is an irrelevant one at the beginning of a between-time that will testify to the obsolescence of autonomy during the ascent of totalitarianism. Thus the pseudo-speculative narrative perspective only goes through the motions of speculation, knowledgeable as it seems to be of the common denominator of homogenising discourse. This denominator is the practice of assigning subject position through exclusionary processes. The opening of the protocol thereby engages in a self-reflective debate concerning the tendency of discourse towards identity fixity and regulation that both attempt to fix, if not totally exclude, difference.

The impression of a still life aesthetic is reinforced through the immobility of the representation. The twin signifiers of death and non-movement are present in the image of corpse and son. The latter is about to become further immobilised by the weight of duty awaiting him as only surviving male in the immediate family. This unsavoury prospect coupled with the proximity of the corpse conveys the impression that persons are somehow assembled into dead-end positions by force of ill-luck and unfortunate circumstance. The son is thereby effectively introduced as someone who is surrounded by death, a position that in fact rarely changes throughout the novel. The sense that he is trapped by circumstance persists throughout as external situations, political or otherwise, not only determine many of his decisions, but in the place of a subjective inner life, form his existential landscape. This kind of ordering that places the son in a position of death and immobility forms the statement of stasis that runs through the entire novel and that informs many of its representations of discourse.[22]

Stasis is also present in the above image of the corpse whose only mode of communication, interestingly, is the faint rustling of dying skin and nails. The paternal corpse is here portrayed as a hollow depository for the far greater force of death, the first whimpering overtures of decay symbolic of the inevitable meek capitulation of the individual to a greater political power that will

---

[22] »Schon drohte ihm die Rolle des Verantwortlichen, der er bisher durch erfolgreiche Abwehr der Vermählung sich entzogen zu haben glaubte. Statt der Obsorge für künftige Familianten sah er sich nunmehr mit der für die Witwe des Verstorbenen belastet. [...] Dazu kam die harte Verpflichtung für das väterliche Haus und die erzwungene Weiterführung einer [...] bisher erfolglos betriebenen Rechtsanwaltskanzlei.« (Ibid., p. 9)

in any case sweep it away. For the corpse is a highly suggestive opening image in a novel that tells of the deficient, diminutive individual in a time of growing totalitarianism. That the faint cadence of rotting tissue is the only sound to emit from this image of stasis also augurs ill for the diagnosis of discourse throughout the novel. The corpse as an empty uncommunicative shell is an immensely powerful generic image of discourse that lingers sotto voce behind nearly all representations of discourse in the novel. It symbolically suggests the impossibility of communication once the subject is assigned a posturing space within the confines of »still life« social order. This accounts for the overwhelming isolation that exists between individuals in the text as they are shown to occupy in Carl J. Friedrich's words »islands of separateness« within the engineered atomisation of totalitarian society.[23]

The hardening corpse also functions as an index for the epistemological limitation, reduction and simplification of the world through any discourse that posits itself to be »in the true« during a certain historical period. The discussion of discourse in the novel which arises through highly stylised discursive tableaux such as the above constantly reminds the reader of the artificial and fictitious nature of most discourse. Thus the protocol does not accept any particular discourse as being »in the true«, subject as discourse is to the political manipulation of man. However, this highly distanced narrative strategy does intimate how that which Hannah Arendt refers to as the mendaciousness of totalitarian discourse, comes to assume the status of transcendental signifier in unique situations. This lie of discourse – the lie of totalitarian representationalism – is exactly the reality that kills truth, as Drach has stated. If the essence of power is understood as the ability to present and make visible a model of social organisation, exposing this lie by divulging the workings of power becomes the raison d'être of the protocol. Claude Lefort has described the totalitarian model in terms of the abolition of heterogeneity as social division, accompanied by the disappearance of the division between state and society. This involves a process of homogenising the social space in order to constitute the totalitarian system. Once the system is established »The representation of a ›natural‹ order is re-established«, but as Lefort points out, this order is far from natural, signified as it is through the conception of a power that is supposedly sufficient unto itself.[24]

---

[23] Carl J. Friedrich / Zbigniew Brzezinski: Totalitarian Dictatorship and Autocracy. Revised Edition, Cambridge: Harvard University Press 1965 (Praeger University Series; U 522), p. 294.

[24] Claude Lefort: The Political Forms of Modern Society. Bureaucracy, Democracy, Totalitarianism. Cambridge: Polity Press 1986, p. 286. For a detailed discussion of how the representation of totalitarian order as natural is engineered, see Hannah Arendt: The Origins of Totalitarianism. New York: Harcourt 1973, p. 389–459. Albert Drach: Die Entwertung aller Werte oder die Wandlung des Etwas in Nichts. In: id., Das 17. Buch der 17 Essays, Nachlaß Albert Drach, Austrian Literary Archive of the Austrian National Library, Wien, p. 3.

The opening paragraph of the novel exposes this representationalist reality, as Drach understands the term, thereby setting the tone for the whole novel. The writing of this engineered reality that excludes the autonomous individual by assigning discursive position begins with the writing of apotheosis through the aesthetic form of the still life. The poverty of the inner life of the individual is communicated not only through the officious nature of the protocol language but also through its visual counterpart: the smallness, the limitation, the outright misery of existence conveyed by the room-sized genre of the still life.[25] Significantly, the room portrayed in this scene is a partitioned space of death, sickness, incapacitation and immobility. The sick-room still life symbolises the historical space of enclosure in which the protagonist is confined and rarely escapes. It is an enclosed space that could be read as a version of the cellular disciplinary space assigned to the docile individual.[26]

Whereas on the surface of things the human subject may be present in this representation, this presence cannot be described in terms of the reassuring metaphorical *praesentia in absentia* of the traditional still life which moreover affirms man's control over his universe of tamed, ordered and arranged objects. Rather, we are dealing with the reverse in this instance and for most of the novel, a kind of *absentia in praesentia*. In other words, humans are overwhelmingly absent as autonomous subjects in the still life tableaux of »Z. Z.«, for the main part present only in their function as objects of the ruling order. Thus humans bear all the traits of things to be manipulated into order in this novel and are accordingly presented in the different still life depictions as objects. This strategy reinforces the sense of a grotesque existence through the reduction of humans to commodities or things.[27]

The overall impression is one of the subject caught in a flat world of inanimate objects that are poised in a certain order and that to an extent confer their artifactual status onto the human subject depicted. This is the web of defining, assigning representationalism in which the son is caught from the outset. The disciplinary partitioning gaze of anti-Semitism is present in the politics of this portrait which assigns the son the position of the inert, the inanimate: the object of the still life, the »other« of society. It is representative of an order »that possesses total knowledge of the detail of social reality« and can thus be seen

---

[25] Seltzer, Bodies and Machines (note 5), p. 139.

[26] »Disciplinary space tends to be divided into as many sections as there are bodies or elements to be distributed [...] the disciplinary space is always, basically, cellular.« (Foucault, Discipline and Punish [note 15], p. 143)

[27] Seltzer argues that in its original form, the still life »necessarily excludes the human subject and the human body since it is precisely the human subject and the human body to which [it] at every point makes reference«. However, the representation of the human subject in the still life seems to reverse the metonymical effect of praesentia in absentia: »[...] the precarious difference between person and thing here« is »the difference between consuming and being consumed.« (Seltzer, Bodies and Machines [note 5], p. 139–140)

as part of the drive to homogenise the social space by enclosing it in the appropriating gaze of power.[28] This opening tableau articulates thus the body of negation, a fact that is reinforced by the detailed depiction of the corpse.

The question as to precisely what body is in a position to order other bodies in this manner is thematised regularly throughout the novel. One chilling key episode explains to a great extent the dominant understanding of power relations in »Z. Z.«, thereby throwing light on the aesthetic choice of the still life. It is the summer of 1936, one year after the Dollfuß murder. Signs of growing anti-Semitism are becoming difficult to ignore in the son's Vienna, particularly after all Jews (the son included) have received the official list citing fourteen Jewish vices. Typically for the son, having ascertained that sexual activity with under aged females is not as yet a recognised vice, thereby rendering the list irrelevant for him, he shoves it carelessly into a drawer meaning to return to it at a later point. In other words, he skates over the accusations that should apply directly to him as a Jewish lawyer and that claim that the legal profession (amongst others) has been all but taken over by conniving Jews.[29]

The son's lack of interest in the latter claim shows to what extent he is utterly alienated from both his inherited legal chambers and his Jewish origins. All that counts is the right to execute a rampant sex life, a cynicism which in itself states where the appropriated other locates its supposedly autonomous existence – in the so-called private sphere, the public areas of profession and racial prejudice perceived as beyond the domain of individual control and therefore irrelevant. Shoving the papers away becomes the action of a subject who knows its place within the social order and who is convinced that individually it can effect little change. Sex is the only hope for self realisation or self expression, but as shall become clear in the final chapter, this private sphere is inseparable from the violence conducted at the broader social level.

As a means of avoiding the growing undertones of anti-Semitism that are becoming apparent in Vienna, the son and his mother go to the mountainous region of Carinthia for a holiday break. However, in a pattern that will become typical of all trips taken during the between time, the holiday destination is already invaded by elements of what the son constantly tries to escape: evidence of Hitler's growing hold on Austria.[30] Foreshadowing the son's journey

---

[28] Lefort, The Political Forms of Modern Society (note 24), p. 288.

[29] »Wieder zu Hause angelangt, fand er ein Flugblatt in seinem Briefkasten, in welchem vierzehn Übel aufgezählt waren, die den Juden zum Vorwurf gemacht wurden, wobei die Anführung damit begann, daß sie neunzig Prozent der Anwälte und Ärzte in der Hauptstadt stellten, auch die Wirtschaft beherrschten, die Zeitungen in Händen hielten und über das meiste Geld verfügten. Daneben war noch erwähnt, daß die Juden [...] sich an Frauen vergingen, die sie mißbrauchten und vergewaltigten. Von Mädchen unter vierzehn war aber nicht die Rede [...]. Der Sohn legte das Blatt in seine Reklamenmappe und hatte vor, gelegentlich darauf zurückzukommen.« (Z. Z. 114–115)

[30] »Sie fuhren nach kärntnerischen Höhen, wo die Urlaubsgäste aus dem Reich bereits teilweise ausgeblieben waren, weil Hitler dieses Reiseziel mit hohen Auflagen belegte, um die Ostmark allmählich zu unterkriegen.« (Ibid., p. 126)

into exile in the autumn of 1938 when he leaves his mother behind in Vienna, mother and son drift further apart on this holiday, the son chasing in vain a girl of mixed origins.[31] He then moves on to a Yugoslavian woman who accompanies him on a mountain climb. In a manner that portrays the private as hopelessly dominated by the public, his hopes of seduction are dashed when she enquires about the political situation in Austria and his position with regard to Hitler's immanent take over.

In the following passage, it becomes clear what understanding of power is most pervasive in »Z. Z.«. Identifying the root of all evil in the between time with the figure of Hitler, the son shows himself to be beholden to a model of power that personifies its source:

> Er selber aber wolle Hitler umbringen. Er fühle die Kraft dazu und die Sendung in sich, er werde den Augenblick und die Gelegenheit dazu herausfinden. Das sei vielleicht gerade das, was er überhaupt auf dieser Welt zu tun habe, denn er sehe in diesem Unhold keine Persönlichkeit, nur eine Personifikation aller Gemeinplätze, die in dem Wortschatz der Halbgebildeten vorhanden und aus diesem ins Volk gelangt seien. (*Z. Z.* 128–129)

This display of heroism is dampened by his companion's reply. Certain death for the son would be the outcome of such an attempted action, she advises. The only path for survival is to accept the situation as it is and simply endure it to the end. With an insight that further emphasises the subordination of the subject during the time of the indefatigable Hitler personification, the son recognises that heroes of warrior ilk are obsolete in the between time:

> Er mußte daher sehr wohl die beiden Ziele auseinanderhalten können, das des Lebenseinsatzes für die Beseitigung einer fleischgewordenen und in diesem Zustand hochgefeierten Personifikation und das des bloßen Überdauerns des durch andere Kräfte, ohne irgendein Zutun seinerseits, zu vernichtenden Popanzes.   (*Z. Z.* 129)

Survival becomes synonymous with passivity. Essentially, the kind of power structure that is here recognised and in a sense obeyed, can be likened to Foucault's understanding of the model of juridical monarchy that conceives of the law and the king as the indisputable sources of all power. In other words, power is personified in the figure of the monarch and this figure in turn rules in conjunction with the law. The totalitarian model of dictatorship differs from the monarchic model however, insofar as the balance between law and monarch is abandoned. The leader now places himself above the law. Such a figure is beyond the limitations of hierarchy, »even the one he might have established himself«.[32] Arendt notes that this form of leadership results in the subordination of all forms of social organisation to the party leader. In the specifically totalitarian scheme, power is no longer simply centralised. It is also disturbingly ubiquitous because the person of the leader infiltrates and dominates all levels of society. This figure goes beyond previous forms of authoritarian rule,

---

[31] »Nach solcher Exkursion [...] löste sich der Zusammenhang zwischen Mutter und Sohn immer mehr.« (Ibid.)
[32] Arendt, The Origins of Totalitarianism (note 24), p. 405.

according to Arendt, because the mere restriction or limitation of freedom is now superseded by the outright abolition of individual freedom within the totalitarian state. Lefort terms this kind of leader an »Egocrat« who, in practising the abolition of difference in order to implement the project of controlled unanimity, »coincides with himself, as society is supposed to coincide with itself«.[33] By implication the society that is dominated by such a figure is enclosed, deprived of freedom, and defined by the body of the ubiquitous leader. As a body that coincides with itself, the body of the egocrat is one that negates difference; in other words, it is the pathological embodiment of the body of negation.[34]

When one considers that all Drach's works thus far discussed steadily work to expose this subject as a fiction of discourse, it is both bitterly ironic and very fitting that this entity should now raise its head in the form of Hitler. For Hitler is the ultimate personification of evil as far as the son is concerned, a product and embodiment of the totalitarian culture that Drach associates with the *Amt*. That Hitler as *Führer* is in the son's eyes little more than a discursively produced image becomes clear in the description that reduces him to the demigod status of the above *fleischgewordene Personifikation* (a personification become flesh and blood). Resentful though he is of the power this entity wields over his person (not to mention entire nations), nonetheless even the son recognises that this personification is indefinitely entrenched in the image of the all-powerful party leader, the omnipresent centre of suppression that characterises the between time.

It should not surprise us thus that at a later point in the narrative, the son refers to the between time as a time in which the incubus or the succubus has a deadly grip on the subject. The personification of Hitler as a font of insurmountable power is here described in the more abstract terms of an insidious evil spirit that insinuates its way into all aspects of the subordinated subject's life. In particular, the choice of the symbol succubus (a female demon who seduces sleeping men) is interesting because it associates the evils of the time specifically with the signifiers »sex« and »woman«. This discussion will be taken up in more detail in the next chapter. Clearly however, this image communicates the perversion of Eros through Thanatos (the degradation of sexual encounters to the will of an evil spirit). It also articulates the dissolution of the public/private divide, underlining the extent to which the developing totalitar-

---

[33] Lefort, The Political Forms of Modern Society [note 24], p. 306.

[34] Foucault argues that whilst we may not yet have »cut off the head of the king«, the juridical-monarchic model does not adequately represent the mechanisms of power in modern society that function »not by law, but by normalization, not by punishment but by control, methods that are employed on all levels and in forms that go beyond the state and its apparatus« (Michel Foucault: The History of Sexuality. The Will to Knowledge. London: Penguin Books 1998, p. 89). Arendt discusses precisely this power complex as it manifests itself in the totalitarian state through the omnipresence of the party leader (Arendt, The Origins of Totalitarianism [note 24], p. 405).

ian state, in the abstract form of incubus/succubus, has invaded even the most intimate lives of its subjects.[35]

Incubus, succubus, personification, apotheosis – these different terms that describe the workings of power in the between time are all consistent with images of stasis and death as non-movement. The above described power model thus produces in its own likeness the order of immobility that is represented by the still life tableaux of the novel. The vertical axis of cultural authority that arranges bodies in cellular, disciplinary positions of decreasing hierarchy is also evoked through these interrelated images. Reading the novel in terms of the statement that assigns position in this hierarchy thus corresponds to identifying the primacy of the culturally determinate body: an egocratic/patriarchial model of the body which takes as its ideological point of departure the »monarchic« position of the centre.

The peripheral and the contingent (aspects of the culturally indeterminate body) are notably played down in this model. In his discussion of power models however, Foucault points out that in fact the image of the sovereignty of the state is not a given at the outset, but is a terminal form that power may take given favourable circumstance. Dictatorship is one such manifestation of power in the above terminal form.[36] Bearing this in mind, it would seem that the assigning/ordering instance of this particular power discourse can be equated with the idol status of the Hitler position. The ontology of the false god, then, determines the body of power in the between time and with this assigns position in its own image and ideology: the still life of the uniform individual/society that coincides with itself to create what Lefort terms the imaginary space of totalitarianism.

In keeping with the ontological image projected by totalitarian power, all other entities are perceived to have emanated from this centre of all existence and are ordered according to this image of the centre. Hence the evil ordering eye of the still life that structures reality and manipulates representation to produce the incapacitated subject who is trapped in this negative ontology. Accordingly, the manner in which subject position is assigned during totalitarianism is played out in the representational device of the still life aesthetic.[37] The related issue of agency behind the assigning function can be explained with reference to the incubus/succubus symbol of death as a general term for Hitler and the society that facilitates his rise to power.

---

[35] »Mag sein, daß solche Unterstellungen für eine Zwischenzeit langen, in denen ein Inkubus oder Sukkubus nicht nur die Form des Teilhabers am Genusse, sondern auch die des Lebenzweckes und des Sinnes des Geschehens übernimmt.« (*Z. Z.* 192)

[36] »The analysis, made in terms of power, must not assume that the sovereignty of the state, the form of the law, or the overall unity of a domination are given at the outset; rather, these are all terminal forms power takes.« (Foucault, The History of Sexuality [note 33], p. 92)

[37] »[...] the scandal of the still life in persons is the reduction of persons to the immobility and, therefore, the inanimation, or suspended inanimation of the commodity itself.« (Seltzer, Bodies and Machines [note 5], p. 143)

In one exceptional situation, the narrative nonetheless betrays a far more incisive knowledge of how power actually works. It is an incident that momentarily releases the representation of power in the novel from the image of the thug party leader, articulating power instead through the alternative image of the contingent. This episode has been correctly identified as an incident of sly civility, Homi Bhabha's term for the faked subservience of the appropriated other.[38] At an advanced point in the plot, the son is unceremoniously marched into the town by his fellow townsfolk so that he can fulfil his Jewish duty of painting and marking Jewish shop fronts. He has no choice but to obey as the braying crowd stampedes his house and eventually bypasses his mother to where he has been hiding in the bathroom. Nonetheless, obedience gets a mimic twist here as the son affects not to know how to wield the paintbrush or use the ladder etc. Determined not to do this degrading dirty work, he slips into the stereotype of the clueless, less able other, pretending to co-operate whilst all the time laughing up his sleeve at his superiors who are unaware that they have been duped to do the job for him.[39]

This incident represents more than simple one-upmanship. Here, the son manages to transgress the discursive image of power in the centralised mode of the unattainable beyond, redistributing it at a local level. The sly civility pose articulates just this manifestation of power at a localised level. The SS men who become the pawns in this ploy represent the centralised ontology of the false god (Hitler) whose engineered position both at the pinnacle of and beyond social hierarchy, it is implied by this local incident, is also potentially fallible. The passage suggests that power is not exclusively attached to the distant concept of the transcendental centre. Rather, it is insinuated that power forms a mobile and unlimited field of energy made up of constantly colliding, changing positions. What essentially occurs in the above episode is a tactical changing of positions from underdog to master and vice versa, whereby this exchange occurs through the transgression of a dominant discursive image of power.

This constellation corresponds to Foucault's general understanding of power which he describes not in terms of the hierarchical ordering principle of the centre, but as »the moving substrate of force relations which, by virtue of their inequality, constantly engender power, but the latter are always local and unstable«.[40] In contrast to the inflexibility implied through the Hitler personifica-

---

[38] Cf. Anne Fuchs: Files against the Self. Albert Drach. In: id., A Space of Anxiety. Dislocation and Abjection in Modern German-Jewish Literature. Amsterdam, Atlanta: Rodopi 1999 (Amsterdamer Publikationen zur Sprache und Literatur; 138), p. 123–162, here p. 152–153.

[39] »So kam es, daß sowohl SA als auch Zivilisten ihm bei seiner Vorleistung behilflich sein, ja sie sogar an seiner Statt übernehmen mußten. Schließlich ergab sich eine Lage, bei der ein SA-Mann den Farbtiegel hochob [sic], ein anderer den Pinsel eintauchte, während ein Zivilist die Leiter ansetzte, auf welcher der Sohn dann gemächlich hinaufstieg.« (*Z. Z.* 261)

[40] Foucault, The History of Sexuality (note 33), p. 93.

tion and image of power, this understanding of power restores to it the positive element of movement so lacking in the still life order described above. As such, the sly civility episode represents a genuine departure from the statement of stasis that largely informs the novel. The son is seen momentarily to transgress his assigned position as appropriated other, asserting himself in the only avenue left open to him, i. e. through the devious manipulation of discourse. In this episode he steps outside his still life persona and takes control of an impossible situation. He disrupts the order of power in so doing, exposing the sovereign image as the carefully crafted fiction that it is. He thereby breaks through the representationalist lie of totalitarian discourse that informs the between time and keeps individuals trapped in a politics of obedience that disempowers them.

However, this incident is very much the exception to the rule in »Z. Z.«. It may be a deviation from the sovereign power model, and a significant one at that, due to the possibilities of subversion it infers through the image of shifting positionality. However, a deviation is what it remains as the son subsequently reverts to type. This is as much a reflection of the controlling power structure of the between time as it is a reflection of the son's personal (and socially induced) inadequacy. The highly atypical nature of the sly civility episode is symbolically indicated through the mother's supporting role during the event. Let us recall that it is she who fends off the irate neighbours who demand the son. In a less than heroic light, the son is depicted as firmly ensconced in his hideaway niche of the bathroom, leaving his mother quite literally to hold the fort. The same disinterestedness that is evident in his lack of reaction to the anti-Semitic pamphlet is again apparent here, as in the mode of the greedy child intent on its own satisfaction he is seen to be guzzling his favourite dessert, lovingly prepared by his mother.[41] After one hour, it becomes clear that the mob is not to be placated, so he emerges and is escorted into the town. Unlike his behaviour towards his mother, she never strays from his side, accompanying him and supporting him throughout the entire ordeal:

> Damals aber kehrte der Sohn mit seiner Mutter heim, wobei sie wie eine Königin dahinschritt und er neben ihr wie ein Rebell ging, welcher sich vorübergehend ihren Anordnungen unterwarf, nachdem er die der Parteifunktionäre nur mangelhaft ausgeführt hatte. Immerhin ist anzunehmen, daß er an diesem Nachmittag zumindest während der Dauer der Heimkehr stolz auf sie sein durfte, weil sie sich noch viel besser als er selbst gehalten und aus freien Stücken nicht von seiner Seite gewichen war.   (*Z. Z.* 265)

This is a rare show and recognition of mother and son solidarity. Normally the mother is viewed by the son as a nagging, worrying burden, whereas here she is presented as the force behind him in this unusual episode. The above forms a very suggestive constellation of images. The maternal space here is not denigra-

---

[41] »In diesem Schlupfwinkel glaubte er sich vorläufig vor der Menge in Sicherheit, wobei er seiner Mutter die Gelassenheit zutraute, beziehungsweise die Gefahr auflud, mit den voraussichtlichen Eindringlingen zu einem Verhandlungsergebnis, nämlich dem ihres Abzuges zu gelangen.« (*Z. Z.* 256)

ted or belittled by the son. Instead, it is revered and recognised for the power that it can lend to the individual. The mother figure remaining alongside her son could be read as the return of the otherwise constantly absent semiotic *chora*, the sly civility episode of mimic man an instance that is both fuelled by and raises this semiotic space. Thus the son, who is otherwise an impoverished weak subject, becomes here momentarily enriched by a maternal presence that is usually scorned.

In an anti-Semitic society that attempts to define the other as banished entity, this amounts to a definite (if isolated) show of resistance as it allows for the return of the other in that disturbing unpredictable, semiotic capacity that undermines the image of the sovereign self. The son's own fleeting openness to this maternal difference in turn generates the difference that is produced by the flexibility and inconsistency of subject position exemplified in the above example. Thetic instability returns as it is implied by the cunning change of power relations that subjectivity is a matter of position and not essence. Thus the local instability of power feeds directly into the instability of the subject who is never quite anchored in its position. Resistance may here be regarded as the openness to otherness as difference that represents risk for both the resisting subject and the symbolic personifications it attempts to resist. It is a resistance to the closure of the symbolic order and an instance that reintroduces the *jouissance* aspect of the drives into a narrative largely characterised by stasis. This episode thus constitutes the short-lived return of the revolutionary subject of poetic language.

The above knowledge and practice of difference only serves to emphasise the tragedy of the matricide at the end of the novel. This final incident taken in conjunction with the above Kristevan reading of the text suggests that the son, who we now know certainly knows better, has opted for a form of coerced obedience to the totalitarian state by expelling from his everyday existence the maternal presence. This is apparent in his decision to leave his mother behind in Vienna as he sets off on the first leg of his exile journey.[42] However, his betrayal of the maternal presence ultimately culminates in the vision of her death at the close of the novel.

It is also this final image that most strongly articulates the motif of travel/motion as homogenous with images of death, exile being both a symptom and consequence of the enclosed space of totalitarianism. Travel in general ironically reflects the opening enclosed space of the sick-room still life and is frequently presented as contaminated by the omniscient presence of the incubus. Along with the interrelated images of corpse and Egocrat, the holiday vignette is another literary form that Drach manipulates in order to expose apotheosis.

All tourist/travel tableaux in the novel evoke this final image of death as the destruction of the semiotic and the resulting regression into stasis. Movement as travel in »Z. Z.« is represented as a kind of running to standstill that antici-

---

[42] »[...] die Mutter [umarmte], einer plötzlichen Eingebung folgend, kurzfristig den Sohn, während die Tochter wegsah. Dabei erklärte ihm erstere ungeachtet bisheriger Beherrschung, daß sie ihn kaum je wiedersehen werde. Der Sohn ahnte zwar, daß sie die Wahrheit sprach, widersetzte sich aber dem ungewohnten Kuß, als wäre er durch diesen in seiner Männlichkeit verletzt.« (Ibid., p. 323)

pates the enforced travel of exile. One year after his sojourn in Carinthia the son goes to France on holidays. Significantly, this time he elects to go without his mother. Also foreshadowing future exile is the holiday destination of 1937 where he will lead a furtive existence in the years during the war, narrowly escaping death in the French concentration camps through a combination of wit and chance.[43] The holiday journey there and back is characterised by many images of spacelessness – the cramped quarters of the train, the visit to the *Comédie Française* and the decision to return to Austria through Switzerland (*Z. Z.* 160, 169, 170). The latter is a ploy to avoid Hitler Germany and suggests the narrowing of the European map specifically for the Jewish other. Unsurprisingly, the motif of spacelessness is repeated in Switzerland. In both countries, the inability of the son to communicate with the natives is highlighted through language difficulties which implies the growing alienation of the Jewish subject from other European nations (*Z. Z.* 162, 168, 175). All of these situations foreshadow the unsentimental journey that Drach's next alter ego, Peter Kucku, will have to endure in a bid to survive extermination at the hands of the Nazis.

Most striking about this particular holiday however, is the depiction of the Eiffel tower. In a deliberate reversal of the semiotics of tourism, the Eiffel tower as the icon of France is described chiefly in terms of its popularity as a convenient launching pad for suicide hopefuls. This information is related in the trite fashion so typical for the protocol, sandwiched between the account of liberally consumed aperitifs which serves only to enhance the mention of suicide. For suicide is a theme that runs consistently through this novel and the next. Moreover, *Unsentimentale Reise* ends in the implied suicide of the Drach figure which continues the overall effect of an aesthetics of death, reflecting in a manner reminiscent of stasis the death of the mother at the end of *»Z. Z.«*.[44]

---

[43] The exile years in France are narrated for the main part in the second part of the autobiographical trilogy, *Unsentimentale Reise. Ein Bericht*, Ungekürzte Ausg., München: Deutscher Taschenbuch Verlag 1988 (dtv; 11226). Ernestine Schlant has likened the movements of the main character – »circles, loops, and arches [...] a desperate sequence of skips and jumps« – to the Dance of Death motif. Similar to the son in *»Z. Z.«*, the circular movement of travel in *Unsentimentale Reise* communicates only that Drach's alter ego, Peter Kucku »cannot leave the magnetic field of the *universe concentrationnaire*« (Ernestine Schlant: Albert Drach's Unsentimentale Reise. Literature of the Holocaust and the Dance of Death. In: Modern Austrian Literature 26 [1993], p. 35–57, here p. 44–45).

[44] »In einem Bistro wurde von Sohn und Schwiegercousin der Frühaperitif genommen, wonach die Autobusfahrt zum Eiffelturm ging, wo alle Etagen zu besichtigen waren, insbesondere aber der zweite Aperitif in der zweiten, der dritte in der obersten eingenommen werden mußte. Von dort wurden sämtliche Ausblicke gezeigt, die Touristen vorzuzeigen sind, einschließlich jener Stellen, von denen sich die meisten Selbstmörder in die Tiefe zu stürzen pflegten.« (*Z. Z.* 168) For the matricide and suicide scenes, ibid., p. 347 and *Unsentimentale Reise* (note 42), p. 368 respectively. The notion of inverse tourism refers to Jonathan Culler's essay: The Semiotics of Tourism. In: id., Framing the Sign. Criticism and its Institutions. Oxford: Norman 1988, p. 153–168.

The overwhelming message is one of non-movement through travel. The final destination of any trip is death. In Carinthia, the presence of the Hitler personification was too dominant to be ignored. In Paris, the utopian image of travel as escape is inverted to become an image of the incubus as suicide. The theme of travel thus represents anything but movement as the deferral of stasis. Rather, it reinforces the sense of apathy that dominates the narrative, refuting as it does the possibility of escape.

To summarise, Drach engages in a dual assessment of totalitarianism in this novel. On the one hand, totalitarianism is presented as a discursive construct, a powerful one certainly, but nonetheless a construct from within the social body that culminates in the figure of Hitler. In other words, Drach's critique of totalitarianism through the use of the still life aesthetic goes some length to show up the tactics of cultural ordering that occur during the between time. On the other hand however, totalitarianism is presented as an insurmountable evil spirit that takes residence in such personifications as Hitler. Yet it is implied by the incubus image that this rendition of evil transcends even the Hitler persona. Or as Drach describes it in his play concerning the Marquis de Sade, evil is not a matter solely of one's assigned position within the social context. Rather, he speculates, true evil must be everywhere present but nowhere resident. It is the capitulation of the son in particular to this latter image of power that forms the basis of his subservience. The coming section will assess representations of the body as articulations of this subservience, exploring the question as to how violence is inscribed on the body in »*Z. Z.*«.[45]

6.3 In the Shadow of the Egocrat: A Micro-Physics of Power

A central image of the body in »*Z. Z.*«, it has been argued, is that of the corpse. Representations of the body in the text are delimited by this mute, defining image as it contours and marks out spaces of controlled legitimacy for the subjected body. Thus we are at a remove from the fragmented body, or as Kristeva terms it, the »material discontinuity« of the thetic position described in earlier chapters.[46] In lieu of the pulverisation of the symbolic self that arises through the semiotic rupture of the symbolic, we now encounter a less mobile articulation of the body. The body as it emerges in »*Z. Z.*« communicates a politics of obedience or docility which, within the psychoanalytic framework, may be interpreted as a symptom of reduced semiotic activity in the representation of the body. As previously argued, this latter development, if pathological, can be read as both symptom and effect of totalitarianism which raises paternal (symbolic) law above all else and accordingly denigrates the maternal

---

[45] »Der wahrhaft Böse müßte durch alle Häute schlüpfen und in keiner seßhaft sein.« Albert Drach: Das Satansspiel vom göttlichen Marquis. Eine Verkleidung in vier Akten. Frankfurt a. M.: Verlag der Autoren 1992, p. 141.

[46] Kristeva, Revolution in Poetic Language (note 18), p. 100.

(semiotic). The totalitarian body thus coincides with the body of negation (the sadistic stiff); its victim other is the negated semiotic.

The body remains nevertheless grotesque in its articulation in this instance. It differs from the grotesque body of the ambivalent self insofar as it is no longer articulated as a transgressive force operating through an ongoing process. The body in this text has been removed from the process. This shift relegates the body to an enclosed, enforced place apart from the process where, according to Kristeva, its only identity is inorganic, paralysed, dead.[47] In terms of self as locative system, the subject of this body no longer occupies the vivacious borderline location of the aphanisic fader. Apart from the process, this corpse-like automaton operates within the space of absolute negation: the *grotta*/grave.

Kristeva's theory of revolutionary language does not readily allow the establishment of this still, »non-revolutionary« space without semiotic disruption. As we have seen, the thetic position as put forward in *Revolution in Poetic Language* always represents a point of semiotic indeterminacy in the symbolic. What if the thetic were to blank this interference, to become more strongly barricaded, however? One could describe this development in theoretical terms by reversing the modus operandi of what Kristeva calls the combinatory moment. The latter denotes the moment of collision between the obscurity of the destructive/creative semiotic process and a symbolic barrier or boundary. The force of the semiotic *chora* encounters thus a moment of stasis »which is viewed as if it were insurmountable« and without which »the process would never become a practice«.[48] In other words, through this clash of the combinatory drives (*jouissance*/stasis; semiotic/symbolic) the thetic position becomes marked out and is thereafter always open to semiotic interference.

With regard to »Z. Z.«, the scandal to be examined is no longer the scandal of semiotic intereference. Rather, it is the scandal of what Kristeva terms hypostasis, as the combinatory moment stops short of combination/collision, becoming instead hostage to the insurmountable image of the static boundary. In other words, it is as if closure of the symbolic is complete and impenetrable whilst the semiotic is excluded from the outset. Position becomes defined through the immobility of this insurmountable wall as the process, arrested indefinitely at this point, fails to transform into a dynamic and exploratory practice. Instead, the ephemeral nature of the subject, subject position and meaning assume the appearance of eternity as they solidify in the (pathological) hypostasis of the symbolic. Material discontinuity, as articulated in the rupture of the symbolic order by the semiotic, tends to recede as the body and the individual are now represented as positioned, contoured and delimited instances of appropriated, mute matter. In abstract terms, the inscription of violence on the body in »Z. Z.« can be seen as this enforced impregnability of the static border, as the individual is truncated if necessary, in order to ensure a more effective appropriation.

---

[47] Ibid., p. 101.
[48] Ibid., p. 102.

In accordance with this shift towards the paralysis and reduction of bodies, the determining image of the body in »Z. Z.« is that of the egocratic body. The latter is a power-invested specification of the corpse that corresponds, to a large extent, to Kristeva's notion of the inorganic body removed from the process/practice and eternally poised at the insurmountable wall of the symbolic. The political implications of Kristeva's inorganic body become manifest in Lefort's description of the Egocrat as the central controlling force of the totalitarian state. There is no room for indeterminacy or material discontinuity in this vision as the Egocrat is shown to coincide with itself in the manner of a self-sufficient, omnipotent figure of power. This particular body merges with the social body as the latter, consistent with the totalitarian project, is increasingly incorporated into the state machinery. In this manner, society becomes invested by power, materialising in the shape of the totalitarian body.

Most interesting however, is Lefort's diagnosis of this body as an inorganic entity due to its very coincidence with itself. Similar to the sign that forbids penetration and that is safeguarded from ambivalence by the impenetrable wall of hypostasis, the totalitarian body that coincides completely with itself represents a society devoid of difference. Certainly the totalitarian society is one populated by »others«; the creation of an easily defined enemy (the Jew) is fundamental to the image of a unified totalitarian body. This process of othering suppresses difference by appropriating the other through a self-reflecting projection of uniformity. The defined place of the other is therefore an integral part of the totalitarian body. It does not initially designate a transgressive beyond of the enclosed system, but a controlled, legitimated if depotentiated »other« space within it.

In this prison of sameness, argues Lefort, »An impossible swallowing up of the body in the head begins to take place, as does an impossible swallowing up of the head in the body«.[49] In other words, part and whole become indistinguishable from one another as difference is erased. Thus a cannibalistic precedent is set by the egocratic body that must eternally devour itself and its parts, in order to purge itself of difference and maintain the protected space of isotropy. The egocratic body is a static body therefore, in which »once the old organic constitution disappears, the death instinct is unleashed into the closed, uniform, imaginary space of totalitarianism«.[50]

It is just this image of the body in the likeness of the Hitler Egocrat that dominates in »Z. Z.« The irony is of course that this body is discursively produced, as noted by the narrative at an advanced stage in the novel. The son's questionable conviction that murdering Hitler would diffuse the present problem of anti-Semitism resurfaces during Christmas of 1937 when it has become clear that the Austrian government will inevitably soon collapse under persistent German pressure. Again, the identification of power with the omniscient

---

[49] Lefort, The Political Forms of Modern Society (note 24), p. 306.
[50] Ibid.

figure of the egocrat/incubus becomes apparent here. However, subservience to the Hitler entity is momentarily refuted as this figure is shown to be simply the pinnacle of centuries of anti-Semitic discourse, an empty form in which the ghost of anti-Semitism may become a flesh and blood personification:

> Bei Vernichtung der Person, die diesen Gedanken verkörperte, würde es sich zwar nicht um mehr als um die Beseitigung einer gänzlich unbedeutenden skrupellosen Kreatur gehandelt haben, wohl aber einer solchen, die durch Einhauchung aller Formeln seit Jahrhunderten angehäufter platter Vorstellungen oberflächlichster Art zur Verkörperung einer Ansicht geworden war, mit der sich banalste Massen aus der Mist verstaubter Literaturabfälle, der Auftragung waschblauer Himmel billigster Ansichtskarten, dem Zusammenklang von Blechmusik aus zehnter Hand mit dem Rhythmus marschierender Versager an den Felsen von Gips ihr deutsches Wesen erlogen und diesem Überkitsch im Zerrspiegel angeblich jüdische Art entgegenzusetzen behaupteten.   (Z. Z. 207)

This furious insight refuses to accord Hitler the egocratic body he projects, instead calling his bluff and rejecting the mythological dimension of evil power conveyed in the incubus image. Instead, the historically and culturally engendered nature of evil is exposed here, that being stupidity and ignorance of the highest degree. We witness the evocation of one of the protocol's chief functions in this respect: the tracing of mendacious language trails as they weave their way through time and into the wrong hands, becoming manipulated pieces of propaganda in the play for absolute power. Hitler's body becomes here a moving mass of ridiculous anti-Semitic hotchpotch, basic, unsubtle, inferior and only worthy of contempt. Thus the image of a world ordered according to the Hitlerite centre shifts briefly, as his body is in this instance no longer the body of an initiating subject that orders its environment into a series of fixed effects. Rather, it is implied that the production of the egocratic image is the effect of a performative discourse that, in its citational persistence, »conceals or dissimulates the conventions of which it is a repetition«.[51]

The conventions, support and tradition of anti-Semitic discourse are exposed as part of a totalitarian propaganda offensive in the above passage. Paradoxically however, this extract is equally the expression of the son's impotence in the face of this discursive image. His burst of outraged cerebral activity is followed by utter passivity as neither he, nor any other Austrian citizen for that matter, takes significant measures against the inevitability of the Berchtesgaden conference, in which the aforementioned vile egocratic personification wields real power in his bullying of the Austrian dictator Schuschnigg. The annexation of Austria, its absorption into the greater German body, becomes only a matter of time after this meeting. Discursive or corporeal, the power emanating from the egocrat's body is real and undeniable. Despite the son's knowledge of the engineered production of this body, the power that it holds

---

[51] Judith Butler: Bodies that Matter. On the Discursive Limits of Sex. New York, London: Routledge 1993, p. 12.

would also appear to be insurmountable, occasionally inciting the protagonist to outbursts of verbal indignation, but little else.[52]

The violence of the power-crazed, egomaniacal Hitler figure is articulated also through the general representation and naming of characters in the novel. The use of personal names is meticulously avoided as we encounter, along with the insistent labelling of the main protagonist as »the son«, the strangest of appellations: *der Schönling* (the dandy), *der Fette* (the slob), *der Musikerkopf* (the musician-head), *die Gliederpuppe* (the jointed doll), *die Alte* (the old maid), *der Goldzahnblecker* (the gold teeth-gnasher/barer), *der Glatzkopf* (the baldy), to name but a few. This pattern of characterisation excludes the personal totally, as the subjected individual is caricaturised through one aspect of its appearance or position in life. It would seem that the above freak-like figures are formed in the likeness of the Hitler personification. They too are personifications, not of themselves, but of the regulated totalitarian body that both dwarfs and reduces them. Reduced thus in stature, they subsist in the shadow of the Egocrat, profoundly alienated from each other, from themselves and from the historical events happening around them during this time.

The image of the *Gliederpuppe* is particularly eloquent in this respect. It is an image of the mechanical, of »ghastly marionettes with human faces«, that pervades all characterisation in the novel.[53] Subordinate to the inflexible egocratic principle of engineered power, characters assume for the main part the function of puppets as they show themselves, either through violence or political passivity, to be the obedient subjects of the state.[54] As if to emphasise this degree of automation, only the young female character of the *Gliederpuppe* manages to move the son to a displaced show of tears. Failing to seduce her, he cries for the loss of a doll that he never had:

Der Sohn [...] hatte es an dem Abschiedsabend besonders darauf angelegt, die geliebte Puppe durch Vernunfts-, Gefühls- und fleischliche Momente an sich zu bringen, wobei er ihr sogar sagte, daß er sie liebe, eine Äußerung, die er in dieser Form schon mehr als ein Jahrzent nicht mehr gebraucht hatte [...]. Im übrigen waren ihm von ihren Körper nur die besonders gerade angesetzten und doch richtig schwellenden Beine bis nicht

---

[52] »Aber während sich der Sohn noch zu nichts aufraffte und niemand sonst etwas tat, um die Fälle zu öffnen, war der Tag bald gekommen, an dem der schulmeisterliche Kanzler nach Berchtesgaden berufen wurde, die Lektion des Führers erhielt und aus dem Untergrund sich die kommenden Recken sammelten, [...] Bombenleger vor jüdischen Juwelierläden, freigesprochene Mörder israelitischer Groschenschreiber.« (*Z. Z.* 207–208)

[53] Arendt, The Origins of Totalitarianism (note 24), p. 455.

[54] This political passivity is presented as a middle-class phenomenon during an early episode in the book; the son goes to a soirée attended by artists, diplomats and the important businessmen of Vienna at that time. The motif of entrapment is presented through the rigid seating plan, the son's cramped position between two unbearable women and the general neglect of political conversation (*Z. Z.* 56–58). This passivity translates into violence a short time later when the son rapes an elderly woman (this incident will be discussed in more detail in the coming chapter), ibid., p. 62–64.

hoch über das Knie bekannt, dazu ihr Puppengesicht samt Lockenkopf. Wie sie
schließlich ging, ohne auf seine Formulierungen einzugehen, [...] sagte sie ihm trotzdem: »Auf Wiedersehen.« Der Sohn aber weinte damals zum ersten Male seit seiner
Kindheit, wie es sich auch schickt, wenn man eine schöne Puppe verliert.   (Z. Z. 135)

This is a show of disaffected emotion that denotes the nature of interpersonal
relations in the novel, i. e. the non-connection of one automaton to the other and
the devaluation of the intimate. The son reduces this young girl to the status of
Heidsieck's grotesque human/thing hybrid; her doll face, curly head and straight
legs are the parts that constitute her body as a product for recreation/consump-
tion. By desiring this kind of body however, the son confirms himself as one of
Adorno's lamentably disaffected subjects: the individual whose interpersonal
alienation stems from reduced libidinal relations (the disappearance of Eros)
between persons of this society. For his declaration of love is dubious, a cunning
trick not practised in ten years, he tells us. That it is necessary to suddenly utilise
old strategies suggests that if ever interpersonal relations were difficult before,
they are now becoming impossible. It is therefore no surprise that even the mechanical doll fails to respond to his advances. This pseudo-libidinal discourse
thus masks a diagnosis of the socio-political world of the between time; it features a form of social fragmentation that anticipates the exclusion of the personal
in the anonymity of the totalitarian mass movement. It also suggests a certain
political strategy of the totalitarian regime as individuals, moored on their respective islands of separateness, are less able to form groups of resistance.

As argued in 2.2, the basic grotesque figure of cross-contamination apparent
in the above person/thing anomaly does not function as a signifier of ambivalent
identity in »Z. Z.«. It is much more the case that we are dealing with the anonymity of the spiritually impoverished in this text as the truncated body of the subjected subject becomes a signifier of a certain micro-physics of power. The latter
phenomenon Foucault describes as a detailed political investment of the body as
the powers that be obtain a hold on it at the level of the physical mechanism. This
practice Foucault calls »working the body retail«, extracting from it the greatest
use by exercising »an infinitesimal power over the active body«.[55] »Working the
body retail« is part of a disciplinary discourse of power that casts the body of the
individual into a strict docility-utility relation, as the power exerted reverses the
course of individual action towards the apotheosis of complete subjection.[56]

In line with the still life aesthetic as a vehicle for the representation of subordination, Foucault mentions the constitution of *tableaux vivants* as one of the
first great operations of discipline. These tables organise the spatial ordering of

---

[55] »Discipline increases the forces of the body (in economic terms of utility) and diminishes these same forces (in political terms of obedience). In short, it dissociates
power from the body; on the one hand, it turns it into an ›apptitude‹, a ›capacity‹,
which it seeks to increase; on the other, it reverses the course of the energy, the
power that might result from it, and turns it into a relation of strict subjection.«
(Foucault, Discipline and Punish [note 15], p. 137–138)

[56] Ibid.

individuals (cells, places and ranks within a hierarchy) and as such may be compared to the taxonomic urge evidenced by the spatial distribution of the symbolic order: the establishment of cellular cogs within patriarchal hierarchy. In other words, »cellular power« goes hand in hand with the reduction of movement, the shift from a world of relative mobility to an enclosed world of still life tableaux. Trapped within and defined by this micro-physics of power, the autonomous person disappears and in its place a disempowered, obedient puppet materialises. The puppet subject, representative of what Foucault terms the »individuality-cell«, could therefore be read as a projection of the body of negation (the egocratic body) and an embodiment of the negated other (appropriated other of the totalitarian state).[57]

Such is the political anatomy of the body in *»Z. Z.«*. In a general distortion of size and dimension that could be described as grotesque, nearly all protagonists are portrayed through synecdoche as reduced players on a stage overshadowed by the presence of the egocrat. The synecdochal representation of character through names or descriptions of the body is furthermore part of the disciplinary discourse of detail that, in keeping with the statement of stasis, assigns position with a degree of precision that expresses just that practice of working the body retail at the level of the individual mechanism. The son's displaced tears form one such instance of this phenomenon. He could not cry at his father's deathbed, now he is an ineffective guardian to his mother, consumed as his energy is by the pursuit of such ever-receding mechanical ideals of the intimate exemplified by the *Gliederpuppe* personification. Thus fragments the family, a possible unit of resistance whilst the son becomes further immersed in his identity as politically inactive, submissive subject of the state.

Names that reduce the person are therefore one means of conveying the practice of »working the body retail«. For instance, the main figure is only ever referred to as a son. That he is beholden to family obligation is communicated through this label, not to mention the anonymity of a term that applies to all men. This label also implies a form of arrested development at an infantile stage. His character is thus portrayed through one aspect of his circumstance, reducing him to just this stunted filial relation. For as will be illustrated in the next chapter, this reduction and precision of identity to the childlike figure of a son forms a hellish, cellular space that facilitates isolation, passivity and selfishness, which together combine to give voice to a form of evil.

The family unit is correspondingly depersonalised, fragmented and reduced, each member referred to only in terms of their prescribed familial position: mother, sister, brother-in-law, niece. None of them have names as such, again underlining the breakdown of family relations under the pressure of mounting totalitarianism. This fragmentation of the family is evoked in the portrayal of the group holiday of 1935 and, like all travel tableaux in the novel, anticipates the irrevocable disintegration of the family in the final incident of the matricide:

---

[57] Ibid., p. 148–149, p. 161.

> Danach sollte die Familie bald in ihre Einzelbestandteile zerfallen, nämlich die Toch-
> ter wohl mit ihrem unmittelbaren Anhang, dem Mann, der Enkelin und der Schwie-
> germutter in ihr Heim, die Mutter in das des Vaters, dessen Witwe sie geworden, zu-
> rückkehren, während der Sohn die Reise noch unterwegs auf einem Schlosse im
> Tschechischen zu unterbrechen vorhatte.   (*Z. Z.* 85)

Interfamilial relations are highly functionalised through the representation of
individuals solely in terms of their identity-cell within the family. If this strategy of pars pro toto illustration is taken at face value, then we are indeed confronted by a species of the reduced individual who is defined according to
position within a certain formation. However, as the son's family seems to
exemplify the atomisation of totalitarian society, each member becoming one
island of separateness detached from the next, the breakdown of the family
from a private unit of possible resistance into a series of disaffected entities
can be taken as symptomatic of the more widespread ordering of society according to disciplinary principles.

Just this phenomenon is presented as a feature of the bureaucratic organisation of local Austrian society. The year is again 1935 and the son finds himself
elected representative of a disgruntled collective of property owners and ten-
ants. On the exploitative scrounge for funds, the state plans to impose a tax
contribution on these property owners. The local suburb (Vienna-Mödling) is
apparently in debt and taxation is one means of raising cash. An assembly of
the protesters is convened, yet although they form the majority, only six of
them show themselves willing to take the matter to a higher authority. This
group then peters out as individuals consider themselves defeated from the
outset. Such is the structure of the pre-Nazi Austrian state machine that it disempowers the individual before a group of resistance can be formed. Local and
central government structures are coordinated to the extent that, as the main
speaker of the assembly points out, the former has never contradicted the latter. Bearing this in mind, it is no wonder that the minute protesting delegation
later disbands. The chancellor officially says that he is against the tax, but this
changes nothing as a different tax is introduced to compensate for the first.[58]

An apparently insignificant episode, the above reveals a lack of cohesion of
individuals at grass-root level that is caused to a great extent by a highly centralised, remote governmental structure. The then chancellor, Kurt von Schuschnigg, may not have been a Nazi supporter, but the above portrayal of Austrian
society shows how in its bureaucratic structure the state could be construed as
implicitly totalitarian. As if to confirm the implications of this picture, Austria
would only a matter of years later excel all expectations in the smooth and

---

[58] »[...] die Abgabe [sei] insofern gerechtigt, als die Stadt große Schulden habe, hinwiederum bitter, weil man sie nur schwer berappen könne, ihre Bekämpfung letzt-
   endlich aussichtslos, weil es noch nicht vorgekommen sei, daß in diesem jetzt vater-
   ländischen Staate das höchste Bundesorgan sich in Widerspruch zu dem höchsten
   Landesvertreter setze.« (*Z. Z.* 41, 67, 69–70)

speedy marriage of its governmental/bureaucratic organisations with the *Alt-reich*.[59] Coupled with the strong tradition of Austrian anti-Semitism, it is no wonder that the body of Austrian society is presented as an (as yet) unofficial limb of the German body. Faced with the impenetrability of such a machine that mobilises persons by separating them, it is almost a foregone conclusion that people, both within and outside the family, will fragment. Practically all of the son's actions are premised on this certainty of failure. As if to emphasise his political uselessness, he announces early on that his concerns are purely cosmetic as opposed to political. In the face of foregone failure, all that may be salvaged is the appearance of looking good whilst sinking fast.[60]

With this picture of a subdued society in mind, the synecdochal naming of characters should not be viewed as an instance of Bakhtinian grotesque materialism. Bakhtin's concept of the grotesque body is defined through its constant mobility as it never ceases to transgress and exceed itself. Whereas the coining of names such as *Glatzkopf* and *Goldzahn* could be confused with the notion that the part laughingly transgresses the whole in a grand show of dynamism and carnivalesque familiarity, it must be noted that the cosmic context of the constantly moving Bakhtinian grotesque body is resoundingly absent in »*Z. Z.*«. In other words, we are only ever presented with the reduced feature of the character in »*Z. Z.*«, the implication being that, due to the absence of a mobile bodily principle, there is no possibility for the renaissance of the self. Instead, the Egocrat's body is the governing somatic principle and this, as has been argued, is defined through its uniformity and distinct lack of movement. Inflexibility as opposed to transgression is the dominant mode of lesser bodies in »*Z. Z.*« as these bodies are distributed across the space of disciplinary monotony.

The politically loaded name *Goldzahn* is a case in hand. Who can read this appellation of the son's Jewish dentist acquaintance without thinking ahead to the macabre Nazi plundering and recycling of the Jewish corpse? This synecdochal tag thus becomes the uncompromising portrayal of the appropriated other as inert matter that will be used for the material gain and perpetuation of the Nazi government.

As illustrated in 1.2, dismemberment is one of the key activities of Drach's *nature morte* aesthetic which he conceives of as a counter aesthetic to the still life programme. To recall briefly the earlier discussion, the *nature morte* aesthetic is embodied in the uninvited monstrous element that disturbs the (for Drach) false harmony of the supposedly genteel still life. In this novel however, images of decay and disintegration are organised in the same way as is synec-

---

[59] Cf. Gerhard Botz: Die Ausgliederung der Juden aus der Gesellschaft. Das Ende Wiener Judentums unter der NS-Herrschaft (1938–1943). In: Eine zerstörte Kultur. Jüdisches Leben und Antisemitismus in Wien seit dem 19. Jahrhundert. Hg. von Gerhard Botz, Ivar Oxaal und Michael Pollak. Buchloe: Obermeyer 1990, p. 285–311.

[60] »In der Zwischenzeit war es für ihn nicht unbedingt nötig, sich Mut zu machen, denn er hatte gar nichts zu verlieren. [...] Trotzdem wollte er in der von ihm übernommenen Sache, wenn schon ein Mißerfolg unvermeidbar war, in Schönheit scheitern.« (*Z. Z.* 55)

doche, that is according to the analytical, dissecting practice of the still life, disciplinary order.

The son's solo trip to France in 1937 reflects this tendency. He is led around the great world capital of Paris by a friend of the family. Bypassing the palace of justice, they end up at the markets where the son is distracted by a display of butchered meat:

> Dort hatte das in kleinste Teile zerschnittene Tierfleisch, wie es übrigens auch nicht anders in sonstigen Fleischerläden zu Schau gestellt wurde, schon seine anatomische Gestalt verloren.   (Z. Z. 167)

This impression is narrated anecdotally and seems to be part of a list of arbitrary phenomena a visitor may observe in the capital city of Paris. However, far from the distracting magnificence of the stereotypical tourist landscape, the dissected meat reflects not just the son's situation, but the predicament of all characters in this between time as in the manner of true still life objects they materialise on the inert matter side of the culture/nature divide. This image is indirectly suggestive of the other's situation as an inferior material effect of a greater power that determines its position and value. The above vignette, which features the son character pausing half-disinterestedly in front of this display, functions like a narcissistic parody, for he can only be looking at a symbolic version of his own present and future degradation as a dismembered, disempowered other subject of the state. Nonetheless, the irony of the juxtaposition culture/nature should not be overlooked here. The hop from the ministry of justice to the meat markets is but a short one. This constellation of places in itself seems to suggest the underlying barbarism of a sophisticated European culture (French or otherwise) that dissociates individuals from power by dissecting them and organising them into the cellular spaces of the totalitarian social structure.

Far from disturbing harmony in the mode of Drach's *nature morte* aesthetic, the image of dissected meat represents yet another evocation of the corpse and by association the static totalitarian body, the *Amt*. It is also a confirmation of the reduced state of individuals who in the manner of dead flesh can no longer understand themselves spiritually, but only anatomically. Consistent with the totalitarian ideology that Drach identifies behind the still life aesthetic, it instead represents the perversion of a hostile order too mechanically instigated.

The level of self-alienation in the novel derives in general therefore from a culturally and politically determined understanding of one's body as docile. This is clear in the examples of non-Jews who are also portrayed through synecdoche as caricatured Aryans. The *Musikerkopf* is one such mindless character whose Aryan roots are implied in the loaded portrayal of his blond locks.[61] However, the particular violence inflicted on the Jewish body is given main emphasis throughout the novel. It is thematised early on in the son's under-

---

[61] The *Musikerkopf* (he supposedly resembles Beethoven) is also referred to as »den Blondschopf« (ibid., p. 110, p. 112).

standing of his own appearance. This becomes apparent in the aftermath of the father's death as the son's physical similarity to the deceased (and to his sister who is by now present at the death bed) is assessed. The terms of comparison are rendered through a discourse that recognises the norms of anti-Semitism. Most curious is the son's insistence on the colour of his eyes; they are, atypically for a Jew it is gathered, a piercing blue. Tellingly, he refers to his eyes, the so-called windows to the soul, as a pair of highly functionalised objects: they are *Blickgeräte* (glance-gadgets). His observation of his own body is thus influenced by ruling anti-Semitic prejudice which determines the typical appearance of the Jew. He may regard his eye colour as a deviation from an imposed racial norm, but the point is however, that irrespective of similarity or dissimilarity to this norm, he nonetheless measures himself according to it. It is thus fitting that his eyes should be mere utensils for the function of seeing, for in this racist, anti-Semitic society the body of the individual (and in particular of the Jewish individual) does not belong to the self. It is devoid of character, a depleted, empty, appropriated automaton. Here it assumes the form of mute matter, the individuality-organism that is soulless and lacking in personality. For the above understanding of the body states that the eyes are no longer a site, »symbolic or otherwise«, for the expression of individuality.[62] A further colonised facial »territory« in »Z. Z.« is the mouth/voice to which we now turn.

6.4 The Ventriloquist's Dummies

One final image of the appropriated body is that of the dismembered mouth. According to Bakhtin's understanding of the grotesque face, the mouth as a gaping, devouring abyss is the central feature. In line with his dynamic concept of the grotesque body, this mouth is a positive signifier of destruction and regeneration. It is an open orifice and therefore constantly in a state of change.[63] This is in direct contrast to the closed, flat and almost total aphonia of the mouth as it is presented in »Z. Z.«. For just as characters do not control the placing of their bodies, they are also appropriated by the language that they speak but do not own. The characters of »Z. Z.« are almost exclusively a cast of mutes as they speak a language of the time that is not theirs. In the same way that their bodies are constituted in the likeness of the egocrat, their speech or verbal »self«-expression often exposes them as the helpless dummies of an evil puppet master: the egocratic ventriloquist.

---

[62] Ibid., p. 13. With this grotesque description of the son's eyes, Drach manages to contradict the argument put forward by Bakhtin that the eyes (along with the ears) do not intrinsically lend themselves to grotesque representation (Michail M. Bakhtin: Literatur und Karneval. Zur Romantheorie und Lachkultur. Frankfurt a. M: Fischer 1996 [Fischer-Taschenbücher; 7434: Fischer Wissenschaft], p. 16).

[63] Ibid.

This alienation from the language one speaks is communicated for the main part by the persistent use of reported speech. As earlier suggested, this is an aspect of the narrative that simultaneously captures and constitutes speaking individuals in the panoptic gaze of implicitly totalitarian power. The intervening perspective of indirect speech has the distancing effect of reducing the autonomy of the speaking characters as the reporting instance is shown to have the final word on the form and content of verbal exchange. In other words, the speaking voice is separated from the speaker and appropriated by an alien perspective. This intervening instance quite literally belittles the speaking characters as they become freeze-framed within the greater context of the reporting instance.

In contrast to the sense of exchange specific to Bakhtin's view of the grotesque mouth, the mouth in *»Z. Z.«* is presented as stuffed, stiff and mute. On holidays in 1935, communication between estranged son and mother is hampered by a dust that blows into their mouths. Thus they never really talk about the recent death of the father, turning into themselves and away from each other in yet another instance of family fragmentation.[64] Correspondingly, a Jewish colleague of the son (the dandy) who is known for his laconic nature is presented as a caricature of almost all indirect speaking instances in the novel. He eases himself into the act of speech with all the awkwardness of a jointed doll, moving his lips without showing his teeth, increasing the impression that he is not really speaking. Instead, he functions as a mere mouthpiece for a greater discourse that requires a reduced level of personal participation. Opening the mouth slightly suffices for the voicing of »personal« news which in any case turns out to be a form of Jewish anti-Semitism. Thus the use of indirect speech is particularly interesting when observing the speaking Jewish characters of the novel. The irony of their situation is articulated by the reporting perspective that shows them up as appropriated and obedient subjects of the anti-Semitic state.[65]

One telling incident is the discussion that takes place between the selfsame character and another Jewish colleague, both acquaintances of the son. The subject of the heated debate is the position of the Austro-Jew with regard to the Nuremberg Laws implemented by the Nazi government in neighbouring

---

[64] »Auf der Wegstrecke [...] hantierte der Sohn mit den verkümmerten Gefühlen gegenüber der eigenen engeren und weiteren Familie, und auch die Mutter suchte nach einer Eröffnung in seiner Richtung. Weil aber der Wind von der entgegengesetzten Seite kam, wehte er Staub in ihre Münder, die er auf diese Weise vorübergehend stopfte.« (*Z. Z.* 86)

[65] »Sobald aber der Schöne wieder seine Lippen bewegte, und er tat dies wie beim Essen, ohne die kleinen Zähne zu zeigen [...], obwohl sie durchaus echt waren, machte er bloß eine rein persönliche Mitteilung, nämlich die, daß er demnächst eine eigene Kanzlei eröffnen werde [...]. Er fühle sich nämlich tagsüber müde, was gar nicht verwunderlich sei, wenn man in Betracht ziehe, daß er die Nächte hindurch [...] Bridge spiele. Das trage ihm ebensoviel, als die Kanzlei ihm tragen könne. Wozu jüdle er auch so gut und wozu sei er denn ein As in diesem Spiel [...], wenn nicht um den Leopoldstädter Juden das Geld abzunehmen.« (Ibid., p. 51–52)

Germany. The son is the typically passive spectator of this conversation which illustrates two different reactions to these racist laws. The fat lawyer (*der Fette*) is presented as pure matter: he has a bloated head, sweats out of all pores and talks incessantly.[66] His reaction to the laws is zealously to excavate his family past for Aryan forefathers who could be of use to him when the Nazis eventually assume control of Austria. A busybody of irritating, know-all advice, this character is ridiculed by the level of his own zeal. Though his view of political events is accurate, the energy he puts into meeting the imposed racial norms is portrayed as a subtle form of passivity through the distancing effect of reported speech. In the manner of a docile subject, he is investing time and money in the research of his origins which have been evaluated by a neighbouring nation. His flurry of activity ill conceals the complete lack of protest at this state of affairs as the lot of the Jew is unquestioningly swallowed:

> Darauf meinte der Fette, [...] man dürfe doch nicht glauben, daß der gegenwärtige Zustand anhalten werde. Einstweilen müsse man eben mitmachen, und später sei es nötig, sich entweder anzupassen oder zu verschwinden, beides aber zur richtigen Zeit.
>
> (*Z. Z.* 50)

This pro-active behaviour is met with scepticism by the tall, well-groomed dandy (*der Schönling*) who is not convinced of Hitler's immediate arrival. However, it is less blind denial of facts than competitive resentment that causes the dandy to reject the other's approach. For he has not started his own uprooting of the family tree perhaps because it is premised on failure from the outset, as suggested in the coming extract. What we encounter in this scenario is a pair of competing Jews who are fatally measuring themselves against an Aryan yardstick. The use of reported speech is thus most appropriate. Neither character speaks a language independent of this anti-Semitic discourse as their understanding of themselves and each other is defined through their identity as Jewish others. That they are dissociated from power in this language is implied through the use of the subjunctive which undermines the authority of whatever either asserts. In this way, they materialise as sound-biting instances of a greater discourse – that of the egocratic ventriloquist – that towers over, determines and divides them:

> Auch diesen Vortrag billigte der Schönling nicht, [...] weil er sich im Anbetracht der eben im benachbarten Deutschland verabschiedeten Nürnberger Gesetze angegriffen fühlte, zumal er von Vaterseite keinen sogenannten arischen Großvater aufzuweisen hatte [...]. Das gar nicht entgegenkommende, geradezu fröstelnde Schweigen des Schönlings veranlaßte den beredten Fetten zu dem Teilgeständnis, daß er bereits an seinem Stammbaum arbeite, aber noch die genauen Daten seiner mütterlichen Großmutter vermisse. Hier ließ sich der Schöne plötzlich hören, indem er seine Verwunderung Ausdruck gab, daß der Bekenner nur so wenige brauchbare Ahnen noch ausständig und so viele verwendbare schon gefunden habe.
>
> (*Z. Z.* 49–50)

---

[66] »Der andere, aus fettem Material hergestellt und mit einem großen gedunsenen Kopf versehen, war zwar nicht nachlässig, aber auch nicht ansprechend verkleidet, schwitzte aus allen Fugen und sprach ohne Pause.« (Ibid., p. 48–49)

The above research of Aryan ancestry again gives voice to the perversion of family and blood relations under the pressure of totalitarianism. It also shows the entrapment of the atrophied Jewish subject in a hypertrophied discourse that diminishes any resistance. For the estranged colleagues are missing the point here, capitulating to the undisputed authority of anti-Semitic norms by indulging in petty infighting. They become true disciplinary subjects as all their energy is channelled into a relation of subjection, here the unquestioning recognition of the validity of anti-Semitic norms. Hence the image of the dismembered mouth as both characters (in particular the slob lawyer) attempt to appropriate a language that in fact appropriates them. Their ignorance of this state of affairs is conveyed through the pointlessly yapping effect of reported speech. In essence, neither has anything to say that might break the circle of entrapment. Because their discussion only affirms existing norms that are in fact levelled against them, they are both ultimately silent, their heated garrulousness thereby becoming the stiff, repetitive and pointless movement of the aphonic mouth described above. The dismembered mouth is thus a mouth removed from the body that uses it. It is a mouth stuffed with anti-Semitic claptrap to the extent that there is no space for personal or resisting articulations. In short, it is a means of citing the conventions of egocratic authority via the body of the appropriated.

Synecdoche in this novel is therefore at some remove from the metonymical discontinuity of the Kristevan thesis. The dismemberment of character in »Z. Z.« goes as far as to reverse the anthropomorphic effect that Jakobson associates with synecdoche and that imbues the world of the generic still life.[67] In a disturbing reversal of fortunes, the world of objects no longer evokes and implies the absent human form. Instead, the human subject is now structured in the likeness of the inert – butchered animal, fatty material, mute machine – as the egocratic automaton attributes its form to the world of human objects. Hence the impression that the disjointed parts of the subjected body amount through reduction to an apotheosis of the self. The diminutive figure of the son-child is the most narrated form of this apotheosis. The coming chapter focuses on this image of arrested development as, on the one hand, a condition symptomatic of the bloody scrabble for survival, and on the other, as a diagnosis of the melancholy disposition.

---

[67] Jakobson makes the point that in proseworks featuring synecdoche and metonymy, the subject tends to be distributed into the objects around him: »[...] statt des Helden ist eine Kette von seinen vergegenständlichten Zuständen und umgebenden Gegenständen – belebten wie unbelebten – unterschoben.« (Roman Jakobson: Randbemerkungen zur Prosa des Dichters Pasternak [1935]. In: id., Poetik. Ausgewählte Aufsätze 1921–1971. Hg. von Elmar Holenstein und Tarcisius Schelbert. Frankfurt a. M.: Suhrkamp 1993 [Suhrkamp-Taschenbuch Wissenschaft; 262], p. 192–211, here p. 205) Seltzer identifies just this bias in the still life in which objects are really representations of the human body that is absent: »[...] a reaffirmation of the body [...] whose agency is neither seperable from nor reducible to natural bodies and material possessions.« (Seltzer, Bodies and Machines [note 5], p. 139)

Chapter 7
The Time of Evil Children

> [...] even if children have the power to forget
> the world of adults for a time, they are never-
> theless doomed to live in this world.
>
> (Georges Bataille)

7.1 The Spectre of Absolute Negation

This chapter examines the complicated relationship between evil, survival, and guilt in »Z. Z.«. Identifying the body of the Egocrat as the classificatory body of totalitarian culture, the previous chapter examined the appropriation and ordering of bodies according to this image of total domination. The coming analysis evaluates the effects of domination on the son who bears the morally suspect identity of victim and victimiser. His victimisation of others is best described as a kind of concupiscent cannibalism (devouring others in order to sustain the self) which in the Holocaust context, it is proposed, may be read as part of a discourse of survival. Implicit in this understanding of victimisation as a survival weapon is the view that to arrive at this dubious point the son himself has first been indelibly branded as victim.

Blatantly misogynist, the sexual victimisation of others has already been presented as consistent with the excluding tactics of anti-Semitic discourse. However, the discursive site demarcated by this excessive consumption of the female other becomes more complex when one considers that it is the point of convergence for not only the sexist and the anti-Semitic, but also the familial, the infantile, the criminal, the guilty and perversely also for survival. The son as Jewish other himself knows the violence of exclusion, yet he visits this violence upon women, most notably upon his mother. It is thus within these converging tableaux of the apparently sexual that the interrelationship of guilt and evil is to be located.

»Total domination«, says Hannah Arendt, »is possible only if each and every person can be reduced to a never-changing identity of reactions«.[1] She argues that this form of rule achieved its ultimate expression in the extermination camps of the Third Reich, but was preceded by a gradual manipulation of the self-perception and socio-political position of the individual. The prerequisites for

---

[1] Hannah Arendt: The Origins of Totalitarianism. New York: Harcourt 1973, p. 438.

dominating a man entirely are firstly, the destruction of his rights, »killing the juridical person in him«;[2] secondly, the murder of the moral person, an act that destroys any hope of solidarity between like-minded protesters; and thirdly, »the killing of man's individuality, of the uniqueness shaped in equal parts by nature, will, and destiny«.[3] Once man is depleted of rights, conscience and spirit there emerges »a world of conditioned reflexes, of marionettes without the slightest trace of spontaneity«, in other words, a corrupt world of moral indifference in which evil rules. Accordingly, Arendt sees this process of desensitisation as indispensable to the introduction of the extermination camps. Echoing the main argument of the last chapter, she states that »the insane mass manufacture of corpses is preceded by the historically and politically intelligible preparation of living corpses«.[4]

These three stages on the road to total domination are at work in »*Z. Z.*«. As illustrated in the previous chapter, this process begins by ostracising the Jew via the Nuremberg Laws to a place of lawlessness outside jurisdiction. The killing of moral conscience and the murder of the individual, however, become particularly apparent in the world of sexual behaviour depicted in the novel, which could be described as the world of conditioned reflexes par excellence. As such, representations of sex continue the discourse of discipline/appropriation identified in the ordering of bodies in the last chapter, but with the added complication of what appears, via the son character, to be victim conspiracy in the act of victimisation. This twist may be more fully understood when one acknowledges the ghostly substratum of extermination that is provoked by the sexualised victim/victimiser anomaly. The period of 1935 to 1938 is as yet ignorant of the coming reality of the extermination camps. However, the representation of sex in openly aggressive terms thematises the disturbing mutation of victim into victimiser, effectively transporting the future spectre of the Final Solution, along with the inevitable trauma of survival, into the between time of the novel.

One could argue that as early as 1935 spiritually and emotionally the son is already in the concentration camps. This is clear from the sexual cruelty of which he is capable. However, on a more general note this behaviour gives voice to what Zygmunt Bauman terms the psychological sealing off of Jewish victims that became manifest in the Aryan/Other racial divide of society as exemplified by the Nuremberg Laws. This isolation of the victim thus paves the way for the complete »ghettoisation« of the son's outlook, i. e. the conviction that existence can at best merely be eked out and that survival is a matter only for the fittest.[5]

Why choose the sexual as a vessel for the portrayal of the above extermination society? Arendt's analysis of totalitarian structures offers a two-pronged explanation for this choice. Firstly, totalitarian domination, in contrast to other

---

[2] Ibid., p. 451.
[3] Ibid., p. 454.
[4] Ibid., p. 457.
[5] Zygmunt Bauman: Modernity and the Holocaust. Oxford: Polity Press 1989, p. 124.

forms of tyranny, invades the individual sphere vis-à-vis »the iron band of terror«, effectively destroying »man's capacity for experience and thought just as certainly as his capacity for action«.[6] The son is thus to be regarded as enslaved to this iron grip nowhere more vehemently than when sexually active, an insight that reinforces the sense of total domination articulated in the novel. Secondly, this invasion results in the complete isolation of the incapacitated individual, described by Arendt as »that impasse into which men are driven when the political sphere of their lives where they act together in the pursuit of a common concern, is destroyed«.[7] Thus the sexual, signifier of the so-called private sphere, ultimately communicates this impasse, i. e. the political superfluity of the individual in totalitarian society. Each time the son attempts a sexual conquest, he inadvertently evokes the impasse of the political, psychological and spiritual ghetto. In other words, each time he victimises an other he feeds the socially engineered moral corruption that anticipates the game of survival in the extermination camps.

Clearly, Arendt's argument implies that individual evil can be understood as a result of extraordinary circumstances »under which conscience ceases to be adequate and to do good becomes impossible«.[8] Further complicating matters is the survival game through which »the consciously organized complicity of all men in the crimes of totalitarian regimes is extended to the victims and thus made really total«.[9] This is the anomaly we are faced with in »Z. Z.« where »the distinguishing line between persecutor and persecuted, between murderer and his victim, is constantly blurred«.[10]

Consistent with this view of individual evil as an effect of one's designated place under totalitarian domination, Bauman argues that »the voice of individual moral conscience is best heard in the tumult of political and social discord«.[11] In his view, evil is more a question of the relationship between authority and subordination than the personality of the cruel individual. It follows on from this view that if inhumanity can be explained through the organisation of social relations, then »cruelty is social in its origin much more than it is characterological«.[12]

Bauman's analysis centres in this respect on the cruelty of Jewish victims to their fellow sufferers. His views are particularly relevant for an understanding of the son in »Z. Z.« because he attempts to rationalise the highly problematic *voluntary* nature of the behaviour of Jews who co-operated with Nazi authority to their own detriment and to the detriment of other Jews. Bauman claims that it is misguided to judge as inherently evil those Jews who got sucked into the doomed »save what you can« game of survival. Such was the extent of their

---

6 Arendt, The Origins of Totalitarianism (note 1), p. 474.
7 Ibid.
8 Ibid., p. 452.
9 Ibid.
10 Ibid., p. 453.
11 Bauman, Modernity and the Holocaust (note 5), p. 166.
12 Ibid., p. 166.

imposed isolation and helplessness, such was the extent of Nazi expertise in the fostering of a choiceless obedience that it becomes rationally clear as to why co-operation with their masters would have appeared a reasonable policy of survival to many Jews.

This kind of game is a strategy of the rulers and not the victims, Bauman is quick to point out. It ensures the unwitting collaboration of the victims in the certainty of their own destruction, even as they imagine that obedience will save them. This state of affairs exposes the perversion of reason in a morally bankrupt world determined by the certainty of death. Reason, argues Bauman, is a good guide for individual behaviour only when the rationality of both actor and action converge. In other words, the autonomous actor will use his powers of deduction to follow a desired path of action which should bring about the envisaged result. The predicament of the Holocaust victim who plays the »save what you can« game, however, articulates not the logical cohesion of actor and action, but the radical divergence of action from the actor. In other words, the Jewish victim participant in the survival game is utterly alienated from what he does, believing that his action will lead him to a certain desired point (survival) when in fact the opposite will emerge. As such, he unwittingly demonstrates the monstrosity inherent in reason cast adrift from teleological goals of progress, and so exposes the illogical logic of a society that paradoxically articulates development as destruction.[13]

The son is one such doomed participant in the shady struggle for survival. Sex is the signifier of this misguided rationale, the son's behaviour an articulation of the »save what you can« game. For if ever the representation of Eros could time and again evoke the Death Instinct, thereby implicating annihilation as the end result of all survival endeavours, then it is in »Z. Z.« that we repeatedly encounter this twisted momentum. As will later be illustrated, the matricide hangs over all images of sexual conquest, effectively transforming what in other circumstances might simply be construed as evidence of Eros into the monotonous mouthpiece of death. Certainly, the sexual and the feminine are constantly associated with disease, decay and mortality.[14] Yet the son persists in his pursuit of women, and with that the associated semantic territory of putrefaction, at first glance seeking some sort of escape from his own predicament. Ultimately however, he is enacting the above fatal ritual of the reverse teleology that is survival. This arrangement voices both Arendt's description of the isolated impasse of the dominated individual (the sex ghetto as it were) and Bauman's view that moral corruption under the impossible circumstances of

---

[13] Ibid., p. 129–142.

[14] The connection between sex, the female, the Jew and moral corruption is graphically rendered in the following excerpt: »Er merkte, daß die Welt einen krummen Gang ging, er hörte, wie einer von dessen Jüngern sich vom Schleim eines ihm verkrüppelten Mädchens reinigte, und auch vielleicht von dem der dreizehnjährigen Jüdin, die vorher angeblich von ihrem Bruder entjungfert worden«. (*Z. Z.* 113)

Nazi rule is a form of socially engendered evil. Observe a telling remark concerning the son at an early stage in the novel:

> Die Frage, ob Sexus allein das Leben rechtfertige, konnte sich einem immer wieder stellen, der sonst nichts hatte. (*Z. Z.* 113)

The above reduction or ghettoisation of individual space (political, professional and social) to the physical/sexual represents the moral murder of man. It has already been preceded by the destruction of the juridical person clearly thematised when the son recognises that his right to work will inevitably be withdrawn in the wake of the Nuremberg Laws.[15] This state of affairs explains in part the total dissociation of the sexual from the pleasure principle. In the absence of a reasonable professional occupation, sex becomes the central focus of the son's entire existence. In this manner, all sexual activity assumes the appearance of a work model. According to the above logic, sex is all that can be saved and this reality becomes the professional project of the son. Nowhere is this more evident than in the mode of expression chosen to describe the rape scene:

> *Nach getaner Arbeit* schickte der Sohn die Bettgenossin heim und ließ sich auf inständiges Bitten nicht herbei, sie wenigstens bis zum Haustor zu begleiten. Dafür übergab er ihr den Schlüssel, wodurch sie in die Lage gelangen konnte, nächstens wiederzukommen, wenngleich ein Stelldichein erst für einen Abend in achttägiger Entfernung zur Zeit der Haustorsperre festgesetzt wurde. (*Z. Z.* 64, my emphasis)

Tasteless though it may be, describing a rape in the hygienic terms of an ordinary day's work is curiously apt in a society that will increasingly concentrate the execution of violence in the comparatively invisible, anonymous bureaucratic/professional sphere. The son's sexual behaviour may in this instance be read as a biting commentary on the redeployment of violence through bureaucracy that, according to Bauman, distinguishes modern mass extermination from other forms of genocide.[16] Certainly, the son reveals a degree of both opportunistic and organisational prowess in the above extract. In the manner of a parasitic entrepreneur, he attempts to extract maximum sexual profit from this one incident. Thinking ahead to future demand and potential logistical problems, he gives his by now totally subdued victim a house key so that she can slip into his room unnoticed by others. The peculiar conflation of violence, work and sex evokes again the domination of Eros by Thanatos and the sense of a wilfully misleading path of survival that guides the individual unerringly towards his own demise.

The above analysis suggests that the nature of evil as exemplified in the son character is indeed a social and not a characterological issue. Hunted into an

---

[15] »Sein Hang zur Pflichterfüllung war außerdem ziemlich gering, denn er liebte weder seinen Beruf noch die Sparte von dessen Ausübung. Auch rechnete er sich aus, daß das Regime nicht lange halten und er dann keineswegs würde Rechtsanwalt bleiben können.« (Ibid., p. 55)

[16] Bauman argues that the segregation, enclosure and re-distribution of violence into isolated territories leads to the concentration of violence (Bauman, Modernity and the Holocaust [note 5], p. 97).

existential ghetto of sterile sexuality, this position articulates the humiliation of the Jewish subject whose human rights are systematically destroyed. Yet one must ask whether this perspective exonerates the son of all culpability. This is an extremely difficult question, made all the more treacherous by Drach's choice of representing the socially engineered »evil« of the Jewish victim through the sexual. What are we meant to understand by the rape scene, for example? In this circumstance, the son forces himself on an elderly woman who arrives at the family home to express her condolences some time after the father's death. He pushes her into his bedroom, knowing all the time that she will not scream or otherwise draw attention to herself or to his actions. He knows that he has happened upon the victim par excellence, a disadvantaged, unattractive, isolated and timid older woman. Not even her tears deter him from his course of action.[17]

In my view, the degrading experience of existential reduction to the sex ghetto, along with the desire through momentary violent empowerment to rid oneself of this victim stigma, are accurate, but inadequate, explanations for this level of cruelty. Nonetheless, it is also insufficient to claim in this particular instance that the son possesses untapped resources of individual iniquity which emerge given favourable conditions. Let us return instead to the earlier suggestion that the sex ghetto of 1935 to 1938 functions as the imaginary place of absolute negation, the imaginary place of the Final Solution.

Arendt argues that one of the skills of totalitarian organisation is the ability »to build up, even under nontotalitarian circumstances, a society whose members act and react according to the rules of a fictitious world«.[18] The defining characteristic of this fictitious world is the transformation of anti-Semitism into a principle of self-definition, resulting in »the organization of an entire texture of life« according to this ideology.[19] The son as rapist contributes to and reflects the consistency of this dichotomous social texture, yet his acts of violence are accompanied by a curious *physical* detachment which suggests, on the one hand, the appropriation of his person by the anti-Semitic gaze, and on the other, the unreality of a fictitious existence in which he does not entirely believe. The latter modus vivendi explains in part the complete lack of remorse that features strongly in his abuse of the female other. This inability to engage emotionally with his own predicament and the violence he visits upon others is communicated through the occasional image of the unblemished body. Note the distribution of wounds after the rape scene:

> Während sie ihr Kleid anlegte, zeigte sie gewisse Wundmale, die auf ihren ruhmlosen Widerstand zurückzuführen waren, während der Sohn völlig unbeschädigt geblieben schien.
>
> (*Z. Z.* 64)

---

[17] »Als er aber ihre seidige Haut rühmte [...], hörte er sie leise wimmern, später heulen, wobei die Tränen, mit denen sie ihren befürchteten Fall beklagte, sich mit dem Schweiß seiner Anstrengung, diesen herbeizuführen, vermischten, während sie glaubhaft versicherte, sie hätte bisher niemals einem Manne angehört.« (*Z. Z.* 63)

[18] Arendt, The Origins of Totalitarianism (note 1), p. 364,

[19] Ibid., p. 363.

It would seem that the son has remained to some extent physically absent from his own act of violence, an impression that is matched only by a resounding and conscious emotional absence:

> Er nahm sich nicht mehr die Zeit, nach dem Vorgefallenen traurig zu werden, [...] auch nicht ein Schuldgefühl aufkommen zu lassen [...] Statt dessen schlief er gegen sonstige Gewohnheiten sofort und befriedigt ein und verharrte in seiner gründlichen traumlosen Abwesenheit, bis ihn die Mutter, [...] am Morgen weckte.   (*Z. Z.* 64–65)

The above dreamless absence of sleep could be taken as a motif for the son's stance on his own brand of sexual violence and on the political issues of his time. A marionette operating according to the conditioned reflexes extolled by his society, he seems to be separated from his acts by a resilient membrane of personal disengagement. This remarkable (because paradoxically obedient) truancy further reinforces the sense of a fictitious texture of life in which he is suspended until the very end of the novel. For within the logic of the narrative, it is fitting that in the above extract it should be the mother who awakens the son. Only the final recognition of matricide in the closing pages will ultimately rouse the son out of this soporific myopia. Until then he remains detached.

Nonetheless, as historical circumstance continues to mount tangible pressure on the Jew, the son's desire to escape the texture of a life so unreal as to be bizarre intensifies. This becomes clear in early 1938 when he tries to order paper for his legal practice. The supply agent asks him whether he really believes that any renewal of paper orders is necessary, given the diminishing job market for Jews in the professions. The following extract casts both sex and the notion of evil as either characterological or social in an entirely new if more disturbing light:

> Aber der Sohn wollte dem Agenten das nicht glauben, was er selber bereits wußte. Vielleicht fand er sogar in der Bestätigung seines Wissens Anlaß zum Widerspruch oder wollte zuerst *am eigenen Leibe erfahren*, was kommen würde, bevor er versuchen mochte, diesen etwa nackt und bescholten, statt bekleidet und noch ohne angelastete Schuld in Sicherheit zu bringen.   (*Z. Z.* 210, my emphasis)

The above implies that subsistence in a fictitious world arises primarily through the detachment from one's body, which in the last chapter was diagnosed as an effect of totalitarian appropriation. In this extract, the son still perceives himself to be without guilt, again emphasising the degree of his estrangement from his own actions. Surprising however, is the need to feel guilt and shame, the need to be physically blemished in order to validate his experiences both present and future. This indicates a level of insight as yet absent from his deliberations on existence in the between time. It implies that he is already intimately acquainted with the logic of survival particular to the Jewish Holocaust survivor, recognising that there will be no survival of the between time and therefore no escaping the Final Solution that will not be tainted by guilt. It would seem that the experience of a guilt tattooed onto the body, ironically as yet an abstraction, is the only means of divesting the between time of its fictitious texture. This abstract relationship to evil via the body provides an alternative reading of the rape scene and other scenes of sexual turpitude. No longer solely a means through which to rid oneself of the victim slur, the sexual now intuits through the recognition of imminent guilt the scene of total victimisation, that is the self-imposed lifelong guilt sentence of the Jewish Holocaust survivor.

This projection through the sexual into the Holocaust and after is far more sinister than the »save what you can« game of self-preservation/destruction. The need to bear the mark of evil, to experience it on one's flesh in order to make it real, acknowledges the disturbing abstraction of the incubus/succubus image of ignominy. This desire recognises the subterranean presence of a form of evil that transcends even the variegated discursive slovenliness that constructs the Hitler personification. Beyond the scrabble for a survival that is always provisional, the need to bear the mark of evil evokes the space of self-destruction that comes to fruition in the imaginary gas chamber at the end of *Unsentimentale Reise*. For evil, in this abstract respect, articulates via the default of repetition the unsignifiable, which in this context can be none other than the apprehension of the total annihilation of an entire race. Evoking (as opposed to signifying) the unsignifiable through the intensifying effect of repetition is a discursive strategy that Drach uses in his attempts to convey a sense of evil beyond the banal. Thus lingering behind the predictability of everyday evil in *»Z. Z.«* skulks a spectre of malignancy that can be likened to the Sadian ideal of absolute negation.

How does this malignancy communicate itself in discourse, however? Deleuze's theory of sadistic language provides the lead for linguistic analysis here. He identifies the spectre of absolute negation in the combination of two discursive levels in the Sadian work. The first level is located in the individual descriptions of the acts of sexual violence that form the Sadian quotidian. This concrete level of description houses what Deleuze terms the descriptive or imperative factor at work in Sadian literary discourse. It generally represents the personal element of violence or the perverse individual tastes of the sadist that emerge during each act.[20] The son's choice of the hoary and decrepit spinster as victim articulates a version of this perverse taste of the sadist who, in the practice of his sport, is drawn to the weak, the infirm, the powerless. This choice signifies a destructive consistency that informs all descriptions of female victims throughout the novel. Hence the symmetry of violence between the rape of the spinster and the later tryst with the ice-skating minor.[21]

This linking symmetry indicates a further characteristic of the descriptive level of this type of discourse, however. Ultimately, the descriptive level is com-

---

[20] Gilles Deleuze: Masochism. Coldness and Cruelty. New York: Zone Books 1989, p. 19–20.

[21] The son cunningly seduces a girl whom he suspects to be under fourteen: »Die Wiedersehensfeier wurde vom Sohn mit Absicht mit einem Kinobesuch vollzogen. Es würde wohl niemand annehmen, er werde ein Mädchen, das er auch nur im Eventualfalle für unter vierzehn halten konnte, ganz ohne Hehl ausführen und sich mit ihm zeigen, so daß man allgemein wußte, daß er mit ihm ginge, das heißt geschlechtlichen Umgang unter Mitverantwortung der Umwelt mit der Kleinen betrieb.« (*Z. Z.* 107)

posed of variations on the unvarying theme of sexual violence/victimisation. As such, its primary trait is not one of content. Rather, the defining moment of the descriptive level is the rhetorical feature of repetition. This informs what Barthes has termed the rule of exhaustivity, i. e. the prolific activity of the Sadian libertine as he moves from one victim to the next.[22] However, this spurious proliferation of »activity« is counterbalanced by the monotonous invariability of sexual victimisation. Nowhere is the redundancy of this monotony more apparent than in the son's lacklustre enumeration of female targets midway through the narrative. No less than sixteen women are listed in a single tedious paragraph, a tactic that divulges the complex function of repetition in the novel.[23]

»Beneath the sound and fury of sadism«, says Deleuze, »the terrible force of repetition is at work«.[24] In other words, through the intermediary of an unvarying descriptive level in the narrative of everyday victimisation, a second more abstract and more radical level of violent discourse is evoked. This level Deleuze terms the demonstrative, clarifying further the function of the descriptive level, i. e. the demonstration of an unsignifiable idea of negation through the intensifying rhythm of repetition. According to Deleuze, the sadist's task is to think the Death Instinct (the unsignifiable idea of absolute negation) in demonstrative form. This clarifies Barthes's claim that the Sadian universe is a purely discursive universe in which, apart from discourse and its ordering rhetoric, there is no concrete referent. The function of Sadian discourse, he states, is to conceive of the inconceivable.[25] Deleuze argues this representation of the inconceivable (the Death Instinct) in terms of the sadistic demonstration through repetitive rhetoric of the violence of vacuous reason. Just this empty and potentially dangerous formality of reason is revealed through the incongruity of actor and action in the »save what you can game«. In the sadistic parody of reason, this divergence of the actor from the act, of the means (destruction qua sexual behaviour) from the end (survival) is articulated through

---

[22] Roland Barthes: Sade, Fourier, Loyola. Paris: Seuil 1971, p. 35.

[23] »Bei dieser Gelegenheit erinnerte er sich des Wundermädchens, das er in Gesellschaft der Tochter in einem Haus erblickt [...]. Auch die im Brautkleid boxende Gattin des Facharztes durfte er später nicht mehr allein sehen, schließlich aber doch in Gesellschaft einer Nonne, die er einmal unvollständig ausgezogen hatte [...]. Weiters gerieten vorübergehend in sein Rückblickfeld die Ruthenin bei den Ölquellen, die Polin am Bach, die Indianerin vor ihrer Hochzeit mit dem Tierarzt, die Funktionärstochter auf der Fahrt zur Pariser Ausstellung, die Zwölfjährige, die er ablehnen mußte, die junge Jüdin, die ihn nach Untergang und Annäherung im Bade nicht wollte, das Mädchen vom Kanalmeer, die beiden Schweizerinnen, die schließlich über ihn hinwegplauderten, die knorrige Jungfrau, die er in Besitz genommen hatte, [...] das Eismädchen, dessen Mündigkeit in Zweifel stand, die er sich aber trotzdem unterschob, und schließlich jene, die er als Fünfzehnjährige mit Tränen ungenossen verabschieden mußte [...]. Zuletzt sah er noch die Jugoslawin auf dem Berge.« (*Z. Z.* 202–203)

[24] Deleuze, Masochism (note 20), p. 120.

[25] Barthes, Sade, Fourier, Loyola (note 22), p. 41.

the substitution of repetition for pleasure. That pleasure has been replaced by the bottomless abyss of repetition in »Z. Z.« becomes clear in the son's acknowledgement of his failure to extract any satisfaction from his repeated attempts to claim the female other:

> Und schließlich waren auch die sogenannten Liebesgenusse des Sohnes, [...] bloße Verschlingungen und Verrenkungen, die für Sekunden Lustersatz vortäuschten.
>
> (Z. Z. 192)

The above reduction of sex to the desperate contortions of conditioned reflex communicates the desexualisation of Eros that accompanies the disappearance of pleasure. This is due to the altered function of repetition in relation to the pleasure principle. Repetition in this case no longer denotes »a form of behaviour related to a pleasure already obtained or anticipated«, says Deleuze.[26] Instead, »it runs wild and becomes independent of all previous pleasure. It has itself become an idea or ideal«.[27] On this eternally rotating axis of monotonous »erotic« repetition, the demonstrative function emerges at its most vehement. It gives voice to the inarticulated, i. e. the notion of negation (an act that, besides death, has no ultimate goal or meaning). It is through this evocation of nothingness that the abstract idea of absolute evil comes to light. For these acts of repeated destruction signify the limit of evil mentioned by Bernstein in the last chapter: the expropriation of death from the victim Jew. In other words, the conflation of means and ends in the sexual simulation of survival politics denotes precisely that undoing of the categorial syntax between life and death that Bernstein holds responsible for »the making of death systematically continuous with life«.[28] The rhetorical feature of repetition communicates this collapse of the distinction between life and death, and thus functions as the indirect expression of a speculative ideal that cannot be entirely contained by the descriptive level of sadistic discourse. It may only be dimly grasped through the alternatively condensing and proliferating ritual of repetition.

This form of repetition – the repetition that, by substituting Thanatos for Eros, destroys and erases – is a strategy of discourse that points to the weakened fetish function of language. The sixteen listed female conquests are therefore not so much distractions from the implications of the interim period and the time immediately succeeding it. Rather, »the endless repetitions, the reiterated quantitative process of multiplying illustrations and adding victim upon victim« communicate the dolorous dirge of what Deleuze terms »an irreducibly solitary argument«.[29] This »argument« is the anaphora of nothing envisaged by the sadistic imagination and delivered by a discourse unable to

---

[26] Deleuze, Masochism (note 20), p. 120.

[27] Ibid.

[28] Jay M. Bernstein: Disenchantment and Ethics. Cambridge: Cambridge University Press 2001 (Modern European Philosophy), p. 383.

[29] Deleuze, Masochism (note 20), p. 20.

defer the spectre of absolute negation. Indeed, the son's treatment of women suggests a deliberate reversal of the process that Kristeva calls syntactical passivation. The latter describes the means by which the phobic individual becomes phobic; it sublimates its aggressivity into fear by placing itself in the position of object.[30] By trying to effect a reversal of this sequence, the son attempts to metamorphose from object to subject, from victim to perpetrator. This is the other side of the sadist's solitary argument: the refusal to say »I am afraid of ...« and the refusal to be the object of another's actions. By abandoning the vertiginous skill of the phobic speaker who yaps endlessly in order to overcome anxiety, by opting for a brand of discourse that features (and does not defer) the space of absolute negation, the son locates himself as subject in the *grotta* space. He is thus to be differentiated from his Jewish colleauges (*der Fette* and *der Schönling*) who in the last chapter both evidenced the linguistic prowess of the phobic individual. By contrast, with each repeated sex scenario, the son travels quite a way down the path towards sadism and destruction. The bitter irony of this shift should not be missed, however, for as already argued, it is precisely through his treatment of the female other that the son confirms himself as a disciplined body of the anti-Semitic state.

From this perspective, the space of repetition in »Z. Z.« (the scene of the sex ghetto and the redundant »save what you can« mechanism) demarcates a space of absolute negation that approximates the inconceivable: the unsignifiable space of extermination that apprehends the Holocaust. Beyond the intricacies of saving what one can, beyond the social production of intense individual cruelty, the vacuous signifier of repetition communicates the inexorable rhythm of coming apocalypse, as yet shapeless and undefined, but utterly monstrous in its persistence and finality. The recurrent motif of the sex ghetto thus conceals within it a sneaking knowledge of the cramped quarters of the gas chamber. The son as concupiscent cannibal who devours the female other, embodies the grotesque subject of the grave: locative system of self as corpse.

However, his inability to physically or emotionally register his own cruelty represents his utter incomprehension of human depravity (that of his own and of others'), a kind of uneasy obliviousness concerning the rhythm of evil in which he is trapped. In this manner, it may be argued that, although the son is suspended within and propagates the totalitarian texture of life, he is nonetheless profoundly alienated from the logical extremity of this society. The spacelessness of the gas chamber, although everywhere evoked, remains an abstraction for the son in the same way that his own practice of violence remains abstract. One could say that throughout »Z. Z.«, he is eternally poised on the brink of a horrific discovery both displaced and evinced by the repetition mechanism in the portrayal of »erotic« violence.

---

[30] Julia Kristeva: Powers of Horror. An Essay on Abjection. New York: Columbia University Press 1982 (European Perspectives), p. 39–40.

7.2 Divine Intoxication: Simulating Infantile Sovereignty

> MARQUIS: [...] Ein Kind, noch nicht um seine
> Natur gebracht, quält zahme Kreatur und zer-
> bricht sein Spielzeug. Man lehrt es, das sei
> verboten, die Dinge hätten gedient und könn-
> ten noch dienen. Was weiß ein Kind von der
> Vergangenheit? Was denkt ein Kind von der
> Zukunft? Es greift nach dem Augenblick, um
> ihn auszutrinken.
> (Albert Drach, *Das Satanspiel vom göttlichen
> Marquis*)

The above brink position that straddles both the descriptive and demonstrative
levels of the Sadian discourse of evil denotes a certain texture of life in which
time is reduced to the mechanical repetition of a survival reflex. In this world,
there exists no progressive vision for the future. Instead as we have seen, the
future becomes a shadowy premonition of the evil immanent in the present, as all
survival endeavours appear to lead to a blank point of destruction. Entangled in
the fictitious stratum of infinite sexual activity that ill conceals the substratum of
extermination, the son occupies a warped version of the zone referred to by
Georges Bataille as the eternal present. The latter describes the existential mode
of the child who blatantly disregards the adult world, ignoring its constraints,
interdictions and laws. This mode and its particular understanding of time as
eternal repetition further explain the son's sense of physical disconnection with
regard to the historical period in which he finds himself.

In his treatise on the representation of evil in literature, Bataille emphasises
what could be termed the revolutionary nature of this evil child who, by virtue of
its rejection of what may be roughly termed the symbolic (adult/patriarchal)
order, bears traits similar to Kristeva's mercurial subject of enunciation. Bataille
divides the world into two distinct modes: the adult or »Good« mode of reason
and teleological vision on the one hand, and on the other, the child's mode of
divine intoxication which he equates with »Evil«. The child rejects the imposed
convention of the adult world which is organised according to a vision of the
wholesome progression of time. Instead, this self-indulgent figure immerses
itself in the business of being without constraint, which gives rise to a form of
existence characterised by a preference for living exclusively in the present. The
origins of »Evil« in this respect are to be located in a non-relationship to time. In
short, in the world of »divine intoxication«, evil is an attribute of timelessness.
Whilst »Good« can be generally understood as an orientation towards the future
which envisages a teleologically ordered system of progress and improvement
for the benefit of society as a whole, »Evil« renounces this vision and redirects
its gaze towards the eternity of the self-obsessed child's world.[31]

---

[31] »Good is based on common interest which entails consideration of the future. Divine
intoxication, to which the instincts of childhood are so closely related, is entirely in

In this childhood world of divine intoxication, the principle activity resides in the infinite transgression of adult law and with that the rejection of its measured temporal orientation. Whilst the son may in many ways be likened to the evil child of the eternal present, the revolutionary aspect of the divinely intoxicated mode disappears, as his person assumes the characteristics of the sadist whose crimes establish a norm of repetitive cruelty in the interim universe. Transgression as *jouissance* and pleasure simply disappears as the repetition mechanism of survival takes over. Transgression or crime becomes in this sense modes of obedience within the contours of a society that takes as its defining norm the violation of the other.

Accordingly, the adult order depicted in the novel is not representative of »Good«. On the contrary, it is warped in the likeness of the Egocrat. The son as disciplined subject of the state and ruthless survivor is a product of this egocratic order which, as a form of sacrificial society, could be described as a modern version of the monotonous sadistic universe.[32] The insurgent characteristics of the child's paradise fade against the background of an order that literally demands the sacrifice of others for its continuance. »Good« is therefore not to be located in the general world of adulthood which is in any case stunted. Rather, it is implied (if not actually present) in the lost world of benign parents, both in the obsolete world of the deceased gentleman father and most importantly in the disappearing world of the mother. Furthermore, it is just the sense of this loss that instils in the child sovereign the ruminations of a terrible melancholy disposition, a condition that will be dealt with in a later section.

Despite the reduction of *jouissance* (divine transgression) in the novel, elements of Bataille's evil childhood world are nonetheless evoked. In what has been termed a reductionist and synecdochal mode of representation, the main protagonist is only ever referred to through his function as someone's child: *der Sohn*. The family situation of the opening sequence, complete with the constellation of changing roles and functions of family members in the aftermath of the father's death, serves also to emphasise the son in his existential mode as child. Only half-heartedly and with great apprehension does he turn his attention to the daunting tasks ahead: responsibility for his widowed mother and control of his father's failing legal practice. Money problems herald the end of those halcyon days when he could spend his cash in a frivolous manner on girls and books.

---

the present. In the education of children preference for the present moment is the common definition of Evil.« (Georges Bataille: Literature and Evil. Essays. London, New York: Boyars 1997, p. 22)

[32] Barthes argues that the repetition of crime in the Sadian work accounts for the monotony of the text. By contrast, the discourse is not responsible for the sense of monotony: the limitations of the referent, Barthes suggests, free up the possibilites for discourse (Barthes, Sade, Fourier, Loyola [note 22], p. 41). This contradicts Deleuze's view of Sadian discourse as conducted according to the rule of repetition that destroys and erases (Deleuze, Masochism [note 20], p. 114).

Interestingly, references to futurelessness abound in these opening pages and persist as a central metaphor throughout the novel. With the death of his father and the prospect of unavoidable responsibility, the space of the eternal present is evoked through the helplessness of the child all by himself who cannot cope with adult responsibility and the orientation towards the future that this involves. Instead, we are told of his own lack of orientation with regard to this future beleaguered and rendered invisible by the weight of duty now fallen on the child's shoulders. The son's inability to clearly envisage a future in which he assumes the role of adult can be read as simultaneous with his retreat, evident from these opening pages, into the child's world of the eternal present.[33]

The space evacuated by the father's death remains largely unoccupied as from this point onwards the world of the child is more insistently profiled. The unfilled space of the father is a central motif of the novel as the son stagnates in his child identity. The sense that an era of benign patriarchs has been superseded by the malignant is conveyed in the sequences that portray the evil patriarch: the Hitler incubus. This shift is conveyed in bodily terms as we are told that the son and his sister both feel themselves to have been ripped out of a familiar physical context. This sense of disorientation is not to last, for as we have seen, the body of the ego-crat inserts itself all too readily into the space vacated by the deceased father.[34]

In this arrangement of relations (the absence of the father, the inability of the son to evolve into a replacement paternal figure), the impotence of the truncated individual is again underlined. Even the attention given over to the description of father/son physiognomy serves only to bring home more sharply the image of stunted growth:

> Den sehr buschigen Schnurrbart, wie er zur Zeit vor dem Ersten Weltkrieg üblich gewesen war, hatte sich der Sohn nicht zugelegt. Er wäre ihm auch kaum gewachsen, bei seinen ziemlich flaumigen Haarwuchs.   (*Z. Z.* 12)

A yet more lyrical symbol of the child's world is evoked in this sequence. After each family member has paid their respects, the son and his half sister retire into the garden to discuss family matters. More accurately, the son is led childlike by his sister into the garden, where notably it is she who comes to the conclusion that their youth is now over. The image of forlorn and abandoned children who now must don the yoke of responsibility and bid farewell to a relatively carefree existence – the childhood paradise, as it were – is presented in terms of the lush garden space, the last refuge from the problems of the family. At the same time, this garden haven represents a disappearing ideal of

---

[33] »Er empfand einen Abgang an Güte, der dauernd zu werden versprach [...]. Aber das war nur der Anfang der Wirkung von ihm gefühlten Entbehrung. Schon drohte ihm die Rolle des Verantwortlichen.« (*Z. Z.* 9)

[34] »Sicher aber ist, daß sich die zurückgelassenen Waisen als aus einem auch körperlichen Zusammenhang herausgerissen empfanden, wenngleich derselbe durch keine Nabelschnur symbolisiert wurde und sie vorläufig nicht wußten, wie das Weggefallene zu ersetzen wäre.« (Ibid., p. 14)

individual space, as in the same paragraph the political situation of Austria at the start of the catastrophic between time is thematised:

> Das war am neunzehnten des schon angeführten Monats und im Jahre neunzehnhundertfünfunddreißig, somit im zweiten einer Diktatur, aber schon unter dem anderen Kanzler, nachdem der erste zuvor ermordet war, mithin in einem Zeitraum, gezeichnet von einem gewissen Beginn, aber zu einer noch ungewissen Periode führend, die weder der Sohn noch die Tochter vorausempfanden, da sie die Zukunft nicht wußten und außerdem ohne Hinblick auf allgemeine Ereignungen mit ihren privaten Angelegenheiten und den Folgerungen aus denselben zureichend beschäftigt waren, daher auch öffentlichen Schwierigkeiten keinen Einlaß in diesen Garten gaben, der von ihnen zumindest von jetzt ab rückwirkend als ein Paradies betrachtet wurde.   (*Z. Z.* 11)

This garden is a place of refuge to which the son consistently returns, particularly when he wants to forget the cares of adult responsibility and indulge his daydreams. It symbolises one aspect of the child immersed in the eternal present. Whereas in the above paragraph it is portrayed as a paradise lost, and so may seem from this nostalgic perspective to be far removed from Bataille's world of the evil child, it is clear that as the novel progresses and as the noose of historical circumstance tightens ever more persistently its hold on the individual, this garden comes to symbolise exactly that forbidden world of the child which represents the violation of »Good«. However, it should again be noted that in the depiction of »Good«, »Z. Z.« deviates significantly from Bataille's theory. In contrast to his vision of the transgression of a rather more patriarchal adult order, the violation of »Good« in the novel is portrayed via the betrayal of the specifically maternal world.

Withdrawal into the garden may nonetheless be read as a decisive opting out of historical reality and the pressure for the Jew coextensive with it. Contrary to this initial escapist interpretation however, the confined garden space also becomes a puerile variation on the sex ghetto that articulates the socially engineered isolation of the individual outside jurisdiction and fast losing moral orientation. The son's constant procrastination of decisive action for himself and his mother reflects this inability to deal with the external historical world. Instead of deciding on a practical route of flight, he buries his head in the sand and initiates a crazed consumption of others' bodies, the overriding characteristic of which is predictable repetition. This repetition of events serves to create an atmosphere of timeless circularity which, as already illustrated, is itself the index of evil's repetitive momentum.

This is the other less benign aspect of the eternal present which equates the glorious infinite with dull repetition. On the one hand, Bataille's mode of divine intoxication appears to be activated as time and again the son parasitically gorges himself through the same act on the bodies of others. However on the other, the timeless world of the evil child communicates a truly wretched state as the eternal present is symbolically invoked through the signifier of base physical release, an intoxication so fleeting that it must be ceaselessly repeated in order to ceaselessly elicit this world. As shown by the dispassionate and often insulting tone relating these events, the women involved are mere objects, the means to an end. In this respect, the central image of the main protagonist becomes that of the onanistic child all by himself, selfish, self-obsessed and driven to please (save) only himself.[35]

It is in the garden space that the mode of divine intoxication is most clearly conflated with the scene of sadistic crime. Barthes argues that the essence of the sadistic world is the repetition of crime. This is a principle that permeates the sadistic world but that is most clearly on display in the secretive Sadian place, a place where the victimiser is alone with his victim. Significantly, the secret place of crime is enclosed. However, in the Sadian narrative this enclosed space is everywhere, quite simply because it is the only space depicted in the Sadian world. Hence Barthes's claim that in the Sadian universe one only ever travels or moves in order to enclose oneself further.[36] This truth is borne out when the tranquil garden haven is invaded by SA men. The son is literally hunted out of his garden haven by the thug minions of Hitler's regime, reinforcing the sense that there is simply no escaping the fundamental essence of crime in this world (*Z. Z.* 270). More eloquent than this incident however, is the ubiquity of the cramped sexualised ghetto in the novel, a disturbing testimony to the dominance of the Sadian-style crime as a behavioural code in the between time.

The garden ghetto of *»Z. Z.«* assumes the features of the secretive Sadian place of original crime nowhere more clearly than in the episode depicting the son's first forays into the world of adultery. He dramatically breaks the law of the maternal world in this incident by frolicking under a tree with the wife of a friend. His mother happens upon this display of seedy »divine intoxication« and puts a temporary end to it by asserting her values of correct behaviour. She claims that if the son is ever to repeat this form of adultery (particularly unpalatable because it offends the value of friendship) she will quite simply die. On the surface of it, her protest is moral in the sense that reasonable good society judges that adultery is wrong. However, beyond the moral, this protest is also existential in the sense that obeying this law becomes a matter of her life and her death. Needless to say this protest is futile. The mother's redundancy in a sacrificial world that advocates the survival of the fittest is emphasised in this defence of friendship, which for reasons outlined in the previous section cannot play a meaningful role in the totalitarian context.[37]

---

[35] Onanistic images of the child under the bedclothes reiterate the theme of negation, crystallising the solitary »argument« of the son's sadistic behaviour: that all sexual escapades are intended to fill a vacuum, but instead evoke only the Death Instinct. One masturbation scene features him thinking of corpses; the other takes place on the eve of 1936 and a marked increase in Hitler's influence in Austria. It is furthermore no accident that this latter scene in particular profiles the child's inability to replace his father and his obsession with the ice-skating minor (Ibid., p. 47, p. 98–99).

[36] Barthes, Sade, Fourier, Loyola (note 22), p. 21–23.

[37] »[Die Mutter] [...] erklärte ihm kurz, so sehr sie auch an ihrer Heimat hänge, habe sie es bisher doch für selbstverständlich und natürlich gehalten, daß er nicht ohne sie

Who is the victim in the above garden space? Atypically, it is not in this case the sexual conquest of the son, the wife of his Jewish doctor friend with whom he will travel into exile at the end of the novel. Rather, the victim is the mother, but her sacrifice is not ultimately realised until the final scene of adultery in which the son knowingly goes against her wishes by fornicating with the same woman. During this concluding incident the doctor friend is in the next room, the connecting door ajar so that both adulterers have a good view of the person they betray. The subtext of this incident is again the kind of back-stabbing betrayal of fellow Jews in a time of desperate measures. Most significantly however, the son is aware of betraying his mother and in so doing putting her to death. With this terminal scene in mind the scene of the garden crime tends to foreshadow her crucifixion.[38]

Consistent with the fundaments of the Sadian world in the garden scene, the mother ultimately becomes the prototypical victim of all crime. Her »murder« infiltrates all sexual escapades from this point onwards. Moreover, in the light of the garden incident past victims such as the old spinster become even more disturbingly the necromantic images of impending matricide. Thus it would seem that within the brutality of the survival scrabble, the betrayed mother comes to signify all that must be sacrificed, abandoned and left behind in order to emerge alive from the ordeals of anti-Semitism, exile and imprisonment.

Via this image of the repeatedly rejected mother, the mode of divine intoxication comes to resemble the reiterative vengeful *fort-da* game of the vindictive child, who attempts to counteract its infantile passivity with the vigorous activity of the rejection game. In this scenario, the child rejects the mother by whom it perceives itself to be abandoned. The womanising incidents of »Z. Z.« reveal time and again how this rejection game is transposed onto the female other as the son attempts to assert control over his own immediate universe: the reversal of syntactical passivation. In keeping with Freud's argument, this game yields little pleasure, however, as the child subject appears through its repeated refusal of the m(other) to march to the death-beat of *Unlustvolles*, an eerie manifestation of the subject's subservience to the Death Instinct. Behind the acquisition drive of divine intoxication is the rejection drive and aggressivity of the abandoned child who feels that it must survive alone.[39]

---

gehen würde. Nun aber wisse sie wohl, daß er nur das im Sinne habe [...] er möge aber wissen, sobald er zum andern Male mit dieser Frau das ausführe, was er soeben getan habe, werde sie sterben.« (*Z. Z.* 310)

[38] »Der Sohn faßte nun den blitzartigen Gedanken, diese kurze Frist [...] dazu zu benützen, die blonde frühere Ringerin trotz Nähe des Gatten und noch verschlossener Tür noch einmal und diesmal zu vollständigem Genusse an sich zu bringen.« (Ibid., p. 346)

[39] »Indem das Kind aus der Passivität des Erlebens in die Aktivität des Spielens übergeht, fügt es einem Spielgefährten das Unangenehme zu, das ihm selbst widerfahren war, und rächt sich so an der Person dieses Stellvertreters [...]. Wir werden so davon überzeugt, daß es auch unter der Herrschaft des Lustprinzips Mittel und Wege genug gibt, um das an sich Unlustvolle zum Gegenstand der Erinnerung und seelischen Bearbei-

It would seem then that during the battle for survival, the sadistic universe is the only realm in which the alternately procrastinating and victimising child of divine intoxication may be sovereign. Yet this sovereignty is but a sham when one considers that the maternal space (the semiotic) and not the symbolic must be violated in order to create the eternal fictitious mode of an intoxication that is, as suggested by the logic of *fort-da*, devoid of pleasure. This can only mean further doom as the son figure stagnates into a caricature of Bataille's evil child, becoming in the sadistic context of a society that demands sacrifice, obedient as opposed to rebellious, victim as opposed to victimiser. In line with this automated dichotomy, overtures of discursive transgression in the violation of the family unit via matricide, along with the associated implication of incest, fail to result in the poetic cross-contamination of syntagmatic units that for Barthes is the literary achievement of the Sadian text.[40] The final scene in which matricide, adultery and by implication incest converge (the sexualisation of the matricide through adultery effects the latter impression) communicates only the complete destruction of the family at the hands of the depraved victim child, who in turn is the lowest of concubine lackeys in the infernal court of the Egocrat.

7.3 Infernal Sobriety: Apotheosis of the Eternal Present

> No one can make a thing of the second self
> that the slave is without at the same time es-
> tranging himself from his own intimate being,
> without giving himself the limits of a thing.
> (Georges Bataille, *Writings*).

Implicit in the above argument is the view that the texture of divine intoxication as survival weapon is inseparable from the texture of sacrifice as practised by the technologically advanced yet curiously barbaric society that makes possible the Final Solution. Behind the sullen refrain of divine intoxication hangs the listless apparition of the mother victim, itself a phantom oracle of the

---

tung zu bearbeiten.« (Sigmund Freud: Das Ich und das Es. Metapsychologische Schriften. Frankfurt a. M.: Fischer 1999 [Fischer-Taschenbücher; 10442: Psychologie], p. 202–203)

[40] For Barthes, the family unit in the Sadian work is a lexical field; to transgress this field means naming beyond the lexical division of the family which assigns parental position (Barthes, Sade, Fourier, Loyola [note 22], p. 141). This transgression thus amounts to transgressing the patriarchal order that instigates the paternal metaphor. Deleuze's reading of the Sadian work argues the opposite perspective, i. e. that any transgression is in fact an evocation of the Death Instinct which is transmitted in the work as an idea of patriarchal reason. The latter perspective, which favours the primacy of the paternal metaphor, provides a more suitable angle for reading Drach's representations of totalitarianism.

gassed Jew. The sacrificial society thus conducts an incessant discourse on the necessity of decimating waste in the course of its own survival. Drach clearly translates this racist cultural politics into one striking episode in the novel, simultaneously cloaking and emphasising the primitive nature of sacrifice through his use of medical discourse. Before returning to the text however, let us assess the proximity of sacrifice and the sacrificial society to the mode of divine intoxication.

Bataille's theory of sacrifice is closely linked to his theory of infantile sovereignty. The society that sacrifices is one that, like the evil child of divine intoxication, is fully immersed in the present. In other words, sacrifice as the highest form of expenditure is also »the antithesis of production, which is accomplished with a view to the future; it is consumption that is concerned only with the moment«.[41] Such sacrifice involves a consecration of pure loss as the excess or surplus of a given society/system is squandered after it has been extracted from society's mass of useful wealth. Condemning surplus to the ritual of sacrifice enables society to economically extend its existence at the unproductive but functioning level of status quo.[42]

In contrast to the transgressive activity of divine intoxication, it would seem that sacrifice is a symptom of society in a state of stasis. Accordingly, Bataille describes excessive society in terms of a state of saturated development, a dead end or apotheosis:

> Only the impossibility of continuing growth makes way for squander. Hence the real excess does not begin until the growth of the individual or group has reached its limit.[43]

In this respect, the sacrificial ritual implicit in the exclusion tactics of anti-Semitism becomes the purging reflex of a society keen to rid itself of perceived impurities. Sacrifice could thus be seen as the survival ritual of a paranoid totalitarian society that is fearful of distortion through the inclusion of strangers within its ranks. The son as would-be sovereign infant parodically reflects this greater social maxim.[44]

Just this image of individual, family and society in a state of unproductive saturation is thematised by »Z. Z.« in an episode concerning the mother's ill-health. Hindered by a troublesome gall bladder, she becomes the victim of unprofessional and indifferent surgeons during her operation. Instead of identifying and treating the source of the problem, healthy parts of her body are removed in a willy nilly fashion whilst the colicky area worsens:

---

[41] Georges Bataille: Essential Writings. Ed. by Michael Richardson. London: Sage 1998 (Theory, Culture & Society), p. 63.

[42] Ibid.

[43] Ibid.

[44] Ibid., p. 73.

> Immerhin war an diesem Tag auch die Operation der Mutter des Sohnes zur Zufrie-
> denheit der Ärzte, wenn auch nicht zu einer solchen der Operierten verlaufen. Sie
> sah so elend und dünn wie ein Faden aus, als Sohn und Stieftochter sich bei ihr ein-
> fanden. Auch hatte man ihr bloß die Geschwülst aus dem Darm entfernt, dazu was
> sie an Weiblichkeit im Innern hatte.   (*Z. Z.* 189)

The above extract is possibly the most literal version of matricide depicted in
the novel. It is not enough that the mother should be reduced to the status of
the imprisoned, exposed and incapacitated on the operating table. She must
also concede part of her identity as female when without her consent her re-
productive organs are removed. This is the most extreme image of the general
indignity of the appropriated Jewish other under totalitarianism. In what could
be construed as a grim parody of the coming matricide, the operating surgeons
become obedient conspirators of the state as they play their localised role in
the general destruction of the female other. High priests of sacrifice, they break
down the body of the female sacrificial victim in a manner that recalls the
analytical gaze of anti-Semitism. Her children are the passive on-looking audience in front of the altar (operating table). The violence of this intrusive act is
likened to a rape (and indeed symbolically evokes the earlier rape) as part of
the mother is amputated without her consent.

That she can no longer reproduce reinforces her superfluity. However, it
also reflects the non-productive, frankly destructive nature of all representations of sex in the novel, which in turn explains the lack of pleasure that is
associated with the sexual. The mother's sterility can be understood as the
central image around which all sterile representations of copulation orbit. Tellingly, the only pregnancy that arises from all the exaggerated sexual activity of
the novel ends in abortion.[45] Taken in conjunction with the constant references
to futurelessness, it would seem that the society of the between time has reached
a point of apotheosis from which it cannot progress, but at best uphold through
the sacrifice mechanism. The existential law by which the son abides can be
fully contextualised through this mechanism. Either one sacrifices an other, or
one becomes the other that is sacrificed. Hence the drastic nature of survival
that reveals the victimised other at its most depraved.

This depravity is strongly articulated through the issue of blood donation.
The mother's health could be much improved by an injection of blood from a
willing donor. In a benign society that does not demand the sacrifice of others
for its perpetuation, the sharing of a resource such as blood would not pose any
conflict of interests. However, in the sacrificial society of the eternal present
blood symbolises life, the most essential currency from the perspective of
those under potential threat. In the mode of selfish children concerned only

---

[45] An affair with the wife of a local musician results in pregnancy and abortion: »Bald
nach der gänzlichen Einigung stellten sich aber Folgen ein, welche die Frau ohne
Befragung des Sohnes beseitigen ließ, deren Kosten er nachträglich aber auf sich
nehmen mußte.« (*Z. Z.* 134)

with their own well being, good health and ability to survive future tribulations, neither son nor stepdaughter is willing to donate blood to their mother. Instead, the mother's suffering escalates as both, it is implied, conserve their resources for activities of an amorous nature:

> Ein Blutspender war nicht eingetroffen. Auch die Stieftochter der Blutbedürftigen, welche zwar Blumen gebracht hatte, war zum Opfer des Inhaltes ihrer Adern nicht bereit, wiewohl sie von den Ärzten hiezu für tauglich angesehen wurde. Sie bezog diese Tauglichkeitsvorstellung vielleicht auf ihr gutes Aussehen und setzte es in Zusammenhang mit den Abenteuern des jüdischen Assistenzarztes, denen sie sich bereits zuzählen konnte. Wahrscheinlich war sie aber bloß feige in Bezug auf ihren besonderen Saft, wie dies auch der Bruder, der richtige Sohn der zu Rettenden, gewesen sein mochte [...]. Immerhin bekam die Mutter statt Blut Injektionen verschiedenster Art, so daß sie bald so zerstochen war, wie Nadelkissen es nach langem Gebrauch zu werden pflegen. *(Z. Z.* 189)

The above reiterates the lack of resistance (here referred to as cowardliness) that is typical of a society divided against itself. Again, Drach chooses to portray this lack of solidarity through the fragmentation of the family. However, the mother-son relationship comes under more intense scrutiny a short time later. In a manner consistent with Bataille's theory of sacrifice, the lot of the ailing mother worsens further. Far from receiving aid from her nearest and dearest, the son is presented not only as reluctant to part with his own blood, but determined to extract from the maternal victim's body the useful wealth that he can. In a telling passage, this wealth takes the form of his mother's heart which he is imagined as tearing out of her body at the command of some girl. Within the sacrificial society of the between time, each and every sexual act comes to signify survival of the self through domination of another, this other taking the ultimate form of the mother:

> Allerdings kam es dem Sohne manchmal selbst so vor, als bemächtige er sich des Herzens seiner Mutter, um es für eines der Mädchen oder eine der Frauen zu verausgaben, die er nicht einmal liebte, aber wenigstens haben wollte. *(Z. Z.* 191)

In light of the above image, every sexual act amounts to an articulation of matricide, a betrayal of the chora. It is evident to what extent the son has become enslaved to a code of survival that clearly necessitates the violation of the semiotic and the quashing of difference. The above illustrated amputations of the mother's body recall the wounded body of the raped spinster victim and the contrasting numbness of the son's physical being. It would seem yet again that whatever pain the son cannot feel (emotionally or physically) his mother must endure.

However as previously asserted, this mode of survival in fact predisposes the son to the morbidity of the melancholy sufferer. For the matricide is silently accompanied by the distress of bereavement which persists throughout the novel. It is just this wretched state of loss that commits the son to the half-life of survival, at all times overshadowed by the depravity of the self and the knowledge of what was wilfully sacrificed in the bloody »save what you can« game.

7.4 Contours of the Culpable

> Denn wenn unter Seele etwas zu verstehen ist, das Menschen von Tieren unterschei-
> det [...], so muß mein Abschied vom Leben und dessen Inhalt [...], bereits erfolgt
> sein. [...] Wo nun auch kein Zweifel mehr bestehen kann, weil das Unvermeidliche
> unwiderruflich eingetreten war, hatte sich der Tod vollzogen und war nur noch der
> Ausdruck des Mitgefühls ausständig.
>   [...] Hatte aber einer das Sein bloß in Schein verwandelt, das heißt, sich damit
> abgefunden, als ein Spuk zurückzubleiben, dann wäre es überhaupt fraglich, ob er
> als Adressat des Beileids würdig sei.[46]

Thus speaks the survivor figure of the final novel in the Holocaust series, *Das
Beileid*. The above described post mortem subsistence is in many ways the
inevitable effect of the narrow sepulchral space that informs the everyday in
»Z. Z.«. The emaciated soulless phantom figure of this passage has departed
any semblance of a meaningful life, a chasm of guilt and bestiality separating
him from the land of the living. Similar to the son in *»Z. Z.«*, this protagonist
goes through the motions of living, affecting the appearance of animation.
Internally, however, he is dead. This is the bitter paradox of survival. Guilt and
the memory of deeds done, measures taken, persons abandoned make of survival a form of deprival, lack and loss. As such, survival does not entail the
grateful embrace of life. Rather, it is the morbid predicament of him who has
blood on his hands and who must live with the knowledge of his own inhumanity. The flip-side of the *»save what you can«* game is the melancholy position of the survivor's retrospective. Yet elements of this quintessentially sad
perspective are already present in *»Z. Z.«*.

Similar to the articulation of absolute negation, the representation of lament
and private mourning is subtly effected. During a time that restricts the expression of the private integrity of the appropriated, sorrow is sidelined as the survivor's cunning appears to motivate existence. In keeping with the marginalisation of subjective affect, the literal depiction of trauma is avoided in favour
of suggestive connotation. Whilst verbose expressions of guilt and sadness
may be absent from the otherwise turgid protocol language, certain constellations suggest the fundamental disposition of melancholia. In *»Z. Z.«*, melancholia takes the form of a subliminal mood that, like the spectre of evil as
absolute negation, emerges in the void of non-representation, that is in the
abstract space of Thanatos that is repeatedly connoted throughout. It is in this
realm of unspoken sorrow that the protocol metamorphoses into an inadvertent
confessional of the delinquent survivor who exposes his ruthlessness through
the protocol tactic of writing against the self.

Melancholia Kristeva describes as an overwhelming sadness, likening it to
the apparition of a black sun in the cosmos of the melancholy sufferer.[47] This

---

[46] Albert Drach: Das Beileid. Nach Teilen eines Tagebuchs. Graz, Wien: Droschl 1993,
p. 7.

source of despair directs its rays towards the depressed, condemning them to the monotony of a devitalised existence that »is ready at any moment for a plunge into death«.[48] The sufferer is powerless in the face of this black sun which, within Kristeva's array of images, functions as a metaphor for the debilitating power of Thanatos. The despondent melancholic occupies the twilight zone of the phantom sentenced to function in the land of the living whilst all the time having surrendered to the sadness of death. This limbo subsistence somewhere »on the frontiers of life and death« denotes the melancholy complex that is nowhere more emphatically borne out than in the imaginary suicide of *Unsentimentale Reise*, the tardy attempt to merge in death with that which was sacrificed along the survival route.[49] In *»Z. Z.«* however, this sadness amounts to a less direct articulation of guilt which, although obscure, nonetheless testifies to the lead weight of a lethal melancholia that subtly poisons the book, forming a steadily seeping wound that continues through *Unsentimentale Reise* to *Das Beileid*.[50]

Consistent with the emphatically external protocol representation of the individual discussed in the previous chapter, the survivor's prison of affect is portrayed mainly through the convoluted discourse concerning the feminine. Kristeva speaks of the particular significance of »death-bearing women« in the melancholy psyche, the tendency of the sufferer to obsess over the spectre of death that it associates with the castrated female body.[51] The clear view of castration afforded the melancholy sufferer by the female body testifies, on the one hand, to the flimsiness of fetishist discourse in the task of concealing the castrated state of the death-bearing body, and on the other, to the disturbing lucidity of the melancholy person.[52] Thus the depressed individual is predisposed to a disturbing perspicacity that constantly confronts him with the possibility of his own castration and the eventuality of death. In *»Z. Z.«*, this lucidity translates into the unspoken knowledge of the form survival will take: the castration of the surviving self that cohabits with the dead and that lives with the guilt of survival at all costs, especially that of matricide. For it may be argued that the profile of melancholia reflects the profile of saving what one can.

Locating death in the female figure (in particular the mother figure), the melancholy sufferer tries to avoid Thanatos through a process of extreme exclusion, a form of matricide that attempts to remove all manifestations of the

---

[47] Julia Kristeva: Black Sun. Depression and Melancholia. New York: Columbia University Press 1989 (European Perspectives), p. 3.

[48] Ibid., p. 4.

[49] Ibid.

[50] »In meinem Zimmer, das eng ist wie ein Sarg, liege ich und möchte weinen. Aber Tote weinen nicht, und Tränen sind überhaupt nicht erlaubt auf einer unsentimentalen Reise. Ich weiß nicht, ob ich die Gashähne geschlossen habe, als wir nach dem halbrohen Essen noch Tee bereiteten, aber ich erhebe mich nicht, um nachzusehen. Das Zimmer scheint nach Gas zu riechen.« (Albert Drach: Unsentimentale Reise. Ein Bericht. Ungekürzte Ausg., München: Deutscher Taschenbuch Verlag 1988 [dtv; 11226], p. 368)

[51] Kristeva, Black Sun (note 47), p. 27.

[52] Ibid., p. 4.

chora from the sufferer's world. This process Kristeva terms the non-integration of the *chora*.[53] It evidences the intense, sadistic hostility of the melancholic towards the maternal. The actual removal of the mother's womb, the imagined removal of her heart, her exclusion from the exile trip and her betrayal at the end of the novel signify the offensive of non-integration that is launched against the maternal in »Z. Z.«.

However, similar to the misguided concupiscence of the son, non-integration is the site of a deadly paradox. Like the »save what you can« game of survival, it steers the player (the melancholic) towards certain death even as this person tries to avoid it. For the hostile melancholy sufferer, after ridding itself of the deathly female castration spectre, is consumed by a terrible anguish for the lost *chora*. It is this anguish – the outer manifestation of depression – that delivers the sufferer into the hands of a living death similar to the existence of the Holocaust survivor described in the opening pages of *Das Beileid*. Having rid itself of the despised *chora*, this person now longs for nothing other than the reinstatement of the banished »Thing«, as Kristeva terms it.[54] This melancholy predicament contours the anomaly of survival to a degree: the ubiquitous and bitterly ironic evocation of death at every twist and turn in the murderous battle to outlive others.

That the melancholy person is both unable to escape the abyss of Thanatos and (metaphorically speaking) illiterate when it comes to reading the potentially restorative function of the semiotic becomes clear in this individual's attempt to deflect Thanatos by means of nonintegration of the *chora*. This misguided tactic reveals the extent to which depression hinges on a paranoid suspicion of the *chora*, a misunderstanding so immense that it lays the foundation for destructive hostility against the very force that could deliver the despondent, through *jouissance*, from the fear of absolute negation. From this perspective, the perspicacity of the melancholy person who locates death in the castrated female body is in fact a form of blindness that holds the feminine to ransom for perceived wrongs. Thereafter ensues a loss so engulfing that not even the rituals of desiring metonymy can distract from the blanks in the psychic apparatus. These voids register the death-like condition of non-being. However, without the support of substitution the registered loss can neither be deferred, compensated for nor worked out within the psyche.[55] For this very reason, the discourse of melancholia differentiates itself from the discourse of mourning; the signifying metonymies of compensation and loss refer to an active fetish function in language and provide a form of catharsis – however ephemeral or unconscious – for the speaking subject who has separated from the (m)other.

In the son's case, this sense of loss translates into an estranged experience of the absurd that lends the everyday its meaningless flavour: the mechanical division of time into work, eating, sleeping, and the pursuit of women for rec-

---

[53] Ibid., p. 18.
[54] Ibid., p. 13.
[55] Ibid., p. 14.

reational purposes.[56] Nothing satisfies him and at all times he is niggled by the conviction that something fundamental is lacking in his life. His lacklustre approach to his existence suggests that he lives in a void of non-being typical for the melancholy person, and that the loss that informs this void cannot be compensated for via the pursuit of women that he frankly does not desire. He thus hangs in a vacuum of despair which he notably terms the between time.[57]

This daily listlessness arises from the twin complex of hostility and suffering that characterises the melancholy individual's perspective on the *chora*, i. e. a complete inability to mourn loss. Thus we encounter a species of disaffected suffering in the depressed person who cannot identify or is unaware of the nature of its loss. This ignorance of an emotion that quite simply »wracks« the individual is addressed in the son's misplaced tears for the loss of the *Gliederpuppe* that he in fact never really possessed or knew.[58] Taken against the backdrop of the dry-eyed son at the paternal bedside, these tears expose the emotional disaffection of the melancholy sufferer. Whilst the act of crying for something that one never knew or never had certainly registers the loss of some »Thing«, the displacement of this loss onto the automaton obscures the nature of the lost object. The identity of the lost »Thing« is verbally addressed only in the final sentence:

> Da wußte er plötzlich, daß er seine Mutter ermordet hatte, *wenngleich er im Zeit-*
> *punkt geirrt haben konnte.*   (*Z. Z.* 347, my emphasis)

The italicised sub-clause suggests that matricide as a general principle of hostility/melancholy has in fact encompassed the whole novel. The citation depicts the moment where guilt, like an arrow straight to the heart, is introduced as a matter of conscience, yet, as implied by the above mentioned temporal confusion, it has arguably been the silent companion of all hostility towards the maternal throughout the text. For the first time, the source of the black sun's rays is here directly equated with the denigration of the maternal.

On the surface of things however, the novel tends to repudiate the expression of sorrow. In order to locate the lived emptiness of the melancholy sufferer, we must read between the lines, as it were, and apprehend those registered voids of non-being which Kristeva terms the »nonrepresentative spacing of representation that is not the *sign* but the *index* of the death

---

[56] »Später [...] hatte er es hingenommen, daß sein Dasein in Stunden unterteilt war, die der Arbeit gehörten, und andere, die der Erbauung dienten. Dazwischen lagen Essen und Trinken, das ihm sowohl die Mutter als auch die Schwester so gut als möglich zurichteten, an das er sich aber so sehr gewöhnte, daß diese Funktionen mechanisch wurden.« (*Z. Z.* 140)

[57] »Daher konnte es keinen Sinn für das Leben ergeben, sich durch Gnade in Gott geborgen zu wissen, aber auch nicht durch die guten Werke, die zumeist ihren Gehalt an Güte späterer unangebrachter Benennung verdankten und häufig durch viel schwerwiegendere andere [...], aufgehoben werden. So zumindest dachte der Sohn damals über diese Dinge, und darum lebte er nicht anders als in einer Zwischenzeit.« (Ibid., p. 143)

[58] Kristeva, Black Sun (note 47), p. 3.

drive«.[59] As suggested above, the female body as an insufficiently functioning fetish object accounts for one aspect of the Thanatos index. The son's obsession with this very body thus exposes him as an angst-ridden melancholy sufferer. A second related aspect of this index is to be located in the son's preoccupation with corpses. From this perspective, woman, castration, the corpse and death form an associative, connotative chain of sorrow in which the son is imprisoned as surely as he is trapped in the role of the ruthless survivor.

One particular incident comes to mind in the portrayal of the melancholy condition. Significantly, this incident is situated at the beginning of the novel and so sets the aggressive-melancholy tone for all following romantic encounters. Featured in this scenario is the son's ideal of the perfect woman. She is a young girl, glimpsed by the son and his sister whilst one day walking in the forest. Poised at the window of her small dwelling, she makes an idyllic impression of wholesome coherent beauty on the son. Some time later the selfsame maiden appears at the son's legal chambers on the pretext of business. A date is set as the son in his usual opportunistic manner loses no time in securing a rendezvous for the maximisation of further possibilities.

As it begins to rain on the agreed Saturday however, overtures of the melancholy mood become manifest as a sense of failure and doom seems to enshroud the entire event. The son finds his enthusiasm waning as he struggles through the rain to the agreed meeting point. That the feminine represents danger for him is implied by the damp distortion of his body as the rain blurs the shape of his suit. Supporting the impression of impending doom, he finds himself hoping against hope that she will not be there. The sense of losing the self in the face of the *chora* that is typical for the melancholy sufferer, the fear of parcelling or disintegration of the self as Kristeva calls it, is communicated in this sudden reluctance of the otherwise womaniser.[60]

What follows could be construed as the use of non-integration as a narcissistic support for the threatened self. Kristeva argues that the individual who fears disintegration takes refuge behind the defence of sadness which, if nothing else, »reconstitutes an affective cohesion of the self«.[61] However, she also points out that this defence is suspect as it does not rule out suicide per se, but merely destruction of the self that takes the form of disintegration/parcelling. Instead, self-destruction in the world of the melancholy sufferer becomes a form of archaic regression, an offering-up of the numbed self to Thanatos in the hope of a reconstituted, fortified, if depressed unity of the self.

Contrary to the son's hopes, the girl is present. In contrast to his drenched state, she is barely wet. Moreover, she has no problem hopping over the stony

---

[59] Ibid., p. 27.

[60] »Indessen war es nur so, daß sich seine Vorsätze, wenn er welche gehabt haben sollte, mit dem zunehmenden Naß, das schon sein Gewand erheblich aus der Form brachte, durchweichten und daß er, je näher er dem ersehnten Endziele kam, um so heftiger wünschte, sie würde gar nicht da sein.« (*Z. Z.* 38)

[61] Kristeva, Black Sun (note 47), p. 19.

paths and muddy ways whilst he finds himself struggling, becoming bogged down, sinking into the mire. All aspects of his bedraggled person and reluctant outlook along with the characterisation of the solid, surefooted dry girl communicate the melancholy individual's deep fear of the *chora*. That no sexual encounter takes place only emphasises the impression of melancholy non-integration. In this manner, the son's stream of irrelevant small talk defers the recognition of castration (death as disintegration) because it defers the possibility of a sexual encounter with the death-bearing (castrated) woman. This incident stands out in the context of the son's otherwise insatiable sex drive. Within the anti-Semitic model of society depicted in the book, it seems to express both reluctance and dismay in the face of the sex ghetto, itself an imaginary space of absolute negation. In this particular case, the latter space is avoided, but not for long.[62]

By the time of his second rendezvous with this woman, the inevitable »cadaverisation« of the sexual has begun complete with parodied images of castration. Notably, no copulation takes place, but the sense of castration, emasculation and underlying death is evoked by the presence of an accidentally discovered corpse. The pair arranges to meet in the woods, this dark cavernous location a fitting site for the discovery of castration. As if to reveal her castrated state, the death-bearing woman emerges from a hiding place at the centre of the forest, and from this moment on the son's identification of death with the feminine is complete.

This identification is initially rendered indirectly in the form of a small but aggressive dog brought along by the girl. We learn that the son's negligence had brought about the death of his father's pet dog shortly before he died. The son now plunges himself into the language of death by delivering an obituary in honour of the deceased dog. The damage is done, however, as the memory of the father's death has been introduced into the forest space and the scene of attempted seduction. Moreover, the son's sense of guilt is thematised by his regret concerning the family pet. The death-effect of these seemingly trivial interruptions gathers momentum as shortly thereafter the son and girl, in search of a quiet place for some routine sexual activity, discover the corpse of an old man. This apparition of death, which to the son's mind assumes the identity of his deceased father, puts paid to any notions of romance. In effect, the idea of the son's castration is introduced via these sinister images – the forest, the remembered animal corpse, the discovered corpse, the ghost of the father – that both displace and evoke the void of non-being that is female castration.[63]

---

[62] »Zwischen Wirklichkeit und Wunder war eine Annäherung nicht leicht zu finden, obwohl die kleine Dame neben ihm über den nassen Weg schwebte, in dessen weiches Erdreich er geradezu einsank. Und als sie in der Folge über den Kies und die Felsenstufen sich nach oben und unten schwang, während seine Schritte nichts von ihrem Gewicht abgeben konnten, [...] mußte er sich in seiner Annahme bestätigt finden, daß das, was er sagte, nicht das war, was er sagen sollte und wollte, [...] alles Anknüpfungen, wo kaum etwas zu verknüpfen war.« (*Z. Z.* 39)

[63] »Aber wie sie bei einer Lichtung eintrafen, die den Wald in zwei Teile unterbrach, verbellte der Hund einen größeren Gegenstand, der auf einem Kotzen lag. Und so-

However, the completion of the castration ritual is too delivered in an indirect manner. A football from a neighbouring field lands suddenly in the loins of the corpse. The girl laughs uncontrollably at this event before competently kicking the ball back in the direction it came from. The son, by contrast, is horrified both by the indignity of what has occurred to a corpse in which he glimpses his father (and himself) and by the heartlessness of the mocking girl. His castration thus takes place in the drama objectified before his very eyes: the might of the female other who raises death in the form of a doubly offensive figure: the castrated male corpse.[64]

The female body henceforth becomes the malfunctioning fetish object par excellence. Kristeva specifies this very unreliability of the fetish when she claims that fetishism is a stasis that functions as a thesis.[65] In other words, similar to the depressed offensive of non-integration, fetishism denotes an automatised condition of stasis that has not moved beyond a certain fixation even whilst it affects the signifying function of the thesis. Following this logic, it is inevitable that the female body as fetish in »*Z. Z.*« will become the ultimate index of the castrated melancholy condition and a powerful image of death. As if to reflect this, the son finally admits what he has suspected since the first rendezvous: that the miracle of female beauty is dead, that he is lamed by the whole unpalatable experience, and that the stench of ugliness pervades the air. Nothing but the fumbled attempt at an embrace comes of this second meeting and they part without arranging a further rendezvous.[66]

»Depressive persons cannot endure Eros«, says Kristeva, a perspective that throws some light on the son's inability to keep alive within his own mind the vision of beauty initially associated with the miracle girl.[67] In many ways, the above incident is one of the first scenes of the son's surrender to melancholia.

---

bald sie näher traten, erwies sich dieses Objekt der Verbellung als ein alter Mann, dessen Gesicht im Zwielicht den Sohn an seinen Vater erinnerte, ja zeitweilig dessen Züge annahm [...]. Diese Kenntnisnahme erschwerte sohin dem Sohn die Bereitschaft zum Liebesspiel.« (Ibid., p. 44)

[64] »[...] aber der Sohn [wurde] von seinem Hang zur Verstocktheit abgebracht, sondern es bedurfte hiezu eines Fußballes von einer nahen Wiese, den ein Stürmer oder Eckballer über das Goal hinausschoß und der in der Lendengegend des Todbetroffenen landete. Das brachte die Begleiterin zum Lachen, welches mit den vorgängigen makabren Umständen nicht in Zusammenhang zu bringen war. Auch schoß sie den Ball zurück.« (Ibid., p. 45)

[65] Julia Kristeva: Revolution in Poetic Language. New York: Columbia University Press 1984, p. 115.

[66] »Inzwischen waren sie wieder im Walde angekömmen, und der Sohn zeigte sich trotzdem noch entschlossen, aus dem toten Wunder eine wirkliche Liebschaft zu gestalten. Allein der aufgelegte Kotzen des verstorbenen Höhlenbewohners sowie dieses Verstorbenen vermeintlicher Gesichtsausdruck lähmten seinen Angriffswillen, auch spürte er im Unterleib das mißratene Goal, und schließlich stank das verendete Wunder in seine empfindliche Nase.« (Ibid., p. 46)

[67] Kristeva, Black Sun (note 47), p. 20.

He has witnessed the spectre of decay that is ill-concealed by the apparent beauty of the female body and all sexual encounters are thereafter poisoned by this knowledge. The shift from the comely maiden in the window to the flat-footed kicker of balls (both literally and metaphorically) represents what Kristeva calls the inversion of the matricidal drive into the death-bearing image of the female other.[68] The entire episode could be summed up as a failed ritual of desiring metonymy that implies the unrepresentable condition of melancholy non-being through the connoted images of the castrated female body and the human corpse. In this way, both the girl and the dead vagrant function as an index of the son's fundamental melancholy predicament. It is he alone who sees in the corpse his own father. Even as this connection incapacitates him however, it does not constitute a mourning. All we are told is that the son deals with this discovery in silence. In the same way, it is he alone who witnesses the transformation of the girl from swan to duckling, a metamorphosis that finalises the irreversible initiation of death into his world.[69]

In this manner, it becomes clear as to why the son holds the feminine to ransom for perceived wrongs in the society of the time. The descent of an entire world into condoned barbarism is registered in the shift from beauty to ugliness in the representation of woman. The son's sense of complete isolation as a Jew, of abandonment by his fellow countrymen is reflected by his disappointment in the ugliness of his surrounding world, clearly evidenced in this instance by the sudden ugliness of the girl. The personality of the despondent child king who has lost the primordial object but cannot grieve pervades the entire text, as the son in his role as victimiser and murderer wreaks revenge on a world that has let him down. In this context, the lost object could be described as a sense of belonging in his land of birth, the cradle of the family unit and the belief in a benign deity who guides his earthly offspring at all times. These three orientational points in the son's life are progressively eroded and, leaving him only with the sullen emptiness of the melancholy sufferer, his days are spent in the destructive mode of the depressed.

The lament for things lost, however, emerges in each evocation of the parental (in particular the maternal) corpse. This understanding of the corpse as the index for repressed lament casts the sexual abomination of the female other in a different light. Convinced of the ugliness of the world, convinced of its spiritual, familial and maternal impoverishment, the son's crazed devouring of the female body no longer solely enacts the vindictive taming of the other manifest at the wider social level. Rather, this consumption also signifies the desperate swallowing-up action of the melancholy cannibal who attempts to repudiate loss by de-

---

[68] Ibid., p. 28.

[69] »Darauf betrachtete der Sohn ihre Beine näher, während er sich bisher mit dem Gesicht des Mädchens beschäftigt hatte [...]. Er traf ihre Tragstücke, hiezulande Füße, auch Sprudler geheißen, mit einem Blick, der nichts mehr verschönte [...]. Er fand das zur Schau Gestellte muskulös, teilweise behaart und nicht so proportioniert, wie er nach der Ansicht im Fenster bisher geglaubt hatte.« (Ibid., p. 45–46)

vouring the female object. This act testifies to the inability of the son as Holocaust survivor to forget other victims who did not outlive atrocity, exposing that aspect of memory that situates the self with the dead/lost others.[70] The inability to forget demarcates the melancholy prison of affect of this despondent cannibal. The images of castration, matricide, the corpse and sexual cannibalism which together weave the melancholy tapestry in »Z. Z.« thus manifest »the anguish of losing the other through the survival of self«, a hard fact of the »save what you can« game.[71] The misogyny of the victimised son becomes from this angle an attempt to remain close to the ingested other, the sorrowful articulation of a melancholy solidarity in death that could not be realised in life.

7.5 Suffer Little Children

The discovery of the vagrant corpse in »Z. Z.« evokes the scene of the discovery of death experienced by the child Drach in the short story *Lunz*.[72] In the latter narrative, the boy Drach glimpses a drowned corpse and decides to outwit death by becoming an artist. Hence the child in flight who avoids death as total negation through the *jouissance* of creative language composition. In »Z. Z.«, we encounter the reverse image of the child in flight, i. e. the evil child of infernal sobriety who is mired in melancholia and trapped in the repetitive cycle of growing evil. The point of difference concerning these contrasting figures centres on the function of art as fetish in the clever, flirtatious deferral of death. For certain constellations in »Z. Z.« thematise the failure of art, and in particular of writing, to postpone the eventuality of absolute negation.

This failure is documented to an extent by the relative muteness of the son. True to melancholy type, his speech is a facade that ill conceals a subterranean knowledge of death or of the buried »Thing«. This is nowhere more apparent than in an episode that documents his attempts to write artistically during the between time. Shortly before the Christmas of 1937, the son departs Vienna on a secret trip to the mountains. He arrives at a deserted resort that is covered in snow, remote and far removed from the accelerating anti-Semitism of the increasingly Hitlerite city. Below him lie the dangers of the ravines and gorges that he has had to traverse to arrive at this winter oasis. Overall, this concealed corner of Austria represents a haven of temporary respite from external pressures.

---

[70] Lawrence L. Langer describes this form of memory as an aspect of the buried self; those that did not survive are buried in this subterranean space of memory, much like Kristeva's buried »Thing« (Lawrence L. Langer: Holocaust Testimonies. The Ruins of Memory. New Haven, London: Yale University Press 1991, p.14).

[71] Kristeva, Black Sun (note 47), p. 12.

[72] Albert Drach: Lunz. Eine Erzählung. In: id., Ironie vom Glück. Kleine Protokolle und Erzählungen. München, Wien: Hanser 1994, p. 7–34.

It is typically also the site of an (atypically) chaste love affair. The son finds a guest house in which he is the sole visitor. The only other person present is the blond, blue-eyed landlady whose husband is away. In an unconventional and strangely poignant pose, the son is depicted leaning against her knees as he writes a play in which he decimates Hitler. It is an image of peaceful domesticity that contains an exceptionally benign portrayal of the feminine. Despite her Aryan good looks, despite her political naivety (she appears to support Hitler), the son stresses the warmth of the encounter and transposes her into his play as the innocent companion of Hanswurst (the Hitler figure). Before his departure, the landlady promises to visit him before Easter stating that only her own death will prevent her arrival (*Z. Z.* 201).

The son returns to Vienna by train and on this trip a second person he has encountered enters his mind as he begins to think of writing another literary work. This character is none other than the eastern Jewish pedlar who some time previously arrived at his practice without wares, stating simply that he had come *um dazusein* (to be there, *Z. Z.* 139). From this moment, the son cannot free himself of the suspicion that this humble figure could be God, a benign presence that must not announce itself and that does not intervene to save the day, but that simply *is*. This impression is symptomatic of the son's melancholy state, his need to rid himself of the radical, sullen atheism that is a feature of the depressed.[73] The innocent figure of the Jewish pedlar, similar to the naive landlady, is later transposed into the son's literary repertoire as the character Zwetschkenbaum. In both cases, it would seem that their virtue arises from a complete lack of cynicism that appears to the restless, listless son as the spiritual calm that evades him.

Once he arrives in Vienna however, all literary thoughts and spiritual speculation recede as 1938 is heralded and the prospect of annexation approaches ever faster. The passing of the benign that is suggested by the father's death is re-emphasised by the burlesque death of the landlady and the heartless murder of the pedlar. She is killed in a motor accident involving an SA vehicle. Naturally, all SA members involved survive whilst the innocent personification of femininity dies away (*Z. Z.* 254). The vision of innocence incorporated in the pedlar deity meets a more pronounced end at the hands of the Nazis. The son hears of the beating to death of a pedlar without wares at the concentration camp of Buchenwald (*Z. Z.* 308). Thus the prophecy of the death of God implied by the ascent of the Egocrat and the rule of the incubus is realised in this modern-day crucifixion. Only the matricide awaits fulfilment as the logical conclusion of this chain of destruction that repeatedly articulates the reality that, for Drach, kills truth. It would seem that in these wispy, transient renditions of the benign, truth appears as a state of innocence that is too fragile for the world of »*Z. Z.*«.

Furthermore, language composition is no longer the adequate defence against death as stasis that it once was in the childhood idyll of *Lunz*. The first

---

[73] Ibid., p. 5.

sketches of a play and the first reflections on a prose work do nothing to prevent the death of the two inspirational figures involved. It would seem that the work of art as fetish and the language game of *jouissance*, both of which through the cunning of transgression alternately reveal and defer death, have entered a context in which the deft negotiation of the death drives is no longer a realistic option. Flight from destruction through the creative productivity of language is not possible as the principle of Thanatos everywhere assumes precedence. The protocol work of »Z. Z.« becomes from this point of view the work of art as slipshod fetish par excellence. As illustrated throughout these final chapters, the novel writes and rewrites stasis thereby creating imaginary spaces for the articulation of death. It could therefore be argued that »Z. Z.« as work of art assumes the tone of a lament, becoming an ode to the castration (death) of an entire community, victims and survivors alike, hence tirelessly implying the unsignifiable: the dark secret that can be neither prevented nor concealed by the playful manoeuvres of fetishist discourse – the Final Solution.

The despondent child of the between time thus becomes the point of articulation for a form of absurdity that is in essence tragic. Aware that truth and God are dead, the son experiences not the freedom of absurd man who realises that he is without a master. Rather, the son is aware that the absurd world is a world of sin without God, which in the absence of the benign »merely confers equivalence on the consequences« of evil actions.[74] The rhetoric of repetition in »Z. Z.« represents from this point of view the ethic of quantity that supersedes the quality of experience in the absurd world, which time and again communicates the maxim that »what counts is not the best living but the most living«.[75] The tragedy for the son however, is the overwhelming sense of nothingness with which he lives and the dreadful nostalgia for a benign deity that would somehow rescue the world from an evil that is as absurd as it is inexorable. This lament for the lost God is as profound as the silent mourning for the murdered mother. It testifies to the frail presence of good in the ruins of the son's cynical person. Finally, the voice of grief that emerges in this hopeless longing is the keening of the abandoned child left to his own devices in the desert of the absurd that is the restricted space of the doomed, the between time:

> Mag sein, daß solche Unterstellungen für eine Zwischenzeit langen, in denen ein Inkubus oder Sukkubus nicht nur die Form des Teilhabers am Genusse, sondern auch die des Lebenszweckes und des Sinnes des Geschehens übernimmt, ohne daß diese Auf- oder Unterlage Dämonie für sich hat, so daß bei Abwesenheit Gottes nicht einmal die Gegebenheit des Teufels vorausgesetzt werden durfte. Auf diese Weise klaffte das Nichts einerseits aus den Abgründen um ihn und in ihm, andererseits aus allen Nähten und Bindungen, die ihn selbst oder was auch immer mit der Außen- oder der Innenwelt zusammenfügen oder auch nur in irgendeine Ordnung bringen sollten, selbst in eine bloß willkürliche und provisorische.   (*Z. Z.* 192)

---

[74] Albert Camus: The Myth of Sisyphus. Harmonsworth: Penguin 1975, p. 65.
[75] Ibid., p. 59.

Conclusion
Concentration Camps of the Mind and the Child in Flight

In his well-known work on Holocaust narratives, James E. Young develops the above concept of the psychological concentration camp.[1] During his discussion of the Polish writer Tadeusz Borowski, Young argues that the Holocaust becomes a new referential topos or paradigm for both past and future events in this writer's works. Of this writer Young says that »when he left Auschwitz, it became clear that his mind – his meaning-making capacity – was still interned«.[2] This new and harshly focused epistemology ensures that »not only has the writer's future been turned into a great camp of the mind, but so has the past of his heritage«.[3]

May one argue this angle with regard to Albert Drach? This dissertation has unearthed precisely the above space of enclosure in Drach's autobiographical work. In many respects, the space of absolute negation that has featured so dominantly in the last two chapters refers directly to the »concentration camp of the mind« – or living death – of the survivor-scribe. With reference to Young's discourse on the Holocaust, the *grotta* motif of the evoked space of burial in these texts may thus be considered a means of reading the above paradigm of internment through the literary category of the grotesque. In effect I have, with the help of psychoanalytic theory, re-worked this obscure dimension of the grotesque specifically for readings of the Holocaust in Drach's work. A further project would be the application of this analytical model to the works of other Holocaust survivors. A question worth pursuing would be that pertaining to the manifestation of trauma in literary language; could the findings of this thesis potentially correspond to the Holocaust accounts of other writers? In other words, could one generally expand the theory of failed language fetishism within the wider debate concerning Holocaust narrative?

In conclusion, let us not forget the contrapuntal archetype identified in certain of Drach's other literary works: the child in flight. Against the above image of the timeless internalised camp, the child in flight represents a departure from the space of internment. This topos of mobility therefore also signifies an alternative epistemological universe within the Drach literary repertoire, one

---

[1] James E. Young: Writing and Rewriting the Holocaust. Narrative and the Consequences of Interpretation. Bloomington, Indianapolis: Indiana University Press 1990.
[2] Ibid., p. 105.
[3] Ibid., p. 106.

which implies (qua literary strategy of ambivalence) that the traumas of the past do not necessarily »seal« the survivor-scribe, »himself and his mind, his grasp of all the world, into figures deriving from Auschwitz«.[4]

I have argued that this universe is spatially configured through the topography of transgression: the surface network of grotesque indeterminacy, *jouissance* and movement. Remaining with this perspective, one could surmise that the referential paradigm of the Holocaust is rejected by these works. Young says of Borowski that all he knows »is now apprehended – and thereby reorganized – in the figures of captor and slave, oppressor and oppressed«.[5] In contrast to this, I have argued that those of Drach's works organised according to the strategy of *jouissance* constantly feature difference: the post-modern or post-colonial encounter with other and self as other. This being the case, the figures of master/slave, captor/captive do not survive intact in these narratives, as seen – most clearly perhaps – in the analysis of *Das Goggelbuch*.

It is through this literary embrace of the general paradigm of cultural hybridity that one may identify Drach's poignant plea for an ethics of alterity in post-Holocaust society. This plea ultimately represents a position that wishes to prevent the continued displacement of others into spaces of internment. It also represents the struggle to survive in, enlighten and perhaps to forgive an imperfect world.

---

[4]   Ibid.
[5]   Ibid.

Bibliography

Primary Sources

The following bibliography refers only to works cited in the course of this book. For a more complete bibliography of Drach's primary works, the secondary literature and newspaper articles concerning the author and his works, see *Albert Drach*, ed. by Gerhard Fuchs and Gunther A. Höfler, and Matthias Settele, *Der Protokollstil des Albert Drach*, cited below. The unpublished work from the Drach literary remains of the Austrian Literary Archive is cited in as complete a form as possible.

Published Works

Autobiography

Drach, Albert: »Z. Z.« das ist die Zwischenzeit. Ein Protokoll. Ungekürzte Ausg., München: Deutscher Taschenbuch Verlag 1990 (dtv; 12218).
– Unsentimentale Reise. Ein Bericht. Ungekürzte Ausg., München: Deutscher Taschenbuch Verlag 1988 (dtv; 11226).
– Das Beileid. Nach Teilen eines Tagebuchs. Graz, Wien: Droschl 1993.

Other Protokolle/Novels

Drach, Albert: Untersuchung an Mädeln. Kriminalprotokoll. Ungekürzte Ausg., München: Deutscher Taschenbuch Verlag 1995 (dtv; 12043).
– »O Catilina«. Ein Lust und Schaudertraum. München, Wien: Hanser 1995.

Collections of Short Stories/Protokolle

Drach, Albert: IA UND NEIN. Drei Fälle. München, Wien: Hanser 1992.
– Das Goggelbuch. In: Albert Drach: Die kleinen Protokolle und das Goggelbuch. München, Wien: Langen-Müller 1965, p. 245–303.
– Lunz. Eine Erzählung. In: Albert Drach: Ironie vom Glück. Kleine Protokolle und Erzählungen. München, Wien: Hanser 1994, p. 7–34.
– Martyrium eines Unheiligen. In: ibid., p. 133–185
– Vermerk einer Hurenwerdung. In: ibid., p. 69–90

Plays

Drach, Albert: Das Satansspiel vom göttlichen Marquis. Eine Verkleidung in vier Akten. Frankfurt a. M.: Verlag der Autoren 1992.

Unpublished Works

Essays

Drach, Albert: Essay I. Die Abschaffung Gottes und dessen Ersatz durch die Behörde. In: Albert Drach: Das 17. Buch der 17 Essays. Nachlaß Albert Drach, Austrian Literary Archive of the National Library (ÖLA), Wien.
– Essay IV: Zur Lösung der Antisemitenfrage. In: ibid.
– Essay VII: Stilleben. In: ibid.

Other Manuscripts

Drach, Albert: Eigenhaendige Literarische Einfuehrung. In: Albert Drach: Bildnisse der Erfolglosen, ein Wiener Lied aus unserer Zeit. Nachlaß Albert Drach, Austrian Literary Archive of the Austrian National Library, Wien, dated July 31 1929.
– Wurmfortsatz. Zum Protokoll »Wie man Zwetschkenbaum steinigt«, Nachlaß Albert Drach, Austrian Literary Archive of the National Library (ÖLA), Wien.

Letters

Letter from H. J. Mundt, Kurt Desch Verlag, München, to Albert Drach, 30 December 1957, Nachlaß Albert Drach, Austrian Literary Archive of the National Library (ÖLA), Vienna.

Secondary Sources

Adorno, Theodor W.: Erziehung nach Auschwitz. In: id., »Ob nach Auschwitz noch sich leben lasse«. Ein philosophisches Lesebuch. Hg. von Rolf Tiedemann. Frankfurt a. M: Suhrkamp 1997 (Edition Suhrkamp; N. F. 844), p. 48–63.
– Standort des Erzählers im zeitgenössischen Roman. In: id., Noten zur Literatur I. Hg. von Rolf Tiedemann. Frankfurt a. M.: Suhrkamp 1981 (Suhrkamp-Taschenbuch Wissenschaft; 355), p. 4–48.
– Über epische Naivität. In: id., Noten zur Literatur. Frankfurt a. M.: Suhrkamp 1958, p. 50–60.
Arendt, Hannah: The Origins of Totalitarianism. New York: Harcourt 1973.
Auckenthaler, Karlheinz F.: »Ich habe mich erst als Jude zu fühlen gehabt, als mich der Hitler als einen solchen erklärt hat«. Albert Drachs Beziehung zum Judentum im Leben und Werk. In: Modern Austrian Literature 27 (1994), No. 3/4, p. 51–69.
Bachtin, Michail M.: Die Redevielfalt im Roman. In: id., Die Ästhetik des Wortes. Frankfurt a. M.: Suhrkamp 1979 (Edition Suhrkamp; 967), p. 192–251.
– Literatur und Karneval. Zur Romantheorie und Lachkultur. Frankfurt a. M: Fischer 1996 (Fischer-Taschenbücher; 7434: Fischer Wissenschaft).
Barthes, Roland: Die Lust am Text. Frankfurt a. M.: Suhrkamp 1974 (Bibliothek Suhrkamp; 378).
– Sade, Fourier, Loyola. Paris: Seuil 1971.

Bataille, Georges: Essential Writings. Ed. by Michael Richardson. London: Sage 1998 (Theory, Culture & Society).
– Literature and Evil. Essays. London, New York: Boyars 1997.
Bauman, Zygmunt: Modernity and Ambivalence. Cambridge: Polity Press 1991.
– Modernity and the Holocaust. Oxford: Polity Press 1989.
Beller, Steven: Vienna and the Jews 1867–1938. A Cultural History. Cambridge: Cambridge University Press 1990.
Benjamin, Walter: Der Erzähler. Betrachtungen zum Werk Nikolai Lesskows. In: id., Illuminationen. Ausgewählte Schriften. Hg. von Siegfried Unseld. Frankfurt a. M.: Suhrkamp 1969, p. 409–436.
– The Origin of German Tragic Drama. London: NLB 1977.
Benson, Ciarán: The Cultural Psychology of Self. Place, Morality and Art in Human Worlds. London, New York: Routledge 2001.
Bergson, Henri / George Meredith: Laughter. Essays on Comedy. New York: Doubleday 1956.
Bernstein, Jay M.: Disenchantment and Ethics. Cambridge: Cambridge University Press 2001 (Modern European Philosophy).
Bhabha, Homi: The Location of Culture. London, New York: Routledge 1994.
Botz, Gerhard: Austria. In: The Social Basis of European Fascist Movements. Ed. by Detlef Mühlberger. London: Croom Helm 1987, p. 242–280.
– Die Ausgliederung der Juden aus der Gesellschaft. Das Ende Wiener Judentums unter der NS-Herrschaft (1938–1943). In: Eine zerstörte Kultur. Jüdisches Leben und Antisemitismus in Wien seit dem 19. Jahrhundert. Hg. von Gerhard Botz, Ivar Oxaal und Michael Pollak. Buchloe: Obermeyer 1990, p. 285–311.
– Der 13. März 38 und die Anschlußbewegung. Selbstaufgabe, Okkupation und Selbstfindung Österreichs 1918–1945. Wien: Verlag der SPÖ 1981.
Brennan, Timothy: The National Longing for Form. In: Nation and Narration. Ed. by Homi K. Bhabha. London: Routledge 1990, p. 44–70.
Brockhaus-Enzyklopädie in 24 Bänden. 19., völlig neu bearb. Aufl., Mannheim: Brockhaus 1986–1995.
Butler, Judith: The Body Politics of Julia Kristeva. In: Ethics, Politics, and Difference in Julia Kristeva's Writing. Ed. by Kelly Oliver. London, New York: Routledge 1993, p. 164–178.
– Bodies that Matter. On the Discursive Limits of Sex. New York, London: Routledge 1993.
Camus, Albert: The Myth of Sisyphus. Harmonsworth: Penguin 1975.
Connerton, Paul: How Societies Remember. Cambridge: Cambridge University Press 1989 (Themes in the Social Sciences).
Cuddon, J. A.: A Dictionary of Literary Terms and Literary Theory. 4th Edition, revised by C. E. Preston. Oxford: Blackwell 1998.
Culler, Jonathan: The Semiotics of Tourism. In: id., Framing the Sign. Criticism and its Institutions. Oxford: Norman 1988, p. 153–168.
Deleuze, Gilles: Masochism. Coldness and Cruelty. New York: Zone Books 1989.
Derrida, Jacques: Structure, Sign, and Play in the Discourse of the Human Sciences. In: id., Writing and Difference. London, New York: Routledge 1978, p. 351–370.
Epps, Brad: Grotesque Identities. Writing, Death, and the Space of the Subject (Between Michel de Montaigne and Reinaldo Arenas). In: Journal of the Mid-West Modern Languages Association 28 (1995), p. 38–55.
Fischer, André: Inszenierte Naivität. Zur ästhetischen Simulation von Geschichte bei Günther Grass, Albert Drach und Walter Kempowski. München: Fink 1992 (Theorie und Geschichte der Literatur und der schönen Künste; 85).

Foucault, Michel: Discipline and Punish. The Birth of the Prison. London: Penguin Books 1991 (Penguin Social Sciences).
– The Archaeology of Knowledge. London: Routledge 1995.
– The History of Sexuality. The Will to Knowledge. London: Penguin Books 1998.
– The Order of Things. An Archaeology of the Human Sciences. London: Routledge 2000.
Freud, Sigmund: Das Ich und das Es. Metapsychologische Schriften. Frankfurt a. M.: Fischer 1999 (Fischer-Taschenbücher; 10442: Psychologie).
Friedrich, Carl J. / Zbigniew Brzezinski: Totalitarian Dictatorship and Autocracy. Revised Edition, Cambridge: Harvard University Press 1965 (Praeger University Series; U 522).
Fuchs, Anne: Files against the Self. Albert Drach. In: id., A Space of Anxiety. Dislocation and Abjection in Modern German-Jewish Literature. Amsterdam, Atlanta: Rodopi 1999 (Amsterdamer Publikationen zur Sprache und Literatur; 138), p. 123–162.
Gilman, Sander L.: Jewish Self-Hatred: Anti-Semitism and the Hidden Language of the Jews. Baltimore, London: John Hopkins University Press 1986.
Gross, Elizabeth: The Body of Signification. In: Abjection, Melancholia, and Love. The Work of Julia Kristeva. Ed. by John Fletcher and Andrew Benjamin. London, New York: Routledge 1990 (Warwick Studies in Philosophy and Literature), p. 80–103.
Heidsieck, Arnold: Das Groteske und das Absurde im modernen Drama. Stuttgart: Kohlhammer 1969 (Sprache und Literatur; 53).
Horch, Hans Otto: Heimat und Fremde. Jüdische Schriftsteller und deutsche Literatur oder Probleme einer deutsch-jüdischen Literaturgeschichte. In: Juden als Träger bürgerlicher Kultur in Deutschland. Hg. von Julius H. Schoeps. Stuttgart, Bonn: Burg 1989 (Studien zur Geistesgeschichte; 11), p. 41–65.
Horkheimer, Max / Theodor W. Adorno: Dialektik der Aufklärung. Philosophische Fragmente. Frankfurt a. M.: Fischer 1991.
Huemer, Peter: Albert Drach im Gespräch, 9. 1. 1992 Österreich 1. In: Prozesse 2. Mitteilungsblatt der Internationalen Albert Drach-Gesellschaft 1998, p. 14–26.
Iser, Wolfgang: Das Komische – ein Kipp-Phänomen. In: Das Komische. Hg. von Wolfgang Preisendanz und Rainer Warning. München: Fink 1976 (Poetik und Hermeneutik; 7), p. 398–402.
Jakobson, Roman: Randbemerkungen zur Prosa des Dichters Pasternak [1935]. In: id., Poetik. Ausgewählte Aufsätze 1921–1971. Hg. von Elmar Holenstein und Tarcisius Schelbert. Frankfurt a. M.: Suhrkamp 1993 (Suhrkamp-Taschenbuch Wissenschaft; 262), p. 192–211.
– Zwei Seiten der Sprache und zwei Typen aphatischer Störungen. In: id., Aufsätze zur Linguistik und Poetik. Hg. von Wolfgang Raible. München: Nymphenburger 1974 (Sammlung Dialog; 71), p. 117–140.
Kafka, Franz: Die Verwandlung. In: id., Die Erzählungen. Hg. von Roger Hermes. Frankfurt a. M.: Fischer 1997, p. 96–161.
– Ein Bericht für eine Akademie und andere Texte zum Rotpeter-Thema. In: ibid., p. 322–337.
Kayser, Wolfgang: Das Groteske. Seine Gestaltung in Malerei und Dichtung. Oldenburg, Hamburg: Stalling 1957.
Konzett, Matthias: The Politics of Recognition in Contemporary Austrian Jewish Literature. In: Monatshefte 90, No. 1 (Spring 1998), p. 71–88.
Kristeva, Julia: The System and the Speaking Subject. In: id., The Kristeva Reader. Ed. by Toril Moi. New York: Columbia University Press 1986, p. 24–34.
– Black Sun. Depression and Melancholia. New York: Columbia University Press 1989 (European Perspectives).

- Desire in Language. A Semiotic Approach to Literature and Art. Oxford: Blackwell 1980.
- Powers of Horror. An Essay on Abjection. New York: Columbia University Press 1982 (European Perspectives).
- Revolution in Poetic Language. New York: Columbia University Press 1984.
Lacan, Jacques: Kant avec Sade. In: id., Écrits. Paris: Seuil 1966, p. 765–790.
- Écrits. A Selection. London: Tavistock 1977.
- The Four Fundamental Concepts of Psycho-Analysis. Ed. by Jacques-Alain Miller. New York, London: Norton 1981.
Langer, Lawrence L.: Holocaust Testimonies. The Ruins of Memory. New Haven, London: Yale University Press 1991.
Lefort, Claude: The Political Forms of Modern Society. Bureaucracy, Democracy, Totalitarianism. Cambridge: Polity Press 1986.
Lodge, David: The Modes of Modern Writing. Metaphor, Metonymy, and the Typology of Modern Literature. London, New York: Arnold 1997.
Lukács, Georg: Die Theorie des Romans. Ein geschichtsphilosophischer Versuch über die Formen der großen Epik. 2., um ein Vorwort vermehrte Aufl., Berlin: Luchterhand 1963.
Melzer, Gerhard: Endzeit ohne Ende. Albert Drachs jüngstes Buch, »Ja Und Nein«. In: Neue Zürcher Zeitung, February 2 1993, p. 17.
Menasse, Robert: Das Land ohne Eigenschaften. Essay zur österreichischen Identität. Frankfurt a. M.: Suhrkamp 1995 (Suhrkamp-Taschenbuch; 2487).
Menninghaus, Winfried: Ekel. Theorie und Geschichte einer starken Empfindung. Frankfurt a. M.: Suhrkamp 1999.
Millner, Alexandra: Im Sekundenspiegel. Zu Albert Drachs *Das Goggelbuch*. In: id., Spiegeltexte. Das Spiegelmotiv in der deutschsprachigen Gegenwartsliteratur dargestellt an Texten von Elfriede Jelinek, Adolf Muschg, Thomas Bernhard und Albert Drach. (PhD) Wien 1999, p. 164–185.
Mohr, Peter: Spät entdeckter Individualist. Schriftsteller Albert Drach feiert seinen 90. Geburtstag. In: Main-Echo, December 17 1992.
Monster Theory. Reading Culture. Ed. by Jeffrey Jerome Cohen. Minneapolis, London: University of Minnesota Press 1996.
Musner, Lutz: Memory and Globalization. Austria's Recycling of the Nazi Past and Its European Echoes. In: New German Critique 80 (2000), p. 77–92.
Noll, Alfred J.: Die böse Justiz: Enttäuschungsreflexion bei Albert Drach. Eine Notiz. In: In Sachen Albert Drach. Sieben Beiträge zum Werk. Mit einem unveröffentlichten Text Albert Drachs. Hg. von Bernhard Fetz. Wien: Wiener Universitäts-Verlag 1995, p. 71–85.
O'Neill, Patrick: Fictions of Discourse. Reading Narrative Theory. Toronto, London: University of Toronto Press 1994 (Theory, Culture).
Oliver, Kelly: Introduction. Julia Kristeva's Outlaw Ethics. In: Ethics, Politics, and Difference in Julia Kristeva's Writing. Ed. by Kelly Oliver. London, New York: Routledge 1993, p. 1–22.
Plato: Timaeus. London: Heinemann 1966.
Pratt, Mary Louise: Imperial Eyes. Travel Writing and Transculturation. London, New York: Routledge 1992.
Pulzer, Peter: Spezifische Momente und Spielarten des österreichischen und des Wiener Antisemitismus. In: Eine zerstörte Kultur. Jüdisches Leben und Antisemitismus in Wien seit dem 19. Jahrhundert. Hg. von Gerhard Botz, Ivar Oxaal und Michael Pollak. Buchloe: Obermeyer 1990, p. 121–141.

Raulet, Gérard M.: Vorwort. In: Verabschiedung der (Post-)Moderne? Eine interdiszi-
plinäre Debatte. Hg. von Jacques le Rider and Gérard Raulet. Tübingen: Narr 1987
(Deutsche Text-Bibliothek; 7), p. 7–20.

Reich-Ranicki, Marcel: Über Ruhestörer. Juden in der deutschen Literatur. München:
Piper 1973 (Serie Piper; 48).

Rozenblit, Marsha L.: The Jews of Germany and Austria: A Comparative Perspective.
In: Austrians and Jews in the Twentieth Century. From Franz Joseph to Waldheim.
Ed. by Robert S. Wistrich. New York: St. Martin's Press 1992, p. 1–18.

Russo, Mary: The Female Grotesque. Risk, Excess and Modernity. New York, London:
Routledge 1994.

Sartre, Jean-Paul: Überlegungen zur Judenfrage. Hamburg: Rowohlt 1994 (Gesammelte
Werke in Einzelausgaben; Politische Schriften 2).

Schlant, Ernestine: Albert Drach's Unsentimentale Reise. Literature of the Holocaust
and the Dance of Death. In: Modern Austrian Literature 26 (1993), p. 35–57.

Schmidt-Dengler, Wendelin: Wider die verzuckerten Helden: Ein Gespräch mit Albert
Drach. In: Albert Drach. Hg. von Gerhard Fuchs und Günther A. Höfler. Wien,
Graz: Droschl 1995, p. 9–27.

Schobel, Eva: Albert Drach. Ein lebenslanger Versuch zu überleben. In: Albert Drach.
Hg. von Gerhard Fuchs und Günther A. Höfler. Wien, Graz: Droschl 1995, p. 329–
375.

– Ich bin ein wütender Weiser. Ein Gespräch mit Albert Drach. In: In Sachen Albert
Drach. Sieben Beiträge zum Werk. Mit einem unveröffentlichten Text Albert Drachs.
Hg. von Bernhard Fetz. Wien: Wiener Universitäts-Verlag 1995, p. 14–16.

– Unerbittlich, zynisch, zärtlich. Albert Drachs eigene Auswahl seiner kleinen Protokolle und Erzählungen. In: Süddeutsche Zeitung, December 17/18 1994, p. 4.

Seltzer, Mark: Bodies and Machines. New York, London: Routledge 1992.

Settele, Matthias: Der Protokollstil des Albert Drach. Recht, Gerechtigkeit, Sprache,
Literatur. Frankfurt a. M.: Lang 1992 (Europäische Hochschulschriften; 1/1343).

Shaked, Gershon: Die Macht der Identität. Essays über jüdische Schriftsteller. Königs-
stein/Ts: Jüdischer Verlag bei Athenäum 1986.

Smith, Anna: Julia Kristeva. Readings of Exile and Estrangement. London: Macmillan
1996.

Stallybrass, Peter / Allon White: The Politics and Poetics of Transgression. London:
Methuen 1986 (University Paperbacks; 922).

Sterling, Charles: La Nature Morte de L'Antiquité au XXe Siècle. Paris: Macula 1985.

Thompson, Philip: The Grotesque. London: Methuen 1972 (The Critical Idiom; 24).

Tschizewskij, Dimitri: Satire oder Groteske? In: Das Komische. Hg. von Wolfgang
Preisendanz und Rainer Warning. München: Fink 1976 (Poetik und Hermeneutik;
7), p. 269–278.

Wagner, Richard: Das Rheingold. Der Ring des Nibelungen. Kompletter Text und Erläuterung zum vollen Verständnis des Werkes. Hg. von Kurt Pahlen. München: Goldmann/
Schott 1982 (Goldmann-Taschenbuch; 33072: Goldmann/Schott: Opern der Welt).

Peter Wehle: Sprechen Sie Wienerisch? Von Adaxl bis Zwutschkerl. Erw. und bearb.
Neuausg., Wien: Ueberreuter 1980.

Wistrich, Robert S.: Sozialdemokratie, Antisemitismus und die Wiener Juden. In: Eine
zerstörte Kultur. Jüdisches Leben und Antisemitismus in Wien seit dem 19. Jahrhundert. Hg. von Gerhard Botz, Ivar Oxaal und Michael Pollak. Buchloe: Obermeyer 1990,
p. 169–180.

Yuan Yuan: The Lacanian Subject and Grotesque Desires. Between Oedipal Violation and
Narcissistic Closure. In: The American Journal of Psychoanalysis 56 (1996), p. 35–47.

Young, James E.: Writing and Rewriting the Holocaust. Narrative and the Consequences of Interpretation. Bloomington, Indianapolis: Indiana University Press 1990.

Ziarek, Ewa: Kristeva and Levinas. Mourning, Ethics, and the Feminine. In: Ethics, Politics, and Difference in Julia Kristeva's Writing. Ed. by Kelly Oliver. London, New York: Routledge 1993, p. 62–78.

Index

Adorno, Theodor W. 2, 17, 28–29, 34, 39–42, 46, 68, 105, 132, 137–138, 151, 178

Arendt, Hannah 163, 166–167, 177, 187–190, 192

Auckenthaler, Karlheinz F. 15

Bakhtin, Mikhail 25, 34–39, 41–42, 52, 54, 63, 87, 93–94, 98, 101, 103, 128, 137, 181, 183–184

Barthes, Roland 53, 80–82, 87, 94, 97, 103, 195, 199, 202, 204

Bataille, Georges 14, 187, 198–199, 201, 204–205, 207

Bauman, Zygmunt 3–4, 15–16, 22, 39, 188–191

Beethoven, Ludwig van 182

Beller, Steven 22

Benjamin, Walter 43, 102

Benson, Ciarán 42

Bergson, Henri 93–94

Bernhard, Thomas 150

Bernstein, Jay M. 28–29, 34, 41, 151–152, 154, 196

Bhabha, Homi 4–5, 7, 17–18, 53, 77, 81, 86, 91, 93, 107–109, 111, 113, 115–121, 123–125, 130, 153, 169

Borowski, Tadeusz 219–220

Botz, Gerhard 18, 20, 156, 181

Brzezinski , Zbigniew 163

Butler, Judith 27–28, 176

Camus, Albert 218

Cohen, Jeffery Jerome 53–54, 107

Connerton, Paul 33–34, 63

Cuddon, John Anthony 87

Culler, Jonathan 172

Deleuze, Gilles 31–33, 45, 66–71, 90, 152, 154, 158, 194–196, 199, 204

Derrida, Jacques 47–48, 53, 95

Dollfuß, Engelbert 156, 165

Epps, Brad 25, 43–44, 46–47, 49, 60, 62

Fischer, André 1–2, 76

Foucault, Michel 4–7, 116–118, 127, 158–160, 164, 166–169, 178–179

Freud, Sigmund 5, 7, 14, 32, 44–46, 48–49, 65, 68–69, 154, 203–204

Friedrich, Carl J. 163

Fuchs, Anne 16, 83, 169

Gilman, Sander L. 15–16, 156

Gross, Elizabeth 26, 30, 34, 51

Heidsieck, Arnold 34–35, 37, 39–42, 46, 52, 68, 83, 178

Hilsenrath, Edgar 2

Hitler, Adolf 15, 161, 165–169, 172–173, 175–177, 185, 194, 200, 202, 217

Homer 75, 77

Horch, Hans Otto 21

Horkheimer, Max 17, 28, 132

Huemer, Peter 75–76, 78

Iser, Wolfgang 95

Jakobson, Roman 100, 104, 186

Jelinek, Elfriede 150

Kafka, Franz 14, 51

Kayser, Wolfgang 26, 34–39, 41, 45, 52

Konzett, Matthias 17, 20, 108

Kristeva, Julia 1–3, 5–8, 13–14, 23, 26–29, 31–32, 38, 42–48, 53–60, 62–66, 69–70, 73, 79–82, 84–85, 91–92, 97–98, 100, 103, 105, 111–113, 133, 139, 158–160, 171, 173–175, 186, 197–198, 208–212, 214–216

Lacan, Jacques 5, 51–52, 62, 67, 115,
    117, 119, 125–126, 128, 149–150
Langer, Lawrence L. 23, 49, 156, 216
Lefort, Claude 8, 163, 165, 167–168, 175
Lodge, David 100, 104
Lueger, Karl 19
Lukács, Georg 77

Melzer, Gerhard 104
Menasse, Robert 19
Menninghaus, Winfried 14, 27, 29–30,
    45
Meredith, George 94
Millner, Alexandra 150
Mohr, Peter 82
Mundt, Hans Josef 2
Muschg, Adolf 150
Musner, Lutz 134, 155

Nietzsche, Friedrich 14
Noll, Alfred J. 102–103

O'Neill, Patrick 79
Oliver, Kelly 27, 29, 59

Plato 130
Pratt, Mary Louise 115–116
Pulzer, Peter 20

Raulet, Gérard M. 22
Reich-Ranicki, Marcel 21

Rimbaud, Arthur 18
Rozenblit, Marsha L. 20
Russo, Mary 25–26, 35, 38, 52

Sade, Donatien Alphonse François
    Marquis de 173
Sartre, Jean-Paul 14–15
Schlant, Ernestine 172
Schmidt-Dengler, Wendelin 75, 77
Schobel, Eva 2, 4, 18, 21, 74–75
Schuschnigg, Kurt von 156, 176, 180
Seltzer, Mark 153, 164, 168, 186
Settele, Matthias 1–2, 10
Shaked, Gershon 17
Smith, Anna 3–4, 26–29, 58–59, 64
Stallybrass, Peter 26, 80
Sterling, Charles 14

Thompson, Philip 26
Tschizewskij, Dimitri 52

Wagner, Richard 148
Waldheim, Kurt 134
Wehle, Peter 121
White, Allon 26, 80
Wistrich, Robert S. 20

Young, James E. 219–220
Yuan, Yuan 9, 26

Ziarek, Ewa 28–29, 44–45

Acknowledgements

I would like to convey my heartfelt thanks to the following individuals and organisations for their support and encouragement:

The Council for the Humanities and the Social Sciences

The DAAD and the ÖAD

The staff of the Austrian Literary Archive (ÖLA) of the National Library, Vienna, in particular Hr. Prof. Wendelin Schmidt-Dengler, Fr. Doktor Eva Schobel, and Hr. Doktor Bernhard Fetz.

My supervisor, Dr. Anne Fuchs

This thesis is for Michael J. Cosgrove and Marie T. Hughes